Dear Roy and

We hope you
enjoy some happy retreats

love,
Sara and Walter
(Dad)
May '79

"Why should not the New Englander
be in search of new adventures?"
THOREAU: *Walden*

Country Inns and Back Roads

VOLUME XIV

BY THE BERKSHIRE TRAVELLER

Norman T. Simpson

THE BERKSHIRE TRAVELLER PRESS

Stockbridge, Massachusetts 01262

THE BERKSHIRE TRAVELLER TRAVEL SHELF

Country Inns and Back Roads, North America (1979)
Country Inns and Back Roads, Europe
Farm, Ranch, and Country Vacations (Revised 1979)
New Brunswick Inside Out (Revised 1979)
Canada's Capital Inside Out (Revised 1979)
Montreal Inside Out
Great Montreal Walks
The Inn Way . . . Switzerland
The Inn Way . . . Caribbean
A Guide to Music Festivals in America

(See last page for information
for other Berkshire Traveller Press titles)

COVER PAINTING: Nancy B. Simpson
BOOK DESIGN AND DRAWINGS: Janice Lindstrom

Library of Congress #79-50012
ISBN 0-912944-52-8
Printed in U.S.A.
Printed in Dalton, Massachusetts by The Studley Press

PREFACE TO THE 14TH EDITION

In its fourteen years of publication, this book was never intended to be a *complete* guide to country inns in North America. It contains my continuing experiences in visiting a carefully selected group of inns in each region. The purpose is to encourage travelers to visit country inns, whether included in this book or not, and to experience this unique type of personal hospitality.

A new edition is published every twelve months, because there is constant movement among country inns. Many are making improvements and changes every year, some inns go out of business and others change owners. Also, I am constantly searching for new inns to be considered for inclusion.

From the very beginning, I have always looked for inns that I felt would continue to operate for many years to come. Consequently, there are a number of inns I have been writing about each year since the late 1960s. In this edition, the listing in the Table of Contents indicates the year that the inn was first included in *Country Inns and Back Roads*.

When an inn changes ownership, it is my general practice to omit it from subsequent editions until the new innkeeper has had the opportunity to become firmly established. A steady stream of letters has assured me that this sense of continuity is most important.

Incidentally, I receive many letters from readers each year, and through them I am richer for some lasting friendships. Many of them recommend inns that I have not visited; some share their inn-going adventures, and a few have criticisms. In the latter case, the information is passed on to the individual inn. I am in continual contact with each inn and try to revisit as many inns as possible each year.

If the reader finds as much about *people* as he does about crewel bedspreads, Yankee pot roasts, and curly maple tables, it is because I believe the real heart and soul of the inn is the innkeeper, his family, staff, and guests. The setting, food, accommodations, service, furnishings, diversions, and surroundings, of course, are of prime importance, but the main factor that makes a country inn so unique and enjoyable is personal involvement.

In 1966, the *first* year that *Country Inns and Back Roads* was written, I invited the twelve innkeepers and their wives for dinner, and discovered that they were delighted to have the opportunity to exchange ideas and to help solve the problems unique to country inns. We had such a good time that first evening that we decided to meet again the following year and thereafter. From those early meetings has evolved something that I can see now was inevitable: the formation of an informal, independent innkeepers' association that would provide a forum for innkeepers to exchange ideas continually and to supply each other with practical and moral support. These meetings continue and the association is thriving. Membership invitations are extended to inns selected for *Country Inns and Back Roads*. At the most recent annual meeting held at the Maryland Inn in Annapolis we had innkeeping guests from Norway, Scotland, and Germany. These were from inns featured in *Country Inns and Back Roads, Europe.*

I do not include lodging rates in my descriptions, for the very nature of an inn means that there are lodgings of various sizes, with and without baths, in and out of season, and with plain and fancy decoration. Travelers should call ahead and inquire about the availability and rates of the many different types of rooms.

Rates are comparable to those at hotels, motels, and resorts in the same geographic area. To me, this represents a travel bargain, for there is so much more offered at a country inn.

The italicized paragraphs following the account of my visit to each inn provide factual information and travel directions. In a few instances, I have included some outstanding country restaurants that do not have lodgings. This is carefully noted in the information paragraphs.

"European Plan" means that rates for rooms and meals are separate. "American Plan" means that meals are included in the cost of the room. "Modified American Plan" means that breakfast and dinner are included in the cost of the room. Some inns include a Continental breakfast with the lodging.

For new readers, welcome to the wide, wonderful world of country inns as an interesting, alternate style of travel. The warm, generous, friendly spirit of innkeeping continueth. Visiting country inns is one of the best ways really to get to know America and Americans.

Norman T. Simpson
Stockbridge, Massachusetts
February 27, 1979

Contents

(The year in parenthesis indicates the first year that the inn appeared in CIBR)

(The year in parenthesis indicates the first year that the inn appeared in CIBR)

(The year in parenthesis indicates the first year that the inn appeared in CIBR)

CANADA

(The year in parenthesis indicates the first year that the inn appeared in CIBR)

Country Inns
and Back Roads

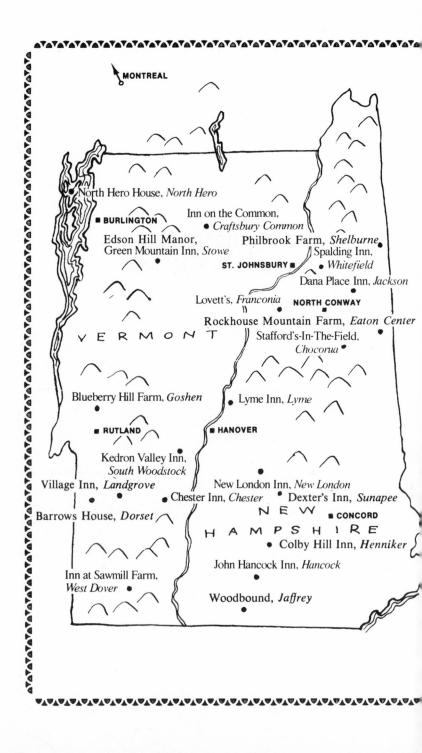

MONTREAL

North Hero House, *North Hero*

■ BURLINGTON

Inn on the Common,
● *Craftsbury Common*

Edson Hill Manor,
Green Mountain Inn, *Stowe*

Philbrook Farm, *Shelburne*

Spalding Inn,
ST. JOHNSBURY ■   ● *Whitefield*

Dana Place Inn, *Jackson*

Lovett's, *Franconia*   NORTH CONWAY

Rockhouse Mountain Farm, *Eaton Center*

V E R M O N T

Stafford's-In-The-Field,
Chocorua ●

Blueberry Hill Farm, *Goshen*   ● Lyme Inn, *Lyme*

■ RUTLAND   ■ HANOVER

Kedron Valley Inn,
South Woodstock

Village Inn, *Landgrove*

New London Inn, *New London*

● Chester Inn, *Chester*   ● Dexter's Inn, *Sunapee*

Barrows House, *Dorset*   N E W   ■ CONCORD

H A M P S H I R E

● Colby Hill Inn, *Henniker*

John Hancock Inn, *Hancock*

Inn at Sawmill Farm,
West Dover ●

Woodbound, *Jaffrey*

Northern
New England

Eastern Time Zone

M A I N E

CALAIS■

■ BANGOR

Asticou Inn,
Grey Rock Inn,
Northeast Harbor

Whitehall Inn, *Camden*   Jordan Pond House,
Pilgrims Inn,   *Seal Harbor*
Deer Isle

Squire Tarbox,   Claremont Inn,
Westport Island   *Southwest Harbor*

Homewood Inn,
Yarmouth

PORTLAND ■

Black Point Inn, *Prouts Neck*

Captain Lord, Old Fort Club, *Kennebunkport*

Island House,
Whistling Oyster,
Ogunquit

Dockside Guest Quarters, *York*

Vermont

BARROWS HOUSE
Dorset, Vermont

"This is exactly what the gazebo is going to look like." Charlie Schubert handed me two photographs of a handsome Victorian gazebo which he planned to erect on the front lawn of the Barrows House in the spring. "We're also putting in Vermont hot tubs next to the tennis court and swimming pool. We'll be able to use them in both summer and winter. There's nothing like coming off the cross-country ski trails and popping into a hot tub."

A group of *CIBR* innkeepers were gathered at the Dorset House to talk over common innkeeping problems, and to enjoy one of Sissy's delicious dinners. Earlier, we had all gathered around in the kitchen while she demonstrated some meal preparation.

It is difficult for me to realize that the Schuberts have been at the Barrows House for seven years. I guess it's been about nine years since I first met Charlie and his father when they stopped and paid me a short visit in Stockbridge while on their way to Vermont to look at country inn property. The Barrows House was for sale at that time, and the Schuberts, including their son Carlie, have been hard at work ever since.

In the intervening years, Charlie and Marilyn who, by the way, is a former airline stewardess, have added considerably to the on-the-ground facilities, including a swimming pool and tennis courts. They also have a very vigorous cross-country ski program with a well-stocked shop, just a few paces to the rear of the inn.

"I think we've become a sort of mini-resort-inn," said Charlie. "Many of our guests spend a great deal of time right here, but when the spirit moves them, they can go antiquing in the little villages like Pawlet and Wells up and down the Mettowe River, or they can drive into the mountains to Weston and perhaps have lunch at the Chester Inn. Sissy can pack a lunch if they like. In the winter, it's just a short drive to Bromley or Stratton Mountain for downhill skiing."

The Barrows House is a traditional New England white clapboard building with black shutters, set considerably back from the main road of the village. It has a rather large English garden on the east side with many varieties of annuals including phlox, lilies, iris, tulips, and peonies. The entire setting is like a small park with elm trees, sugar maples, birches, locusts, and various evergreens.

One of the two front parlors has a welcome fireplace and a whole wall of books. There are several different couches and comfortable chairs. Even in February, the Christmas plants were still in bloom. I

found myself a nice Boston rocker and toasted my toes.

In the other parlor which also serves as the reception area, there were some American primitive-style paintings of both the village of Dorset and the inn. Two young boys were seated on the floor playing with Lincoln logs, and there were all kinds of games on the shelves lining the room.

Upstairs, there are a group of old-fashioned bedrooms with flowered wallpapers, early attic country furniture, and lots of books and magazines.

Charlie continued talking between bites of his veal piccata, and we all kept the dishes of vegetables flowing around the table. When the time for dessert came, he insisted that I try the sour cream spiced apple cake. "Don't tell Marilyn," he said, "but I like it better than the cheesecake."

BARROWS HOUSE, Dorset, Vt. 05251; 802-867-4455. A 26-room village inn on Rte. 30, 6 mi. from Manchester, Vt. Modified American plan omits lunch. Breakfast and dinner served daily to travelers. Swimming pool, tennis courts, paddle tennis, bicycles, xc skiing facilities, including rental equipment and instruction, on grounds. Golf, tennis, trout fishing, and Alpine skiing nearby. Charles and Marilyn Schubert, Innkeepers.

Directions: From Rte. 7 in Manchester, proceed 6 miles north on Rte. 30 to Dorset.

BLUEBERRY HILL FARM
Goshen, Vermont

I'm sure that many of our readers are familiar with that impressive magazine *Vermont Life*. In the winter, 1978 issue, Brian

Vachon and photographer Hanson Carroll combined their talent to present an interesting and colorful photo-journal story of Blueberry Hill Inn and Innkeepers Tony and Martha Clark and their sons, Tim and Christopher. Mr. Carroll's beautiful photographs of cross-country skiers against the background of the inn, as well as some vivid interior shots showing the kitchen with a meal in preparation, made me want to throw my skinny skis on the car and head for Goshen immediately.

Here is a portion of that article: ". . . Blueberry Hill may be one of the most 'at home' inns that ever opened its doors to Vermont travelers—casual hikers in the fall, following observers of nature in the summer but preceding those travelers that Blueberry Hill most charitably caters to; cross-country skiers who will spend their days skiing around it and their nights nestled in its warm embrace. The inn at Blueberry Hill Farm - from November's first timid snowfall to March's last blustery gasp - is home to those particular people who like their skiing uphill as well as down, and everywhere in between."

I first visited the Clarks in midsummer of 1972, when the idea of opening up an inn exclusively for cross-country skiers was just taking shape in their minds. I followed up with a mid-December trip that same year, and already there was a great deal of progress.

In the 1973 edition, I wrote of that visit: "Here in the beautiful green mountains of Vermont, cross-country skiing is just about everything. On the day of my visit, it was cold; I mean *really* cold. Nevertheless, the inn guests were out on the trails in full force, and every once in a while, a little group of them would ski to the rustic lodge where Martha keeps two tremendous kettles of soup on the potbellied stove for anyone who needs to be warm. Most everyone did.

"The inn is very definitely family-style. Everyone sits around the big dining room table and there is one main dish for each meal, which Martha cooks in the farmhouse kitchen. This main dish is likely to be something quite unusual, as she is sort of a country cook with gourmet tendencies.

"The bedrooms are plain and simple with hot water bottles on the back of the door and handsome patchwork quilts on the beds. It truly is visiting a Vermont farm in the Vermont mountains." Well, things have really happened since 1972, and Blueberry Hill Inn has become nationally famous. Tony is a recognized authority on cross-country skiing. The reservation book for winter opens on September first, and it's only fair to say that all the weekends are fully booked almost immediately.

I'd like to share with you a letter I had recently from Martha, telling about *summer* at Blueberry Hill: "We're now open from June through October as well as from December through March for skiing. Summertime here in the Green Mountains is just fabulous. My vegetable and flower gardens are the best they've ever been. Guests gave a hand to Tony while he took down two nearby barns. Our little restaurant went off very well, with Elsie doing a super job with busy crowds on Saturday nights. Tony, by the way, does the omelets on Sunday nights.

"There's great fishing in our streams, hiking, and biking, and nearby tennis, and always a refreshing dip in the pond (I'll bet you didn't even know we had one!). Many guests who don't have their own gardens enjoy helping us pick the vegetables from ours. They can even help clear trails.

"Be sure to stop in at Blueberry Hill this summer. We'll all be here and would love to see you."

A few important observations about Blueberry Hill: there are no babysitting facilities for young children. Reservations for winter accommodations should be made as early as possible, as the inn is often booked solid for weeks at a time for winter.

BLUEBERRY HILL FARM, Goshen, Vt. 05733; 802-247-6735. A mountain inn passionately devoted to cross-country skiing, 8 mi. from Brandon. Modified American plan omits lunch. All rooms with private baths. Meals not served to travelers. Open from June to November; December to April. Closed Christmas. Swimming, fishing, and xc skiing on the grounds. Tony and Martha Clark, Innkeepers.

Directions: At Brandon, travel east on Rte. 73 through Forest Dale. Then follow signs to Blueberry Hill.

CHESTER INN
Chester, Vermont

Chester is an old Vermont village with many nineteenth-century homes and buildings, including a striking group of stone houses at the eastern end of town. It has one of the longest main streets of any village I have ever visited, possibly rivaled only by Pennsburg, Pennsylvania. Dominating the center of Chester is a Victorian building that reflects many architectural influences. The porch runs across the entire first floor and there is a second balcony over the center section. The block-long, narrow village green is directly in front of it. This is the Chester Inn.

The innkeeper-owners for the last three years have been Tom and Betsy Guido who moved to Vermont from Cleveland. Although neither of them had any prior experience in the inn business, they came armed with a lot of nerve and determination to do well. Before I share a letter from Betsy Guido which will really bring a lot of us up to date with their progress, I'd like to point out that the Chester Inn is a busy place in all seasons. In winter, it is convenient to several major ski areas, and warmer weather guests use it as home base while exploring Vermont's back roads and antiques. Now to portions of Betsy's letter:

"This was the year of 'revamping'. Our dining room has new carpeting, and a few new Hudson River Valley paintings grace its walls. The lobby, warm and inviting, has been repainted. Our real pride catches the visitor's eye as they approach the stairway leading to the upstairs guest rooms. Bold brown print wallpaper with bluebirds giving a Chinese effect decorates the stairwell, while on one wing of the first floor is a green leaf motif and on the other wing is a small yellow and blue floral. We're redecorating two more rooms this winter and its a lot of fun searching for antiques.

"The lounge also will see some changes. Because we need an area for our houseguests to enjoy some quiet moments, we are partitioning off the end area and furnishing it with a game table for bridge, and good backgammon and chess sets.

"In the spring, we will be painting. The bulldozers have been here and done some landscaping. We have made a much larger area around the swimming pool. Since our own children have a swing set and sandbox, it now becomes an integral part of the inn. Mothers of small children can comfortably send their youngsters off to play.

"The brook is lovely with large rocks and rushing water. It's a private place to contemplate and enjoy the beauty of what makes Vermont unique.

"Our food continues to be a great source of pride, and Tom receives many compliments. Everything is homemade . . . from soups and daily-made French bread to garden fresh salad tossed at the table. Our entrées and vegetables are cooked to order, and our veal dishes are still the most popular including veal Piccata, veal Estragon and veal Hungroise. Our lamb is raised locally.

"We devoted ourselves to the Connecticut Valley antique car club for a weekend. It looked terrific to see the shiny vintage Bentleys and stately Rolls Royces lined up on the green in front of the inn.

"Come for the Fourth of July celebration if you can. It is one of the big events of the year. Everything from auctions to water polo, fondly, Betsy."

So, things go well at the Chester Inn.

CHESTER INN, Chester, Vt. 05143; 802-875-2444. A 30-room village inn on Rte. 11, 8 mi. from Springfield, Vt. Convenient to several Vt. ski areas. Lodgings include breakfast. Lunch and dinner served to travelers daily except Mondays. Closed from late October to mid-November and April to mid-May. No children under 4 in dining room. No pets. Pool, tennis, and bicycles on grounds. Golf, riding, Alpine and xc skiing nearby. Tom and Betsy Guido, Innkeepers.

Directions: From I-91 take Exit 6. Travel west on Rte. 103 to Rte. 11.

EDSON HILL MANOR
Stowe, Vermont

There were five of us. Four ladies from Quebec and me. Joyce, Betty, Gisele, and Lisette—two English and two French—enjoying the midday sunshine on the terrace at Edson Hill Manor. It was late

21

March and the snow was still very deep on the slopes of Mount Mansfield. The inn looked very story-bookish with snow piled very high on the roof. There were some early-returning birds who didn't know that Vermont has a very late winter. The cross-country ski trails were the same bridle trails that I had taken on horseback during the previous autumn. The Edson Hill touring center was very busy that morning renting skis, applying wax, and giving advice.

On my last visit at the end of September, Liz Turner had invited me to "meet the horses" and we had walked down the mountain from the main house past the sunlit terrace, flagstone swimming pool, the putting green, and the trout pond with the rowboat. The air at fifteen

hundred feet was clear and sharp. The same robins and chickadees chattered noisily among the many varieties of trees to be found in the high Vermont forest—most of which already had some brilliant autumn shades.

Innkeeper Liz Turner remarked that she was glad I was there. "The fall colors are almost at their height; it's one of the very best times of year."

The barn was busy with horses stamping and snorting and guests getting ready for a morning ride. "We try to fit our riding program to the horsemanship of our guests," she said. "We can accommodate first-time riders or people who really want to improve their riding technique. I've been teaching advanced riding for quite a few years. During the winter our entire stable is turned into a cross-country ski shop where our guests can rent all the equipment they need. We have miles and miles of trails on our own property and good instructors."

Horseback riding and cross-country skiing are just two of the outdoor activities available at Edson Hill. There is golfing, fishing, tennis, and hiking nearby. For the guests who might be in a more contemplative mood, there's a beautiful view of the valley and mountains beyond, dozens of places to curl up quietly with a book, and it takes just about thirty seconds to be on one of the walking trails into the woods.

Vermont backroading in the area is some of the best. The inn has a road and tour map for all of them. In the summertime, almost everybody rides up to the top of Mount Mansfield on the gondola. As might be expected, the view is just tremendous.

Edson Hill Manor is a gracious and luxurious home. The atmosphere is low-key, informal, and simple. In the living room is a beautiful oriental rug, a spacious fireplace flanked by comfortable divans, and pine-paneled walls hung with paintings - some by owner Larry Heath's mother. There are floor-to-ceiling windows with elegant draperies. Bookshelves full of books are everywhere. The same sense of casual luxury extends to the bedrooms, many of which have fireplaces, private baths, and spacious closets.

It was in the 1978 edition that I shared my first adventures at Edson Hill Manor, and during the late summer and early fall, I received several letters from readers who expressed gratitude for the information that there were horses available in the summertime.

Now, Gisele, who had such pretty blue eyes, turned from her conversation with the other girls, and said, "We have a wonderful idea. We've done enough skiing for today and we must return to Montreal late this afternoon. Why don't we all go up to the top of Mount Mansfield in the gondola and look at the view."

I'll never get a better offer.

EDSON HILL MANOR, Edson Hill Rd., Stowe, Vt. 05672; 802-253-7371. A 16-room resort-inn about 6 mi. from the center of Stowe, high in the Mt. Mansfield area. Mod. Amer. plan, winter; European plan, summer. Breakfast, lunch, and dinner served to travelers, winter only. Open mid-December to mid-April; mid-June to end of October. Closed Memorial Day. No pets. Horseback riding, swimming, practice golf, xc skiing, fishing on grounds. Mountain climbing, downhill skiing, back roading nearby. Laurence P. and Dorothy Heath, Owners. Elizabeth Turner, Innkeeper.

Directions: Exit I-89 at Waterbury/Stowe. Follow Rte. 100 north to Stowe village, turn left on Rte. 108 north, turn right on Edson Hill Rd. immediately past Buccaneer Motel.

GREEN MOUNTAIN INN
Stowe, Vermont

For almost thirteen years I've been having a great deal of fun writing about Parker Perry, the innkeeper at the Green Mountain Inn. I have referred to him in the past as Savonarola, Stein Ericksen, and as a member of the Loyal Opposition in the English Parliament. I've suggested that he was a man born out of his time; a man with a bit of Viking blood; or perhaps a touch of Charlemagne. All of these things and more are true.

During my annual visit with him recently, I picked up a few more famous quotes from Innkeeper Parker:

"I've owned this place since 1944. The food here has been good ever since and was pretty good before then. It has always been authentic New England, nothing French, Spanish, Chinese, or Italian. No Greek, Japanese, or Polynesian—just things like roast beef and Indian pudding, rice pudding with raisins, homemade cookies, and all those other New England treats. They are served every day at lunch and dinner.

"My wife and I own an old New England inn that was built in 1833. People ask me when I am going to retire—I tell them never. No leisure towns, no nursing homes, no retirement village for me. I'll drop dead tasting the soup in the kitchen at the Green Mountain Inn just before we open for dinner.

"Take fresh calves' liver. Have you ever eaten fresh calves' liver? Not unless you know where to go. We serve it every day of the year. It's never frozen, it is always fresh, which isn't so easy to arrange. It requires a 70-mile trip once or twice a week to get the liver fresh, but it's worth it. I like it and I think most everyone else does too."

And there, somewhat disconnected, are some thoughts from the innkeeper himself about the Green Mountain Inn.

The inn is located on the main street of Stowe, Vermont, one of the most picturesque towns in the Northeast. In winter it becomes one of the ski capitals of the country with great downhill runs on Mt. Mansfield, Vermont's highest peak, and many cross-country trails throughout the area.

In summer, Stowe changes its mantle of white for a many-hued cloak of summer colors. Back roading in all directions offers delightful surprises in the forms of covered bridges, country stores, old houses, and many antique shops. The Stowe Area Association is happy to provide travelers with a series of back-road tours that would take at least a week to complete. There are many activities including golf, tennis, swimming, and lots of hikes and walks in the area for the more active-minded.

The Green Mountain Inn reflects the influence of Dottie Perry who is extremely fond of flowers. In all seasons, the inn is graced with her beautiful fresh flowers and dried arrangements. Both Perrys are very fond of reading, and as a result, bookcases scattered throughout the inn are filled with all kinds of reading materials from novels to travel books.

What a pleasant way to wrap up a fun-filled day at Green Mountain Inn—curled up in bed with a good book!

GREEN MOUNTAIN INN, Main St., Stowe, Vt. 05672; 802-253-7301. A 61-room village inn on Rte. 100, 36 mi. from Burlington, 6 mi. from Mt. Mansfield, Vermont's highest peak. Modified American plan omits lunch. Breakfast, lunch, dinner served to travelers daily. Open mid-December to mid-April, late May to late October. Golf, tennis, riding, hiking, bicycles, Alpine and xc skiing nearby. Parker and Dorothy Perry, Innkeepers.

Directions: From I-89, take Exit 10, and proceed north on Rte. 100 to Stowe.

INN AT SAWMILL FARM
West Dover, Vermont

It was three o'clock on a bright winter's afternoon when I drove from Wilmington, Vermont to West Dover on the twisting, winding road that ascends into the mountains alongside the creek which now was frozen over with ice formations that created weird and wonderful ice-sculptures. Although there had been lots of snow, the efficient state road crews had cleared the way, and other cars with ski racks of cross-country and alpine skis were proceeding on their expectant ways. Passing through West Dover, the Congregational Church was on the right, and I could see the snow-covered tennis

courts and buildings of the Inn at Sawmill Farm. I drove over the bridge into the parking lot and once again was ready for a pleasant visit at this very popular Vermont country inn.

The first thing that impressed me was the new entrance area which is depicted in Jan Lindstrom's sketch. I passed through the new front doors and up the stairs to the reception area. On this particular visit it so happened that Innkeepers Rodney and Ione Williams were visiting their daughter who lives in London.

There were a number of things that had been added and changed since my last visit. The first was a new residents' lounge which has a handsome view of the mowing (Vermont for hill), and Mount Snow to the north. The room has a gorgeous view of the sweep of valley which I don't remember ever seeing before. There are many books and magazines—copies of *Antiques Magazine, Architectural Digest, History of Art,* and *Architectural Record*—a table for bridge in one corner, and some beautiful antique decoys. All of these reflect Roger and Ione Williams' continuing interest in the beautiful things in the world. There are also traditional and contemporary water colors and oils of outdoor scenes. There was a checkerboard in one corner and other games a-plenty.

Lodging rooms have been both added and redecorated, and again I was smitten with the beautiful quilted bedspreads, the bright wallpaper and white ceilings, the profusion of plants in the rooms, and all of the many books and magazines which add to the guests' enjoyment. There were several new suites. One had an extremely attractive summery wallpaper with a matching quilt and overlooked the swimming pool.

I took a walk outside, before the December sun set completely. The swimming pool was now dormant, but in a few months it would be the scene for more good times. I walked to the brow of the little hill overlooking the pond. The view of the village, usually obscured by the apple orchard, was clear and idyllic. I could see some cross-country ski trails stretching out beside the banks above the Sawmill River.

Some of the guests, having finished skiing at Mount Snow, were now gathering in the big living room, eagerly awaiting dinner. I looked at the evening menu and noted that among other things there was dried, cured, Irish smoked salmon, escargots, backfin crabmeat, and clams casino. Some of the entrées were veal and peppers, braised duck, roast duck, frogs' legs Provençal, fresh oysters, Icelandic lobster tails, rack of lamb for two, steak au Poivre flambé, and sweetbreads.

Warming myself in front of the fire, I had a conversation with another guest who had visited many other inns. "Of course they're all different," he said, "and I enjoyed them all very much. But, for me, this is a very special place. In fact, I think it's a model for all country inns."

INN AT SAWMILL FARM, Box 8, West Dover, Vt. 05356; 802-464-8131. A 19-room country resort-inn on Rte. 100, 22 mi. from Bennington and Brattleboro. Within sight of Mt. Snow ski area. Modified American plan omits lunch. Breakfast and dinner served to travelers daily. Closed Nov. 7 through Dec. 7. No children under 8. No pets. Swimming, tennis, and trout fishing on grounds. Golf, bicycles, riding, snowshoeing, Alpine and xc skiing nearby. Rodney, Brill, and Ione Williams, Innkeepers.

Directions: From I-91, take Brattleboro Exit 2 and travel on Vt. Rte. 9 west to Vt. Rte. 100. Proceed north 5 mi. to inn. Or, take US 7 north to Bennington, then Rte. 9 east to Vt. Rte. 100 and proceed north 5 mi. to inn.

THE INN ON THE COMMON
Craftsbury Common, Vermont

I was languishing in the bath at the Inn in Craftsbury Common. It had been a beautiful day, particularly the events of the afternoon. I had driven the short distance from Stowe through Hartwick up Route 14, and then followed the signs through Craftsbury Village to Craftsbury Common, to find Michael and Penny Schmidt attending to some mid-afternoon chores in preparation for dinner that evening. It was the second week in March and the snow was still piled high in all directions in the northern kingdom of Vermont. Penny

said, "It's really the end of the season, but the true cross-country skier doesn't give up without a fight. We have some people flying in from Florida tonight that have never been on cross-country skis before."

Michael and Penny, after summering in this part of Vermont for many years, purchased the Inn on the Common in 1973, and have made it an extension of their own thoughts and ideas. For example, although Penny actually plans and prepares the dinners, she dresses for dinner and takes her place at the head of one long table, and Michael sits at the head of the other and they both enjoy dinner and conversation with their guests. The dining room and the living rooms with their beautiful antiques, many, many books, and welcome fireplace are, in effect, *their* dining and living rooms, and guests can't help but feel at home.

Upon my arrival, Penny took me in tow immediately to show me the new Craftsbury Sports Center which has a complete ski touring facility. "We also have a trail which goes from the front of the inn over the fields to the Center," she said, as we were looking at the maps which show the courses of the many trails. There was the familiar and reassuring aroma of pine tar and cross-country ski wax. There were many skis available for rental. It was a little late in the day to take a run, but I planned to get up early in the morning.

We returned to the inn and joined Michael in front of the fire for a late afternoon mug of hot mulled cider, and the two of them enthusiastically filled me in on the activities.

"The house across the road, where incidentally, you will be staying tonight, has been a huge success. We had just finished rebuilding it when you were here last. It was filled with guests almost immediately and there are two very popular rooms with wood burning stoves." Michael went on, his face aglow, "In the summer-time, we have very many enthusiastic tennis players among our guests. The swimming pool has also made a great deal of difference and the croquet-for-blood games go on almost everyday." Mean-while, through the colonial windows I could see snowflakes falling on this late winter's day. Summer did seem some distance away.

I decided to excuse myself while they continued with the preparations for the evening and after sampling the almond soup, found myself in the bathtub dreamily contemplating a short nap before dinner. My room certainly invited guests to prolong their stays in this Vermont upcountry village. It had exposed beams with adze marks, and the tones of grey and brown were accentuated by the white plaster ceilings. Four very comfortable chairs all covered with bright colors, a low settee, and two twin beds with the colorful patchwork quilts, completed the picture.

I arose from the bath, toweled off briskly, and then donned the colorful terrycloth bathrobe which is supplied each of the inn guests, since the baths are "down the hall." Mine was a bright yellow check with a monk's cowl. A few moments later, with the wood stove crackling merrily, I was perusing a book on Vermont, which Penny generously offered to loan me for my visit, and I felt my head nod. I set the alarm in my room to allow me time to dress and join the other guests at 8 o'clock for dinner. It was going to be a good evening.

THE INN ON THE COMMON, Craftsbury Common, Vt. 05827; 802-586-9619. An 11-room inn in a remote Vermont town 35 mi. from Montpelier. Shared baths. Modified American plan omits lunch. Breakfast and dinner served to houseguests only. Open from May 15 to Oct. 20 and Dec. 20 to Mar. 31. Attended pets allowed. Swimming, tennis, croquet, lawn bowling, xc skiing, snowshoeing, on grounds. Golf, tennis, swimming, sailing, horseback riding, canoeing, fishing, xc and downhill skiing, skating, hiking, and nature walks nearby. Michael and Penny Schmitt, Innkeepers.

Directions: From Exit 7, I-89N, take Rte. 2 east to Rte. 14 north until 8 mi. north of Hardwick. Watch for marked right hand turn, go 2 mi. to inn. From Canada and points north, use Exit 26 on I-91 and follow Rte. 58W to Irasburg. Then Rte. 14 southbound 12 mi. to marked left turn, 3 mi. to inn.

KEDRON VALLEY INN
South Woodstock, Vermont

I'd like to share with you some of the history and heritage of the Kedron Valley Inn, which is recounted on the back of the menu. The valley is named after the brook which flows right through the

community. Actually, very little has changed in South Woodstock since its original settlement. According to this account, "The beautiful meadows, pasture, uplands, and timbered hills are natural and unspoiled by most civilized 'improvements'. The fields and forests are rich in many varieties of flora and fauna. Should any early pioneer of Kedron Valley rise from his resting place to have a look around, it is doubtful that he would find very much different than when he was alive and well. The citizens of South Woodstock are still country people at heart. We still look up when a plane flies over. And we don't have to look both ways before crossing the road, except during the tourist season. And we, the Kendall family, owners and proprietors of the Kedron Valley Inn, are very proud of the fact that the Kendalls were here from the beginning. Running in a single blood stream, our children are the seventh generation to live in the Kedron Valley."

The present Kendall family is composed of Paul and Barbara and their two sons, Dane, twenty, and Chip, twenty-one. In addition, Paul's mother is still very active in the inn, and I've written several times about her wonderful pies.

The inn, as well as its annex, is built of beautiful dark red brick with very white mortar and has been in continuous operation since 1822. The annex was for many years the store and post office of South Woodstock. The old safe is still built into the wall.

The KVI is tucked away in a mountain fastness near Calvin Coolidge's birthplace. However, Paul and Barbara are not content to get by on pastoral charm and Yankee reputation alone. They take pains to serve good food, keep spotless rooms, and continually look for ways to improve the inn.

Many of the rooms are in the main house, and are in the traditional country inn, early-attic style. Some motel-type lodgings in a Vermont log house are a few steps away.

In 1978, the inn was opened for its first full *winter* season. Superb snow conditions provided excellent cross-country and downhill skiing, and lots of horse-drawn sleigh rides. The cross-country ski activities are aided by a complete ski shop with rentals and supplies, and several miles of well-marked and maintained trails. Instruction is also available. Other outdoor winter activities include paddle tennis and ice skating on the pond.

In the spring, everyone at the inn becomes involved with maple sugaring. Much of this is done in the old-fashioned way, using a team of horses and a sled for gathering the sap. Then it's taken to the new "sugar house" for boiling down to syrup for canning and shipping. It's wonderful to visit there in the late winter and see how it's done, from tapping the trees, to gathering, boiling, and best of all, tasting.

In the summertime, it's a very active place for people who enjoy horses. There are trail rides and surrey rides. One of the highlights of the season is a competitive fifty-mile trail ride in September which has become an annual event. The pond and sandy beach provide a respite for warm summer days.

The Kedron Valley Inn is a traditional Vermont inn that reflects the changing vacation interests and enthusiasms of America. Many guests who visit and revisit, enjoy the quiet atmosphere, beautiful mountain scenery, and an opportunity to sit in the rockers on the front porch and watch an occasional car pass by.

KEDRON VALLEY INN, Rte. 106, South Woodstock, Vt. 05071; 802-457-1473. A 34-room rustic resort-inn, 5 mi. south of Woodstock. Near Killington, Mt. Ascutney ski areas. European plan and modified American plan offered. Breakfast, lunch, and dinner served daily. Closed Sunday evenings November to May. Closed Christmas Day. Swimming, riding, sleigh rides, carriage rides, paddle tennis, hiking, and xc skiing on the grounds. Tennis, golf, and bicycles nearby. Paul and Barbara Kendall, Innkeepers.

Directions: Take Exit 1 from I-89 and follow Rte. 4 to Woodstock. Proceed south on Rte. 106 for 5 miles. Or, take Exit 8 from I-91 and follow Rte. 131 for 8 mi. Proceed North on Rte. 106 for 12 mi.

NORTH HERO HOUSE
North Hero, Champlain Islands, Vermont

I was lunching in the beautiful new greenhouse-dining room at the North Hero House, which has been set aside by innkeepers Roger and Caroline Sorg for non-smokers. All the glass in the walls and ceiling brings the entire outdoors completely inside, and it is even further beautified by baskets of hanging flowers. The room is air

conditioned and cleverly arranged so there is no direct sunlight on any of the tables.

"Roger and I designed it," said Caroline, "and we worked on it during many fall and spring weekends."

Because this lunch is an annual occasion for me, I had the opportunity to catch up on all of the Sorg family activities. On that particular day, David Sorg had just been accepted at Western Maryland University and we all gave a rousing cheer. His younger sister, Lynn was passing the relish tray at lunch and also running the craft shop, which is getting more interesting Vermont things on each of my visits.

"There have been some changes and some additions and improvements," said Roger. "Let's take a walk around and I will show you what I mean."

We strolled down to the grass-covered steamship dock which has been in existence since the late 1890s, and in recent years has been improved by the Sorgs. There were many guests and staff members lying in the sun with their eyes closed. I nodded to Marie and Mike, and we made a date to play a little tennis later on.

After a short session in the sauna which is located right on the lake shore, I ran out and plunged into the water and played on an enormous inner tube which, Caroline explained, was her Christmas present to Roger. Mr. Goodspeed, the college professor from West Viginia, with whom I have had so many conversations over the years, was again running the motorboat for waterskiing guests. Two guests came by with a string of bass, walleyes, and northern pike, and still another was launching one of the Sunfish sailboats.

We were joined by a number of the guests on a float-boat ride among the neighboring islands. Roger explained that the lake itself was the only highway in early times before the islands were connected by ferries or bridges. A great deal of history involving the French, Indians, English, and Americans has developed in this otherwise tranquil upper Vermont countryside.

Upon our return, I looked over the final phase of the new family accommodations which would be ready in 1979 in the remodeled Cove House. They include a bedroom, a private bath, and a sitting room complete with the old original fireplace. "This room used to be the cobbler's shop," explained Caroline. "It will also have its own porch right next to the shore." Other accommodations are in the main inn and in other lakeside houses which have also been renovated by Roger and Caroline, without losing any of their early 19th-century atmosphere.

Vacation activity at the inn which is maintained for twelve weeks every summer, includes water skiing, sailing, snorkeling, fishing, tennis, bicycling, golf, and horseback riding. It's also in a great location for backroading, antiquing, and just simply rocking on the porch and gazing at Lake Champlain.

On July 21, 1979 there will be a "first" at North Hero House. Two of the staff members of many summers, Tom, the maître d', and Michelle who has been the assistant manager, hostess, and waitress over the various summers, will be married on the steamship dock. Tom is a dental assistant at the University of Pennsylvania, and Michelle is finishing up her senior year at the University of Vermont. I hope to be present on that happy day myself.

It was another happy day for me in the summer of 1972, when I first visited North Hero House and met all of the Sorg family. They truly make innkeeping seem like fun.

NORTH HERO HOUSE, Champlain Islands, North Hero, Vt. 05474; 802-372-8237. A 22-room New England resort-inn on North Hero Island in Lake Champlain, 35 mi. north of Burlington and 65 mi. south of Montreal. Modified American plan. Breakfast, lunch, and dinner served daily to travelers. Open from late June to Labor Day. No pets. Swimming, fishing, boating, waterskiing, ice house game room, sauna, bicycles, and tennis on grounds. Horseback riding and golf nearby. No credit cards. Roger and Caroline Sorg, Innkeepers.

Directions: Travel north from Burlington on I-89, take Exit 17 (Champlain Islands) and drive north on Island Rte. 2 to North Hero. From N.Y. Thruway (87 north), take Exit 39 at Plattsburg and follow signs "Ferry to Vermont." Upon leaving ferry, turn left to Rte. 2, then left again to North Hero. Inn is 15 min. from ferry dock on Rte. 2.

THE VILLAGE INN
Landgrove, Vermont

"Happiness is children riding our pony cart." Kathy Snyder and I were taking a walk on the Vermont dirt road that runs in front of the Village Inn, when we caught sight of some of the younger inn guests enjoying an outing on the pony cart. "We just love families with

children," she went on, "and I think they like us because we really have a number of activities that children enjoy. There's horseback riding, cross-country skiing, tennis, rides on the Bromley chair lift and Alpine slide."

I reflected that, in my opinion, one of the reasons the young people like to visit the Village Inn is because of the wonderful Rafter Room. It is a recreation room with a big fireplace, log beams across the low ceiling, and plenty of games like ping-pong, skittles, and bumper pool. "Yes, that's true," she responded, "It's all very well and good to think children are happy during the wintertime on our cross-country ski trails or perhaps downhill skiing, but there comes a time at the end of the day when they all gather back here at the inn. That's why we took particular pains to have an area where they can really have a good time, and we found that with games and other diversions, they could work off what seems to be their unending supply of energy. In winter, we have a couch in front of the fireplace that holds twelve kids."

My most recent visit was at the height of the summer activities and everybody was enjoying the swimming pool. The tennis court sign-up sheet indicated that it was also a very popular activity.

"There are quite a few guests backroading today," Kathy added. "We give them maps and a box lunch, if they wish."

The Snyders have been at the Village Inn for eighteen years. During this time, their two children, Heidi, who is now nine years old and in the fourth grade, and Kimberly, who is eleven and in the sixth grade, have become quite familiar to inn guests. "Heidi likes to ride one of her Shetland ponies over to the inn from where we live nearby," explained Kathy. "She frequently gives the children a ride. Kimberly is a regular innkeeper. She does all kinds of things to help out." To furthur engender the family feeling, Jay's parents moved to Vermont in 1977 and are both quite active at the inn.

There's a great deal of emphasis on Vermont-style home-cooking with dishes like roast beef, leg of lamb, baked potatoes, summer salads, strawberry shortcake, apple and blueberry pies, and similar hearty country fare.

The guest rooms at the Village Inn span a wide variety of tastes. Because the inn is family-oriented, there are several rooms that would be adaptable for whole families, as well as bunk rooms. There are also rooms in a newer section which are furnished in a more contemporary style. Lodgings include a hearty breakfast.

"Before I forget," exclaimed Kathy, we had a wonderful time at Christmas. Among others, there were two very large families gathered from all over the country. It was delightful, and their stockings covered the fireplace mantle."

The Village Inn, high in the Vermont mountains in Landgrove, is the place where both adults and children can have a beautiful country inn experience.

THE VILLAGE INN, Landgrove, Vt., 05148; 802-824-6673. A 21-room rustic resort-inn in the mountains of central Vermont, approximately 4½ mi. from Weston and Londonderry. Lodgings include breakfast. Breakfast and dinner served to travelers by reservation during the summer except Wed. dinner. Open from Nov. 23 to April 15; July 1 to Oct. 17. Children most welcome. No pets. Swimming, tennis, volleyball, pitch and putt, xc skiing, fishing on grounds. Downhill skiing, riding, indoor tennis, paddle tennis, antiquing, backroading, Alpine slide, golf, summer theatre nearby. Jay and Kathy Snyder, Innkeepers.

Directions: Coming north on I-91 take Exit 2 at Brattleboro, follow Rte. 30 to Rte. 11 and turn right. Turn left off Rte. 11 at signs for Village Inn. Bear left in village of Peru. Coming north on Rte. 7 turn east at Manchester on Rte. 11 to Peru. Turn left at signs for Village Inn. Bear left in village of Peru.

Green mountain by-way

New Hampshire

COLBY HILL INN
Henniker, New Hampshire

Country inn hospitality has abounded for many years at the Colby Hill Inn. "As far as we have been able to discover, the original inn was built in 1821 by John S. Bartlett on 75 acres of land." Don Glover was explaining some of the interesting history of the inn. "He developed it into a good farm to provision his tavern. It consisted of what is now the two-story house and an addition to the north of only one story. This new section was all in one room and called 'Bartlett's Hall.' It was used for dances and meetings of various sorts. Several times it sheltered a private school. After the burning of the second meeting house of the Congregationalists in Henniker in the winter of 1883, the church hired Bartlett's Hall in which to hold Sunday services.

"In 1836, it was sold to Oliver Pillsbury and ceased to be a tavern. The Pillsburys were excellent farmers and held possession through their son until about 1866, when it was purchased by Lewis Colby. The road from which the present inn takes it name ran up to Colby Hill in those days.

"George Rice and his son Elmer, the next owners, continued to farm for a number of years and also ran a retail milk route in the town. Subsequent proprietors continued it as a farm until 1959, when it was restored as a place of entertainment."

This New Hampshire village, home of New England College, with its white clapboard houses and its church spires rising in the blue sky, is an ideal location for this trim little inn which is now owned by the Glover family, including the senior members, Don and June, classmates of mine at Bucknell University, and their son Don, Jr., who is now the manager and chef. They acquired it a few years ago from my good friend Bettie Gilbert who now lives right across the village street in a beautiful red house. "I wanted more time to travel," she said.

To provide a better picture of the atmosphere at the inn, here is an excerpt from a letter I received from a recent guest. "The inn was just as you described it. The house, the furniture, the paintings, the wide floor boards were all a feast to the eyes. We especially enjoyed looking out the dining room window and watching two large birds roosting in the doorway of the barn. We realized they were live turkeys.

"I took a swim after dinner while my wife watched the sunset behind the mountains. As I swam back and forth, a mist rose on the lower field and gradually enveloped the bottom of each of the hills so that only the top edge was clearly visible. It was similar to a Japanese print."

The inn is rather small and the dining room with its pewter serving plates and gay linen is a popular meeting place for people from the surrounding countryside and villages. It has many country antiques, a group of old post office boxes, a solemn grandfather's clock, and a handsome fireplace with its own baking hearth in the main parlor.

Don, Jr., brought a wealth of experience to the kitchen of the inn, and besides the freshly baked bread there are such interesting menu items as beef kabob Teriyaki, fresh seafood, crab Imperial, shrimp Scampi and usually a fresh fish of the day. June Glover has her own little baking corner and does the chocolate cakes, the cinnamon buns, the biscuits, and the applesauce. Their garden provides some interesting things for the table, such as juice from their tomatoes and jelly made from wild grapes that grow out behind the barn.

Thanksgiving and Christmas dinners are quite an occasion and are served to inn guests only. "We all sit down to the table with our guests," said Don, "and it is like being one big family. We always have turkey with all the trimmings."

"I shall certainly always be grateful to George W. Rice," said Don. Puzzled, I inquired just why. "Because he's the man who built the beautiful barn in 1893. We have more people stop and want just to run their hands over the old barn wood and roam around inside. For barn lovers, it is really a monument."

COLBY HILL INN, Henniker, N.H. 03242; 603-428-3281. An 8-room inn on the outskirts of a New Hampshire college town.

European plan. Some rooms with shared baths. Breakfast served to houseguests only. Dinner served to travelers Tuesdays through Sundays. Open year-round. No children under 6. No pets. Swimming pool on grounds. Tennis and xc skiing one short block; alpine, 3 mi., golf, canoeing, hiking, bicycling, and fishing nearby. The Glover Family, Innkeepers.

Directions: From I-89, take Exit 5 and follow Rte. 202 to Henniker. From I-91, take Exit 3 and follow Rte. 9 through Keene and Hillsborough to Henniker. At the Oaks, W. Main St., one-half mile west of town center.

DANA PLACE INN
Jackson, New Hampshire

Each year I get at least one good long letter from every inn in *CIBR*, and this time I think I will share some of Mal and Betty Jennings' letter which is something of an almanac of the Dana Place seasons, as well as a letter.

"Our winter season was the best yet with a strong, steady growth of cross-country skiing. It's a major activity here in the snow season.

"It stayed cold for most of the season and we did not close until the second week in April. We greatly enjoyed hosting the March regional meeting of the *CIBR* innkeepers, and thought that Chris, our chef, did a great job with his cooking demonstration. This was his second big performance of the winter — his first being a joint cooking venture with world pro skier Hank Kashiwa. This was filmed for inclusion in a movie produced by Volvo to publicize the World Cup ski races to be held annually at Cranmore Mountain. The camera crew returned on another date to film some of our guests enjoying fondue in the dining room.

"We reopened in mid-May to accommodate the hoards of skiers taking advantage of the great spring skiing at Tuckerman's Ravine (*for expert skiers only*). In-between times we managed to fit in a week in Bermuda with the kids, which we enjoyed immensely. Chris, eighteen, is now a freshman at Bates College in Maine, and Page, our fourteen-year-old daughter, is a freshman in high school. Page worked all summer as part-time waitress and chambermaid. She is also our resident babysitter. Chris's first letter from college said it was a little difficult adjusting, but that anything beat washing dishes at the Dana Place." I have a feeling that every innkeeper's child has a deep and abiding hatred for the dish machine, because they get called on when the regular dishwasher doesn't show up for work.

"Summer was beautiful and September was dazzling. I think people are discovering how beautiful northern New England can be

just before the great numbers of people arrive to look at the foliage. It's always good the last week in September and not at all crowded. We have always had an unusual number of people traveling with *CIBR* at that time from west of the Mississippi. It's great tennis weather, too.

"At Thanksgiving time, we closed and took the kids to Cape Cod. Last year we stayed in Provincetown and had dinner at the Red Inn which we all enjoyed a great deal.

"It's always amusing to me when people ask what on earth we do for two months when we close. Now, instead of spending a good half-hour explaining what has to be done between seasons, I just say, 'catch up,' and as there is still plenty of 'catching up' to do, I'll close. Betty sends her very best wishes and we hope to see you before too long. Cordially, (Mal and Betty)."

I feel that there's very little I could add to Mal's letter that would give any reader a better picture of what life is like at this beautiful little inn in the Mount Washington Valley of upper New Hampshire.

DANA PLACE INN, Route 16, Pinkham Notch, P.O. Box 157-B, Jackson, N.H. 03846; 603-383-6822. A 14-room resort inn, 5 miles from Jackson, N.H. in the heart of the White Mountains. Rates include lodging and full breakfast. Lunches served on winter weekends only. Dinners served to travelers daily from late May to late October and from mid-December to late April. Closed Thanksgiving Day. Two tennis courts, natural pool, trout fishing, xc skiing on grounds. Hiking trails, indoor tennis, 5 golf courses, downhill skiing nearby. Malcolm and Betty Jennings, Innkeepers.

Directions: Follow Rte. 16, north of Jackson Village toward Pinkham Notch.

DEXTER'S INN AND TENNIS CLUB
Sunapee, New Hampshire

There was a light mist (euphemism for rain) in Sunapee, New Hampshire. The guests at Dexter's Inn were dividing into two groups. Some were out antiquing and taking back road tours or perhaps visiting nearby Hanover, the home of Dartmouth College. Another group was seated inside watching the tennis tournaments on television, already dressed in their tennis togs ready to run outside in case the weather should let up again. I walked across the lawn to the tennis courts which were wet and then past the swimming pool, the rose garden, the horseshoe pits, and across the grass to a nice hammock strung out for somebody to use, and yellow umbrellas which were folded until after the rain had stopped. The mountains were slightly obscured by mist, but there was an air of expectancy and an occasional movement of the clouds overhead.

Tennis and cross-country skiing are really the watchwords here at Dexter's Inn. There are nine-and-a-half miles of cross-country ski trails which are used for walking in the summer and fall. Three all-weather courts are constantly in use with the active tennis program. Incidentally, the last week in September is one of the best times to visit New Hampshire; the leaves are already turning, and it's not crowded.

The lodging rooms at Dexter's are fun. The accent is on very bright and gay colors in wallpaper, curtains, and bedspreads. Ten rooms in the main house are reached by funny little hallways that zig-zag around the various wings.

The front parlor has a baby grand piano, a lovely old antique desk loaded with copies of newspapers and magazines, a very inviting fireplace, and lots and lots of books. There's also a little gift shop.

There are other bedrooms with a rustic flavor located in barns across the street. These I visited briefly noting the country wallpaper which makes an interesting contrast with the barn siding. The newly decorated rooms were very attractive.

Recreation for the younger set during rainy days or after tennis or skiing is provided in the recreation room in this barn which has a small pool table, a television set, and other games. "I think that kids need an area like this when they're on vacation," was the way Frank Simpson put it.

Like many other country inns, Dexter's is pretty much a family operation. Innkeepers Shirley and Frank Simpson are always on deck, and their youngest son Aaron is available quite frequently during the winter, and always in the summertime. Michael, who is a biology teacher at a New Hampshire school, spent his fall reshingling the roof of the annex. The Simpsons' daughter, Holly, from Keene, left her gardens and anti-nuke activities to come and help out during the very busy season of October. "Although none of them are here exclusively," said Frank, "it's still a family-operated organization."

I was now in the dining room indulging in a between-meal snack—a homemade brownie with vanilla ice cream, when one of the guests came running in from the outside, yelling, "The sun, the sun!" Immediately all was activity as tennis players made a beeline for the doorway in a flurry of tennis rackets, tennis balls, and people returning to their rooms for hats.

The principal summertime activity at Dexter's Inn was again underway.

DEXTER'S INN AND TENNIS CLUB, Stagecoach Rd., Sunapee, N.H. 03782; 603-763-5571. A 17-room country inn in the western New Hampshire mountain and lake district. Mod. American and European plans available. Breakfast, lunch, and dinner served to travelers by advance reservation. Lunches served only July, Aug.; Dec., Feb. Open from mid-June to mid-October; December 26th through mid-March. Closed Thanksgiving and Christmas Day. Pets allowed in Annex only. Three tennis courts, pool, croquet, shuffleboard, 12½ mi. of xc skiing on grounds, downhill skiing and additional xc skiing nearby. Frank and Shirley Simpson, Innkeepers.

Directions: From North & East: Use Exit 12 or 12A, I-89. Continue west on Rte. 11, 6 mi.-just ½ mi. past Sunapee to a sign at Winn Hill Rd. Turn left up hill and after 1 mi., bear right on Stagecoach Rd. From west: use Exit 8, I-91, follow Rte. 103 east into N.H.-through Newport ½ mi. past Junction with Rte. 11. Look for sign at "Young Hill Rd." and go 1½ mi. to Stagecoach Rd.

JOHN HANCOCK INN
Hancock, New Hampshire

I was in a rocking chair on the front porch of the John Hancock Inn on Friday afternoon of Labor Day weekend. The weekenders had not yet arrived, and for the moment I had the inn and the village almost to myself. The sun shone through the trees, slanting across the porch floor boards, lighting the petunias, and catching the American flag fluttering in a light breeze.

The porch had other rocking chairs and a long, ancient deacons' bench, but for the moment, I was the only occupant. The village green to the right of me with its gazebo, handsome church, and town hall, beckoned to a few strollers. Across the street, the Hancock Cash Market was now beginning to attract a few townspeople who came in to stock up for the busy weekend. To the left, up the village street, I could just see the corner of the Hancock Toy Store.

The homes of the village are a tasteful combination of late 18th-century and Victorian buildings. The trees on either side arch high over the streets and many of the houses have front gardens. It is a small, remote, New England hamlet with very few intrusions of commericalism.

The bell in the steeple tolled four as a young lady on a ten-speed bike came whizzing down the village path, said "hello," and ran inside the inn. An early arriving waitress.

Pat Wells who, with her husband Glynn, is innkeeper of the John Hancock, came out and settled down in the adjacent rocking chair. "1979 is going to be a landmark year for our town," she said. "It's 200th birthday! Although the inn is ten years short of *its* bicentennial, what better way can we celebrate with the town than by keeping it proud of its inn?

"We will begin with a joint effort. The Bicentennial Committee has planned a festive New Year's Eve for residents and friends: a concert and ball at the town hall along with a dinner buffet here at the inn. We love being involved with this sort of gala. I'm looking forward to the beginning of a year of celebrations."

Apparently the John Hancock Inn has had many celebrations during its almost 200-year life. It is New Hampshire's oldest operating inn, opened in 1789. In my many visits I have learned that besides offering comfortable country inn lodgings and a rather extensive menu, it is very much the center of village social activity. There are weddings, parties, political rallies, and many informal town meetings held in its low-ceilinged parlors and dining rooms.

Pat and I rocked for a moment, and then I commented on the lovely old New England home just across the street from the inn. "The owners have always lived there. They have been married 52 years and the gentleman has lived 87 years in Hancock. We have many people who have lived here almost all of their lives."

Because I've known Pat and Glynn for a great many years and followed with eager interest their progress, I asked her how she felt about innkeeping now, after a few years.

"The holiday seasons are so busy, with reservations at capacity many weeks in advance. There is really quite a challenge to provide the personal touches that our guests and our family enjoy. The meals have earned scores of new friends, since many times, luncheon and dinner guests discover our lodgings and return to spend more time as houseguests. Our first-time visitors seem amazed to find the richness of the Monadnock region, both in the beauty of the land and in the talents and abilities of our people.

"I guess that we are learning to cope with the pressures and frustrations. We're philosophical about never catching up, and having to get a business education 'on the job.' We've learned to fit family and business together. It is still a great life and we wouldn't trade it for the world. The faith that brought us to Hancock is sustaining us constantly, and life is most certainly richer and fuller than ever."

THE JOHN HANCOCK INN, Hancock, N.H. 03449; 603-525-3318. A 10-room village inn on Rtes. 123 and 137, 9 mi. north of Peterborough. In the middle of the Monadnock Region of southern N.H. European plan. Breakfast, lunch, and dinner served daily to travelers. Closed Christmas Day and one week in spring and fall. Bicycles available on the grounds. Antiquing, swimming, hiking, Alpine and xc skiing nearby. Glynn and Pat Wells, Innkeepers.

Directions: From Keene, take either Rte. 101 east to Dublin and Rte. 137 north to Hancock or Rte. 9 north to Rte. 123 and east to Hancock. From Nashua, take 101A and 101 to Peterborough. Proceed north on Rtes. 202 and 123 to Hancock.

43

LOVETT'S BY LAFAYETTE BROOK
Franconia, New Hampshire

"The building dates back to 1840," said Charlie Lovett, "and we've repainted the exterior with some advice and counsel from the New England Society for Preservation of Antiquities." Charlie Lovett and I were walking around the grounds at Lovett's and he was describing some of the improvements that have been made since my last visit. It was a gorgeous morning in July and we were sharing the moment with a few joyous birds who were raising paeans of praise to the new day. Cannon Mountain, its ski trails now etched in shades of green, seemed even closer than in midwinter.

"In the main inn, we concentrated on the living room with new wallpaper and slip covers. We also spruced up the back dining room with a coat of paint. We redesigned and decorated two rooms in the Stony Hill Cottage, and installed new air conditioning and heating units. You'll notice that we've carefully cut back some of our forest so that there are new vistas for most of the cottages. By the way, we installed Franklin stoves in most of our cottage fireplaces."

"Almost like a club," is one of the frequent comments I receive from the readers who have stayed at Lovett's. It is a sophisticated country inn with considerable emphasis on excellent food and service, and is well into its second generation of one-family ownership. Many of the guests have been returning for years; their fathers and mothers came before them. There is a very definite spirit that pulls everybody together.

Perhaps this is best illustrated by a letter: "My mother, a friend and I spent two days and nights at Lovett's in June. We had traveled over 3500 miles in the New England states and eastern Canada by the time we reached Franconia. Seldom had we experienced warmth and hospitality such as that offered at Lovett's, ranging from the young man who greeted us upon arrival, to our waitress, Barbara. The meals were excellent, especially the omelet creations and the desserts. The ingredients are as tasty as the names are enticing. We are looking forward to another opportunity for a visit."

Summer in Franconia has many delights—antiquing, horse shows, summer theatre, flower shows, auctions, and country fairs. Most of the ski areas run their lifts during the summer and autumn. Shopping seems to intrigue Lovett's guests, and there is a sprinkling of country stores and craft shops throughout the mountains.

On the campus-like grounds of the inn there are small chalets with mountain views and living rooms, many of them with fireplaces. There are also poolside chalets, as well as several bedrooms in the main house and in two nearby houses.

Of the two swimming pools, one has rather chilly mountain water that comes right off nearby Cannon Mountain, and the other has a solar heater; one of the first in the area, I am sure.

With Lovett's impressive reputation for its food, it is difficult to make a choice from the tempting menu.

When I pressed Charlie Lovett to tell me which dish was most favored, he had this to say, "We're particularly proud of our cold bisque of native watercress, our eggplant caviar, and our pan-broiled chicken in brandy, herbs, and cream. People also tell us they enjoy our braised sirloin of beef Beaujolais, and lamb served with our own chutney."

Just for the fun of it, I am going to list a few of the desserts: strawberry shortcake, hot Indian pudding with ice cream, angel cake à la mode, macaroon crumble pie, grasshopper pie, meringue glacé with strawberries, and butterscotch ice cream puff.

When I spoke to Charlie about the letter of commendation, he said, "Well that's simply marvelous. Of course, the whole idea is to run a comfortable inn and we have been trying to do it for over thirty years."

LOVETT'S BY LAFAYETTE BROOK, Profile Rd., Franconia, N.H. 03580; 603-823-7761. A 32-room country inn in New Hampshire's White Mountains. Modified American plan omits lunch, although box lunches are available. Breakfast and dinner served by reservation to travelers. Open daily between June 29 and Oct. 8 and Dec. 26 and April 1. No pets. Two swimming pools, xc skiing, badminton, lawn sports on grounds. Golf, tennis, alpine skiing, trout fishing, hiking nearby. Mr. and Mrs. Charles J. Lovett, Jr., Innkeepers.

Directions: 2½ mi. south of Franconia on N.H. 18 business loop, at junction of N.H. 141 and I-93 South Franconia exit. 2¾ mi. north of junction of U.S. 3 and 18.

LYME INN
Lyme, New Hampshire

The Lyme Inn is a precise, antique-laden gem. Lodging rooms, parlors, and dining rooms are meticulously furnished with wall coverings, fabrics, and paintings chosen to complement this most New England of settings.

The inn rests on the end of a long New England common, and although the village feels quite remote, it is nonetheless just ten miles from Hanover, New Hampshire, the home of Dartmouth College, and inn guests have the opportunity to share some of the sporting and theatrical events taking place there. It is just a few minutes from the Dartmouth Skiway, and there's plenty of cross-country skiing nearby.

Having set the stage, now let's share a portion of Judy Siemons' recent letter which will provide us with an even greater window on the Lyme Inn.

"We finished room number eleven last December after you visited. It really turned out beautifully. We steamed off four coats of wallpaper and part of the wall, too! You should see it now. The old brick has a lovely red patina. We have also started to add more old maps, and baskets, and are using farm tools to decorate the third dining room.

"Our boys have all been very much involved with the inn. Our eldest son, Rick, did dishes, helped out at the front desk, and much to our delight and shock, decided to transfer to the hotel management course at the University of New Hampshire. Gary was our breakfast cook and second cook on busy weekends. Our youngest Rob, splits wood, does odd jobs—and anything else when the spirit moves him, including the dishes when things get rushed. By the way, Fred (her husband and co-innkeeper) does the breakfast during the week, and makes all of the rolls and breads."

Speaking of breakfast, the Lyme Inn is well-known in that particular department. Besides an à la carte breakfast, there are at least eight other full breakfasts with everything from cheese omelets, poached eggs, English muffins, and French toast, to a north country breakfast featuring pancakes.

The main dishes on the dinner menu include hasenpfeffer, weiner schnitzel, rack of lamb, and hunter-style veal.

Bedrooms have poster beds, hooked rugs, handstitched quilts, wide pine floorboards, stenciled wallpaper, wingback chairs, and all kinds of beautiful antiques which guests frequently become very attached to and purchase.

I would estimate that it takes about three days really to enjoy this part of New Hampshire. The Dartmouth College Theatre, the backroads, local shops, fairs, auctions, and the great emphasis on handcrafts in the area, plus the skiing, both cross-country and downhill, would encourage many guests to extend their holidays.

The Lyme Inn is small and intimate. It has nine rooms with private baths and five rooms with shared baths. I feel certain that children would not be comfortable, because there is no entertainment particularly designed for them.

In keeping with its austere New England setting, the inn has only one television set located in a side sitting room. However, there are loads and loads of books. Fred and Judy encourage guests to take home partially-read copies and return them when finished.

LYME INN, on the Common, Lyme, N.H. 03768; 603-795-2222. A 15-room village inn, 10 mi. north of Hanover on N.H. Rte. 10. Convenient to all Dartmouth College activities, including Hopkins Center, with music, dance, drama, painting, and sculpture. European plan year-round. Some rooms with shared baths. Breakfast and dinner served daily to travelers, except dinner on Tuesdays. Closed three weeks following Thanksgiving and three weeks in late spring. No children under 8. No pets. Alpine and xc skiing, fishing, hiking, canoeing, tennis, and golf nearby. Fred and Judy Siemons, Innkeepers.

Directions: From I-91, take Exit 14 and follow Rte. 113A east to Vermont Rte. 5. Proceed south 50 yards to a left turn, then travel 2 mi. to inn.

47

PHILBROOK FARM INN
Shelburne, New Hampshire

We were all together in the great farm kitchen of the Philbrook Farm Inn.

First, there was Maxine McKay who is really, as innkeeper Connie Leger says, "The pulse of the kitchen. She has been here for so many years." Then there was Cilla, the morning waitress who is the fourth generation of her family to work at the inn. Nancy Philbrook, Connie's sister and co-innkeeper, along with a few other assorted neighbors rounded out the gathering. Nancy said, "Come on in, I think we're having a mini-town meeting."

Everybody sat around on stools or leaned up against the counters drinking coffee, joking, and telling stories about the old days. Through the outside door came a very hearty man who has been plowing the town roads since the days when they were rolled instead of cleared. He was retiring after this winter, and everyone laughingly attempted to dissuade him from leaving his job.

Most of the heat in the kitchen came from the ten-burner *woodburning* range built by the Magee Furnace Company of Boston during the 1890s. "Yes," said Nancy, "we do almost all of our cooking and baking on this range. We only use the electric stove in case of emergencies or to keep things warm." Imagine, a country inn where almost all of the cooking is done on a woodburning range!

The Philbrook Farm Inn *is* New Hampshire. There's New Hampshire everywhere I looked: New Hampshire prints, paintings, and photographs—some of them really irreplaceable. There were some tints of old prints, hooked rugs and many, many books about New Hampshire. A whole library of books is just on the White Mountains. Some have been written by former guests.

Another fun activity is looking at the albums, photographs, and mementos of the farm that go back over the years. In one of them I found a copy of a 1952 edition of *White Mountain Echos* which, among other things, had a story about the inn and a photograph showing all of the elm trees in the front. Even in 1952, the headline said, "Philbrooks of Shelburne have played host for generations because innkeepers run in their family."

Wintertime is waking up in the morning to snowstorms, or brilliant sunshine, seeing Mount Washington over the hill in the distance, and also looking at the cross-country ski wax thermometer which gives advice on the correct wax to use. It's looking out over the snow-filled fields, which in summertime have Herefords standing knee deep in the lush grass. Summer and fall are a pure delight.

All of this outdoor activity in all seasons encourges the kind of appetites that most people forgot they had. Consequently, food is on everybody's mind at least three times a day. "It is all homemade with no mixes," said Connie. "There is one main dish each night, and the dinner usually consists of a homemade soup, some type of pot roast, pork roast, or roast lamb. The vegetables are all fresh and we try to stay away from fried foods. Most of the guests enjoy roasts, because these days they are not served as much at home. All the desserts are homemade. There's pie, ice cream, and pudding. For lunches, we serve salads, chowder, hot rolls, hash, macaroni and cheese, and things like that. We always serve a full breakfast with a choice of juice, hot or cold cereal, eggs, bacon, toast or muffins. On Sunday morning, we have New England fish balls and corn bread. On Saturday night, we have a New England baked bean supper. We almost always have roast chicken dinner at Sunday noon."

Back in the kitchen, the meeting broke up, and everybody rinsed out their coffee cups and started the chores of the day. Maxine headed for the next room to do some ironing, and as I left she said, "There's always something to do around here."

PHILBROOK FARM INN, North Rd., Shelburne, N.H. 03581; 603-466-3831. A 20-room country inn in the White Mountains of northeastern N.H., 6 mi. from Gorham and just west of the Maine/N.H. line. American, mod. American & European plans available. 6 rooms with bath, 1 with ½ bath, 13 with shared bath. Breakfast, lunch, and dinner served daily to travelers. Open May 1st to October 31st; December 26th to April 1st. Closed Thandsgiving, Christmas. Pets allowed only during summer season in cottages. Shuffleboard, horseshoes, badminton, ping-pong, pool, hiking trails, xc skiing, snowshoeing trails on grounds. Swimming, golf, hiking, back roading, bird watching nearby. Nancy C. Philbrook & Constance P. Leger, Innkeepers.

Directions: The inn is just off U.S. Rte. 2 in Shelburne. Look for inn direction sign and turn at North Rd., cross r.r. tracks and river, turn right at crossroad, and the inn is at the end of road.

ROCK HOUSE MOUNTAIN FARM
Eaton Center, New Hampshire

Betsi set the delicious piece of apple pie down in front of me and said; "Now that I have been elected selectman in Eaton Center, I hope that I will finally receive from you the respect that I deserved all along!" I sprang up from my chair and made a deep bow. "Madame, henceforth I shall certainly give you all the respect you deserve." Betsi and I have had a wonderful kidding-insulting relationship since my first visit several years ago. It is her father and mother, John and Libby Edge, who started Rock House Mountain Farm, as Libby says, "A thousand years ago." They were joined subsequently by Betsi's brother, Johnny, to make it a continuing family affair. In the course of time, Betsi Edge became Mrs. Betsi Ella, but she still does all of the cooking at the inn.

Guest-friends have been returning to this farm-inn for the tenth, fifteenth, twentieth, and even thirty-second season. "It's a continous stream all summer," said Johnny, when I joined him down at the barn where he was taking care of the stock. "Life is a continual round of arrivals and departures. As you know, when guests leave, we all gather around the front door and ring bells." I was reminded of a similar ceremony at the Milford House in Nova Scotia.

It was a beautiful August morning, and Johnny put out the feed for the horses which were down across the road in the meadow. He whistled sharply and soon they all came galloping up and through the gate and began to enjoy their morning repast. Three German shepherd dogs added to the excitement by barking and chasing

50

each other. What a wonderful experience to be so close to farm animals!

The horses are just a part of the completely self-contained farm environment. They're used for trail rides which are conducted by Johnny. There are also cows, ducks, geese, chickens, pigs, piglets, ponies, and guinea hens. Believe it or not, they all have their own names. The great barn is filled with hay in which the younger guests burrow tunnels and play circus on rainy days.

Besides the fun of being on a farm where guests can milk the cows, feed the calf, help with the haying, hike up to the Indian cave, go on cook-outs, and use the canoes and sailboats at Crystal Lake, there is tennis, golf, soaring, bicycling, hiking, fishing, summer theater, antiquing—lots of things for guests of all ages to enjoy.

Suddenly, I was startled by a caterwauling immediately behind me. When I jumped, Johnny put his hand on my shoulder and said, "Oh, don't worry. That's just our Bourbon Red turkey gobbler from Michigan. He scares everybody."

Since Rock House Mounatin Farm is open from June 15 through October, I remarked to Johnny that he probably had plenty of chances to take it easy during the wintertime when Betsi returns to being a full-time housewife and his mother and father, John and Libby, go to Florida.

"People are always asking me that," he said, with a twinkle in his eye. "Running a farm as well as an inn puts a double load on the work. Fences have to be taken down, wood has to be cut and split, water has to be drained, and generally speaking, the establishment has to be put to bed for the winter. The stock still has to be taken care of and there seems to be as much to do in the winter as there is in the summer when we have all the guests here."

RMF is informal, rustic, and gregarious. The happiest guests are those willing to lend a hand with the chores, "do" the dozens of White Mountain things together, and sit talking around the table long after the remains of one of Betsi's wonderful dinners—lobsters or roasts and pies—have been cleared away.

ROCKHOUSE MOUNTAIN FARM INN, Eaton Center, N.H. 03832; 603-447-2880. A complete resort in the foothills of the White Mountains, (6 mi. south of Conway), combining a modern 18-room country inn with life on a 350-acre farm. Some rooms with private bath. Mod. American plan. Open from June 15th through October. Own saddle horses, milk cows, and other farm animals; haying, hiking, shuffleboard; private beach on Crystal Lake with swimming, rowboats, sailboats, and canoes—canoe trips planned; stream and lake fishing; tennis and golf nearby. The Edge Family, Innkeepers.

Directions: From I-93, take Exit 23 to Rte. 104 to Meredith. Take Rte. 25 to Rte. 16, and proceed north to Conway. Follow Rte. 153, 6 mi. south from Conway to Eaton Center.

SPALDING INN CLUB
Whitefield, New Hampshire

Ted Spalding handed me a letter from a gentleman in Virginia saying, "I think you might find this rather interesting."

The man wrote to say how he had been quite concerned that his two young children would prove "too energetic" for the other guests at the Spalding Inn Club or that they would not find their "type of fun" at this resort-inn in the White Mountains.

"Quite the reverse," the letter said, "they loved every minute of it." Then the letter went on to thank both the tennis pro and the man in charge of the swimming pool for being patient and excellent teachers.

The Spalding Inn Club is an excellent example of the entertainment and hospitality that can be provided for a family with many different preferences. For example, on the inn grounds there are four clay tennis courts, a swimming pool, a nine-hole par-three golf course, two championship lawn bowling greens, and shuffleboard. Five full-size golf courses are fifteen minutes away, and there is plenty of trout fishing, boating, canoeing, and many enticing back roads for motoring. The Appalachian Trail system for mountain climbing is a short walk from the inn.

I personally prefer to have a balance of vigorous outdoor activity plus some quiet times, so I was pleased to find the extensive library, a card room, and a fine collection of jigsaw puzzles. I also enjoyed quiet walks in the nearby woods among the beautiful maple, birch, and oak trees native to northern New Hampshire. There are over four hundred acres of lawns, gardens, and orchards. Ted explained somewhat ruefully that it takes a staff of nine gardeners to keep everything up to snuff!

I like good food, so I was in seventh heaven with a menu reflecting both the mountains of New Hampshire and the seacoast of Maine which is just a few hours away. Delicious clam chowder, oyster stew, lobster bisque, cod fish drops, broiled scrod, and poached salmon are some of the seafood offerings. Pork chops, roast stuffed duckling, roast tenderloin, sweetbreads, Indian pudding, and hot mince pie are a few of their other specialties. They do their own baking, make their own soups and sauces, and even raise some of their own fruits and vegetables.

This lovely old place is a second and third generation resort-inn with an air of quiet dignity. You wouldn't think of going in to dinner without a jacket or tie, and during my trips there I saw some extremely attractive dinner and sports outfits on the guests. Elegant touches include finger bowls and turn-down service.

There are real country inn touches everywhere. The broad porch is ideal for rocking, and the main room has a big fireplace with a low ceiling and lots of books and magazines, a jar of sour balls, apples in baskets, and a barometer to tell you tomorrow's weather.

The inn also maintains completely furnished and equipped cottages. They are available for rental periods of three days or longer from December to April. This makes winter activities, including downhill and excellent cross-country skiing as well as snowmobiling and snowshoeing, available during the beautiful New Hampshire winter.

SPALDING INN CLUB, Mountain View Road, Whitefield, N.H. 03598; 603-837-2572. A 70-room resort-inn in the center of New Hampshire's White Mountains. American plan only from early June to mid-October when breakfast, lunch, and dinner are served daily to travelers. Housekeeping cottages only from mid-December to April. Heated pool, tennis courts, 9-hole par-3 golf course, 18-hole putting green, two championship lawn bowling greens, and bicycles on grounds. Also guest privileges at 5 nearby golf clubs. Trout fishing, boating, summer theater, and backroading nearby. Ted and Topsy Spalding, Innkeepers.

Directions: From New York take Merritt Pkwy. to I-91; I-91 to Wells River, Vt. Woodsville, N.H. exit; then Rte. 302 to Littleton, then Rte. 116 thru Whitefield to Mtn. View Rd. intersection—3 miles north of village. From Boston take I-91 north thru Franconia Notch to Littleton exit; then Rte. 116 thru Whitefield to Mtn. View Rd. intersection—3 miles north of village. From Montreal take Auto Route 10 to Magog; then Auto Route 55 and I-91 to St. Johnsbury, Vt.; then Rte. 18 to Littleton, N.H. and Rte. 116 as above. The inn is situated 1 mi. west on Mountain View Rd.

STAFFORD'S-IN-THE-FIELD
Chocorua, New Hampshire

I'd like to share a letter that was written about a visit to Stafford's-in-the-Field. "I have just returned from the most fantastic experience at Stafford's in the Field, Chocorua, New Hampshire. It was almost unbelievable to me that in today's commercial world, it can still be possible to find a haven so well-run by such a beautiful family.

"From the moment we left the highway and saw Stafford's, I knew this vacation would be something special. Fred and Ramona Stafford are incredible when it comes to hospitality. And, as you stated in your book, Ramona is a superb gourmet cook. Our stay brought back memories of visiting my grandparents long ago in their big old country home on the farm. This inn is an experience that I will long remember and I will make every effort to go back as soon as possible."

That letter was written in 1972, the first year I included Stafford's Inn in *CIBR*. Since that time, many things have been happening at this inn which have made it an even more enjoyable experience.

For one thing, cross-country skiing is one of the big winter attractions. There are open fields and practice slopes for novices and marked trails for more accomplished skiers.

Ramona's gourmet meals continue to surprise and delight all the guests. The lamb curry, served with her own combination of condiments, and the spare ribs cooked with maple syrup, are two of my favorites. Others are chicken breasts in a marinated sauce, and fish crêpes served with a spinach souffle.

In recent years, Fred and Ramona's daughter, Momo has become, under her mother's instruction, an excellent cook who particularly excels in desserts. I can remember on one visit she had just finished a Black Forest cake, and we each ate a piece while sitting in the kitchen.

All three young Staffords, Momo, and her two brothers Hans and Fritz, have beautiful voices. They've appeared many times in local shows and operettas and they've also made yearly appearances at the inn's big barn which has offered Gilbert and Sullivan during the past few summers. The barn is the scene for square dances and other summer entertainment.

Accommodations in the main house are comfortable rooms that have been furnished with country antique furniture. Hans and Fritz did a handsome stenciling job in one of the bedrooms, and Ramona tells me that they are planning to do even more rooms. Other accommodations are in cottages.

As the letter mentioned, Fred and the guests sit together evenings, and I think this is when the dinner party atmosphere is particularly enjoyable for everyone. Many guests enjoy a stroll through the open fields before dinner, walking down the shady paths in the woods surrounding the inn. Winter transforms these paths into ski trails and guests often spend the whole day out on skis with a picnic lunch that is prepared for them by Ramona.

In March, it's maple syrup time, and anyone who wants to help, can. I think it adds to the flavor of the blueberry waffles if one has had a first-hand knowledge of the source of the syrup!

According to my last note from Stafford's just before this book went to press, Ramona's cookbook, which has been in preparation for as many years as I can remember, is now complete and she will have copies available for all of the guests in 1979. Her cookbook would be the next best thing to actually being at Stafford's-in-the-Field.

STAFFORD'S-IN-THE-FIELD, Chocorua, N.H. 03817; 603-323-7766. An 8-room resort-inn with 5 cottages, 17 mi. south of North Conway. Modified American plan at inn omits lunch. European plan in cottages. Some rooms in inn with shared baths. Meals served to guests only. Closed Apr. and May, Nov. and Dec. No pets. Bicycles, square dancing, and xc skiing on the grounds. Golf, swimming, hiking, riding, tennis, and fishing nearby. The Stafford Family, Innkeepers.

Directions: Follow N.H. Rte. 16 north to Chocorua Village, then turn left onto Rte. 113 and travel 1 mi. west to inn. Or, from Rte. 93 take Exit 23 and travel east on Rtes. 104 and 25 to Rte. 16. Proceed north on Rte. 16 to Chocorua Village, turn left onto Rte. 113 and travel 1 mi. west to inn.

WOODBOUND INN
Jaffrey, New Hampshire

On this visit to the Woodbound, I arrived just as the sun was a few points above the tree line silhouetting the birches, beech, hemlocks, maples, and oaks, and casting an orange glow on the white clapboard main building.

After parking the car, I stood for a few minutes taking in the whole scene. The last of the golfers were headed toward the inn comparing score cards. At one of the tennis courts, the game was at "set point." Quite a few people were sitting out on the porch and lawn quietly reading or talking during the few moments before dinner.

I walked into the low-ceilinged dining room noting the unusual number of spiked golf shoes all in a neat row by the door. Inside, there were attractive paintings and photographs of the Monadnock Region of New Hampshire. The fireplace at one end had a long musket hanging over it, and the furniture looked comfortable and homey. I checked the bulletin board to see what had been going on here during the past few days. The children's program and the golf tournament were underway and later in the week there would be a royal circus show. On another evening there would be folk and square dancing with instruction. The nearby Peterborough Players, and the Marlborough Theatre Company were both in production. There were notices concerning the famous Cathedral in the Pines which is just a few paces from the inn. The summer season was in high gear.

The Woodbound is a genial, family resort-inn. Ed and Peg Brummer started it all, and their son and daughter-in-law, Jed and Mary Ellen, are continuing. There is even a third generation of Brummers who are starting to do the inn chores as well. For guests who like active outdoor things, this is a delight. The lake with sailboats, canoes, and swimming is just through the woods. There are

miles of hiking and walking trails, golf, tennis, and shuffleboard. In the wintertime the Brummers have two ski tows, a ski school, 22 miles of cross-country skiing, and even tobogganing.

When I remarked to Ed Brummer that everyone seemed well acquainted, he reminded me that during July and August, guests are accepted only by the week. "Some have been returning here for years with their children and grandchildren," he said. The rest of the year stays of any length are welcome.

After dinner the children were playing on the slides and swings in the backyard. Their parents were chatting or practicing putting on the lawn. Another game of tennis was going on in the twilight. Peg Brummer was putting out some feed for the chickens and other animals which are part of the children's program. For the most part, the guests were just relaxing at the end of another lovely day at Woodbound.

WOODBOUND INN and COTTAGES, Jaffrey, N.H. 03452; 603-532-8341. A 40-room resort-inn on Lake Contoocook, 2 mi. in the woods from West Rindge or Jaffrey. Within walking distance of Cathedral of the Pines. American plan in summer and winter. Overnight European plan available in May, June, and late fall. Breakfast, lunch, and dinner served daily. Open from May 26 to 30; June 9 to Oct. 10; Dec 26 to March 12, with some closed periods. Par 3 golf course, swimming beach, sailing, water skiing, tennis, hiking, children's programs, ski area, touring trails, tobogganing, and skating on grounds. Ed and Peggy Brummer, Jed and Mary Ellen Brummer, Innkeepers.

Directions: From Boston, follow Rte. 2, then Rte. 119 to Rindge where there are directional signs to inn. From New York, follow I-91 to Bernardston, Mass. Proceed on Rte. 10 to Winchester, then Rte. 119 to Rindge and watch for signs to inn.

Maine

ASTICOU INN
Northeast Harbor, Maine

George and Esther Stiles and I were seated in the East Room which is just off the main deck of the Asticou Inn. It was an ideal morning in mid-August, and from the side windows I could see the evergreens around the swimming pool and the three masts of the windjammer *Victory Chimes.* "Isn't she beautiful?" asked Esther. "She arrived last night."

George Stiles, who is the innkeeper of the Asticou Inn, pointed out the fact that the East Room had been added since my last visit. "We needed another parlor for our guests' use," he said, "and this room serves as a quiet place for reading or even playing bridge." The basic color of the room is blue with three very interesting wall hangings and blue and white furniture.

The Asticou is a luxurious summer resort-inn in the now-rare tradition that was popular for so many years in the White Mountains of New Hampshire, the Berkshires, the Maine coast, and certain resort areas in West Virginia, South Carolina, and Palm Beach.

These were the small, extremely well-run resorts where guests would spend a great deal of the summer, reaching them by train and making a trip back to the city at the "end of the season." Now, there are very few of these medium-sized resort-inns that have the many little touches that make them so special, such as beautiful table linen, fresh flowers, and turn-down service. Even today, many guests stay for as long as three or four weeks, but just a few for the entire season. In *Country Inns and Back Roads* I think these beautiful little jewels are typified by the Asticou, the Black Point, the Spalding Inn Club, and the Brazilian Court.

George was most enthusiastic about the guests of the inn. "We've had the same people coming back here for many years, and now their children and grandchildren are returning," he said. "The Asticou is growing with the times. For example, in former days guests used to go swimming in the cold waters of the harbor, but today's guests enjoy our swimming pool because it is just a few steps away from the deck of the inn. I can also tell you that we have tennis courts in our plans.

"Today's guests at the Asticou are much more active. We have so many things here on Mount Desert that attract outdoor-minded people who are concerned about ecology and nature. Our guests stay here on the modified American plan which omits lunch and allows everyone to enjoy the one hundred different activities on Mount Desert Island."

Although the Asticou was for many years a "carriage trade" accommodation, there is a most informal feeling here, with the head waiter, the chef, Allen Weigman, and the front desk personnel all very helpful and friendly. I was particularly impressed with Geneva Wilcox, who seemed to have patient answers to all of the guests' questions.

There are changes at the Asticou, but it is the enduring tradition and the beautiful situation of the inn which make it such a joy. For the most part, because this is an older building, the bedrooms are larger than usual and many of them have a view of the harbor which is one of the most exciting and dramatic in the Bar Harbor area. Most have twin beds as well as double beds.

The furnishings in the dining room and the various sitting rooms are very gay with bright summer colors that offer an immediate holiday atmosphere. The inn is a friendly and relaxing place with backgammon, jigsaw puzzles, many books, and perhaps best of all, the sundeck which offers everyone an opportunity to sit outside and enjoy the panorama of sky, water, and trees.

"It's a funny thing," said George, as we were saying good-by after a short visit, "the Asticou has been here since the days of the Bar Harbor 'cottages' when it was considered a leisure class summer resort. Now it is being discovered by more and more people every year who are looking for the elegance of those days."

ASTICOU INN, Northeast Harbor, Me. 04662; 207-276-3344. A 60-room elegant resort-inn on the northern coast of Maine. Near Acadia National Park, Cadillac Mountain, Abbey Rockefeller Gardens, Thuya Lodge and Gardens, and Jackson Laboratory.

Modified American plan omits lunch. Breakfast, lunch, and dinner served daily to travelers from late June to mid-September. Swimming pool and extensive gardens on the grounds. Bicycles, golf, tennis, sandy beaches nearby. George M. Stiles, Innkeeper.

Directions: Exit Maine Tpke. (Rte. 95) at Bangor. Follow Alt. Rte. 1 to Mt. Desert Island.

BLACK POINT INN
Prouts Neck, Maine

The sun, although still bright in the sky, cast long shadows across the Black Point Inn swimming pool. I stood for a quiet moment at the head of the flagstone terrace and looked out over the waters of the bay. I spotted the bobbing markers for the lobster pots, and in the distance I could see a sailboat beating around the point. Two or three ocean swimmers had made their last dash into the water and were now toweling off, headed back up the steps toward the inn. The flags at poolside, Canadian and American, were now hanging somewhat listlessly as the late afternoon breeze had not yet freshened. I returned to my room through the new rose garden.

Earlier, the lunch served here at poolside can best be described as "bounteous." There were several different kinds of salads and a special plate of corn beef hash which innkeeper Norm Dugas insisted "Was not from the can." A small orchestra played very lightly at one end of the inn terrace. It was like a scene from a Fitzgerald novel.

The Black Point Inn is one of the few remaining American plan hotels that were so numerous on the New England coast sixty and seventy years ago. It has quiet dignity, personal service, and attention to details.

For the active sports-minded, there's just about everything: a good 18-hole golf course, tennis courts, sailing, fishing, swimming, beach walking, and clambering over rocks.

It was in the late sixties that I first visited this inn which, like the Asticou in Northeast Harbor, the Spalding Club Inn in Whitefield, New Hampshire, Hound Ears in Blowing Rock, North Carolina, and the Brazilian Court in Palm Beach, provides some of the last remaining intimate resort experiences.

I noticed that along with the Rolls Royces, Cadillacs, and Lincolns in the parking lot, there was a sprinkling of Porsches, Audis, and VWs. The younger people are also enjoying themselves at the Black Point Inn.

One hundred years ago, a young Winslow Homer, the American painter, found in this section of the rocky Maine coastline the

inspiration and atmosphere in which to create some of his greatest works. In fact, he walked these sandy shores and climbed these same rocks.

Prouts Neck became popular as a summer resort at the end of the nineteenth century, and time has brought few changes to this lovely neck of land which stretches out into the Atlantic. The sea, birds, water, sky, and trees, all of which go to make such desirable tranquillity, are still here today.

The Black Point Inn and all of the beautiful summer homes at Prouts Neck are privately owned. The same families have been coming here for generations and the beauty is well protected.

The inn fits perfectly into the ambience of the community. Gentlemen wear coats, and ladies don colorful dresses for dinner. The same small orchestra plays for dancing in the evening. Families with children over the age of twelve find the inn rewarding; however, younger children may be bored, as the inn has no junior hostess or children's activities or facilities.

BLACK POINT INN, Prouts Neck, Me. 04070; 207-883-4311. An 80-room luxury resort-inn on Rte. 207, 10 mi. south of Portland. American plan. Breakfast, lunch, and dinner served to travelers. Open early June to mid-Oct. No children under 12 between July 15 and August 15. No pets. Pool, bicycles, sailing, dancing, golf, tennis, and ocean bathing all within a few steps. Normand H. Dugas, Innkeeper.

Directions: From Maine Tpke., take Exit 7. Turn right at sign marked Scarborough and Old Orchard Beach. At second set of lights turn left on Rte. 207. Follow 4.3 miles to Prouts Neck.

THE CAPTAIN LORD MANSION
Kennebunkport, Maine

Bev Davis and Rick Litchfield, the personable owners of the Captain Lord Mansion, were filling me in on a few of the intriguing historical details of the building and the town. "During the war of 1812, the British threatened to burn the port if shipbuilding and trade didn't cease. Captain Nathaniel Lord answered the needs of idle carpenters and sailors by engaging them to build this mansion using timbers intended for ships. The carpenters not only topped the house with a cupola, but incorporated hints of their nautical trade throughout the interior.

"Naturally, as the Lord Mansion progressed through several generations of descendents, it acquired all of the trappings and legends that such a building might accumulate. We even have ghosts. One is Sally Buckland, whose portrait hangs in the front sitting room. She has the kind of eyes that actually follow you around, and you can even feel them looking at you when your back is turned.

"In addition to the cupola, the original structure claims one of the few three-story, unsupported elliptical staircases in Maine. Each window is considerably enhanced by hand-sewn draperies, and each displays its original double Indian shutters and blown glass. The beautiful floors with their original pine boards are a handsome complement to the remainder of the furnishings, most of which are antiques of such great history and pedigree that we have conducted tours for all of our houseguests."

The Captain Lord Mansion is an opportunity to be transported into an elegant era of the nineteenth century. It is a mansion of over thirty-five rooms of many descriptions. Most of the bathrooms have marble sinks. Some have light fixtures that are real silver. One of the sitting rooms has the original French imported wallpaper from 1812, and still another has real gold leaf paper.

During the past year, Bev and Rick have made some interesting changes. "We found the perfect piece to accompany the centennial Chippendale table," said Bev. "It is an Austrian lead crystal chandelier and takes everyone's eye. We've added another bathroom so that now eight of the ten rooms have full private baths.

Rick chimed in, "We've tried to make the rooms fit the kind of guests who've been visiting us. We've had a number of women traveling together this summer. They want twin beds, so a few of the doubles have been replaced by twins. By the way, we've started a collection of old steamer trunks. They are most appropriate as luggage racks, and they store extra blankets and pillows. A few of our guest rooms have working fireplaces."

The subject turned to breakfast, and Bev took over: "We have a variation of breads. There's pumpkin bread, zucchini bread, and cranberry bread, and I also make a lot of different types of coffee cake and cinnamon rolls. We also serve hard boiled eggs, juice, and coffee or tea. Most everybody gathers downstairs in the big kitchen. However, we do serve breakfast in bed in the winter to those who request it. Many of our guests say that they have *never* had breakfast in bed, and it's such a romantic idea!"

After breakfast, Rick conducts a tour of the house and tells about the antiques, the history, and some of the legends. Of course, everybody loves to go up into the cupola which provides such a wonderful view of many of the historic houses of Kennebunkport.

"I've never met Captain Nathaniel Lord," said Rick, "nor, for that matter, any members of the Lord family, but fortunately, so much of his way of life has been preserved in this building for more than a hundred and fifty years that I feel I have a very strong tie with him. I've studied the history of the family and love to tell it to our guests."

Bev had the last word: "It's like acquiring a whole new set of ancestors."

THE CAPTAIN LORD MANSION, Box 527, Kennebunkport, ME 04046; 207-967-3141. A 10-bedroom inn located in a mansion in a seacoast village. Near the Rachel Carson Wildlife Refuge, the Seashore Trolley Museum, The Brick Store Museum, and lobster boat tours. Lodgings include breakfast. No other meals served. Not particularly oriented to children. No pets. Open year-round. Bicycles, hiking, xc skiing, deep sea fishing, golf, and indoor swimming and tennis, nearby. Bev Davis and Rick Litchfield, Innkeepers.

Directions: Take Exit 3 from the Maine turnpike. Turn left on Rte. 35, follow signs through Kennebunk across Rte. U.S. 1 to Kennebunkport. Turn left at the Sunoco station at the traffic light, go over the bridge and then the first right around the monument to Ocean Avenue. Go exactly 3/10 mi., turn left, and the mansion will be on the left on a slight rise. Park at rear entrance.

THE CLAREMONT
Southwest Harbor, Mount Desert Island, Maine

The continuing story of the Claremont Inn during the past three years is one of the reasons why I rewrite *Country Inns and Back Roads* every year. At the Claremont as at many, many other inns, the progress and changes are so significant that anything less than a yearly update would be woefully inadequate.

In 1977, for example, just before going to press, I learned that one of the main buildings of the Claremont was being torn down and that only cottages would be available that summer.

I visited again in 1978 to obtain first-hand information about the renovation for the 1979 edition, and found that the changes were marvelously dramatic.

The new building was entirely completed and I could see where, with a little weathering, the natural shingles would blend perfectly with the main part of the hotel. This building contains the new dining room and has a hip roof which repeats the slant of the roof on the main part of the inn. There are beautiful picture windows which allow guests to enjoy the view of the broad lawns, the great sweep of Somes Sound, and the mountains beyond. The interior has a beamed ceiling with a matching central column and wainscoting. There's a free and open feeling about it.

At dinner with owner Gertrude McCue and innkeepers Matt and Joan Landreau, a great deal of the talk centered around not only the new building, but the fact that the Claremont, as the only surviving hotel on Mount Desert Island has been named for inclusion in the National Register of Historic Places.

The suntanned college student waiters and waitresses were busy with platters of sirloin steaks and lobsters. Everybody had already helped themselves at the soup and salad table. Matt explained that seafood is from right outside the door and the vegetables come from the inn garden. "We do our own baking here including all the breads and the desserts as well," he said.

After dinner we wandered through the parlors, all of which have windows overlooking the Sound. There were many people reading, talking, and playing games. In the reception parlor there was a small bright fire in the old fireplace which seemed rather welcome even in August. "Yes, the days are quite warm here, but it cools off quickly at night." said Matt.

As we wandered outside on the lawn, Matt said, "The Claremont has twenty-two rooms in the main building. There are also additional rooms in Phillips House, which by the way, is where we hold quite a few weddings each summer. The two front bedrooms there also have working fireplaces. We also have other rooms in the Clark House and in other cottages.

"Speaking of weddings," said Joan Landreau, "the Claremont is an ideal place for a honeymoon and in one of the bridal suites there's a beautiful brass bedstead, very colorful wallpaper, and of course we always put fresh flowers everywhere."

It's always intrigued me on a visit to Southwest Harbor that there are actually two different aspects to this community. On one side of the small peninsula is a working harbor with lots of fishing boats and the hustle and bustle of people who make their living with the cooperation of the sea. On the other side, it's a more tranquil scene with sailboats and launches. This is the view from the lawn and the boathouse of the inn which is, by the way, the place everybody gathers before dinner.

So the Claremont I'm happy to say has emerged again, now in full operation, and is looking forward to another almost one hundred years of accommodating guests from all over the world.

THE CLAREMONT HOTEL AND COTTAGES, Southwest Harbor, Me. 04679; 207-244-5036. A 22-room rambling summer hotel with rooms also in two adjacent guest houses; on Somes Sound, Mt. Desert Island, 20 mi. south of Ellsworth. Modified American plan omits lunch. Some rooms with shared baths. Hotel open June

20 to Sept. 16. Guesthouse rooms available year around. Eight housekeeping cottages on grounds open May 1 to Oct. 15. Dining room open Memorial Day weekend to Sept. 30, serving breakfast and dinner daily to the public as well as guests. Tennis, rowboats, croquet, badminton, dock, and deep water moorings on grounds. Fresh water swimming, golf, bicycles, riding, boating, and sailing rentals nearby. The McCue Family, Owners; C. Matthew Landreau, Innkeeper.

Directions: From Maine Tpke., exit at Augusta and proceed east on Rte. 3 to US #1. At Ellsworth, pick up Rte. 3 again and follow Rte. 102 on Mt. Desert Island to Southwest Harbor. Follow inn signs approaching and in Southwest Harbor.

DOCKSIDE GUEST QUARTERS
York, Maine

It was dawn on York Harbor. I awakened when the October sun peeked into my east window and illuminated the trees along the shore—the white pines and firs, native spruces, all of which remained green year around. The yellow and oranges of the maples, the rusty greens of the hickories, and the scarlets of the sumacs and beeches were at the height of their autumn glory.

The sundeck of my room, almost at water's edge, looked most inviting, so with camera and binoculars in hand, I put my feet up on the rail and settled back to watch the harbor drama unfold.

The tide was on the way in, the sea was calm, and the first of the lobster boats was gliding out of the harbor. Almost immediately, the "resident flock" of mallard ducks, as David Lusty calls them, came quacking into view and hesitated momentarily looking for a handout. They're really quite tame and serve as perfect decoys to bring literally hundreds of migrating ducks to the nearby marsh.

I thought immediately of all the people who write to me saying, "Can you help us find a country inn located directly on the water — preferably in New England?" Well, the Dockside Guest Quarters fills the bill. David Lusty who is a native "state-of-Mainer," complete with a Down-Easter accent, purchased Harris Island, where the DGQ is located, a number of years ago. He hired a young lady whom he had met in college, and fourteen months later, David and Harriette were married at Dockside Guest Quarters. Over the years it has proven to be a very popular place with honeymooners.

The inn has grown not only to include the original 1880s-style New England homestead called the Maine House, but also other multi-unit cottage buildings of a contemporary design each with its own porch and a view of the ocean. Some have a casual studio feeling. In 1979, a new gift shop has been added.

At breakfast which is Continental style at the Maine House, David enthusiastically made suggestions to all of us about a foliage tour of the Maine coast. As he said, "I think this is the best time of the year to be here."

A few years ago, David and Harriette added the Dockside Dining Room, now managed by Steve and Sue Roeder, serving luncheon and dinner with a great deal of emphasis on food from the waters of the nearby Atlantic. One of the non-sea offerings is a splendid roast duckling, "à la Hickory Stick."

The first order of the day was a guided tour of York Harbor and river in the DGQ launch with the Lusty's son Eric. In his laconic way he said he did it everyday, but never got tired of it.

Pointing due east toward the open sea, he said, "Next stop — Spain."

DOCKSIDE GUEST QUARTERS, Harris Island Rd., York, Maine 03909; 207-363-2868. An 18-room waterside country inn 10 mi. from Portsmouth, N.H. Some larger quarters in newer multi-unit cottages. York village is a National Historic District. American plan available. Continental breakfast served to houseguests only. Dockside Dining Room serves lunch and dinner to travelers daily except Mondays. Open from Memorial Day weekend in May through Columbus Day. Lawn games, shuffleboard and badminton, fishing, sailing, and boating from premises. Golf, tennis, and swimming nearby; safe and picturesque paths and roadways for walks, bicycling, and jogging. David and Harriette Lusty, Innkeepers.

Directions: From U.S. 1 or I-95, take Exit at York to Rte. 1A (the main street of York). Take Rte. 103 (a side street off Rte. 1A) and follow signs to Harris Island Rd.

GREY ROCK INN
Northeast Harbor, Mount Desert Island, Maine

The big news from Janet Millet's trim bed-and-breakfast inn on Mount Desert Island is that "Tree Tops," an English-style cottage which is on the property immediately adjacent to the Grey Rock Inn, and one which I have admired often during the past few years, has now been made a part of the inn.

"You remember, I'm sure, Norman that you stayed in it last year. The former owner was gracious enough to allow me to make it available to guests when she was not in residence. It has a beautiful living room with a fireplace, two bedrooms, and a full kitchen. It is

adaptable for either one couple or two, and also for families traveling with children. I am going to make it available for two-day minimum stays."

I remember it well because it is such a happy little hideaway that would also make an ideal honeymooners' cottage. "Yes," she went on, "the guests may join the remainder of us in the Grey Rock dining room for a Continental breakfast if they desire. It's such fun when everyone gets together."

I think another reason for the good times at the Grey Rock is Janet Millet's own ebullient personality. This is what former innkeeper Bettie Gilbert had to say about her stay: "Janet's breakfasts - Continental indeed! The hot gingerbread muffins, fresh strawberries, and her lovely English china on real linen doilies were charming touches. Logs crackling in the fireplace and a full-rigged schooner in the bay were delightful, not to mention that we had the two rooms and a bath at the end of the hall all to ourselves with a balcony. We wish we could have spent the summer there. And the white wicker, the flowers, and light Victorian touches were so typical of sweet, soft-spoken Janet. I could have hugged her when we left - she's such a dear!"

Grey Rock Inn sits on a rocky promontory overlooking a corner of Northeast Harbor Bay and yacht basin. It has an alpine, parklike setting of evergreens and berry bushes. Janet says that there are forty different varieties of birds who make their homes among the walks and trails that lead deeper into the woods.

Because Grey Rock Inn was built as a private estate in the early 1900s, the bedrooms are quite large. Each faces out and has its own bath. They are cool and shady in the summertime and pleasantly decorated with many delightful feminine touches. Five fireplaces provide a warm welcome on cool evenings.

Many of the guests stay on for additional days because after they get to Mount Desert Island, they find so many things to do. There are quiet places to have dinner including the Claremont, the Asticou, and the Jordan Pond House. I've always enjoyed shopping in the Northeast Harbor shops; they are small and personal. There are also art galleries and craft shops, concerts, and other special events, as well.

"By the way," said Janet, in her charming English accent, "please remind your readers that we have a two-and-a-half-hour island cruise that leaves from the Northeast Harbor town dock and winds its way around the many islands. I've taken it a few times myself and it's always very lovely."

GREY ROCK INN, Harborside Rd., Northeast Harbor, Me. 04662; 207-276-9360. A 12-room village inn in the town of Northeast Harbor, Me. adjacent to Acadia National Park and all of the attractions of this unusual region. European plan. Continental breakfast served to houseguests only. No other meals served. Small cottage available for minimum 2-night stay. Season from early spring to Nov. 1. Children 14 yrs. and older preferred. No pets. Janet Millet, Innkeeper.

Directions: Located on the right-hand side of Rte. 198 approaching the town of Northeast Harbor. Note sign for inn. Do not try to make a right-hand turn at this point, but proceed about one block, turn around and approach the inn on the left up the steep hill.

HOMEWOOD INN
Yarmouth, Maine

I remember the evening very well. It was June 10, 1978— opening night at the Homewood Inn. I joined innkeepers Colleen

and Fred Webster and Doris and Ted Gillette in the dining room, and throughout the meal there was a continual reunion of old friends, not only from the community of Yarmouth, but also the first guests of the season, making this occasion even more festive. Particularly touching were the greetings exchanged by the waitresses with long-time guests.

There was lots of news to catch up on with the Websters, including their trip to the Lamothe House in New Orleans, the Lodge on the Desert in Tucson, and the Rancho de los Caballeros in Wickenburg, Arizona. "We just had wonderful times," said Colleen.

Doris Gillette, Fred's mother, noted that this is the first time in many years that I hadn't been at the Homewood on a Monday night to enjoy the summer clam bake. She and her husband Ted enthusiastically showed me many of the new, original Maine crafts that they had collected all during the spring for their craft shop in the inn.

I've been visiting the Homewood Inn since 1972, and each time I've met guests who have returned year after year. It's a very homey, family-type place. Lodgings are in single and double cottages; many have fireplaces and views of Casco Bay. They are set among the junipers, cedars, maples, and Norway pines. Guests are frequently delighted to find they are sharing the waterside environment with dozens of varieties of land and shore birds. It's a great place for children of all ages and there is much activity for them to enjoy on the grounds.

After dinner, we all gathered around the piano in the lounge, where a local history teacher holds forth each weekend at the piano. Everyone joins in the old songs. Fred suggested that Colleen and I take a stroll through the grounds and join him in his new shop featuring "collectibles," now located in the old Abnaki Cellar in the basement of the Maine House. As we walked past the swimming pool and tennis courts in the twilight, Colleen explained that Fred has become fanatically interested in antiques and was even planning on taking a course on the subject at the university that winter.

As we wandered down to the shore, she remarked that the cottage where I would be staying had needed extensive repairs after the blizzard and storm in February 1978. "The waves were very high and did quite a lot of damage," she said. She also sadly reported that Leon Martin, whom I mentioned in past editions of *CIBR*, who worked at the Homewood as a caretaker since April, 1924, passed away during the spring. "He was really a fixture here and we all loved him." she said.

The next morning before breakfast I took a jog around the beautiful roads of Cousins Island and noted that a few of the guests were already up and about, playing tennis and even dipping an inquiring toe into the swimming pool. It was going to be a beautiful weekend and I imagine many of them would be taking advantage of the sunshine to get an early tan. Some of them were already taking photographs of the water, shore, and sky.

Once again after a hearty Maine breakfast, which was punctuated by lots of joking and good times, I bade goodbye to all of my good friends at the Homewood Inn and took one last lingering look at the splendid Casco Bay shoreline. It was wonderful to know that I would be visiting it again in 1979.

HOMEWOOD INN, Drinkwater Point, Yarmouth, Me. 04096: 207-846-3351. A 46-room waterside inn on Casco Bay north of Portland. European plan. Breakfast and dinner served to travelers daily except Mondays when Continental breakfast and steak or lobster cookout at night available (by advance reservation). Open June 8 through Oct. 14. (Some rooms and cottages with kitchenettes available from May 1 and after Oct. 15.) Bicycles (incl. tandems), pool, tennis, croquet court, boating, hiking, salt water swimming on grounds. Golf, riding, fishing, state parks, theatre nearby. Fred and Colleen Webster, Ted and Doris Gillette, Innkeepers.

Directions: From the south, take Exit 9 from Maine Tpke. (I-95) to Rte. 1-N and follow signs to inn. From the north, take Exit 11 from I-95 at Gray and follow Rte. 115 to Yarmouth. Follow signs to inn.

JORDAN POND HOUSE
Seal Harbor, Mount Desert Island, Maine

Twilight was deepening at the Jordan Pond House and I was taking the opportunity to chat with Jim Brown, the managing director of the restaurant.

We were gazing across the Pond at two low hills that are almost twins. They're called the Bubbles. "You know there is something unique about one of those Bubbles," he said. "There is a boulder on the top of one that must have been dropped by the receding glacier about a million years ago. The nature of the rock is completely different from anything that we have around here. The only force that could have carried it here must have been the glacier as it moved down from the north."

The Jordan Pond House first opened in 1896 and has been operating in much the same style ever since.

Part of that style includes afternoon tea with popovers and homemade ice cream. Visitors to Acadia National Park and Mt. Desert Island actually get in line half an hour before tea time in order to be certain of a place at the rustic tables on the lawn overlooking the pond. Dinner at the Jordan Pond House that evening started with a choice of three soups, almond, cream of broccoli, or cream of cheese with sherry. This was followed by a choice of three entrées: lobster, chicken, or steak.

Most everyone who comes to Maine wants to enjoy a lobster dinner and I was certainly no exception. We had already eaten our popovers and at this point our young waitress, a college student like most of the other staff, brought in two beauties.

These were served with baked potatoes and delicious fresh peas. Sweetener for the iced tea consisted of sugar already melted in water. Incidentally, finger bowls are still a part of the exceptional service.

By this time, the light of day had faded and our friends, the Bubbles across the pond, were but a shadow.

The waitress came for our dessert order and I happily chose strawberry ice cream.

Jim was still warmed up to the subject of some of the phenomena of Acadia National Park:

"Somes Sound, which was also formed by the glacier, divides Mt. Desert Island almost in half. It is the only fjord on the east coast."

After a long browse through the Jordan Pond Gift Shop, Jim and I said good night and walked out to get in our cars. "Isn't it fascinating," he said, "that at one time everything here was covered by a two-mile thick glacier."

JORDAN POND HOUSE, Seal Harbor, Acadia National Park, Me. 04675; 207-276-3316. A country restaurant on Park Loop Rd., 1 mi. out of Seal Harbor. No lodgings. Luncheon, afternoon tea, dinner served daily. Open mid-June to Oct. 1. (Lodgings in other CIBR inns on Mt. Desert Island.) Jim Brown, Managing Director.

Directions: Exit U.S. 1 at Ellsworth. Follow Rte. 3. Or take Rte. 3 to Rte. 198 to park entrance. Jordan Pond House is located in Acadia National Park on Park Loop Rd.

OLD FORT CLUB
Kennebunkport, Maine

Yale Brass and I had just finished two sets of tennis and were seated at courtside enjoying the sunshiny weather in mid-June.

"As you know, I'm an airline pilot," he said "and I've seen a great many parts of the world. However, Kennebunkport is really 'home' for us. I guess it's a *second* home to many of our guests who return each year. We have people from all over the United States, but did you know that this part of the Maine coast is also very popular with Canadians? Kennebunkport seems to be the focal point for them; we have people from all over Canada throughout the summer.

"There used to be a hotel on this property, but Marjorie and I had it torn down. We converted one of the buildings into twelve efficiency apartments which include daily maid service, and an enclosed garage. We also converted a portion of the carriage house into Marjorie's antique shop and gallery. In the section overlooking the swimming pool, we built a club room with a big fireplace, a large terrace, and a kitchen for entertaining. It makes a nice place for our guests to enjoy lobster and steak cookouts."

The apartments Yale mentioned, are meticulously designed in decorator colors with harmonizing draperies, slip covers, and furnishings. All have fully-equipped kitchen facilities. The

dimensions are large enough so that people can stay for longer periods without feeling cramped.

"You probably noticed that we planted many new rose bushes, added more flower boxes, and have continued our beautification projects," he said. "Marjorie is planning more art exhibitions in the shop and possibly a fashion show. She's also mentioned a few painting demonstrations.

"You'll meet Karen and Mario Mesiti tonight. They are the new resident managers and have already become a part of the family. They make certain that guests are introduced, arrange fishing trips, plan backroading trips, recommend restaurants, and make telephone calls for reservations. They will also make a third and fourth for tennis and, in general, attend to everybody's comfort. One of the things that we're happiest about is that many of our guests have developed "Old Fort friendships," and plan to come back when their new friends will also be here."

I like to visit Kennebunkport because it still retains the charm it had when it was the queen of the seas for this part of Maine. The old sea-captains' houses, beautiful streets, and winding river make it a very pleasant vacation experience. The area also has two golf courses, boating, and fishing, and an excellent summer theater is just a few miles away.

Across the pool, the sunlight created a dappled pattern through the trees. Roses climbed the stone wall and the corners of the stone-and-brick garage. Overhead, a few errant clouds chased each other across the blue sky. Yale suggested that we had just about time enough to take a good stroll on the sandy beach "I think this is really the best time of day," he said, "and then we can work up an appetite for dinner. I've got to fly again tomorrow, but I certainly try to be here as much of every summer as possible."

It is difficult for me to believe that this robust, black-haired man and his attractive wife would become grandparents for the fourth time in January. "What do you think of that ?" he said.

OLD FORT CLUB, Old Fort Ave., Kennebunkport, Me. 04046; 207-967-2709 or 3980. A 12-apartment resort-inn on Cape Arundel within walking distance of the ocean in an historic Maine town. No meals are served, but a full kitchen is provided with each apartment. Daily maid service. Balconied club room. Open from Memorial Day to Oct. 15. No pets. Heated pool, tennis court, shuffleboard on grounds. Bicycles, golf, salt water swimming and boating nearby. Yale and Marjorie Brass, Innkeepers.

Directions: Use Exit #3 (Kennebunk) from Maine Tpke. Turn left on Rte. 35 to Kennebunkport and follow signs to inn.

THE INTRODUCTION TO DEER ISLE

I'm sure the Deer Isle-Stonington Chamber of Commerce will not object if I quote from a recent brochure: "It is difficult to pick the most interesting part of Deer Isle. Artists find much in Stonington Harbor with its fishing fleet, the frequent cruise schooners from Camden, fishing boats from Nova Scotia and summer pleasure craft of all sorts. There are others who seek quiet coves, where sand beaches and shores of pink granite form an indescribable composition in colors ranging from the dark green of spruce and fir to the deep blue and sometimes pale translucent green waters. For those who like to be on the water there are excursion boats which run to the outer islands . . . the fishing grounds for cod, haddock, hake, and other fish, and to picnics on the shores of the uninhabited islands.

"Lovers of silversmithing, ceramics, arts, sculptoring, iron-working, and other forms of handicrafts may find shops spread throughout the island. Boatbuilders are also numerous. The towns of Deer Isle and Stonington have a combined population of approximately 2600 year-around residents, many of whom, came first as summer people only to retire here later and become permanent islanders."

On a map of the Penobscot Bay region, Deer Isle is about one hour south of U.S. 1 and a number of roads lead down through the Blue Hill peninsula and over the bridge at Eggemoggin Reach. Have a caution, however, because Deer Isle may prove to be a delightfully incurable malady, as in the case of George and Elli Pavloff of Pilgrim's Inn.

PILGRIM'S INN
Deer Isle, Maine

I was sitting in Elli Pavloff's kitchen, watching the final stages of preparation for dinner at Pilgrim's Inn. Elli had allowed me to sample the hot crab dip which would shortly be taken upstairs to the waiting guests. Delicious. "Tonight we're having a Filipino chicken," she said. "The chicken has been parboiled and broiled with soy sauce, vinegar, and ginger. After surrounding it with fresh fruits and vegetables, the sauce will go over it and it will go into the oven for another half hour. We serve these in individual casseroles for each table. There will also be Indian fried rice with cardamon seeds, cinnamon, and cloves."

George Pavloff came in, and we continued our chat about the early history of the building. "Squire Ignatius Haskell's second wife was homesick, so he imported a master carpenter and builder from Newberryport to build a Great House. Tradition says that it was modeled after Howe's Tavern in South Sudbury, Massachusetts, which later became Longfellow's Wayside Inn. Much of the work was done on the mainland, including the magnificent carvings and paneling, and then floated across to Deer Isle.

"What I think *is* unusual is that the building has remained almost completely unchanged," asserted Elli. "It has the classical colonial feature of two large rooms plus a kitchen on the ground floor. One is the Common Room and the other is called the Tap Room. Both have very large fireplaces and low ceilings. Food during the early times was cooked over one of the fireplaces and then carried upstairs to the formal dining room. We still use the dining room during the early spring and the late fall, but serve in the old barn during the summer.

This early American feeling and design has been lovingly supplemented by George, Eleanor, and Elena Pavloff. Pilgrim's Inn for them is far more than a livelihood . . . it is a way of life. "It means so much to us," said the ebullient Elli. "We looked at so many places because we've known that we wanted to be innkeepers for years. Our search brought us to Deer Isle, and when we saw this building and learned its history and felt the real presence of the past, we knew we had found our inn."

Pilgrim's Inn is just a few steps from the Deer Isle crossroads and is set on a little point of land overlooking both the millpond on one side and the harbor on the other. There are wild roses, nasturtiums, geraniums, lupines, and zinnias on the grounds, as well as some apple and pine trees. A short walk to the edge of the millpond or the harbor is usually in the company of ducks, herons, and cormorants.

Let me share with you a portion of a letter I received from Eleanor and George late last fall: "Elli has gone to carpentry class for help in building our daughter Elena a doll house, which is to be a replica of the inn. She is making a stained glass window for the barn dining area, and hopes to get back to her pottery after that. She will also be serving on the crafts panel of the Maine Arts and Humanities Commission.

"One tradition we intend to continue by popular demand is what we call our Tuesday night "Moveable Feast." Each Tuesday night we give our guests the usual refreshments and then send them all to a pier where a local lobsterman cooks and serves them clams, mussels, and lobsters and then everybody comes back to the inn for dessert and coffee.

"During the summer season, the sunset takes place over the harbor at dinner time. When it's at its height we call our guests away from the dinner table for a few moments. Everyone seems to like this, especially the city folk who have no opportunity to share such comparable sights."

Speaking of sharing, Elli says, "Anybody who is looking for a room with a private bathroom will have the thrill of knowing what fun it is to meet other people on their way to our *semi-private* baths."

PILGRIM'S INN, Deer Isle, Maine 04627; 207-348-6615. A 10-room inn on the Blue Hill peninsula on the Maine coast between Camden and Bar Harbor. Modified American plan includes breakfast and dinner, which is served for houseguests every day from May 1 to Dec. 1. Outside dinner reservations accepted Wednesday through Saturday evenings only. A 4-day minimum stay is required for reservations in August. One room with private bath, rest shared.

The immediate area is replete with all types of cultural and recreational advantages. Golf, sailing, fishing, hiking available nearby. George and Eleanor Pavloff, Innkeepers.

Directions: From Boston, take I-95 to Brunswick exit. Take coastal Rte. 1 north past Bucksport. Turn right on Rte. 15 which travels to Deer Isle down the Blue Hill peninsula. At the village, turn right on Main Street (Sunset Rd.) and proceed one block to the Inn on the left side of the street, opposite the Harbor.

THE SQUIRE TARBOX INN
Westport Island, Maine

The Squire Tarbox Inn is a very quiet place in a section of the Maine coast sufficiently off the beaten track to be unspoiled and natural. It is an expression of the best 19th-century ambience and tradition. The original house, constructed about 1763, was purchased in 1806 by Squire Samuel Tarbox and moved to its present location. The exposed boards and timbers that remain today are original. About 1825, the Squire built the main house in which the original floors, carvings, moldings, and windowpanes have been preserved.

Lodgings are in the main house and in the attached barn, and both are very cozy in a real upcountry manner.

It has always been one of my principal joys while visiting the Squire Tarbox, to sit around the dining room table after dinner and enjoy long conversations which frequently move into the sitting room in front of the fire. Innkeepers Anne McInvale and Elsie White have a number of enthusiasms and interests that are reflected by the unusual number of books and magazines to be found throughout the parlors and lodgings of the inn.

"For our guests who want to sample a slice of New England country life," explained Anne, "we have a friendly game of darts in the barn, a walk down the pine-needled path to Squam Creek, the fragrance of wild strawberries in the summer sun, snuggling into a soft chair with a good book, sunning on the open deck overlooking the woodlands, swimming or fishing in Montsweag Bay, or picking blueberries and raspberries.

"Many of our guests presented weekends at the Squire Tarbox Inn as wedding gifts this year. The result was a steady stream of happy honeymooners. Still other guests sent us packages of their favorite coffee, allowing as how ours was *almost* as good as theirs! It is comforting to know that we do not have to add tennis courts, a swimming pool, etc., to provide people with the kind of experience they are seeking. Incidentally, we have added lovely handmade quilts by Elsie's mother to all of the beds.

"Our menus have some rather exciting changes, including several new flounder dishes, as well as scallops and shrimps. We continue to feature fish or seafood as a choice at every dinner. The rest of the menu is set. It includes soup, salad, three vegetables, and dessert. The favorite soup this year seems to have been our own new apple soup made from old-fashioned varieties of apples such as Red Astrakhan and Yellow Transparent. The favorite dessert is probably the chocolate mint pie which we call 'sin pie' because of its sinfully rich nature.

"As you know, we grow some of our own vegetables, including tomatoes, summer squash, zucchini, green beans, lettuce and cucumbers. We are also able to get a specially-grown variety of tiny sweet corn. We grew six varieties of lettuce, and our guests found it a real treat to have salad made from all of the varieties, served with our special old-fashioned bacon dressing."

THE SQUIRE TARBOX INN, Wesport Island, R.D. #2, Box 318, Wiscasset, Me. 04578; 207-882-7693. A restored Colonial home on Rte. 144 in Wesport, 10 mi. from Wiscasset. European plan. 6 rooms with shared baths; two with private bath. All lodgings include Continental breakfast. Breakfast served to houseguests only. Dinner served to travelers by reservation daily, except Sunday. Open from mid-May to mid-Oct. No pets. Golf, tennis, pool, sailing nearby. Anne McInvale and Elsie White, Innkeepers.

Directions: From Maine Tpke. take Exit 9 follow Rtes. 95 and 1 to Rte. 144, 8 mi. north of Bath. Follow Rte. 144 to Wiscasset-Westport Bridge. Inn is located 6 mi. south of bridge on Westport Island.

THE WHISTLING OYSTER
Ogunquit, Maine

Ogunquit is acutally an Indian word which means: "Beautiful place by the sea." For the past 100 years, an increasingly favorite spot for many people, Ogunquit is a splendid place where writers, artists,

and tourists gather to enjoy the singular delights that are special to this part of the southern Maine coast. I have spent many happy hours strolling the Marginal Way, the natural path that clings to the cliffs high above the sea, where I watched the ocean change its moods quickly and decisively from a gentle splashing on the sandy beach to raucous waves breaking high over the rocks, blending green-blue and moody grey hues.

The Whistling Oyster is located in Perkins Cove right on the waters of this sheltered harbor and it has a splendid view of all of the activities of the busy waterway.

The late afternoon sun reflecting the cove waters created dappled patterns on the walls and ceilings of the Whistling Oyster's outer-deck dining room. Lobster boats were coming in under the drawbridge and many smaller boats darted among the moored pleasure craft. John Parella, whom I have called for years, "the best baritone-innkeeper I have ever met," came toward me once again with his hand outstretched. "I'm so glad you could come today," he said. "We've got a lot to talk about."

There is some drama involved with this restaurant which I have been visiting since the late 1960s. I'll touch just briefly on the fact that in late summer, 1976, the original Whistling Oyster was completely destroyed by fire, and during the following winter and spring, a new building was designed and constructed that included some of the best concepts of the original structure. I am happy to say that the Whistling Oyster has indeed been restored, "beyond my fondest dreams," said John. Once again, he gave full credit to the many people who worked so hard during the reconstruction period. "It is all behind us now," he said, "but you'd be surprised at how many people seem so delighted with the *new* Oyster."

This time John was filled with news about how gratifying it was to keep the restaurant open all winter. "Many people enjoy the coast of Maine in the off-season," he said, "and believe me there is nothing

80

quite as beautiful as Perkins Harbor under a fresh blanket of snow. It never gets very deep except for that one bad blizzard in 1978.

"We're continuing with the special events connected with our Oyster Club," he said. "Some of the highlights, in addition to the International Dinners have been the English Hunt Breakfast, a New England Harvest Buffet, and the traditional holiday celebrations. We initiated a Christmas carol sing last year."

The International Dinners to which John alluded included a number of different evenings devoted to the cuisine of many different countries — there were English dinners, Italian dinners, Russian, French, and Mardi Gras dinners. These were all the creation of chef Bill Cardwell who seems to thrive on continuing challenges.

While John and I were holding this animated conversation, waiters brought in bowls of Captain Blight's Delight and Crabmeat Snug Harbor, two of the menu offerings that I have been enjoying ever since my first visit. Other luncheon items included broiled filet of haddock Amandine and eggs Benedict. Some of the entrées on the dinner menu included duckling flambé, roast rack of lamb Persillé, and shrimps and mushrooms sautéed in garlic butter.

After lunch I couldn't resist another visit to the famous Whistling Oyster gift shop which now occupies considerably more space than the original.

We lingered for a few monents at the front entrance and John had one final thought: "One of our most successful winter events last year was the formal New Year's Eve dinner," he said. "We are going to have another one this coming year, so why don't you drag your tuxedo out of the mothballs and come and join us!"

THE WHISTLING OYSTER, Perkins Cove, Ogunquit, Me. 03907; 207-646-9521. A waterfront restaurant in Perkins Cove at Ogunquit. No lodgings. Lunch and dinner served daily. Open throughout the year. Reservations advisable. Nearby CIBR *overnight lodgings include the Capt. Lord Mansion and the Old Fort Club in Kennebunkport; and the Dockside Guest Quarters in York. John Parella, Innkeeper.*

Directions: From the south, take the York exit from I-95. Turn north on Rte. 1 to Ogunquit Square. Proceed south on Shore Rd. for about 1 mi. to Perkins Cove turnoff.

WHITEHALL INN
Camden, Maine

I certainly knew that I was in Camden, Maine. There again were the flowered-decorated lamp posts and the waterfall at the town landing. Also present was green-clad Mount Beattie and the lovely

Camden Harbor with its colorful Windjammer sailing fleet. They set sail each Monday morning with the tide.

If ever an inn and a setting were made for each other, the Whitehall Inn and Camden are perfectly matched. The buildings of the inn have a neo-classic design connected by a large porch with plenty of comfortable wicker furniture. The inn sits back from the main street among huge elm and pine trees and there are many window boxes and arrangements of summer flowers.

On the first floor there are several parlors and a large lobby, all of which are furnished with Maine antiques. The lounge is furnished with sewing machines ingeniously converted into tables, chess sets which invite competition, and a large collection of unusual shells which are displayed under glass. Lodgings are country style.

Innkeeper Ed Dewing met me at the front door and immediately launched into an update of all of the Dewing family activities.

"Chip and Jonathan are both here at the inn this summer, and they are both also planning to return to the Gasparilla Inn in Boca Grande. Heidi is still very happy as a pastry baker at the Ritz in Boston, but is in a quandry regarding her next step. Where do you go from the Ritz? Such a problem!"

The Dewing family left Boston and came to Camden in the early 1970s to become keepers of this highly reputable village inn. Because their maturing years were spent working at the inn, all three of the second generation are planning careers in the hospitality business.

Ed said that most of the guests still are interested in the Edna St. Vincent Millay Room with its collection of photographs of Miss Millay from the time she was eighteen years old and lived here in Camden. The room has been designed as a tribute to her and contains many volumes of her poems, along with memorabilia that would be of interest to Miss Millay's numerous admirers. It was here at the

Whitehall Inn on a warm August evening in 1912 that young Edna first recited her poem, "Renascence."

The inn is located just a short tree-lined walk from the center of the village. An excellent folder provided by the inn has dozens of suggestions about activities in and around this part of Maine, including golf, sightseeing, art exhibitions, boating, swimming, hiking, and fishing.

The Whitehall Inn has its own island reached by the inn launch in nearby Penobscot Bay. As Ed pointed out, "The island continues to enchant all who visit, and becomes the highlight of their water experience in Maine. It has a lobsterman's shack on it, and is also a game reserve. There are seventeen varieties of wildflowers and many birds in a natural habitat. It's a wonderful place to spend the day in quiet and contemplation."

I believe that a major part of everyone's country inn experience is the food. In reference to the Whitehall Inn, here's a letter I have from a gentleman from Vermont. "Because I have been connected with the food industry most of my life, I instinctively notice the small considerations that lift an establishment head and shoulders above the rest. During the past few years, we have enjoyed quite a few meals at the inn, and this year we were guests for a delightful week. The food is certainly exceptional."

As Ed and I stood on the porch sort of summing things up at the Whitehall, he said: "Actually nothing is new and I think that's why our guests have chosen the Whitehall as their special place. We still don't have any television or air conditioning, no swimming pool, and no disco. We've added new electrical service so that we blow fewer fuses. The Whitehall has been here seventy-seven years and we promise the same beautiful sunrises and sunsets, crisp clean air, days filled with sunshine (a little fog now and then), brilliant fall foliage, picture book villages, friendly neighbors, a bountiful table, and lots of people to look out for everybody's comfort and well being."

WHITEHALL INN, Camden, Me. 04843; 207-236-3391. A 38-room village inn in a Maine seacoast town, 75 mi. from Portland. Modified American plan omits lunch. Breakfast and dinner served daily to travelers. Open, May 25 to Oct. 15. Tennis, bicycles, shuffleboard, day sailing, harbor cruises on grounds. No pets. Golf, hiking, swimming, fishing nearby. Jean and Ed Dewing, Innkeepers.

Directions: From Maine Tpke. take Exit 9 to coastal Rte. 95. Proceed on 95 to Rte. 1 at Brunswick. Follow Rte. 1 to Rte. 90 at Warren, to Rte. 1 in Camden. Inn is located on Rte. 1, ¼ mi. north of Camden.

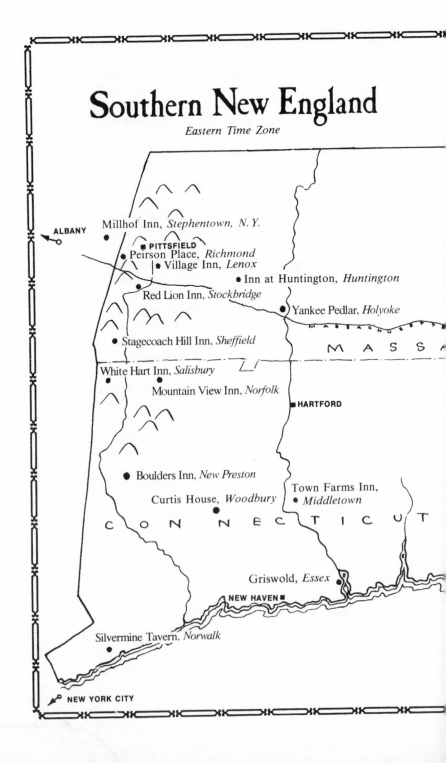

Southern New England

Eastern Time Zone

ALBANY

Millhof Inn, *Stephentown, N.Y.*

PITTSFIELD

Peirson Place, *Richmond*

Village Inn, *Lenox*

Inn at Huntington, *Huntington*

Red Lion Inn, *Stockbridge*

Yankee Pedlar, *Holyoke*

MASSACHUSETTS

M A S S A

Stagecoach Hill Inn, *Sheffield*

White Hart Inn, *Salisbury*

Mountain View Inn, *Norfolk*

HARTFORD

Boulders Inn, *New Preston*

Curtis House, *Woodbury*

Town Farms Inn, *Middletown*

C O N N E C T I C U T

Griswold, *Essex*

NEW HAVEN

Silvermine Tavern, *Norwalk*

NEW YORK CITY

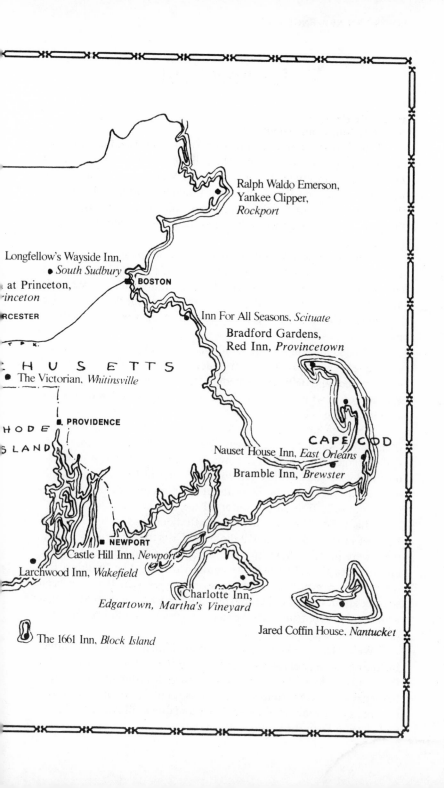

Ralph Waldo Emerson,
Yankee Clipper,
Rockport

Longfellow's Wayside Inn,
• *South Sudbury*

at Princeton,
rinceton

RCESTER

BOSTON

Inn For All Seasons, *Scituate*

Bradford Gardens,
Red Inn, *Provincetown*

H U S E T T S

• The Victorian, *Whitinsville*

HODE

PROVIDENCE

CAPE COD

SLAND

Nauset House Inn, *East Orleans*

Bramble Inn, *Brewster*

NEWPORT

Castle Hill Inn, *Newport*

Larchwood Inn, *Wakefield*

Charlotte Inn,
Edgartown, Martha's Vineyard

The 1661 Inn, *Block Island*

Jared Coffin House, *Nantucket*

Connecticut

BOULDERS INN
New Preston, Connecticut

It was an absolutely crystal clear August day without a wisp of a cloud. I wove my way among the hills on the beautiful roads of northwest Connecticut that lead to Lake Waramaug. I was on my way to see Dick and Jane Lowe at the Boulders. Suddenly I could see the raft just off shore from the inn and people sunning themselves on the dock. I pulled in between the big stone gates and wheeled around to park under the trees.

There was a sort of midafternoon lull. Four people were having a rather relaxed doubles game on the tennis court; I could see a couple walking leisurely down the trail that leads to Pinnacle Mountain. And there was Jane Lowe standing in the doorway with a big smile. "Come on, change into your trunks," she said. "Let's go swimming."

I needed no urging, and in the trice she and I were walking down the stone steps across the lawn under the great maples, oaks, and hickory trees and between the hedges leading out to the water's edge. We sat for a while in a pair of captain's chairs and watched the activity on the lake.

"The lake has remained pretty much the same as it was when my grandfather was here," she mused. "Families would come with horses and carriages. They had large homes where they could stay for weeks on end. I wish you could be here for the Fourth of July. All the people who live on the lake light flares about 9 o'clock and it's just gorgeous to see the reflection on the water all the way around the lake."

This time I discovered that the Boulders has over a hundred kinds of birds, and Dick and Jane supply lists to their guests. I knew there were birds in those hills and on the lake, but I'd never had the faintest idea that there were so many varieties. The Boulders is a family inn in every sense of the word. Every year that I've been writing about them I've heard from families with children of all ages who stayed there from a weekend to two weeks and I'm delighted to say that the kids love it.

Well, they ought to. There are all kinds of boats available, including fishing boats and sailboats, and there's the big barn to play in on rainy days. The barn is also used for the Monday night barbecues. There are simply acres and acres of woods and trails, and in winter, tobogganing, cross-country and downhill skiing, sledding, and skating keep the young folks happy.

The family feeling extends to the operation of the inn. Three members of the fourth generation are now involved. Tuck Lowe was home from Lehigh taking charge of the grounds. West returned from spending a winter in Vail, Colorado, and also contributed a great deal to major maintenance. Pete Franklin is also a member of the family and is really managing the inn, giving Dick and Jane a little more time to concentrate on expansion plans.

And I mustn't forget the food. There are all the dishes which we associate with the country, including pumpkin and apple pie, apple sauce, custards, blueberry pudding, prime ribs with Yorkshire pudding, leg of lamb, and turkey. American plan guests can have the eating time of their lives, young and old alike.

As we came back from our swim, Jane added, "Lots of people come up just to be here in the woods and to watch the sun rise and set over the lake. It's beautiful in any season."

BOULDERS INN, Lake Waramaug, New Preston, Conn. 06777; 203-868-7918. A 30-room year-round resort-inn, 1½ mi. north of New Preston, 20 mi. from Danbury. All plans available. Breakfast, lunch, and dinner served daily to travelers from late May to mid-October and some weekends through the year. European plan and breakfast available rest of year. Monday dinner served to house-guests only. Rooms and breakfast only on Thanksgiving. Closed Christmas. Tennis, swimming, boating, sailing, fishing, hiking, bicycles, xc skiing, tobogganing. Golf and riding nearby. Dick and Jane Lowe, Innkeepers.

Directions: From I-84, take Exit 7 and follow Rte. 7 north to Rte. 202 (formerly 25) through New Milford. Proceed 8 mi. to New Preston then 1½ mi. to inn on Rte. 45.

CURTIS HOUSE
Woodbury, Connecticut

"Yes, since the inn opened in 1754, I believe we are the oldest inn in Connecticut." The speaker was redhaired Gary Hardisty, himself a lifelong resident of Woodbury and a member of a family that has operated the Curtis House since early 1950.

"There have been quite a few changes and alterations over the years, and many different owners. However, since four of them, all unrelated, were named 'Curtis' I believe that this is an appropriate name."

The Curtis House by any name is a real country inn experience. I visited it on a chilly Saturday afternoon in January after a pleasant snowfall the night before. Everything combined to make it idyllically New England. The countryside was at its best in a white mantle, and the towns and villages in northwest Connecticut, with 18th-century homes and churches, gleamed in the bright sunshine.

The drive from the Massachusetts Berkshires (Woodbury is in the Connecticut Berkshires) took about 90 minutes and I was eagerly anticipating lunch. As I opened the old front door, the heavenly odors of hearty New England cooking wafted toward me.

I walked through a narrow hallway, past the stairway to the lodging rooms on two floors above, and entered the low-ceilinged, heavily-beamed dining room. Waitresses were bustling about carrying trays laden with plates of beef pot pie, Yankee pot roast, roast beef hash, scallops, and blueberry pancakes. The room was filled with happy people including quite a few families of students at the local prep school. I was given a quiet table in the corner, and my visit to the Curtis House began in earnest.

My luncheon included a delicious fresh fruit and sherbet cup, hot muffins, and a beef pie. From the desserts, I chose an apple crisp which was served with vanilla ice cream. I noticed that the dinner menu offered these things and much more, including sweetbreads, roast beef, and quite a few fish dishes such as broiled bluefish.

I was delighted to discover that there were 18 lodging rooms in this old inn, many of them with canopied twin or double beds. Twelve of the rooms have private baths. There are four more modern rooms in the nearby Carriage House.

Later, I chatted with Gary Hardisty in the living room with the fireplace and wide floor boards. He explained that the large inn signs outside were the work of Wallace Nutting who included many of the Woodbury buildings in his book, *Connecticut the Beautiful*. Gary explained that Woodbury was one of the antiquing centers of New England and there were many, many antique shops on Routes 6 and 47. The Glebe House, which was the birthplace of the American Episcopal church, is only a ten-minute walk from the inn.

Gary explained that as a rule dinner reservations are not accepted with the exception of New Year's Eve, Mother's Day, Easter, and Thanksgiving.

I learned that almost everything on the extensive menu is prepared from scratch and the inn does all of its own baking. Those warm muffins at lunch really hit the spot.

After spending the remaining part of the afternoon browsing through the village, I left Woodbury and the Curtis House as the setting sun created great red and orange streaks over the snowy hills and the lights of the inn were already casting their warm beckoning glow. This was the way it's been for well over 200 years.

CURTIS HOUSE, Route 6 (Main St.), Woodbury, Conn., 06798; 203-263-2101. An 18-room village inn, 12 mi. from Waterbury. Open year-round. European Plan. Lunch and dinner served daily except Christmas. No pets. Antiquing, skiing, tennis, platform tennis, horseback riding nearby. The Hardisty Family, Innkeepers.

Directions: From N.Y. take Sawmill River Pkwy. to I-84. Take Exit 15 from I-84 in Southbury. Follow Rte. 6 north to Woodbury. From Hartford take I-84 to Exit 17, follow Rte. 64 to Woodbury.

THE GRISWOLD INN
Essex, Connecticut

"Isn't this terrific. I just love concerts." Bill Winterer and I were standing with his children listening to music by the Eastern Brass Quintet at Griswold Square on Wednesday evening, December 13,

1978. Griswold Square is a reproduction of a small village meeting place formed out of the early nineteenth-century buildings across the road from the Griswold Inn. Now they contain attractive shops and galleries. The occasion was the annual Christmas tree-lighting ceremony and caroling, which by now has become a tradition at the Griswold Inn each year.

in Griswold Square as we joined in singing "Hark, the Herald Angels Sing," "Joy to the World," and other beloved Christmas carols and anthems. It was a very touching scene and the moon, almost full, emerged from behind the clouds helping us celebrate it even more.

lights beckoned us to a sumptous meal. When I crossed the road, the dramatic lighting of the 1776 American flag hanging over the front clutching cups of hot chocolate.

"You know, this is one of the joys of innkeeping here," said Bill, "it seems to draw everybody together so much." I would say that this "drawing together" takes place not only at the Christmas season, but also during the rest of the year. In the true tradition of a village inn, the Griswold is the center of all kinds of community activity here in Essex. Apparently this has been true since 1776 when the inn was first opened for business by Sala Griswold. It even survived the war of 1812 when the British Marines destroyed the Essex fleet by fire. They commandeered and occupied the Griswold Inn during their brief Connecticut Valley campaign.

Today, the Griswold Inn has within its many dining rooms and parlors a remarkable collection of marine paintings, prints, ship models, firearms, binnacles, ship's clocks, a pot-bellied stove, humorous posters and prints, a genuine popcorn machine, and heaven-knows-what-all!. Futhermore, it has a dining room constructed from an abandoned New Hampshire covered bridge and still another dining room, where the wall rocks back and forth creating the impression you're on shipboard. There are fresh flowers, warm woods, open fires, candles, and different kinds of entertainment for the guests' edification most every evening.

There are eighteen guest rooms at the "Gris," most of which have private baths and are furnished in early Essex. The newest is called the Oliver Cromwell suite, named after the first warship of the Revolutionary Navy which was built just a few paces from the Griswold Inn. It has a bedroom, living room, bath, porch and a wood-burning fireplace.

The menu is basically American, with a wide selection of fresh and salt-water fish, also beef and lamb dishes which have been popular in this country from the very beginning. A Hunt Breakfast is served every Sunday which includes great long tables of fried chicken, herring, lamb, kidneys, eggs, grits, *(grits?)* creamed chipped beef, and the inn's own special brand of 1776 sausage.

Now the Eastern Brass Quintet accompanied all of us standing in Griswold Square as we joined in singing "Hark, the Herald Angels Sing," "Joy to the World," and other beloved Christmas carols and anthems. It was a very touching scene and the moon, almost full, emerged from behind the clouds helping us celebrate it even more.

The white clapboard exterior of the Griswold Inn decorated with festoons and garlands intertwined with strings of small white lights beckoned us to a sumptous meal. When I crossed the road, the dramatic lighting of the 1776 American flag hanging over the front door really brought a lump to my throat.

GRISWOLD INN, Main St., Essex, Conn. 06426; 203-767-0991. A 16-room inn in a waterside town, steps away from the Connecticut River, and located near the Eugene O'Neill Theatre, Goodspeed Opera House, Ivoryton Playhouse, Gillette Castle, Mystic Village, Valley Railroad and Hammonasset State Beach. Some rooms with private baths. European plan. Complimentary Continental breakfast served daily to inn guests. Lunch and dinner served daily to travelers. Hunt breakfast served Sundays. Closed Christmas Eve and Christmas Day. Day sailing on inn's 44-foot ketch by appointment. Bicycles, tennis, and boating nearby. Victoria and William G. Winterer, Innkeepers.

Directions: From I-95 take Exit 69 and travel north on Rte. 9 to Exit 3, Essex. Turn right at stop light and follow West Ave. to center of town. Turn right onto Main St. and proceed down to water and inn.

MOUNTAIN VIEW INN
Norfolk, Connecticut

I was looking through the 1969 edition of *Country Inns and Back Roads*. It had a yellow and green cover and was seventy-four pages long. Several of the inns I wrote about ten years ago are in this edition of *CIBR*: The Sutter Creek Inn, The Boone Tavern Hotel, The Black Point, The Jordan Pond House, The Whistling Oyster, The Jared Coffin House, Longfellow's Wayside Inn, The Botsford Inn, The Beekman Arms, The Lincklaen House, Moselem Springs Inn, The Larchwood Inn, The Green Mountain Inn, Kedron Valley Inn, The White Hart, and the Mountain View Inn in Norfolk, Connecticut.

Page sixty-three featured an excellent reproduction of a rococo clock and my description of the Mountain View.

"Karl Jokinen, the innkeeper at the Mountain View Inn, has a passion for clocks. He's the only person I have ever met who has a clock from the very first school he attended. It's a plain school clock that goes 'tick-tock,' and has an oak case. But he'll never part with it nor will he part with any of the others in his prize collection. It certainly makes a Swiss symphony when they all strike twelve o'clock at once.

"Karl and Joan love the Mountain View Inn. Their eyes lit up when they told me about how it was just the answer to their search. At that time Karl had nineteen years of experience as a saucier, second chef, and as a chef de cuisine.

"The Mountain View Inn (I continued in 1969) is a rambling white house sitting on top of the hill just down the road from the Yale Summer School of Music in Norfolk. It has broad lawns, many trees, and a tremendous array of flowers. Norfolk is on the Hartford road, and is one of the main roads between southern Connecticut and the Berkshires. It's quite ideal for a country holiday."

I had some very good news on that trip: "All of Karl's baked goods like pumpkin bread, prune bread, prune pie, apple bread, cranberry bread, banana bread, dressings, pies, and rolls will be available at the inn."

In 1970, I reported on the larger-than-usual-lodging rooms. In 1971, Karl told the story about Brazillai Treat, the famous fiddling ghost of Norfolk. In 1972, the new front entrance to the inn made news.

In 1973, I wrote about having duck at the Mountain View, and Karl tells me that it is the favorite item on the menu. 1974 was the year I pointed out that Karl made the small tables in the parlors from old sewing machines, and that steak tartare, chicken Papillote, and veal curry were well-received. In the 1975 edition, I visited on Thanksgiving Day for an abundant feast which I still remember to this day.

December, 1976, found me there for dinner and meeting (then nine-year-old) Jennifer Jokinen who was decorating the mantelpiece. There were old-fashioned Christmas ornaments and little arrangements of choir boys, reindeers, and Santa Clauses, and stockings were hung by the chimney with care. That was the year that Karl announced he was keeping bees and he used the honey in baking breads and rolls. Larry Jokinen at that time was helping his father in the kitchen.

In 1977, I spoke about the wonderful sense of joy which I always found at this inn, as Karl visited the guest tables wearing his white chef's hat. In 1978, I was still writing about the clocks and Karl's duck l'orange and people were still ordering it after reading about it in *CIBR*. Karl reported that he was doing more canning than ever, and the only things "necessary to buy are flour, sugar, salt, and things that really cannot be grown or made. We stay away as much as possible from processed food and stick pretty much to the natural things."

Now, in 1979, things continue to progress. Larry and Ronnie have gone into careers of their own, but Jennifer, at thirteen is a regular little innkeeper. Changes are being made inside the inn, which I believe our readers will find interesting in 1979. Karl was planning a new individual menu with a completely new design and selections; and for ladies, one without prices.

Among the things that have not changed—besides the warmth, hospitality, and concern—is the fact that one of the clocks is still running backwards.

MOUNTAIN VIEW INN, Norfolk, Conn. 06058; 203-542-5595. A 7-room village inn, 40 mi. west of Hartford in the picturesque

Litchfield Hills. European plan. Breakfast and dinner served daily to travelers except Mondays and Christmas Day. Open year-round. Golf, tennis, hiking, swimming, mountain climbing, bicycles, ice fishing, Alpine and xc skiing nearby. Karl and Joan Jokinen, Innkeepers.

Directions: Norfolk is on U.S. 44 which runs east-west. North-south roads which intersect 44 include U.S. 7, I-91, and U.S. 22. Inn is located off Rte. 44, ¼ mi. on 272 South.

SILVERMINE TAVERN
Norwalk, Connecticut

I wish that everyone could visit the Silvermine Tavern on such a day as I had on my last visit. It was mid-August, but a high pressure system from Canada had cooled our hot, humid air to a more bearable temperature. The sunshine was brilliant, and the sky was a clear blue as I drove down a tree-lined street through the residential section of Norwalk to the country crossroads where the Silvermine Tavern and Country Store are located. The Silvermine can be difficult to find and the first-time traveler has to follow the directions very carefully.

It was late afternoon, still a bit early for dinner. I walked through the lobby and found my way to the outer deck which overlooks the mill pond and waterfall. I watched the ducks circle and play in the vicinity of a single white swan who floated serenely, apparently unaware of the majestic picture he was presenting. The sun shone through the trees as they towered over the deck, creating a dappled pattern on the tables and gleaming silverware.

The deck was built around the trees with holes cut in the floor to allow the trees to continue to grow comfortably. There were even rubber cushions lining the holes to prevent injury to the trees as they swayed in the wind. What a pleasant place to relax in the warm afternoon sun.

During the chilly months guests can enjoy the cozy atmosphere of the several different dining areas all of which are decorated with antique oil paintings, prints, wooden farm implements, and other artifacts of our agrarian heritage. There are fireplaces and many old tables and booths conducive to quiet conversation.

The lodging rooms at this inn are typical of many country inn rooms I have seen. They are from medium to small in size, furnished with antique country furniture, and have neither television nor telephones. Lodgings are scattered through the various buildings of the Tavern complex.

At dinner that evening Frank Whitman pointed out some of the offerings on the menu: "There are quite a few New England dishes," he said, "including Indian pudding, bread pudding, honey buns, native schrod, lobsters, scallops, and oysters. Thursday night, we have a buffet that includes roast beef, corned beef, and fried chicken. On Wednesday and Friday night during the summer, there's a barbeque, and our Sunday brunch buffet has as many as twenty-five different offerings on the big tables over there."

(A word about desserts: save room for cream pies, homemade fruit pies, and superior cakes!)

"By the way," he continued, "we find more and more people seeking our country inn atmosphere for weddings. Some come from as far as New York to be married here."

This trip was particularly enjoyable because I ate outside on the deck, but this inn is also a great place when the wind is whistling around corners and the snow is sifting down through the bare branches of the trees.

I don't know what happens to the ducks and the swan in winter—I'll have to ask Frank.

SILVERMINE TAVERN, Perry Ave., Norwalk, Ct. 06850; 203-847-4558. A 10-room country inn in the residential section of Norwalk. Long Island Sound and beaches 6 mi. away. European plan includes Continental breakfast. Lunch and dinner served to travelers daily. Open year-round. Closed Christmas Day and Tuesdays during winter. Golf, tennis, and fishing nearby. Francis C. Whitman, Innkeeper.

Directions: From New York or New Haven via I-95, take Exit 15. Pick up the new Rte. 7 going north. At the end of Rte. 7 (approx. 1 mi. turn right, go to first stoplight, turn right. At next stoplight by firehouse turn right onto Silvermine Ave. Proceed down Silvermine Ave. about 2 mi. to Tavern. From I-84 and Danbury take old Rte. 7 south to Norwalk. Watch for Kelly Greens ½ mi. south of Merritt Pkwy. on the left, turn right on Perry Ave. opposite Kelly Greens. Follow Perry Ave. 2 mi. to Tavern. From Merritt Pkwy. take Exit 39 south on old Rte. 7 and follow directions above.

TOWN FARMS INN
Middletown, Connecticut

Almost a year had passed since my first visit to the Town Farms Inn. Once again, following Bill Winterer's directions, I turned off Route 9 at Silver Street in Middletown, and followed the road through the Connecticut Valley Hospital complex. Cresting the hill, I looked down into the valley next to the Connecticut River, and there was the mellowed-red-brick building with which, by this time, I was quite familiar.

This trip, instead of the hustle and bustle of carpenters, brick layers, cabinetmakers, and electricians at work, all was serene and calm. I walked into the parlor with its burning fireplace already sending forth a cheery glow against the chill of a mid-December afternoon. In one corner, was a striking Christmas tree with small glistening white lights, red bows, and gold garlands and ornaments. I settled down into a deep sofa and immediately ordered a cup of tea — it seemed most appropriate in this elegant atmosphere that reminded me of an English country house-hotel.

This time it was Vicky Winterer who was able to join me for a few moments before we both went over to nearby Essex, Connecticut, to share the excitement of the tree-lighting ceremonies at the Griswold Inn.

"Bill and I have had such a wonderful experience here during the past year. The decorating is complete and we're pleased with the appearance of the grounds." "Of course," she said, as she set her teacup down on the mahogany table, "we still have more plans."

We strolled into the American Indian room which has very low ceilings and beautifully mellowed exposed posts and beams. The ladder-back chairs add a harmonious note. Twin fireplaces were decorated with Christmas garlands and white lights, and all of the candelabras were entwined with garlands of holly. There were red roses in vases on each table.

It was a most interesting contrast to walk into the River Room which is almost two stories high with magnificent chandeliers, a Palladian window, and a full view of the river and shore beyond.

Vicky, referring to the terrace said, "We serve lunches out there during the summer, and everyone applauds when a train goes by."

The inner wall has a new mural which depicts a scene on the river around 1865. The light blue walls are enhanced with beautiful green garlands, and in a little balcony at one end, a stringed trio was beginning to tune up for the evening's entertainment. "We find chamber music most appropriate, but we also have other types as well," she remarked.

Although the Town Farms Inn is at present a restaurant only, Vicky commented on the plans for twelve lodging rooms on the second and third floor. "I'm just not sure when we'll be able to undertake this major project," she said, "but Bill and I are both very excited at the prospect."

Besides the ambience of the Town Farms Inn, its popularity is quite obviously based on the menu. There are a lot of New England dishes, such as Boston scrod, bluefish, lemon sole and Cape Cod scallops. I also noted roast Canadian quail, hare cooked in wine and fresh mushrooms, chicken Cordon Bleu, and beef Stroganoff. There's a handy children's menu, too.

We returned to the parlor once again, and I noticed a rack of newspapers including the *Wall Street Journal*, the *New York Times*, the *Hartford Courant*, the *Wesleyan Argus*, the *Christian Science Monitor*, and *the National Review*. "It sort of reminds me of a club," I remarked.

"Funny you should mention that," she said, "many people who come here say that it has a 'club' feeling. Part of the reason may be that we have quite a few Wesleyan University faculty here both for lunch and dinner, and we do host small dinner parties for the college faculty and staff." She looked at her watch. "I think that perhaps we'd better be going over to the Gris. I know you want to visit a few of the shops in Essex."

TOWN FARMS INN, Silver St., Middletown, Conn. 06457; 203-347-7438. A riverside restaurant just a few minutes from the center of Middletown. Lunch and dinner served daily except Christmas Eve and Christmas Day. Wesleyan Univ. nearby. Long Island Sound about 40 min. away. Bill and Vicky Winterer, Innkeepers.

Directions: From I-91 follow Rte. 9 south to Middletown and take Exit 12 to Silver St. Then proceed ½ mi. eastward, following signs to Connecticut Valley Hospital whose grounds resemble a college campus. The inn is on the left side of the road at the bottom of the hill, a red brick building with a black mansard roof.

THE WHITE HART INN
Salisbury, Connecticut

A country inn in Connecticut with almost equal parts of American main dishes and oriental gourmet favorites? When I mentioned this to John Harney, he laughed and said, "I guess I'm just lucky. A couple of years ago when I was searching for a new chef, Danny Yu Shan Lee turned out to be the man and it was one of the most fortunate moves I ever made."

The night had a festive air. The inn still had some of its Christmas decorations and was sending a cheery light out into the village green. A group of *CIBR* innkeepers, including the Edges from Rock House Mountain Farm in New Hampshire on their way to Florida, had gathered for an afternoon and evening of good innkeeping talk and, of course, good food.

The evening began with a tour of the inn and particularly of the spacious cellar where John blends Sarum Tea, which is one of his major occupations besides keeping a country inn. He showed us many different varieties and exactly how it is blended. "If all the cups of tea consumed annually were placed side by side, it would stretch eleven and a half million miles." he said. "We've been importing teas from East Africa, Ceylon, Indonesia, and China, with the help of Mr. Stanley Mason, who started the business a number of years ago. We're now turning out what we think is the best tea obtainable. Sarum tea, incidentally is available at the White Hart Inn Country Store which is located in one of the former dining rooms of the inn. Many other inns in *CIBR* also serve it."

Meanwhile, John kept up a running commentary on the dining rooms, public rooms, and lodging rooms, as we trooped up and down stairs. There were compliments for the comfortable and inviting country inn bedrooms with their flowered wallpapers and attractive bedspreads.

However, it was at dinner that John, joined by Chef Danny, really shone.

Because they were anxious for us to sample as many of the oriental dishes as possible, we were served a special meal that included barbequed ribs, spring lobster roll, rice paper-wrapped chicken, and sesame seed fantail shrimp. Danny carefully explained how each was prepared and also the section of China where it originated.

Our entrée included generous samplings of roast Peking duck, sweet and sour pork, hot spicy tangy chicken ball, sea treasures, tea-flavored hot spicy lamb, Buddhist delight vegetables, and sweet red bean stuffed honey banana. These are all on the regular menu, and as John says, "They are all hot spicy dishes, but you can order without the hot."

I should hasten to explain that the White Hart menu also includes hearty familiar favorites such as beef Stroganoff, filet mignon, breast of chicken, roast duckling, lamb chops, rainbow trout, and other New England dishes.

At the conclusion of the long dinner, we all stood up and applauded the chef, who repaid our tributes by passing out recipes for most of the tasty morsels we had been eating during the evening. "You will see that Chinese cooking is really quite easy," he said. "I hope that many of you will try these dishes in your inns and also remember to serve Mr. Harney's Sarum tea!"

WHITE HART INN, Salisbury, Conn. 06068; 203-435-2511. A 25-room village inn, 55 mi. west of Hartford. European plan. Breakfast, lunch, dinner served to travelers daily. Alpine and xc skiing, ski-jumping, golf, swimming nearby. John Harney, Innkeeper.

Directions: Exit the Taconic Pkwy. at Millbrook, N.Y. Proceed east on U.S. 44 to Salisbury. Inn is located at Jct. of U.S. 44 and 41.

Rhode Island

THE INN AT CASTLE HILL
Newport, Rhode Island

The October-November issue of *Historic Preservation*, published by the National Trust for Historic Preservation, has a most interesting article which deals with new uses for large estates. Among the ways that these beautiful homes and mansions of the past are being preserved is to convert them into resort-inns. Incidentally, a two-hundred-page compendium of information concerning the problems of preserving great estates is published by the National Trust and it is available from their bookshop at 704 Jackson Place, NW, Washington, D.C. 20006.

The article cites the Inn at Castle Hill as a prime example of a meaningful contribution to the preservation of Newport's architectural heritage and its open spaces along the ocean.

The estate at Castle Hill was built in 1874 by Professor Alexander Agassiz of Cambridge, Massachusetts. He established a laboratory there and studied with twelve Harvard students for twenty-five years, until the marine biological laboratory at Woods Hole, Massachusetts, was built. He donated part of his land to the government because it was the most obvious spot for a needed lighthouse, which was built in 1890. Today, it is a painted white granite tower, forty feet above the sea, and is visible for ten miles on Narragansett Bay.

I first visited the Inn at Castle Hill a number of years ago at the request of Mrs. Eileen O'Connell. It had been purchased by her father, Mr. J.D. O'Connell, a prominent Newport merchant a few years earlier, and she was seeking ways to make it into a viable year-round resort-inn.

Fortunately, a short time later another old innkeeping friend of mine, Paul McEnroe, was engaged by Mrs. O'Connell as the innkeeper and it is under his watchful eye that the Inn at Castle Hill has returned to its former effulgence. Paul was for many years the innkeeper at De la Vergne Farms Inn in Amenia, New York, which unhappily was burned to the ground in the early 1970s. However, he brought a wealth of innkeeping experience with him to Castle Hill.

The Inn at Castle Hill is literally on the edge of a peninsula where the Atlantic Ocean funnels into Narragansett Bay. It's just a few paces from the lawn to the water's edge. From the porches and all of the bedrooms, guests have an uncontested view of both the pleasure craft and commercial ships that ply this beautiful historic

waterway. It is a most advantageous point from which to view the finish of the yacht races which are held in Newport every summer.

Accommodations at the inn vary from the mansion-like rooms (some with enormous bathrooms) to housekeeping cottages which are rented by the week during the summer and fall.

The menu is definitely Continental, and the service with the headwaiter and assistant waiters all moving about very smartly is reminiscent of several fine European restaurants.

The article in *Historic Preservation* mentions that while the kitchen and bathrooms are new, the interior and exterior features of the house remain unchanged. It praises the oak wall and ceiling paneling, the fireplace of hand inlaid wood, and the fact that Agassiz's furnishings preserve its original homelike atmosphere.

I was very proud that the Inn at Castle Hill, which I've been visiting since 1973, has been recognized by such a prestigious organization as the National Trust.

INN AT CASTLE HILL, Ocean Drive, Newport, R.I. 02840; 401-849-3800. A 20-room mansion-inn on the edge of Narragansett Bay. Near the Newport mansions, Touro Synagogue, the Newport Casino, and National Lawn Tennis Hall of Fame, the Old Stone Mill, the Newport Historical Society House. European plan. Continental breakfast served to houseguests only. Lunch and dinner served daily to travelers. Guest rooms open all winter. Lounge open winter weekends. No pets. Swimming, sailing, scuba diving, walking on grounds. Bicycles and guided tours of Newport nearby. Jens Thillemann, Manager. Paul McEnroe, Innkeeper.

Directions: After leaving Newport Bridge follow Bellevue Ave. which becomes Ocean Dr. Look for inn sign on left.

THE 1661 INN
Block Island, Rhode Island

Rita Abrams was explaining many of the Block Island sights: "There are several hundred miles of stone walls here on the island still standing from the days of farming during the early 19th century." We stood on a knoll looking west up the middle of Long Island Sound with Connecticut on one side and Montauk Point on the other. In the distance was Orient Point, Long Island, where I could see the ferry which runs in summertime over to New London, Connecticut.

It was a marvelously clear day with blue sky and light fluffy clouds on the horizon. Gulls and seabirds swooped overhead and behind us were meadowlands and fresh water ponds. I counted twenty sailboats on the Sound. Rita, Justin, and Joan Abrams were taking the afternoon off to get some more saltwater tan and show me the beauties of this unusual place.

"The island is a paradise for bicyclists," explained Joan. "Don't you like the three-speed bikes we have at the inn?" Indeed I did. We were riding them ourselves, looking at the Victorian houses and enjoying the vistas that came at every turn of the road. I learned that there were 360 fresh water ponds brimming with fish, and that 68-degree waters offshore in summer make lobster one of the main products of the island.

Hiking on the beach is one of the most popular recreations here. There are twenty-two miles of beach on Block Island and the fabulous Mohegen Bluffs, 150 feet straight down to the beach. "Our guests walk the beach for hours," said Justin.

With so much emphasis placed on outdoor activity which seems to produce hearty appetites, I found that breakfast and dinner were very important times. There were many intriguing regional dishes, including johnny cakes, Indian pudding, blackberry flummery, Block Island clam chowder, flounder, lobster, and swordfish. All the dishes are made on the premises and the baked stuffed flounder with mussels and clams is a real joy. Another baked stuffed flounder dish has oysters and walnuts.

The 1661 Inn is an old white house partially hidden from the road by thick hedges. There are twenty-one rooms; five have their own private baths, but "sharing the conveniences" has always been part of the tradition of country inns for me. The rooms are decorated with attractive wallpaper and braided rugs.

Block Island is known as one of the best bird observation areas on the Atlantic flyway; I saw many people with notebooks and binoculars.

The big news is the rehabilitation of the old Manisses Hotel by the Abrams family. This Victorian building, just a few steps from the main building of the inn, is one of the vestiges of the great days at the turn of the century when Block Island was a very fashionable resort. It had fallen into considerable disrepair; however, during my visit in July, 1978, the first steps were to convert the cellar into a very intriguing restaurant, and the outdoor terrace into another dining area. According to a letter from Joan Abrams, it became "a huge success as the season progressed. We served everything from a snack to a dinner. Someone has already written to *Gourmet* for the recipe for our homemade clam chowder."

I can hardly wait for my 1979 visit, not only because I enjoy visiting Rita, Joan, and Justin, but I will be very anxious to see what has happened on the upper floors of the Manisses as well.

THE 1661 INN, Box 367, Block Island, R.I. 02807; 401-466-2421 or 2063. A 21-room island inn off the coast of R.I. and Conn. in Block Island Sound. Modified American and European plans. Most rooms with shared baths. Open from Memorial Day through Oct. 4. Breakfast and dinner served to travelers daily. Lawn games on grounds. Tennis, bicycling, ocean swimming, sailing, snorkeling, diving, salt and fresh water fishing nearby. Block Island is known as one of the best bird observation areas on the Atlantic flyway. The Abrams Family, Innkeepers.

Directions: By ferry from Providence, Pt. Judith, and Newport, R.I. and New London, Ct. By air from Newport, Westerly, and Providence, R.I., New London and Waterford, Ct., or by chartered plane. Contact inn for schedules.

LARCHWOOD INN
Wakefield, Rhode Island

"Rhode Island," said Frank Browning, "was the inspiration for the first 'two weeks vacation with pay.'"

This one stumped me. Frank and I had been talking awhile about how Rhode Island, for its size, is one of the most interesting and intriguing experiences around for travelers and vacationers.

"Take fishing," he said. "There are flounder, cod, mackerel, tuna, swordfish, pollock, and marlin in Rhode Island Sound, and just off Block Island, the fishing is some of the best in the world. By the way," he added, with a twinkle, "in season, we have most of those fish on the menu here at the Larchwood."

The point was well made, because earlier that evening I had enjoyed some broiled swordfish which was caught just a few miles from the Larchwood.

"As far as hunting is concerned, some of our guests have bagged partridge, quail, woodcock, and duck, although we tend to think of ourselves more as a place for swimming and fishing."

The swimming is done on southern Rhode Island beaches which are just minutes from Wakefield. People who have discovered them say that they're excellent.

The Larchwood was a well-established village inn in Wakefield for many years under Mr. and Mrs. Hugh Cameron. Frank was the chef, and a few years ago he became the owner. It is a community meeting place, and I noticed that the Rotary Club met there each week, and also that a generous number of businessmen from

Wakefield, as well as nearby Kingston and Narragansett, were enjoying a hearty lunch in the Scottish Lounge.

The Scottish theme established by the Camerons is being carried forward, and the walls of one of the dining rooms known as the Crest Room are covered with Scottish badges and tartans. Here and there I found an inscription from the works of Robert Burns.

"Burns is very important here," said Frank, "we celebrate his birthday on the first Saturday in January."

My visit to the Larchwood also included a tour of the lodging rooms, which are quite large since the inn was originally built as a mansion in the 19th century. There are usually two beds in each room, and the windows afford a view of spacious lawns and beech, larch, blue spruce, and pine trees.

During spring and summer, the rhododendrons, begonias, roses, and forsythia are a colorful display. In fact, the Larchwood, during the first week in June with all the spring plants in bloom is a sight anyone would enjoy.

I couldn't resist asking Frank what he meant by "the first two weeks vacation with pay."

"Oh, that," he said. "It happened in 1524 when the Italian sailor Verrazano was exploring the North American coast. He became so enthralled with Narragansett Bay that he lingered here for a fortnight!"

LARCHWOOD INN, 176 Main St., Wakefield, R.I. 02879; 401-783-5454. An 11-room village inn just 3 mi. from the famous southern R.I. beaches. Some rooms with shared bath. European plan. Breakfast, lunch, dinner served every day of the year. Swimming, boating, surfing, fishing, xc skiing, and bicycles nearby. Francis Browning, Innkeeper.

Directions: From Rte. 1, take Pond St. Exit and proceed ½ mi. directly to inn.

Massachusetts

CAPE COD

Cape Cod is one of the premier travel attractions of New England. It's a peninsula extending out into the Atlantic Ocean, which is shaped exactly like an arm in the position of flexing the biceps. The Cape was formed by glacial deposits, and a great deal of it is in sand dunes which are protected by the National Park Service. The inner Cape consists of the communities of Buzzard's Bay, Bourne, Falmouth, and Woods Hole. The middle Cape has Hyannis, Dennis, Brewster, Harwich, Harwich Port, and other similar towns. The outer Cape is Wellfleet, Truro, and Provincetown.

It takes about an hour to drive from Buzzard's Bay on the mainland to Provincetown on the Mid-Cape Highway, and much longer on the various attenuations of route 6A. The Cape is extremely popular during the two high summer months of July and August, and it is frequently very difficult to find overnight accommodations. The restaurants are quite apt to be totally reserved, especially on the weekends. The Cape particularly appeals to me in September and October, because the sun is still very high and the water is still warm enough for swimming. The Cape weather at this time is usually ideal. I can do my backroading, bicycling, and strolling in comparative solitude.

THE BRAMBLE INN
Brewster, Cape Cod, Massachusetts

As the Cape Cod twilight deepened, each passing moment brought greater brightness from the single candle which complemented the table setting for dinner at the Bramble Inn. Fortunately, I had the pleasure of the company of two very attractive women, Karen Etsell and Elaine Brennan, the alert innkeepers.

The entire ambience was most pleasant. The basic colors are green and pink. For example there are green place mats and pink napkins held in place by very attractive flowered rosebud napkin rings. The walls and woodwork are sparkling white and the floorboards of differing widths have been refinished to a warm, brown patina. There are lots of plants hanging from the ceiling and lots of ivy to provide more accents of green.

"Mmmm, this is a delicious dinner," I exclaimed. What is this dish called?" Karen replied: "It's our Carbonnade de Boeuf Bourguignon. It is tender chunks of beef marinated in Burgundy wine with spices, and then baked slowly with fresh mushrooms, turnips, onions, and carrots. We purposefully have a limited menu because we think that anything we do, we want to do as well as

possible. This is served with salad and freshly baked bread right from our own ovens."

The full name for this inn is the Bramble Inn Gallery and Cafe, and this interest in art on the part of both Karen and Elaine is reflected by the most interesting collection of water colors, oil paintings, lithographs, pastels, and wood lathe art which decorate the walls of the dining rooms.

"We are both very much interested in art," said Elaine, "and both of us like to do various forms of art ourselves, as well as display the works of local and off-Cape artists here in the gallery. Karen studied wood-cut printing and I studied silk screening."

"Elaine is an excellent photographer," asserted Karen. "Last year she had a one-woman show at the Inn at Princeton. She also does off-loom weavings and plans this coming winter to create some nature weavings to display next season."

Brunch and lunch seemed to go on indefinitely here, and the menu includes Cape Cod clam chowder, home-baked bread, cheese plates—including one called breakfast cheese plate (a delightful repast which I grew accustomed to while traveling in Europe), consisting of a light cheese for the morning meal. Most of these are accompanied by fruits. The luncheon plate consists of fruits served with a choice of Brie, Camembert, and Vermont cheddar cheese, and more of that wonderful baked bread. A delicious quiche and two crêpe dishes round out the menu.

During dessert that evening, which was a delicious chocolate mint crêpe, our conversation turned to the fact that this side of the Cape is quite different from the south shore. "It's interesting," said Elaine, "because the Cape has such a variety of aspects. The north shore is quite different, but then all of the places on the Cape have their own personality—Provincetown, Chatham, Hyannis, and Brewster."

That evening I remained overnight in one of the two guest rooms above stairs. Mine, with the double bed, had pleasant country inn furniture, and a blue towel with a matching washcloth were laid out on the bureau for me. The shared bathroom was just outside my door. The other room has twin beds.

After my Continental breakfast the next morning, Karen and Elaine presented me with a copy of their very own cookbook which has recipes for some of the quiche, soup, and cheese dishes which are used at the inn. It also has the recipe for the "Bramble," an old-fashioned Cape Cod delicacy with raisins and cranberries wrapped in a tender pastry and topped with vanilla ice cream.

I think anybody looking for a small, cozy, intimate spot to stay at Cape Cod will enjoy the Bramble Inn.

THE BRAMBLE INN GALLERY AND CAFE, Route 6A, Main St., Brewster, Cape Cod, Ma. 02631; 617-896-7644. A village inn and art gallery in the heart of one of Cape Cod's northshore villages. Lodgings include Continental breakfast. Lunch and dinner served daily except Mondays. Open May through October. Small, intimate inn does not meet the needs of most children. No pets. Swimming, sailing, water sports, golf, recreational, and natural attractions within a short drive. Adjacent to tennis club. Elaine Brennan and Karen Etsell, Innkeepers.

Directions: Take Exit 10 from Rte. 6. Follow to the intersection of Rte. 6A (4 mi.). Turn right, one-tenth mile to inn.

NAUSET HOUSE
East Orleans, Cape Cod Massachusetts

"Please step into our conservatory." Lucille Schwarz led the way from the terrace of the Nauset House into what was at that time a partially constructed greenhouse, which was being added to the inn. Jan Lindstrom's sketch shows it very well.

"Jack and I have had more fun, not to mention a few arguments about this entire project," she said. "This was originally built in 1908 as a conservatory on an estate in Greenwich, Connecticut. It was disassembled, each part was carefully labeled, and then it was sent here by truck. It arrived here all in pieces. As you can see, we've been working hard at getting it reassembled, and I fully expect to have it completed early in 1979. We're going to use it as a covered garden, and our guests will undoubtedly take breakfast or afternoon tea and refreshments in it."

The Nauset House Inn is really a combination of antique shop and bed-and-breakfast inn. There are actually more antiques in the

inn than in the shop. Lucille and Jack have been avid and knowledgeable collectors for some time, and I'm always fascinated to see the new pieces that have been added since my previous visit. There are beds made from sleighs, chairs that once were horse buggies, butter churns, spinning wheels, wonderful marine pieces, and many, many more.

There's a tiny antique shop in the orchard just behind the inn with still more choice selections.

Lodging rooms are in the main house and in the barn where one of the guest rooms has a canopy bed.

Breakfast is the only meal served and all sorts of New England and Cape Cod things are offered, including real maple syrup from the Schwarz's farm in Vermont. Lucille has a very winning way with scrambled eggs. For lunch and dinner they're happy to recommend restaurants on the Cape from Chatham to Provincetown. "Many of our guests go to the Bramble Inn, which is just across the Cape," said Jack, "and quite a few go out to the Red Inn in Provincetown."

Guests at the Nauset House Inn have the entire Cape with its many natural attractions at their disposal. It's particularly enjoyable from late May through early June, and again after Labor Day. It's also fun walking on nearby Nauset Beach, finding it almost deserted.

In my yearly visits to see Jack and Lucille, I found that there have been people from all over the world gathered around the breakfast table and seated under the orchard trees. One of them, T.R. Milligan, a professor of language and linguistics at Manhattan College in Riverdale, New York, who delights in writing poetry, sent a rather lengthy poem about his stay. The last two stanzas I think sum up his feelings about country inns:

The magic of this Inn is not performed
With mirrors. Breakfast helps: French toast itself
Deserving of a toast, and quiche beyond
The reach of stock superlatives. And those
Clocks that grace the wall: like guests, each one
A private face, with independent chime;
And some, perhaps believing time's too short,
Simply never make a sound at all.

Now if a blazing hearth defines a home,
Then the Nauset House has earned the definition.
To meet here is to be well met: good talk
Is made before a fire, and memories forged
Beyond a mere recycled recollection . . .
And so we say: salud, sante', and prost
To the hostess and the host! And to all
Who pass this way, let the good word be:
See you at the Home—and wait for me!

NAUSET HOUSE INN, P.O. Box 446, Nauset Beach Rd., East Orleans, Cape Cod, Mass. 02643; 617-255-2195. A 12-room country inn 90 mi. from Boston, 27 mi. from Hyannis. Breakfast served to inn guests only. No other meals served. Some rooms with shared bath. Open daily from April 1 to Nov. 15. No children under 10 yrs. No pets. Within walking distance of Nauset Beach. Riding and bicycles nearby. Jack and Lucy Schwarz, Innkeepers.

Directions: From the Mid-Cape Hwy. (Rte. 6), take Exit 12. Bear right to first traffic light. Follow signs for Nauset Beach. Inn is located ¼ mi. before beach on Nauset Beach Rd.

BRADFORD GARDENS INN
Provincetown, Massachusetts

The light from the fireplace, so welcome at any time, flickered over the low ceiling of the bedroom and glanced off the polished headboard of the bed and bureau. I pulled the counterpane up under my chin and luxuriated in the delicious comfort of actually having a fire in my bedroom in the morning. Six of the rooms at Bradford Gardens have their own fireplaces, and one has a Franklin stove.

The front window of my room overlooked a corner of Province-town Harbor and the shapes of the old houses, shops, and churches became more visible in the early morning light. The side window overlooked a beautiful rose garden with over 300 plants, and several flowering fruit trees, and many chairs and chaise lounges scattered

about. An outdoor fireplace is also located in this area, and is used by some of the guests for their own cooking should the spirit move them. Breakfast is the only meal served at the Bradford Gardens, but Jim Logan, the innkeeper, is happy to describe the specialties of the various Provincetown restaurants.

I remained in bed until the very last minute and then hustled downstairs to meet Jim and the other guests at breakfast. On this particular morning we had eggs Franciscan. However, there are several different dishes offered on successive mornings. During the summer, lighter breakfasts are served in the Rose Garden.

It's very tempting to stay on and on at the Bradford Gardens Inn because there is so much to do in the immediate vicinity. The inn is located away from downtown Provincetown, but well within walking distance of all of the quaint shops and wharfs, the Pilgrim's Monument, the museums, and the dozens of other things to enjoy. The great Cape Cod National Seashore is only minutes away. It's fun to rent bicycles and use the many special bicycle paths that have been laid out among the sand dunes.

The Bradford Gardens Inn is rather small and quite informal. Guests become acquainted readily because Jim sees to it that everyone enjoys himself.

Each of the lodging rooms has its own character and descriptive name such as the Honeymoon Suite, which has a bedroom and sitting room with a garden view and a Franklin stove; the Jenny Lind Salon which has a beautiful spool bed; the Yesteryear Room with its astonishing brass bed; the Cherry Tree Room which is particularly lovely the last two weeks in June when the famous tree shows off; and the Sun Gallery Room which has its own private entrance, a fireplace, a garden view, and an excellent harbor view. Behind the inn, there is the Loft Lodge, which accommodates six people in two loft bedrooms. It has a deck, patio, fireplace, and includes a full kitchen with a washer and dryer.

I have been visiting the Bradford Gardens Inn since 1973, and it has been great fun to watch its growth during the years. Letters from readers praise the breakfast, the comfortable rooms, many with fireplaces, the growing art collection, and the feeling that there is somebody around who actually cares.

BRADFORD GARDENS INN, 178 Bradford St., Provincetown, Mass. 02657; 617-487-1616. A small 8-room village inn with working fireplaces overlooking Provincetown Bay. European plan includes complimentary breakfast. No other meals served. Open year-round. Within walking distance of Provincetown harbor and shops. Bicycles, swimming, riding, tennis, golf, and dune buggies nearby. Jim Logan, Innkeeper.

Directions: Follow Rte. 6 to Provincetown, turn left at 2nd P'town exit, and left on Bradford St.

THE RED INN
Provincetown, Massachusetts

It was a chilly January evening in 1974, when I drove out to the end of Commercial Street in Provincetown and came to the swinging sign that said, "The Red Inn," and parked my car. I walked over the red brick path to the front door, pausing for a moment to feel the fresh sea air as it swept across Provincetown Harbor.

As I stepped inside there was an interesting contrast. An exceptionally genial fire radiated warmth and good cheer in a low-ceilinged room that seemed to personify the idea of hospitality. There was an antique set of scales heaped with red apples. I reached for one. A young man whom I later learned was Innkeeper Ted Barker's son, invited me to be seated in — of all wonderful places — a great settee in front of this selfsame fire. I sank into the shelter of its depths, stretched my shanks, and prepared to be enchanted.

I learned from conversations with Ted and Marcie that the house was built in 1805 and was opened as an inn in 1915. It has been operating ever since. Almost every table in the different dining rooms has a generous view of the sea. They were kind enough to take me on a tour of all the nooks and crannies including an efficient-looking kitchen. This is Marcie's domain since she is the chief cook and originator of the piquant sauces and entrées.

The menu at the Red Inn is about evenly divided between fish dishes and meat dishes. For example, there were fresh broiled scallops and stuffed shrimp baked with a spice and herb dressing. The shrimps *champignon* were cooked in a mushroom sauce and served on a bed of rice. Naturally, there was lobster fresh from the lobster boats at the Provincetown wharf.

On the other side of the menu were sirloin steak, filet mignon, and steak shish kebab which sounded excellent. Also beef Stroganoff à la Troika which is served with verve and style. And my eye noted a dish I seldom see these days: smoked pork chops.

I eventually chose stuffed filet of sole served in a seafood bisque sauce. Excellent. Ted pointed out that there are many fish dishes available at various times of the year: for example, bluefish, swordfish, and striped bass.

All during dinner my eye kept wandering out to the water and the blinking lights of the buoys, lighthouses, and channel markers.

That was 1974. Since that time there have been some most appropriate additions at the Red Inn, principal among which is the construction of the Garden Room which now seats about another forty people very comfortably. It has windows on all three sides and the seating arrangement is such that every guest can look out over the Harbor, and even see the lights of Long Point in the distance. The floor is of slate, and the windows are adorned with planters, which are also used as dividers to create a feeling of intimacy.

In 1978, there were two sons, two daughters-in-law, and two nephews at the Red Inn, as well as Ed and Marcie. "It's always been a real family operation," said Marcie."

THE RED INN, 15 Commercial St., Provincetown, Mass. 02657; 617-487-0050. A waterside country restaurant with a striking view of Provincetown Harbor. No lodgings. Open for lunch and dinner every day of the year. Within walking distance of all Provincetown lodging accommodations and recreational activities and attractions. Ted and Marcie Barker, Innkeepers.

Directions: Follow Rte. 6 to end of Cape Cod.

CHARLOTTE INN
Edgartown, Martha's Vineyard, Massachusetts

"I guess you'd call us a combination inn, art gallery, and French restaurant," said Gery Conover. "We have five gallery rooms plus a gift shop on the first floor, and the lodging rooms are located on the second floor."

Gery and I were having lunch at the Chez Pierre, which is a French restaurant operated in conjunction with the Charlotte Inn. It had a kind of indoors-outdoors atmosphere with many, many plants arranged around the brick garden and with trees arching overhead. A discreet gate on South Summer Street separated us from the passers-by, who were doing what so many people do in Edgartown—strolling and looking at the beautiful Federalist and Greek Revival houses.

Chez Pierre is noted as one of the top French restaurants on the island, to which visitors come from all over the Cape to dine. It's run by a young couple who take great pride in their cooking.

Gery's two sons, Gery, Jr., 16 and Timmy, 9, stopped off on their way to go sailing in the Edgartown Harbor. "Many of the inn guests find the harbor a very pleasant diversion," he remarked, "and they can rent different types of sailboats and power boats from the boat livery."

"We are open year-round. Good sailing days start early in the spring and extend through the fall. It's interesting, though, how many people come out to visit us during the so-called off-season. Edgartown is delightful when it is more quiet and has fewer visitors. Our guests enjoy shopping in town, walking along the beaches, and biking down to Chilmark which is at the other end of the island. You can really work up a good appetite. It's beautiful here during the Christmas and New Year's holidays. All of the Islanders are very proud of their home decorations."

Like many other Edgartown houses, the Charlotte Inn is a classic, three-story white clapboard with a widow's walk on top. It was the former home of a Martha's Vineyard sea captain. There have been some changes, but basically, the building is the same as it was during the days of Edgartown's whaling heyday.

Following lunch, we strolled through the gallery on the way to the second floor, and Gery pointed out to me that one of the rooms was devoted to the work of Ray Ellis who had a most handsome display of seascapes and beach and harbor scenes in water colors and oils. "Edgartown is a very popular place to paint," he said. "It's also a great place to photograph in all seasons."

Lodging rooms at this inn are individually furnished and great care has been exercised in their decoration. All the rooms are very quiet and have their own private baths. A warm feeling of hospitality and a romantic atmosphere greets each guest. My large room had a working fireplace for guests to use in the winter, and was furnished with antiques including a four-poster queen-sized bed. It had a pleasant view of the garden and courtyard.

As in all the other rooms, there were fresh flowers, lots of books and magazines, good reading lamps, and candlewyck bedspreads.

Guests may enjoy a Continental breakfast served in their rooms.

Later that afternoon Gery, Jr., and Timmy returned in time to lend a hand with the inn chores. "They are both very helpful," said Gery, "and I'm happy to say that Gery, Jr., is really taking to innkeeping with great enthusiasm. He knows the island history and enjoys advising our guests about the best beaches, and the best fishing and sailing."

CHARLOTTE INN, So. Summer St., Edgartown, Martha's Vineyard Island, Ma. 02539; 617-627-4751. A 10-room combination inn-art gallery and restaurant located on one of the side streets in the village of Edgartown, just a few short steps from the harbor. European plan. Rooms available every day of the year. Continental breakfast served to inn guests. Chez Pierre restaurant open for lunch and dinner from mid-March through New Year's Day. Other island restaurants open year-round. Boating, swimming, beaches, fishing, tennis, riding, golf, sailing, and biking nearby. No pets. Gery Conover, Innkeeper.

Directions: Martha's Vineyard Island is located off the southwestern coast of Cape Cod. The Woods Hole-Vineyard Haven Ferry runs year-round and automobiles may be left in the parking lot at Woods Hole. Taxis may be obtained from Vineyard Haven to Edgartown (8 mi.). Check with inn for ferry schedules for all seasons of the year. Accessible by air from Boston and New York.

JARED COFFIN HOUSE
Nantucket Island, Massachusetts

I've been out to Nantucket a number of times. Each time I get the same wonderful twinge of anticipation driving from Falmouth to Woods Hole. There's a point where I can see the whole harbor and be reassured that either the ferry "Nebska" or the "Uncatena" has not left without me. I think this comes from having missed it on an earlier occasion.

Arriving in Nantucket on the ferry, there's the game of picking out the landmarks as the boat makes its way into the breakwater and the dock. The high-spired churches, the waterfront buildings and towers gradually take form. Then, there is the fun of actually going across the gangplank and putting your foot right down smack on Nantucket Island, the same Nantucket where ship-owner Jared Coffin built his house.

The Jared Coffin House is truly extraordinary. It was built in 1845 by one of the island's most successful ship owners. A number of years ago the buildings were restored to their original style both in architecture and furnishings. Today, the JC helps recapture the spirit and feeling of the glorious days of Nantucket's reign as queen of the world's whaling ports.

It's difficult to believe that this sturdily built, Federally dimensioned house is an inn. Only the discreet murmur of voices and muffled clinking of silver from a tree-shaded patio gives its identity away. It seems just like the other handsome houses of Nantucket whaling captains.

It was good to see Phil and Peggy Read again, and I was very pleased when I realized that I would again be spending my visit in the Crewel Room with those splendid four-poster beds and the beautiful antiques. Interestingly enough, I have met three other people in my travels about the country who have also been guests at the Jared Coffin House, and were also put into the Crewel Room.

In reviewing some of the events at the Coffin House in the last ten years, probably the most significant is that Peggy and Phil Read are now the sole proprietors of this classic country inn, as well as being the innkeepers. In 1978, a beautiful 1821 Federal house on Center Street, across the street from the inn on the dining room side, was purchased and has been converted into additional lodgings with six lovely rooms decorated and furnished in keeping with the Federal style.

Nantucket was seriously damaged by the Great Fire of 1846, and the discovery of gold in California and the subsequent discovery of oil in Pennsylvania (see Wells Inn, Sistersville, West Virginia), caused the depletion of the great whaling oil industry on Nantucket. These combined to isolate the island for many years.

Although Nantucket was known for years primarily as a summer resort, it has become more and more popular as an out-of-season resort as well. A visit early in the year will bring unusual glimpses of an early New England spring, while the fall months offer some of the most beautiful days, warm and clear, with vivid colorings of the moors which are unforgettable. And Christmas at the Jared Coffin is really special!

I enjoy just strolling about the winding streets, happily coping with the cobblestones, and bicycling out to look at the Scotch heather, wood lilies, and wild roses on the moors. These also provide a haven for rare birds such as the Swedish Nightingale and the Yellow-bellied Bulbul.

This kind of activity naturally makes for a hearty appetite, and I particularly favor the Jared Coffin specialties such as Quahaug chowder and bay scallops.

Visiting Nantucket is always a unique experience. Staying at the Jared Coffin House is probably the closest thing that I've found to actually feeling like I am a native for a few days.

JARED COFFIN HOUSE, Nantucket Island, Mass. 02554; 617-228-2400. A 41-room village inn 30 mi. at sea. European plan. Breakfast, lunch, dinner served daily. Strongly advise verifying accommodations before planning a trip to Nantucket in any season. Swimming, fishing, boating, golf, tennis, riding, and bicycles nearby. Philip and Margaret Read, Innkeepers.

Directions: Accessible by air from Boston and Hyannis, or by ferry from Woods Hole, Mass. Automobile reservations are usually needed in advance. Seasonal air service from New York and ferry service from Hyannis are available May thru October. (617-426-1855.) Inn is located 300 yards from ferry dock.

WESTERN MASSACHUSETTS

Fortunately, for those of us who live here, western Massachusetts is blessed with some of the best backroading that I've ever encountered. One such road is Route 116 which runs from Adams east through a few of the hill towns such as Plainfield, Ashfield, and Conway. This is a "natural" portion of Massachusetts which is not at all oriented to the tourist, and is home for a great many farmers and woodsmen who take a quiet pride in living and raising their children in this truly rural atmosphere.

Conway is a village located approximately seven miles from the Connecticut River Valley. Many people have sought it out because of its quiet tranquillity, and the preservation of what we've all come to regard as the best of New England's ideals, personified in some of Robert Frost's poetry. This is indeed a Frostian atmosphere, and I think that Reverend Jim Moore of the United Church of Conway has caught the real spirit of the village in this short selection from one of his parish letters which I am reprinting here with his permission.

CONWAY

Birds were softly chattering out in the trees in the graying of very early dawn. Quietly and slowly I went out so as not to disturb but to share in such peace of nature. Up the hill I walked and through the windbreak of trees and shrubs into the freshly mown, sweet-smelling hayfield. The tree-covered ridge to the east was silhouetted against a sky of softest blue which was beginning to be touched with the pink of the sun not yet risen. A mist was rising from the damp depression beyond the hayfield hill and softening the dark trees beyond. On the crest of the hill standing black against the screen of mist in stark contrast to the soft environment stood the machinery of haying, waiting for the drying hot sun to make it needed once more. What a wonder-

fully exhilarating way to begin a new day! What a breathtaking scene it was!!

We should consider ourselves fortunate indeed to live in such a beautiful part of this wonderful world, to enjoy daily its grandeur, to partake of its bounty.

Let us attune ourselves to our senses and fully partake of this beauty, and let our hearts be filled with gratitude that we are here.

THE INN AT HUNTINGTON
Huntington, Massachusetts

It was about two weeks before Christmas. I drove from Stockbridge to Huntington using Route 20 that runs along beside the Westfield River. The moon played hide-and-seek with the clouds as I parked the car and walked toward The Inn at Huntington, noting that there were candles at each of the windows and a large holly wreath at the front door. The brass knocker was the traditional pineapple sign of hospitality.

Inside there was a buzzing of activity as many people were standing in the hallway and parlor talking about the event of the evening. The beautiful brass candelabra was decorated with sprigs of pine, and the candle sconces had holly berries and holiday decorations. I saw both Murray and Barbara Schuman almost immediately. Murray was resplendent in his great white chef's hat. Barbara said, "Welcome to our Early American Feast. Do you have a menu as yet?"

Murray explained that the idea for the annual Christmas feast at The Inn has grown each year. "The first one was an Italian Renaissance Feast with madrigal singers in costume. Last year, we presented an eighteenth-century English Feast accompanied by a baroque quartet. This year we will serve an early American Feast five nights this week."

The evening started when a group of young musicians and singers came down the stairway dressed up in early American costumes, faces aglow with the merriment of the occasion. "These are all students from Gateway Regional High School," whispered Barbara. A trumpet fanfare was followed by a group of carols, then we all repaired to the dining rooms which were arranged so that groups of guests shared long tables.

There were five courses including mock turtle soup, scalloped oysters, jellied port wine with chestnuts, a goose, ham, and capon pie, and Williamsburg pound cake from an eighteenth-century recipe. The young singers and musicians joined the regular staff in bringing the courses to the table.

It was a wonderful evening with delicious food interspersed with more carols and music. It exactly personified Barbara's and Murray's ideas that a country inn should be a part of the community.

They met at the Culinary Institute in Hyde Park, New York, where he was Dean of Instruction and she was librarian. Now their mutual dream of owning a special country inn has culminated in the Inn at Huntington; a total concept of decor, service, and menu with each part complementing the other.

The regular bill of fare is called "European countryside," because as Murray says, "For the present we are focusing on Western cooking and respect the manner with which country cooks know how to blend and combine ingredients and wholesome and delicious dishes with hearty flavors and textures." Some unusual main dishes include roast duckling in a raspberry or a ginger-and-walnut sauce, poached fresh salmon, lobster pocket, sautéed fresh fish with shallots, and several specialties from Murray's internation repertoire gained when he was a student at the prestigious École Hoteliere in Switzerland.

Meanwhile, Barbara has launched what appears to be a most successful idea, combining her love of books with the knowledge gained in the specialized field of cooking and gastronomy. Her new catalog of books, available by mail, lists many rare and valuable out-of-print cookbooks.

Under the influence of such excellent hospitality, fine food, and Dickensian joviality, when the time came for all of us to join the singers in Christmas carols and anthems, we were in fine form.

THE INN AT HUNTINGTON, Worthington Rd., Huntington, Ma. 01050; 413-667-8868. A restaurant featuring European countryside cuisine on Rte. 112 (Worthington Rd.) 1 mi. from downtown Huntington. No lodgings. Dinner served nightly except Monday. Reservations strongly suggested. Open February 1st to December 31st. Closed Thanksgiving, Christmas Eve, Christmas Day. Murray and Barbara Schuman, Innkeepers.

Directions: Huntington is on Rte. 112, off U.S. Rte. 20, halfway between the Westfield and Lee exits of the Mass. Tpke. From Northampton use Rte. 66 to Rte. 112 to Huntington.

THE INN AT PRINCETON
Princeton, Massachusetts

The Inn at Princeton is really a jewel. It was once a mansion, with a lower story of beautiful fieldstone and an upper story of traditional weathered New England shingles. It is set slightly apart from the town in its own spacious gardens and lawns. Like so many other country inns, it represents a wish fulfillment—in this case, for two attractive women who discovered a few years ago that they each wanted to leave the teaching profession and open a country inn.

"It has been tons of fun and tons of work," said Suzanne Reed who, with Liz Sjogren is joint-owner of the inn, "but the moment we saw the house, we knew it had to be ours—it was exactly what we wanted. Although the outside of the building was beautiful, it did require quite a few repairs; but the interior needed to be almost completely done over. We worked after school, on weekends and vacations for months; cleaning, scraping, painting and wallpapering. We scoured the antique shops; begged and borrowed from our families and friends. We both had always been interested in art, and the art work seemed to fall into place. The miniature dollhouse with its tiny furnishings on display on the stairway landing represents part of our individual collections of miniatures."

"Meanwhile," said Liz, "we interviewed many chefs and cooks, and realized that this was going to be a real problem. Then we became acquainted with Walter Hawley, who is a graduate of the Culinary Institute, and he is our chef now. He has been wonderful, and our guests rave about his dishes. He is happy here, because he is able to do the things he likes best—to create his own dishes and experiment with ideas. As a result of his inspiration, we now have a special section on the menu called 'Menu du Chef.'"

From the Sun Room, one of the two dining rooms on the first floor, there is a lovely view through the ten handsome bay windows of lawn, trees, and a country road. The other dining room overlooks the great sweeping valley with rolling fields, and in the evening, the lights of Boston in the distance.

Guests entering through the front door are greeted by a fireplace on the right, and by an expansive living room on the left with a collection of very colorful and cleverly-lit oil paintings and water-colors. An old trunk holds firewood for the living room fireplace. There is an air of style and grace about these rooms with their highly polished parquet floors.

Decorated in attractive period furnishings and bright, cheery wallpaper, the bedrooms have many special touches, such as the cradle I found in one, and cleverly framed old photographs.

A breakfast tray is thoughtfully delivered to each room every morning with juice, coffee and sweetrolls or muffins.

It was a gentle evening in mid-September. We were all out on the terrace of this quiet, rather sequestered inn, when Suzanne said, "I think it has grown dark enough now to see the lights of Boston."

"Really? But Boston is at least fifty miles away," I exclaimed.

"Well, come and see for yourself," she said, and we walked to the end of the terrace which is the highest point on the inn property. Sure enough, there, twinkling in the distance, I could see some of the lights of the Boston skyline.

"Yes, and when it gets pitch dark a little later on they look like little diamonds in the blackness," said Liz.

For dinner that night I had sweetbreads Divan which were served on a bed of broccoli with a most unusual sauce. I was especially fond of the squash which was wonderfully spiced. I also had the opportunity to meet Walter who came out of the kitchen wearing his jaunty chef's hat. Among the other items of Continental cuisine are paupiettes du veau, lamb chops en croute, and scallops Provençale. Dessert was a fresh strawberry torte — delicious.

After dinner, I decided to take another short constitutional on the terrace with Elite and Easter, two friendly dogs from the inn. Sure enough, now that the night was inky black, the distant lights of Boston seemed ever so much closer.

THE INN AT PRINCETON, Mountain Rd., Princeton, Ma. 01541; 617-464-2030. A 5-room village inn 60 mi. from Boston and 14 mi. from Worcester near Mt. Wachusett State Reservation. European plan. Dinner served to travelers Wednesday thru Sunday, from 5-9 p.m. Open year-round. Closed Christmas. No pets. Not oriented for younger children. Tennis, swimming, skiing, hiking nearby. Suzanne W. Reed and Elizabeth A. Sjogren, Innkeepers.

Directions: From Boston: Rte. 2 west to Intersections of Rte. 2 and 31. From Conn. and Mass.: Mass. Tpke. to Rte. 122A to Holden Center, right at Rte. 31. From Vt.: I-91 to Rte. 2 to Rte. 31.

THE INN FOR ALL SEASONS
Scituate Harbor, Massachusetts

What do innkeepers do on their day off? On this particular day, a considerable group of innkeepers all came together at the Inn for All Seasons to renew old acquaintances and to enjoy one of Elaine Wondolowski's marvelous dinners. This particular meeting was something special, because a similar meeting planned the preceding year had to be canceled as a result of the great blizzard that had inundated all of the Massachusetts coast.

"I'm delighted that we have such a wonderful day, today," said Elaine. "I'm not at all superstitious, but I don't believe I could endure another ordeal like last year." We were all gathered in the parlor of the inn which is decorated in a mixture of turn-of-the-century and Art Nouveau. The wallpaper is black with gold stripes and flocking; the corner cabinets have little china pieces; and there is a chest of drawers with a marble top. A ceramic zebra stands on the piano, and there are elegant beaded curtains at the window.

Elaine explained some of her philosophy: "Everything has to be pleasing. We try to have the colors and the mood of the season reflected in both the atmosphere and in the menu. It changes four times a year. We serve heartier meals in the fall and winter, and light, more delicate foods in the spring and summer. I think that we could call our cuisine 'Continental,' because it allows our chef Tom Jablonski, a graduate of the Culinary Institute, the opportunity to express his imagination with Spanish, French, Italian, and other European dishes.

Elaine warmed to her subject: "Tonight we're having Crab Crown Pompadour which is one of our specialties; we originated this dish in our kitchen. We have it on the menu year around. It's prepared in a casserole lined with buttered croutons and filled with an egg custard, seasoned with chives, and then filled with selected crabmeat. It is then inverted and looks like a crown, bejeweled with a pompadour sauce and chopped truffle. Another thing we do is to offer our guests the option of having salad *before* or *after* dinner. It is always served with a chilled fork and plate. We change the house dressing four times a year as well.

"We've originated a lot of things in our kitchen, including chocolate cheescake, and I guarantee you we make the best pecan pie anywhere. We've had requests from *Gourmet* magazine for the recipe many times. We always share our recipes. That includes the people who come to our Dining Seminars, which are held at various times during the year and enable our guests to talk directly to chef Tom, who explains the dinner and discusses the preparation and presentation. Our manager, Bert Patterson is frequently the host."

Dinner was a rousing success—something that I know pleased both Tom and Elaine very much, because who could be more discriminating than keepers of other country inns? All of us spoke glowingly of the beautiful white dining room and the gleaming silverware and graceful stemware. There were so many little touches that make the room extremely attractive, both in the evening and for breakfast in the morning.

Elaine, of course, responded generously to the request for some of her recipes, but when it came to the secret of the dessert, which was a Trifle, she laughed and said, "Oh, Trifles are simply a matter of inspiration."

Inspiration—there was certainly a generous amount of this highly desirable ingredient at the Inn for All Seasons.

INN FOR ALL SEASONS, 32 Barker Rd. Scituate Harbor, Mass. 02060; 617-545-6699. An 8-room inn in a picturesque south shore sea town, 32 mi. from Boston. Shared baths. European plan. Continental breakfast, lunch, and dinner served to travelers daily except Mondays. Reservations for all meals advised. Open year-round. Children over 12 years old and attended pets allowed. Bicycles, fishing, golf, swimming, tennis, antiquing, and deep-sea fishing nearby. Elaine Wondolowski, Innkeeper.

Directions: From Boston, take Southeast Expressway south to Rte. 3. Continue south on Rte. 3 to Exit 31. Turn left at bottom of ramp and take right on Rte. 123 at traffic light. Go approximately 8 mi. to traffic lights intersecting Rte. 3A. Come across Rte. 3A, and follow signs for Scituate Harbor. At end of town take a right turn at set of traffic lights on to Jericho Rd. Take second left after Pier 44 on to Barker Rd. The inn is two blocks up on the right.

LONGFELLOW'S WAYSIDE INN
South Sudbury, Massachusetts

When I visit Boston, I prefer to stay overnight at the Wayside Inn in South Sudbury. It is set back from the road in the quiet countryside, amidst the trees and meadows. On many a morning I've heard pheasants in the nearby wood. It's hard to believe it is only 35 minutes from Copley Square.

On an early spring evening, I was back at the inn having dinner with innkeeper Frank Koppeis and it seemed quite natural in such a historical setting for our thoughts to be turned backward in time.

125

After all, the Wayside was one of the focal points of the events of the stirring days at the start of the American Revolution.

Frank was saying: "I'll bet Zeke Howe really had those Sudbury militiamen worked into a lather before they took off for Old North Bridge in Concord. He was the Colonel, you know, and I'll bet there was a lot of pounding on these old tables and shaking of fists in the direction of Boston. As they were nearing Concord, I believe it was he who is quoted as saying, 'If any blood has been shed, not one of the rascals shall escape.'"

"Gosh," I thought, "things like that happened here and the inn was already nearly seventy-five years old at that time!"

Today, the Wayside Inn, which became Longfellow's Wayside Inn as the result of the poet's famous "Tales From A Wayside Inn" is remarkably restored and preserved. It shares with the Beekman Arms in Rhinebeck, New York, the distinction of being the oldest continually operating inn in America.

Among the famous rooms which are a part of the inn today is the old Bar Room, the Longfellow Parlor with much memorabilia of the famous poem, the Longfellow bedchamber with a pencil-post bed and canopy, the Early Kitchen, the Old Ballroom, and the Old Kitchen. Most of these rooms are still in public use.

Dinner that evening was Massachusetts duckling in orange sauce, some baked Cape Cod scallops, and baked Indian pudding with ice cream. The muffins were from meal, stone ground at the Old Grist Mill just down the road. I felt that if I were going early American, I might as well go all the way!

Rooms at the Wayside Inn are furnished with antiques, but I'm happy to report that the beds are most comfortable and the conveniences have considerably improved since Ezekiel Howe's day. My favorite room is reached by a creaky staircase in the old part of the inn where the ceilings are quite low. I laid out my clothes very carefully on the chair in case Col. Howe should call *me* to arms, as well!

LONGFELLOW'S WAYSIDE INN, Wayside Inn Rd., off Rte. 20, South Sudbury, Mass. 01776; 617-443-8846. A 10-room historic landmark inn, midway between Boston and Worcester. Within a short distance of Concord, Lexington, and other famous Revolutionary War landmarks. European plan. Lunch and dinner served daily except Christmas. Breakfast served to overnight guests. Francis Koppeis, Innkeeper.

Directions: From the west, take Exit 11A from Mass. Tpke. and proceed north on 495 to Rte. 20. Follow Rte. 20 east to inn. From the east, take Exit 49 from Rte. 128. Follow Rte. 20 west to inn.

PEIRSON PLACE
Richmond, Massachusetts

"Basically I think we have two types of guests. We have permanent residents and those who visit us between Memorial Day and Columbus Day."

Margaret Kingman and I were seated by the pond at the Peirson Place, and so placid was the surface that it mirrored a willow tree by the waterfall. It was early fall, and already the sugar maples, oaks, ash, hickory, birch, and walnut trees on the grounds of this delightful, historic hideaway were beginning to feel the faint touch of autumn's brush.

"I've spent years researching the history of this property," she said. "It's a Historical Landmark in Berkshire County. We have two houses here, plus a great many outbuildings—this beautiful big barn behind us, and 150 acres of wooded hillside."

Margaret warmed to the subject, "The smaller of the houses is called Cogswell and was built in 1762 by Joseph Cogswell. He had to buy it twice, once from the Indians and once from the Colonial Government Proprietors of Berkshire County. A few years later Nathan Peirson built a tannery on this land, thereby starting a connection through a later marriage between the two families. Joseph Cogswell and his four sons were minute-men serving at Bennington, Bunker Hill, and Valley Forge. Nathan Peirson was a lieutenant in the Revolutionary Army for which he supplied boots and saddle leather, and which enabled him to build a new tannery here in 1784.

"The main house was built in 1788 on the site of the first tannery, and the Cogswells and the Peirsons were united when Nathan's oldest daughter married a grandson of Joseph Cogswell.

"I think that the Peirson Place has probably changed very little

127

outwardly from the steel engraving in the *History of Berkshire County,* published in 1875. Our front hall still has the original French wallpaper of 1789. Ells have been added to both houses and we have modern bathrooms, instead of 'curtained washrooms.'"

The Peirson Place is really very unusual. Within this circumference of history and natural beauty, Margaret has created an intimate bed-and-breakfast inn that is markedly different from other accommodations in the Berkshires. She has many guests who have been returning year after year because they enjoy the shaded quiet of the Victorian gazebo and the tranquility of the woods. Many follow the birdwatcher's path or the unusual trail for the blind, perhaps the only one I've ever heard of which allows sightless people to enjoy the woods and fields by "smell and tell." During my short visit, I saw many guests riding bicycles, and some were swimming in the pond and enjoying the use of the sauna.

Breakfasts or afternoon teas are great fun here because guests have been to Tanglewood, Jacob's Pillow, or the Berkshire Playhouse, or perhaps visited Williamstown, or the nearby Hancock Shaker Village, so the conversation is quite lively. The fresh croissants and crumpets disappear just about as quickly as the attractive young girls in their red-checked cobbler's aprons can bring them in.

Accommodations are in a wide variety of environments, including the main house which has very sumptuous rooms, and the barn. There are more frugal but most interesting quarters-hosteling facilities. "We make refrigerator space available for guests who wish to picnic by the pond, and there are dozens of good restaurants here in the Berkshires."

While we were chatting, a bird flashed across the pond and into the forest. Noting my perplexed look, Margaret said, "That is a black-throated blue warbler. He's one of over 100 summer visitors who return to us. Birdwatchers just love us here. We also have more than 25 permanent residents, including ring-necked pheasants and ruffed grouse."

"Permanent and summer visitors." Now I was beginning to understand.

PEIRSON PLACE, Richmond, Mass. 01254; 413-698-2750. A 10-room country house, 6 miles from Pittsfield on Rte. 41 near all of the scenic attractions of the Berkshire hills: Tanglewood, Hancock Shaker Village, marvelous backroading in western Massachusetts, eastern New York, and southern Vermont. Various accommodations: 4 rooms with private baths, 6 rooms share 3 baths. Lodgings include morning coffee and pastry, afternoon tea, and all of the facilities in the woods and the nearby fields. Pond, sauna, badminton, darts, boating, hiking on grounds. Tennis, golf, horseback riding, etc. nearby. No pets. No facilities to amuse children under 12. Open every day from Memorial Day through Columbus Day. One-day rentals not accepted on weekends during Tanglewood season. Margaret Mace Kingman, Innkeeper.

Directions: From Boston: Take Massachusetts Turnpike to Exit 1. Follow Rte. 41 north through Richmond. Peirson Place on left-hand side. From New York: Leave Taconic State Parkway at Rte. 295 and continue east to Rte. 41. Turn left.

RALPH WALDO EMERSON
Rockport, Massachusetts

"When it comes to rocks, ocean, and sky, I think we have more than our share," said Gary Wemyss. Gary pointed out to the breakwater about three miles in front of the "Emerson," as it is known to most of its guests. "In 1946 it was about three times the length it is now, but the storms and heavy seas have beaten it down until now in places it is barely visible. The far left end originally formed a harbor of refuge for sailing ships, but the builders ran out of money and gave up the construction.

"There is a reef out there beyond the breakwater known as Dry Salvages which was an inspiration for the T.S. Eliot poem. The town is trying to get the federal government to rebuild the breakwater because it protects us in winter's heavier storms."

Preoccupation with reefs, the ocean, and the swooping gulls is one of the big attractions at this country inn in Pigeon Cove. It is run by Gary Wemyss, the son of the innkeepers at the Yankee Clipper, which is about a mile away. The two inns make an interesting contrast because the Emerson is built along somewhat conventional

129

lines and has many rooms overlooking the water, whereas the Clipper is tucked away among the rocks overlooking the water and is much smaller. Then, too, the Clipper is open year-round, but the Emerson closes during the cold weather.

Gary pointed to two lighthouses which, he explained, were located on Thatchers Island. "They are the only twin lighthouses on the eastern seaboard. However, only one of them has a working light. People like to sit out here in the evening and watch the stars over the ocean and the circling beam from the lighthouse."

Gary and I started to walk down the veranda steps toward the swimming pool when a young boy, still wet from his swim, collided with me. I asked him if the water were cold. "Oh, no," he said, "they have heated water."

"And a sauna and whirlpool bath to relax in afterward," added Gary.

Gary explained that the guests include people of all interests and ages. "I think they mix well here," he said. "We find that the easiest thing is to not make any distinction in any way. Everyone seems to enjoy the things that are here—the village, the shore, and of course, the proximity to the sea. There is a real feeling of being relaxed and away from urban pressures, and I think that draws a lot of people together. It is such a relief just to have a few days' holiday."

Well, any kind of a holiday usually includes an emphasis on food, and at the Emerson the emphasis is on food from the nearby ocean waters, especially lobster. "People come to this part of New England for lobster, so we try to serve it as frequently as possible," Gary explained. "Sometimes our guests go up to the Clipper for dinner or people staying there come down here. It is part of the advantage of having two inns run by the same family."

Ocean, rocks, sky, reefs, lighthouses, bobbing lobster pots, plenty of homecooked food—all close to Rockport, Massachusetts, one of the most picturesque towns on the New England coast—that's what the Ralph Waldo Emerson is all about. It has provided vacationers with diversion and relaxation for many years.

RALPH WALDO EMERSON, 1 Cathedral Ave., Rockport, Mass. 01966; 617-546-6321. A 36-room oceanside inn, 40 mi. from Boston. Modified American and European plans. Breakfast and dinner served to travelers daily. Snack bar luncheon in season. Season: July 1 through Labor Day. Open Memorial Day through Nov. 1. No pets. Pool, sauna, and whirlpool bath on grounds. Tennis, golf nearby. Courtesy car Gary Wemyss, Innkeeper.

Directions: Take I-95 to Rte. 128 to 127 (Gloucester). Proceed 6 mi. on Rte. 127 to Rockport and continue to Pigeon Cove.

YANKEE CLIPPER
Rockport, Massachusetts

The granite boulders loomed around me as I gingerly negotiated the rocky path, grateful that I had worn my rubber-soled deck shoes. With the aid of some strategically placed rope railings, and following Fred Wemyss's directions, I picked my way down to the water's edge. On this warm September morning it was like a totally different world. There were small tidal pools in which I could see bright green moss and several species of marine life. Overhead a few gulls dipped and swooped, bright spots of white against the clear blue sky. I sat with my back against a warm granite boulder, enjoying the sun and salty sea air.

At dinner the previous evening I had heard the whole story of the inn. In 1946 Fred and Lydia Wemyss were here on vacation, when the idea of turning a private estate into an inn occurred to them. They have been here ever since.

"These have been wonderful years for us," Fred told me. "Our son, Gary, and our daughter, Barbara, have both grown up here. Gary stayed in the innkeeping business with us and is the manager of the Ralph Waldo Emerson in Pigeon Cove. The most satisfactory part of innkeeping has been the hundreds of people that have become good friends."

Rockport has been an artist colony for over forty years. Once it was a sleepy fishing village, but then it was "discovered" by artists during the Depression of the thirties. Some of the most important people in painting have either visited or lived in Rockport. Now it attracts all kinds of creative people, including photographers, writers, and craftsmen, as well as artists.

The Rockport Art Association's annual exhibitions are always a big event. Rockport has been referred to as one of America's most highly paintable locations with its open ocean, snug harbors, picturesque fishing boats, and great, gorgeous rocks.

131

The town is filled with fetching little houses with beguiling roof lines, inviting gardens, and winding elm-shaded streets. Furthermore, I am sure there must be at least a hundred different fascinating shops in this little seaside community.

My reverie was broken by a sailboat's passing not fifty yards from where I sat sunning myself. I decided to return to the inn and went back up the path to the grassy lawn with its carefully tended flower beds, the beautiful terrace, and the grape arbor. Lunch was being served under the shade of the old New England apple trees.

I strolled under the butternut tree to the pool whose water was dappled by the brilliant early fall sun. Experimentally, I stuck my finger in and found the water surprisingly warm. Fred explained later that the pool is heated.

I wandered over to a quiet corner near a beautiful old stone wall and found myself surrounded by a profusion of flowers and shrubs. I realized that there must be literally dozens of intimate spots in the inn just like this. In fact, that is a good word to describe the Yankee Clipper—intimate!

YANKEE CLIPPER, Rockport, Mass. 01966; 617-546-3407. An intimate 26-room inn on the sea, 40 mi. from Boston. European plan available year-round. Modified American plan from May 15 to July 1 and Sept. 5 to Nov. 1. Breakfast and dinner served daily. Lunch served during July and August. Meals served to travelers by reservation only. No pets. Ocean view, shoreline walks, many antique shops and other stores nearby. Fred and Lydia Wemyss, Innkeepers.

Directions: Take I-95 to Rte. 128 to 127 (Gloucester). Proceed 6 mi. on Rte. 127 to Rockport and continue to Pigeon Cove.

THE RED LION INN
Stockbridge, Massachusetts

I have a friend from New York City who came to Stockbridge for a few days in February. I joined him for lunch in the Widow Bingham's Tavern at The Red Lion and he fixed me with an accusative eye.

"You're always talking about Stockbridge in the summer," he said, "how we should come up to Tanglewood, the Berkshire Playhouse or Jacob's Pillow, play golf, and walk through the hills. I want to know what's the matter with winter?"

He happened to catch me after I had just taken a generous spoonful of one of The Red Lion's homemade cream soups, so I could only spread my hands in surrender. "Ruth and I came up Sunday afternoon. It is just about three hours from New York on the Taconic Parkway. We walked into the lobby and saw the fireplace. She ran over, pulled up a chair and said, 'I'm not going to budge for the next three days.' I felt the same way.

"We had a delicious dinner. I had roast beef and she had fillet of sole. Afterward we came back to the lobby and the fire for about an hour and a half and struck up an acquaintance with some people from Buffalo. The four of us went downstairs to the Lion's Den—what a marvelous decorating job!—for the live entertainment and made even more new friends.

"The next morning, after breakfast, the first thing we did was stop in at Country Curtains where Ruth has been ordering curtains by mail for years. She had the measurements for our newly decorated bedroom, so we picked out something right on the spot. Then we wandered about the town, went into the Old Corner House and saw

the Norman Rockwell paintings, stopped at a few of the attractive shops, visited The Pink Kitty and Vlada's, walked up the hill and took a long hike into the country. The snow started to fall, but I imagined that that was a device on your part to create local atmosphere!"

I started to protest, but he just continued: "The interesting thing about that walk was that we met two other people who were staying at the inn. They came for the weekend, but because they were having such a good time, including a morning's browse in the library, they decided to stay two more days.

Well, the fact of the matter is that Stockbridge is a five-season town; winter, spring, summer, autumn, and fall foliage. I see many visitors who are guests at the inn as they pass the window of my office on Pine Street doing just as my friends had been doing—enjoying a quiet New England town with fresh air, lots of trees, and friendly local people, many of whom migrated here from the city themselves.

The Red Lion Inn fits well into the ambience of the village. It is the community meeting place, where we all go for club meetings, wedding parties, dances, and political rallies. In the summertime, its broad porch with many rocking chairs is a meeting place for locals and travelers alike. Nestled behind the inn among the trees and flowers is a summer dining area called, "The Courtyard." It's just the right touch on a warm day.

While we were lunching, State Senator Jack Fitzpatrick, and his wife Jane, who are the owners of the inn, stopped at our table and graciously invited us for a tour of the inn to see some additions to its impressive antique collection.

RED LION INN, Stockbridge, Mass. 01262; 413-298-5545. A 95-room historic village inn dating back to 1773 in the Berkshire Mountains. Adjacent to Tanglewood, Norman Rockwell's Old Corner House Museum, The Berkshire Playhouse, Jacob's Pillow, Chesterwood Gallery, Mission House, and major ski areas. European plan. Breakfast, lunch, and dinner. Open year-round. (From Nov. 1 to May 1, only 30 rooms open.) Outdoor heated pool. Tennis, golf, boating, fishing, hiking, mountain climbing, and xc skiing nearby. Betsy Holtzinger, Innkeeper; Jack and Jane Fitzpatrick, Owners.

Directions: From the Taconic State Pkwy, take Exit 23 (N.Y. Rte. 23) to Mass. Rte. 7. Proceed north to Stockbridge. From the Mass. Tpke. exit #2 Lee, follow Rte 102 to Stockbridge.

STAGECOACH HILL
Sheffield, Mass.

I like to arrive at Stagecoach Hill just at dusk as the carefully tended stone walls along Route 41 become vague shapes, and occasionally my headlights reveal some deer out in the meadow. This route is aptly named Undermountain Road, for along this stretch I feel as if I am driving directly underneath the imposing, protective influence of Mount Race.

Entry is through ponderous Victorian doors and up a short flight of stairs to a lounge area, dimly-lit by candles flickering in red jars. Except in the warm summer months, additional light is provided by fires on two raised hearths.

More candles grace the dining rooms, which are most inviting with their red tablecloths, white napkins and gleaming silverware.

The walls have sporting and hunting prints and a generous sprinkling of photographs and prints of the English royal family, including Queen Victoria, Queen Mary, and King George.

Innkeepers John and Ann Pedretti, who will be remembered by many Berkshire visitors as the former owners of the Toby Jug restaurant in nearby Lenox, have made some very welcome additions to this old red brick building, part of which was once the town poor house over one hundred years ago. "We are creating six typical country inn bedrooms upstairs in the main building," explained John. "They'll all be decorated in character with the architecture, and there will be colonial prints, wallpaper, and appropriate furniture. Ann is from England, and she is most meticulous about things like that."

In addition to doing all of the cooking, Ann also does the extremely neat lettering on the blackboard menu which on my last visit showed such interesting main courses as baked scallops, duckling Bigarade, steak and kidney pie, and roast prime rib of beef served with Yorkshire pudding. "I learned to cook several different veal dishes because John is from northern Italy and he loves them. I also do a New England oyster pie," she said.

In looking at the menu, I realized that it was a choice of either an à la carte or table d'hote, or a mixture of each. Certain appetizers are offered at no additional charge, as well as certain desserts.

Ann, who is from a town near Manchester, England, met John a few years ago in New York where she was a fabric designer. (Small wonder that she has such a keen interest in redecorating the rooms!)

Oddly enough, they moved to England for two years in the early 1970s, and then returned to the Berkshires, and are happy and contented that they have found such an English inn in such a beautiful setting. "It might well be Cheshire or Derbyshire," she said.

The "Coach" as it's known locally, is an ideal distance from either Boston or New York. Its situation in the Berkshires makes it ideal for a visit in any season, because there are several ski areas within a very short drive, and also good cross-country skiing. In summer, all of the Berkshire recreational and cultural advantages are most accessible.

Returning to Stockbridge from Sheffield, once again I was impressed with the idea that the inn, with all of its trees, red barns, and its babbling brook would be a marvelous setting for Alfred Noyes' poem *The Highwayman.* How does it go? I remembered just a few snatches about *"riding up to the old inn door,"* and "Tess, *the landlord's daughter"* warning the highwayman that he was in danger.

STAGECOACH HILL INN, Undermountain Road, Sheffield, Mass. 01257; 413-229-8585. Inn with British overtones on Rte. 41 midway between Salisbury, Conn. and Great Barrington, Mass. European plan. Dinner served nightly except Wednesday. Closed Christmas Day. Near South Berkshire ski areas, Tanglewood, Jacob's Pillow, and all summertime attractions. John and Ann Pedretti, Innkeepers.

Directions: From Mass. Tpke., take Exit 2 and follow Rte. 102 west to Stockbridge. Take Rte. 7 south to Great Barrington, then follow Rte. 41 south to inn.

THE VILLAGE INN
Lenox, Massachusetts

It was one of those delightfully warm days in late April when I drove the few miles from Stockbridge to Lenox, taking the winding road up Prospect Hill past Lake Mahkeenac, entering Lenox through the woods from the south.

As many times as I have driven this road it has always given me a real lift to see the lake, hills, and open marshes where so many birds reside in all seasons. It is a reflection of the many moods of New England from the gentler one of this day to the rugged wind-whistling days of January—that same unpredictable weather that delighted Melville but distressed Hawthorne. Both lived in the Berkshires and in fact, tradition says, met in a nearby cave on a rainy day.

The crocuses and daffodils were in luxuriant profusion in

Lenox, and there were signs of early May flowers on the lawns of the Village Inn, where I was about to meet my friends, John and Peggy Rogers, Mary and Harry Harrison, and perhaps Rhoda Miller and Natalie Robertson would be joining us. It is an equal distance for most of us to meet and enjoy a pleasant luncheon.

The village of Lenox, with its tree-lined streets, has an interesting history dating from colonial days and continuing through the eighteenth and nineteenth centuries. In many ways, the Village Inn reflects quite a few of those historical events. The building itself dates back to the American Revolution and has been operated for over a hundred and fifty years as an inn. Hand-hewn trees of stout size fastened with wooden pegs support its roof and floors, and its attic and earth-floor cellars have abounded with ancient steamer trunks, crockery, letters, and other possessions of generations of guests, innkeepers, and their employees who have lived within these walls.

It is a two-and-a-half-story yellow clapboard building with a basic Federal design that has been adapted to meet various needs over many years. The two rear wings were well-constructed barns moved from another part of Lenox and joined to the inn about one hundred years ago. They form an L-shaped sheltered terrace and lawn on which there are a number of beautiful maples, a small fountain, and an American flag. Plantings of iris, daffodils, petunias, peonies, roses, and tulips brighten the picture throughout the warmer weather.

The inn is open every day of the year serving "all-morning breakfast" from eight a.m. until eleven-thirty. Lunch goes from noon to two-thirty. Because there is no evening meal served, a great deal of emphasis is placed on lunch, which is Marie Judd's particular interest. "We have all kinds of quiches such as mushroom and quiche Lorraine, also a wide variety of crêpes." There are other hearty luncheon dishes, including asparagus spears served with cheese sauce and bacon. I am very fond of the particularly good homemade soups which are served in bucket-shaped bowls. Larger appetites favor the luncheon steak which is served with garlic bread and salad.

Guests at the Village Inn are delighted with the bulletin board which lists literally dozens of suggestions for activities in all seasons of the year. One of these is cross-country skiing, and there is an excellent group of marked trails nearby at the Pleasant Valley Sanctuary. I have skied there myself several times, and also walked the same paths which become nature trails in summer.

Other nearby attractions for year-round entertainment are the Clark Art Museum in Williamstown, the Norman Rockwell museum in Stockbridge, and the Berkshire Museum in Pittsfield. In the summertime, the Boston Symphony performs at Tanglewood, and

the Berkshire Playhouse gives performances in nearby Stockbridge. Jacob's Pillow is just a short distance away in Lee.

The spotlessly clean lodging rooms are models for a country inn.

Luncheon was over and we resolved to meet again next week. As I walked across the street to pass the time of day with my friends at Squire's Antiques, I looked back at the Village Inn once again: "It belongs in Lenox," I said to myself.

THE VILLAGE INN, Church St., Lenox, Mass. 01240; 413-637-0020. A 25-room inn in a bustling Berkshire town 4 mi. from Stockbridge, 8 mi. from Pittsfield, and 1 mi. from Tanglewood. Lenox is located in the heart of the Berkshires with many historical, cultural, and recreational features. Breakfast and luncheon served daily to travelers. Open every day of the year. No pets. Swimming pool privileges across the street from inn. All seasonal sports including xc skiing and down hill skiing available nearby. Richard and Marie Judd, Innkeepers.

Directions: After approaching Lenox on Rte. 7, one of the principal north-south routes in New England, exit onto Rte. 7A to reach the Village Center and Church Street. When approaching from the Mass. Tpke. (Exit 2) use Rte. 20N about 4 mi. and turn left onto Rte. 183 to center of town.

THE VICTORIAN
Whitinsville, Massachusetts

Walking into an imposing mansion that sits regally above the street on a grassy slope, a visitor would expect to find rich wood paneling everywhere, spacious rooms and halls, high ceilings, a stately staircase, tall doors, and windows, and many large fireplaces. The Victorian has all of that, but who would also expect to find handtooled leather wainscoting in a charming third-floor room with lovely arched windows, or intricately tiled floors in the bathrooms, or a dressing-room in one bedroom with full-length mirrors mounted on the mahogany, walk-in closet doors? Marty and Orin Flint are still marveling at their good fortune in finding this fine example of Victorian architecture which was kept in excellent repair by the Whitin family—for whom the town of Whitinsville was named.

Looking in on the six bedrooms, I was impressed with the sense of graciousness and comfort inherent in all of them with their roomy, tiled bathrooms. The third-floor rooms have a shared bathroom.

Being a bit early, I still had my choice of their three dining rooms—the formal, stately blue and gold room with its blue moire-covered walls, ceiling-high windows draped with gold swags, gilt-edged mirrors, and a beautiful chandelier; or the book-lined, softly-lit dining room with its huge fireplace and two bay-window dining nooks. The third room was engaged for a private party.

I'm particularly partial to book-lined rooms, and so we sat down near some shelves that featured a set of "Tom Swift and His Adventures." Seeing a book by Edward Everett Hale, I thought I'd stump them with a question on what famous story he had written. Quick as a flash, Phil, the waiter, replied, *Man Without a Country.* Orin explained Phil actually taught French and was pinch-hitting that evening for one of their waitresses. The sense of camraderie and cooperation between the staff and the innkeepers is a pleasure to see, and I'm sure contributes to the enjoyment of their guests.

Although Marty is no longer doing the cooking, they are very pleased with their new chef, who is continuing to uphold the high standards she has set. Making a choice from their French menu proved to be a difficult job. Marty said, "Our most popular dishes are filet of beef with Madeira sauce and shrimp Scampi—but I think my favorite is lamb chops Souvarov, which are done like a beef Wellington with pastry jackets."

"Fricassee de Lapin" caught my eye—rabbit braised with wine and vegetables. Or I could have had prime rib, frogs' legs Provencale, oysters Florentine, filet of sole stuffed with salmon mousse, boneless breast of chicken with cream and seasoning, blanquettes de veau—chunks of veal with onions and mushrooms in a cream sauce—or boiled lobster. Salad is served in the Continental manner after the main course.

To choose between the desserts, as might be expected, is pure torture. I got to sample several, since we all chose a different dish—the crêpe with glazed fruit and a generous dollop of ice cream was superb; the apricot sherbet (which really isn't sherbet) is like nothing I've ever tasted: absolutely marvelous; the strawberry Chantilly looked like a huge piece of feathery-soft, pink and white cake—and tasted like some heavenly ambrosia.

A gracious conclusion to dinner at the Victorian is a tiny goblet of mulled wine served to every diner, compliments of the host and hostess.

As I drove down the curving driveway, I thought it is true that the house looks very grand and imposing, but the spirit of warm and friendly hospitality makes everyone feel delightfully "at home" in the Victorian.

THE VICTORIAN, 583 Linwood Ave., Whitinsville, Mass. 01588; 617-234-2500. A Victorian mansion with six lodging rooms available in a quiet town 15 mi. from Worcester, Ma. and 40 mi. from Narragansett Bay in R.I. European plan. Dinner served to travelers daily except Mondays. Lunch served to travelers daily except Mondays and Saturdays. Overnight guests receive Continental breakfast. Very small pets only. Lawn games, ice skating, fishing on grounds. Golf and tennis nearby. Orin and Martha Flint, Innkeepers.

Directions: From Providence, follow Rte. 146 north and take the Uxbridge exit. From the traffic light in Uxbridge, proceed north on Rte. 122 approximately 1½ mi. to Linwood Ave. (there will be a sign on the corner saying "Whitinsville — Left"). Bear left here. The inn is a few hundred yards around the corner. From Worcester, follow Rte. 146 south to the Whitinsville-Purgatory Chasm exit. Proceed into Whitinsville and keep right at the set of traffic lights onto Linwood Ave. The inn is on the left at the other end of Linwood Ave. — about 1½ mi.

Mid Atlantic

Eastern Time Zone

LAKE HURON

ONTARIO

Grandview Farm, *Huntsville*

LAKE ONTARIO

TORONTO

Little Inn, *Bayfield*

Oban Inn,
Niagara- On- The- Lake

Clarkson House,
Lewiston

Asa Ransom House,
Clarence

STRATFORD

Holloway House
East Bloomfield

LAKE ERIE

Glen Iris Inn, *Castile*

N E W

P E N N S Y L V A

Eagles Mere Inn, *Eagles M*

WILLIAMSPO

INTERSTATE 80

Tavern, *New Wilmington*

PITTSBURGH

PENNSYLVANIA TPK.

Century Inn, *Scenery Hill*

Hickory Bridge Farm, *Orrtanna*

Fairfield Inn. *Fairfield*

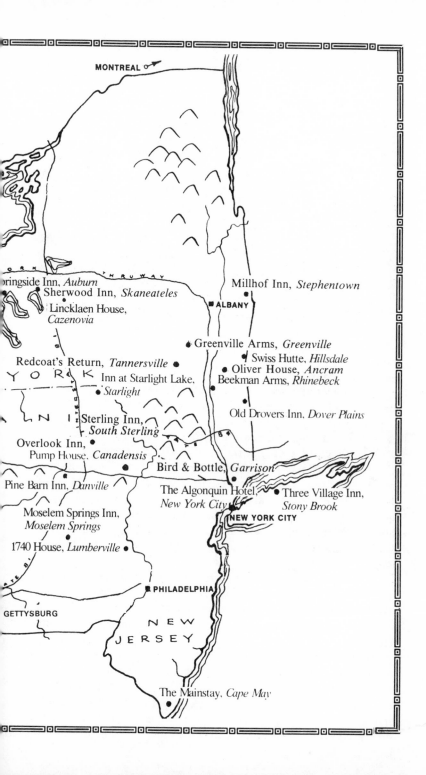

MONTREAL

ringside Inn, *Auburn*

Sherwood Inn, *Skaneateles*

Lincklaen House,
Cazenovia

Millhof Inn, *Stephentown*

ALBANY

Greenville Arms, *Greenville*

Redcoat's Return, *Tannersville*

Swiss Hutte, *Hillsdale*

Oliver House, *Ancram*

Inn at Starlight Lake,
Starlight

Beekman Arms, *Rhinebeck*

YORK

Old Drovers Inn, *Dover Plains*

Sterling Inn,
South Sterling

Overlook Inn,
Pump House, *Canadensis*

Bird & Bottle, *Garrison*

Pine Barn Inn, *Danville*

The Algonquin Hotel,
New York City

Three Village Inn,
Stony Brook

Moselem Springs Inn,
Moselem Springs

NEW YORK CITY

1740 House, *Lumberville*

PHILADELPHIA

GETTYSBURG

N E W

J E R S E Y

The Mainstay, *Cape May*

New Jersey

THE MAINSTAY INN
Cape May, New Jersey

I have a lot of news about the Mainstay, but first, let me explain that the building is an Italian Villa built in 1872 by Southern planters to serve as a very elegant gambling club in the residential area of Cape May. In 1896, the house was sold to a wealthy Philadelphia family who added a wing in the back to house six maids.

Tom and Sue Carroll bought it in 1977 from a retired Baptist minister who ran it as a guesthouse for nearly thirty years. Many of the furnishings are original pieces custom-built for the house. A pair of matching love seats and two brass chandeliers are identical to those found in a plantation in Natchez, Mississippi. The copper bathtub enclosed in a wood frame is like one in Washington Irving's house.

In addition to the ten-foot mirrors, ornately carved headboards, and marble-topped dressers, there are other unusual Victorian features. Under the beds are chamberpots which roll out on wooden trays. The original mosquito nets are attached to small pulleys in the ceilings.

Most of the guest rooms are very elegant and spacious with twelve-foot ceilings, while others in the maids' wing are small and cozy.

A recent letter from Sue Carroll had lots of news. "We have added two huge porch swings at each end of the veranda. Each is large enough for two persons to stretch out on, and they are rarely vacant. At last we finished renovating and 'Victorianizing' our dining room. Our fancy eight-foot chandelier was polished and electrified in Philadelphia and is really dazzling. Our guests seem to enjoy having breakfast in the dining room where we serve from mid-September to mid-June. The rest of the year we serve out on the veranda.

"Cape May is looking more beautiful than ever. We were declared a national landmark and had a big celebration. All over town people spruced up their Victorian buildings, and new shops and restaurants are popping up. "The Cape May *Ocean Wave* of June 1872 had an interesting notice about our place: 'The new club-house — in the design of this model building which now adds so much to the attractiveness of Columbia Avenue, Mr. S.D. Button, the architect, has won for himself additional honors . . . It is symmetrical in proportions, airy and cheerful in its appointments and finished in that unpretentious elegance so foreign to mansions of the shoddy order.'

"We have just returned from a wonderful trip following *CIBR* all the way. This included a delightful evening with David Thomas at the Fairfield Inn and visiting Nancy Jean Hamett at nearby Hickory Bridge Farm. Then we moved on to the Century Inn and thoroughly enjoyed Bob and Nancy Sheirer. The inn was beautiful. We loved the Buxton Inn and Granville, Ohio.

"Since we are Victorian freaks, we were thrilled by the Golden Lamb. They were decorated for Christmas in the most astonishing profusion of antique ornaments that left us green with envy. At Pleasant Hill we were amazed with the authentic details in the rooms. Such elegant buildings! We had a very nice visit with the Dedmans at the Beaumont Inn and admired that beautiful red brick building with the white pillars.

"We were warmly welcomed at the General Lewis and 'oohed and ahed' over their antiques.

"Now, we're back home, filled with inspiration and are busy papering and painting because we've got to keep up with all those inns we visited."

Funnily enough, I've had many other of our *CIBR* innkeepers say exactly the same thing to me after they have visited the Mainstay.

THE MAINSTAY INN, 635 Columbia Avenue, Cape May, N.J. 08204; 609-884-8690. A 9-room inn in a well-preserved Victorian village just one block from the ocean. Modified American plan. Breakfast served to house guests. Open every day of the year from April to October; weekends in March and November. No pets. Boating, swimming, fishing, bicycles, riding, golf, tennis, and hiking nearby. Tom and Sue Carrol, Innkeepers.

Directions: From Philadelphia take the Walt Whitman Bridge to the Atlantic City Expy. Follow the Atlantic City Expy. to exit for Garden State Pkwy., south. Go south on the Pkwy. which ends in Cape May. The Pkwy. becomes Lafayette St.; turn left at first light onto Madison. Proceed 3 blocks and turn right onto Columbia. Proceed 3 blocks to inn on right side.

New York

THREE VILLAGE INN
Stony Brook, Long Island, New York

On a fresh August morning, I was sitting in one of the beach chairs under a tree on the terrace in front of my cottage at the Three Village Inn. Seagulls circled over the scene which included the broad lawn leading down to the marina with its many sailboats and cruisers to the marshes beyond and the low cliffs on the northern shore of Long Island in the distance. A friendly robin lighted on the rustic fence and began poking his way through the entangled rambler roses.

The previous afternoon, I had taken the ferry from Bridgeport, Connecticut to Port Jefferson, Long Island, a trip that took an hour and thirty minutes and then followed route 25A through one or two villages, arriving at Stony Brook just about six-thirty in the evening. Once again it was Whitney Roberts, who has literally grown up in this inn, who greeted me with the news that his father and mother, Monda and Nelson, would be joining me for dinner a little later on.

The Three Village Inn is, at all odds, a Long Island institution and tradition. The Roberts family has a background of innkeeping which began with Whitney's grandfather who came from Rockland,

Maine and opened a restaurant called "The Maine Maid" in nearby Jericho, Long Island. Many of our readers may remember this highly reputable restaurant.

Monda and Steve came to the Three Village Inn many years ago when all of their children were quite young. For many years, they guided the destiny of the inn, and through the understanding and generosity of the previous owners, have now themselves become the proprietors.

Originally, accommodations were found only in the main house of the inn, but since 1971, the year of my first visit, several cottages have been refurbished or built to accommodate guests. These are furnished with colonial reproductions. Monda Roberts says that they are quite a favorite with honeymooners, and with people who like to escape from New York City for a weekend. Some of them have fireplaces.

There are plans to change the entire east wing of the inn so that the two ground-floor bedrooms will benefit the handicapped. Many of the guests will remember that this wing for many years was occupied by the Three Village Garden Club Ladies' Exchange which has decided to move across the street to larger quarters.

In addition to walking along the sandy beach behind the inn and watching the boats from the marina, there's a great deal to do on the north shore of Long Island, which is rich in colonial history. There's quite a gathering at twelve o'clock noon each day at the Stony Brook post office where an enormous carved wooden eagle with a twenty-foot wingspread slowly flaps its wings.

From the very beginning, Nelson and Monda Roberts have placed a great deal of emphasis on food. They are very particular about not using foil for the baked potatoes, baking them in rotation for the evening and using fresh vegetables whenever they are available. The menu is one of the largest I have ever seen. It includes a great deal of fresh seafood as well as generous helpings of beef, pork, veal, and lamb. The extra touch of serving fruit sherbet with the main meal is something I have always enjoyed.

This time Whitney was very enthusiastic about the fact that his younger brother Larry has joined the family operation and originated the idea of the "In and Out Room" which offers very tempting luncheon buffets. Decorations feature oil paintings and prints of three and four-masted schooners, and in the main dining area there is a boat model in a glass case that even has little tiny lights running up and down the rigging.

The Three Village Inn has been a way of life for the Roberts family for almost thirty years and by the looks of things, they've had fun doing it.

*THREE VILLAGE INN, Dock Rd., Stony Brook, L.I., N.Y. 11790;
516-751-0555. A 7-room village inn with 15 adjacent cottage/motel
accommodations, 5 mi. from Port Jefferson, N.Y., on Long Island's
historic north shore. Near the museums of Stony Brook. European
plan. Lunch and dinner served to travelers daily. Closed Christmas.
No pets. Golf, swimming, and boating nearby. Nelson and Monda
Roberts, Innkeepers.*

*Directions: From L.I. Expressway, take Exit 62 and travel north on
Nichols Rd. to Rte. 25A. Turn left on Rte. 25A and proceed to next
light. Turn right on to Main St. and travel straight ahead to inn.
Available from New England via L.I. ferries from Bridgeport during
the summer. Ferry reservations advisable.*

HOTEL ALGONQUIN
New York City, New York

A country inn in the city! I first became intrigued with this idea
when Andy Anspach, the manager of the Hotel Algonquin, wrote me
a letter back in 1970. At that time he had visited several of the inns
included in this book and suggested that the Algonquin had the same
qualities of warm, personal hospitality. I decided to spend a few days
at the Algonquin and found it such a refreshing experience that I've
been staying there ever since.

Among the very nice things that have happened as a result of
including it in *Country Inns and Back Roads,* is that a number of
people, despairing of ever finding a good small hotel in New York,
have written us letters of thanks. (I think this is one of the most
rewarding aspects of writing this book every year.)

One lady wrote: "One of the reasons that I enjoy staying at the
Algonquin is that the garage is located right across the street.
Parking in New York is a problem and it's a great feeling just to drive
into that garage and not worry about the car until I am ready to
leave."

Another letter said: "One of the Algonquin's joys is the late
evening supper buffet. What a pleasure to know that after the theatre
or the pro basketball or hockey game, we'll be able to swing into that
warm friendly lobby and have a choice of so many different
dishes. One of my favorites is Welsh rarebit. With the special salads,
fluffy cakes, apple pie, ice cream, lobster Newburg, and similar
goodies spread out on large tables, it's like being invited to your own
birthday party."

This small hotel was made famous fifty years ago when the
Algonquin Wits, Benchley, Parker, Mencken, and others of their ilk,
met there to enjoy the food and shred literary and artistic reputations.

One of my greatest disappointments in recent years was the fact that I was in Italy visiting villas and country houses at the time that the Algonquin Hotel was given a seventy-fifth birthday by their neighbors, the *New Yorker* magazine. This was most appropriate, because legend has it that the *New Yorker* was actually brought to life in a room in the Algonquin during the 1920s.

Today, guests are liable to see the most interesting people in the elevator—and hear the most interesting conversations. Recently, standing in front of an Algonquin elevator, a fragment of a conversation floated over to me. A voice of some depth and quality was saying, "And I told them I would not sign a two-picture contract."

I'm still trying to place that voice.

ALGONQUIN HOTEL, 59 W. 44th St., New York, N.Y. 10036; 212-840-6800. A quiet, conservative 200-room country inn in the heart of Manhattan. Convenient to business, theatres, and shopping. European plan. Breakfast, lunch, dinner and late supper buffet served to travelers daily except Sunday dinner. Open year-round. No pets. Very near bus, rail and air transportation. Garage directly opposite entrance, with complimentary parking for weekend visitors arriving after 3 p.m. Fri. or Sat. for minimum 2-night visit. Andrew Anspach, Innkeeper.

Directions: 44th St. is one-way from west to east; 43rd St., from east to west. Garage is accessible from either street.

149

BIRD AND BOTTLE INN
Garrison, New York

"This place hasn't always been an inn," explained Nancy Noonan. "It was built in 1761 and called Warren's Tavern. It was the place where the Albany stages stopped to change horses. During the American Revolution, a group of Connecticut soldiers encamped here for some time, and I imagine that the old place saw a lot of activity then."

Nancy and I were standing on the bridge which spans the brook immediately behind the Bird and Bottle Inn. It afforded me an excellent view of the original building and the wings that had been added at each end. It was mid-April and the spring flowers were just beginning to show off their fresh colors. The forsythia was almost gone, but the tulips and daffodils which Nancy and Tom had planted around the old wooden fence were starting to bloom.

"We're right across the river from West Point," Nancy continued. "It is not hard to imagine all of the secret meetings and discussions that probably took place here leading up to Benedict Arnold's defection. That didn't come until later on in the war, but I am sure that Mr. Warren, the landlord, must have had an interesting time keeping the Tories and the Patriots separated. This area had decidedly divided loyalties.

"Warren sold the tavern in 1832 to a man named Justice Nelson, and it became a farm for three generations. It was re-established as an inn in 1940 and has been one ever since."

Nancy and I had just finished a delightful inspection of the three lodging rooms at the inn. All of them are furnished in early American antiques and have either a canopied or a four-poster bed. All have private baths and wood-burning fireplaces. "There are two double rooms and a suite," she said, "and we're planning on one more. We serve a Continental breakfast for our houseguests."

Dinner that evening was prepared by Tom at my table, using a chafing dish. It began with crêpes filled with lobster, crab, sea bass, and shrimp. The entrée was delicious duck in orange sauce. I almost chose the roast pheasant which is served with special sauce and truffles.

In searching for the right combination of words to describe the Bird and Bottle, it occurs to me that "country chic" fits. The buildings are very old with low ceilings and wide floor boards, and the country antique furniture just belongs.

For the most part, the food appeals to the more sophisticated palate. I always allow extra time for the meals since each dish is prepared individually. I might add, that Tom seems to be everywhere at once.

"It's interesting," said Nancy, "Tom loves to prepare food at the table and he takes great care with our menu. In spite of this, our most popular dessert still is good old homemade American apple pie."

BIRD AND BOTTLE INN, Garrison, N.Y. 10524; 914-424-3000. A 4-bedroom country inn, rich in antiquity located on Rte. 9, a few miles north of Peekskill, N.Y. A short distance from Boscobel Restoration, U.S. Military Academy at West Point, and Sleepy Hollow Restorations. Dinner served Monday through Saturday, and all day Sunday. Closed Mondays and Tuesdays from Nov. to Memorial Day. Thomas and Nancy Noonan, Innkeepers.

Directions: From NYC: cross George Washington Bridge and follow Palisades Pkwy. north to Bear Mtn. Bridge. Cross bridge and travel on Rte. 9D north 4½ mi. to Rte. 403. Proceed on Rte. 403 to Rte. 9, then north 4 mi. to inn. From I-84, take Exit 13 and follow Rte. 9 south for 8 mi.

BEEKMAN ARMS
Rhinebeck, New York

For many years I have been sharing with our readers some of the historical significance of the Beekman Arms which is, according to the beautiful new sign on the front lawn, "The Oldest Inn in America." It is in the historic River Valley. I'm sure everyone knows about this beautiful section of the country because as innkeeper Chuck LaForge says, "Washington Irving was our first press agent."

The inn's origins go back to the early 1700s, and by 1769 it had increased to two full stories with a roomy attic which later became a

ballroom. When trouble arose between the Indians and the white men, the entire community would take refuge within its walls.

During the Revolution, George Washington and his staff enjoyed the inn's fare, and the window from which the Commander-in-Chief watched for his couriers is still there. Those were anxious days, and Lafayette, Schuyler, Hamilton, and Arnold also spent many hours at the inn. In fact, over the years, hundreds of men who helped fashion the destiny of our nation partook of the inn's hospitality.

There have been courtships, weddings, political rallies, quarrels, assignations, plots, counterplots, concerts, balls, and parties galore. In short, it's now rounding out its third century of being the center of community activities.

I was made even more aware of this on my last visit just a few days before Christmas of 1978. It was one of those days when leaden skies and sullen winds were harbingers of a real snowstorm.

Inside, Earl Bebo put another log on the fire for a group of very excited ladies who were here for a Christmas holiday lunch. He also lit the little candle sconces, and the true cheeriness of the inn began to pervade the atmosphere. I commented on the attractiveness of the American primitive furniture, with which all the dining rooms and parlors of the inn are now outfitted, and Earl replied that the Water Wheel Wood Works in nearby Pine Plains is also making specially designed furniture for the inn's lodging rooms. "In 1979 we will have completed transforming four rooms into two with private baths. This means that we will have sixteen rooms with private baths."

A beaming Chuck LaForge, my friend of many years, greeted

me exuberantly, and we continued our stroll about the inn as he proudly pointed out many things that had taken place since my last visit.

In the Tap Room with its beautiful paneled walls, there's a blackboard which told everybody that the luncheon that day started with Bavarian lentil soup, followed by pepper steak or braised short ribs of beef, or sardines on toast points served with raw onions, plus cole slaw and/or potato salad.

More and more of the village businessmen and curious and expectant travelers were filling the inn at lunchtime, and there was a wonderful air of pre-Christmas hustle and bustle as the attractive waitresses chatted with the guests and made note of their luncheon orders.

The village of Rhinebeck grew up around the original crossroads tavern. It is within an easy driving distance of a great many of the restored and preserved homes of the Hudson Valley. One of the delightful diversions for visitors is to walk around the corner to the Firehouse Gift Shop which, along with other shops, is housed in what used to be the old Rhinebeck Firehouse.

Today, the Beekman Arms is much more than a historic inn which thousands of people visit because of its fascinating authentic colonial decor; like many other country and village inns, it is very much the center of all community activity. Decisions, great and small, have been made within its walls for almost three hundred years.

It's a living link to America's past.

BEEKMAN ARMS, Rhinebeck, N.Y. 12572; 914-876-7077. A 13-room village inn with an adjacent 4-room guest house, 1 mi. from Amtrak Station at Rhinecliff. Short drive to F.D.R. Library and Home in Hyde Park. European plan. Lunch and dinner served to travelers daily. Closed Christmas. Open year-round. Golf nearby. Charles LaForge, Innkeeper.

Directions: From N.Y. Thruway, take Exit 19, cross Rhinecliff Bridge and pick up Rte. 199 south to Rte. 9. Proceed south on Rte. 9 to middle of village. From Taconic Pkwy. exit at Rhinebeck and follow Rte. 199 west 11 mi. to Rte. 308 into village.

THE REDCOAT'S RETURN
Tannersville, New York

"If there's one thing that I think innkeepers should have in great abundance," asserted Tom Wright, "it is a sense of humor!"

That the Redcoat's Return abounds with a wonderful sense of

humor is almost immediately obvious to even the first-time visitor. The name alone gets it off the mark. Peggy Wright explains it this way. "Tom is British, but he's been in this country a long time, and he and I thought this would be a great name for an inn kept by a Briton in the Catskills. A lot of people comment on it. We've even carried it through to the new inn sign which has a painting of Tom on one side and of me on the opposite side."

This wonderful sense of humor also includes the new brochure for the inn which carries on the cover the legend: "England is ten minutes from Tannersville." The brochure has a complete history of the beautiful old house which starts with its days as a "summer boarding house" in 1910. There's a marvelous description of what life in the Catskills was like for the summer visitors.

When Tom and Peggy Wright, who call themselves refugees from Manhattan, took over in the fall of 1972, the first project was to winterize the hotel completely and to convert it into an English country inn. For the past few years, Tom has been not only the chef, turning out prime ribs with Yorkshire pudding, poached filet of sole, roast duck in orange sauce, steak and kidney pie, as well as English-style fish and chips, but also the carpenter enlarging rooms, and adding bathrooms. "I would stop hammering and sawing," he said, "and run downstairs and check the sauce and test the roast. I'm happy to say that a great deal of the remodeling is done, and I can spend more time in my beloved kitchen."

The Redcoat's Return is in the center of the Catskill Game Reserve and there is a wealth of recreational activities available to the guests in every season of the year. Hiking trails actually lead from the inn into the mountains where there are magnificent views of the Hudson Valley. There's a lot of golf, swimming, tennis, and horseback riding nearby. During the winter season, there's downhill skiing at Cortina Valley, Hunter Mountain Ski Bowl, and Windham Mountain. There's also plenty of cross-country skiing throughout the area.

Lunch is not served at any time at the Redcoat's Return. It will close for one week in early November, and anyone planning to visit at that time should call ahead for details.

Although I have visited in the summer, my favorite time to drive over is in mid-December, when the inn is already decorated for Christmas. It's especially cozy on a chilly night when there's snow on the ground, and the wind whistles through the trees. On the last visit I found the red setter contentedly sharing the couch with the cat, and some good "Fats" Waller records being played lightly in the background.

Yes, the Redcoat's Return has all the ingredients of an ideal country inn, including generous dollops of humor.

THE REDCOAT'S RETURN, Dale Lane, Elka Park, N.Y. 12427; 518-589-6379. A 12-room English inn approx. 4 mi. from Tannersville, N.Y., in the heart of the Catskill Mts. Within a short drive of several ski areas and state hiking trails. European Plan. Lodgings include breakfast. Dinner served daily except Thursdays; no lunches served. Open from Memorial Day to Easter. Closed 1 week in early Nov. Please call for details. No pets. Hiking, nature walks, trout fishing, croquet, skiing, swimming, ice skating, riding, tennis nearby. Tom and Peggy Wright, Innkeepers.

Directions: Exit 20 or 21 from N.Y. Thrwy. Follow 23A to Tannersville; turn left at traffic light onto County Road 16. Follow signs to Police Center 4½ mi. Turn right on Dale Lane.

GREENVILLE ARMS
Greenville, New York

I was swinging on one of the swings at the Greenville Arms, going higher and higher almost as if on the backward swoop I would swing right into the swimming pool. I could look down on the beautiful lawn to the volleyball court, and then on across the fence to the field where there were horses grazing, and a farm beyond. I pumped again, straining to go higher. Now, I could look into the uppermost branches of the twenty-six-year-old blue spruces, but not nearly as high as the fir trees that were planted fifty years ago. I could see the balustrade on the top of the Greenville Arms, and to my left,

155

the converted barn with the connecting porch, that was once part of the hayloft.

I had driven over from the Berkshires by way of the Rip Van Winkle Bridge and Route 32. The town seemed quiet and relaxed with a few kids bicycling and the Greenville Memorial Library sleepily basking in the sun.

There were the gentle sounds of a summer Sunday—birds flitting about among the tall trees on the village streets with their pleasant white clapboard homes, and the hollow sounds created by a stroller's footsteps on the slate sidewalks. The sky was blue with white clouds, and a gentle Catskill Mountain breeze relieved what would otherwise have been an uncomfortably warm day.

It was at the height of the summer, just a few days after the Fourth of July. All of the flowers carefully planted and nurtured by Ruth Stevens were in full bloom. The geraniums, impatiens, clematis, peonies, and roses, sent forth their colorful message. There were other guests seated around the poolside tables and children using the wading pool. Some had been visiting the Catskill Game Farm nearby, and another family had spent part of the day at Howe Caverns in Cobleskill.

The Greenville Arms is a Victorian country mansion with several interesting porches, cupolas, gables, and corners. It's well-shaded with tall trees and beautifully landscaped with bushes and shrubs. Lodging rooms are in the main house and also in the converted barn to the rear. Throughout, the atmosphere could best be described as "homey and inviting." There is even an old-fashioned water cooler on the front porch.

I left my high-flying swing to join Ruth Stevens over a lemonade, and she told me about her menu: "There's a set meal on

Saturdays, Sundays, Tuesdays, and Thursdays. On the other days, our guests have choices. A typical Sunday meal would be fruit cup, roast turkey, dressing, mashed potatoes, squash, peas, relishes, celery, cottage cheese, breads, and a choice of sundaes. Monday night, we might have a choice including a New England boiled dinner. Tuesday night we have roast beef, Wednesday night a choice might include roast loin of pork. Thursday night we have baked chicken. Friday night, the choices include a baked haddock. Saturday night we always have baked ham.

"There were five sisters in my family, and four out of five of us became innkeepers. We all learned cooking from my mother. We all grew up here in the Catskills. I guess my cooking is kind of old-fashioned, but our guests tell me they've enjoyed it for the last twenty-six years."

Holding to this tradition, the Greenville Arms has weekly rates which include two meals a day as well as the use of all the sports and recreational equipment on the premises. "The difference in rates is based on the type of accommodations. It's most necessary to call ahead for reservations, not only for rooms, but for meals as well."

Winter guests enjoy skiing at Windham Mountain and in spring there's trout fishing and hiking. There are many historical houses and places nearby. In the summer and fall, guests can go horseback riding, play golf, or spend the day in the mountains.

As we were strolling about the grounds around the swimming pool, I found a penny. "Pick it up and you will have good luck all day," said Ruth. The date on it was 1976, the first year that I visited the Greenville Arms.

That was one of my luckier days.

GREENVILLE ARMS, Greenville, N.Y. 12083; 518-966-5219. A 20-room country inn with many resort features 20 miles from Catskill, N.Y., on Route 32. Modified American or European plans. Breakfast and dinner served to travelers by reservation only. Open every day; no meals served Thanksgiving and Christmas. Children most welcome; cribs, cots, and highchairs available. Pets accommodated in nearby kennels. Pool and lawn sports on grounds. Riding, golf, skiing, hiking, backroading, antiquing nearby. Ruth Stevens, Innkeeper.

Directions: Exit N.Y. Thrwy. at 21B. (Coxsackie-New Baltimore). Turn left on 9W South 2 mi. to traffic light. Turn right on Rte. 81W 13 mi. to Greenville. Turn left at traffic light. Inn is second house on right. Via Taconic Pkwy., exit at Ancram on Rte. 82W over Rip Van Winkle Bridge and follow Rte. 23 to Cairo. Turn right on 32N, 9 mi. to Greenville.

OLD DROVERS INN
Dover Plains, New York

Menus are some of my favorite reading, particularly menus from country inns. This time I was reading the portable menu at the Old Drovers Inn. It was hanging on one of the low beams next to the fireplace, but innkeeper Trav Harris is prepared to move it to any corner of the dining room so that everyone may contemplate the culinary marvels awaiting his choice. There are the famous Old Drovers cheddar cheese or cold lemon soups, also onion or Russian cabbage soup.

A second course could be, among others, a paté of duck livers, Portuguese sardines, or a shrimp cocktail. Choosing an entrée involves deciding between dishes like roast duckling, curry of turkey or lamb with chutney, sautéed calves liver, beefsteak and kidney pie, shrimps rarebit, rainbow trout, or julienne of veal served Zurich style (that's veal sautéed in butter and white wine with mushrooms, shallots and sour cream served over rice).

The desserts that evening included one of the inn's famous sweets: fresh key lime pie. There was also strawberry meringue glacé, peach Melba, pecan pie, and apple cheese cake. This last is apple pie with cheese cake on top garnished with walnuts and coconut.

I've gone into some detail about this menu because luncheon and dinner are the main reasons why most people visit Old Drovers Inn. The atmosphere in the dining room is romantic, to say the least, with red leather benches, low wood ceilings, and an attractive combination of rough beams and stone walls. Lining the walls, just below the ceiling, is a collection of glass, copperware, and brass. An old musket hangs over the fireplace. Oversized glass hurricane lamps protect the candles on the tables, and it is great to come in on a chilly day to this beautiful room with a cheery fire crackling in the fireplace. The atmosphere reminds me very much of English country house hotels I've visited.

The three somewhat sumptuous lodgings on the floors above are reached by a box-like staircase hung with marine prints. A most comfortable sitting room on the second floor has a fireplace, deep-cushioned chairs, and plenty of books and magazines. The Federal Room, where breakfast are served, is decorated with some interesting Hudson Valley murals.

There is a handsome, double-sized sleigh bed in the corner bedroom which also has its own fireplace and is wood-paneled. Another bedroom has twin beds with beautiful quilts, more handsome paneling, a tall chest of drawers, and a fireplace. The curved ceiling in one room indicates that before its conversion into a spacious bedroom, it must have been part of the ballroom. These rooms, by the way, are usually booked considerably ahead.

Dining at the Old Drovers Inn is an elegant, luxurious experience, and the prices reflect the skillful preparation of top-quality food and drinks, fine tableware, and expert service. Innkeeper Harris says, "Guests spending the night and taking dinner and a full breakfast should plan on sixty to seventy dollars each."

A dining experience like this must be savored in the most leisurely and unhurried fashion. But imagine, with all of this, I can still order browned turkey hash served with mustard sauce and delicious, crispy, crunchy-on-the-outside-and-soft-on-the-inside popovers!

OLD DROVERS INN, Dover Plains, New York 12522; 914-832-9311. A 3-room authentic 18th-century luxury·country inn midway between New York City and the Berkshires just off New York Rte. 22. European plan. A full breakfast available to house guests at à la carte prices. Closed on Tuesdays and Wednesdays and for 3 weeks prior to Dec. 30 each year. Luncheon served weekdays from noon to 3 p.m. Dinner served weekdays from 6-9 p.m., Saturdays and holidays from noon to 9:30 p.m., Sundays from 1-9 p.m. Located in historic Dutchess County in the scenic foothills of the Berkshires. Travis Harris, Innkeeper.

Directions: From New York follow Saw Mill River on Hutchinson River Pkwy. to I-684 which leads into Rte. 22 at Brewster. Go north to Dover Plains.

THE OLIVER HOUSE
Ancram, New York

Donald Chapin was telling me about the ongoing restoration plans at the Vauxhall, a restored Greek Gothic villa which is maintained as part of the Ancram restoration. We were seated in front of the fireplace in the parlor at the Oliver House, which is also a part of the restoration. All of the ideas, designing, innovation, and inspiration come from Donald and his cousin John-Peter Hayden, Jr. They are, indeed, lighted from within to restore and preserve an elegant Victorian way of life.

"The Vauxhall is now complete in the sense that it's decorated. Over the years we're going to put the front porch back on, and we're going to move the staircase so that it will complete the final and ultimate restoration. It was the original Livingston House, named for the people who founded the town. It was built in 1740, and redone in 1842 in its present style. It sits in the center of the park and overlooks the 'kill,' that's the Dutch word for creek. We have five lodging rooms available there now, bringing our total to ten."

Along with Oliver House and Vauxhall, the Ancram restoration includes the Ancram Opera House, which is the home of the Gotham Light Opera Guild where live concerts and recitals are offered beginning April first. During the summer there will be seven or eight performances a week, and in 1979 it will feature Franz Lehar's, *The Merry Widow*. Donald explained that at Christmastime there will be a full schedule of performances and other galas. "We have a film program every weekend as well."

Across the village street from the Opera House, is the Johann Strauss Atheneum which is the only operetta museum in the world. There are playbills, posters and photographs depicting the works of the Great operetta composers such as Victor Herbert, Strauss, Lehar, and many others.

At the crossroads is Simon's General Store which dates back to 1874, and today has all kinds of beautiful china, sachets, soaps, elegant gifts, homemade apple and blueberry bread, cheese, candies, and lovely German silk flowers.

John-Peter joined us bubbling over with enthusiasm about Sundays at the Oliver House. "This is a Victorian restoration," he said. "The Victorians observed the Sabbath and we decided that Sunday is going to be a special day and our whole schedule at the Oliver House is built around it. Everybody wakes up early on a Sunday morning and comes down for breakfast until ten-thirty. At eleven-thirty there's a church service at our restored 1855 church, the Oratory of the Holy Spirit. Dinner is served here at the inn at one-thirty. There's one sitting and a set meal that might be a chicken dish or pork or lamb. Something roasted. We never broil anything here. We are trying to do the things that other restaurants don't do.

"There's a four o'clock Vesper Service at the church followed by afternoon tea back here at the inn at five-thirty. I love this because it gives me the chance to show off all the different cakes. We don't serve dinner on Sunday night."

At the Oliver House there are five Victorian furnished bedrooms which share one large bathroom. Each of these rooms has been furnished individually in Victorian furniture of varying designs.

Dining is in the Palm Room with its potted palms and lovely crystal chandeliers. For up-to-date information about the many different events in Ancram, I suggest readers send their names and addresses to the *Ancram Standard* in Ancram, New York 12502, for a complimentary copy of a sprightly paper which has it all.

THE OLIVER HOUSE, Part of the Ancram Restoration, Columbia County, Rte. 7 and N.Y. Rte. 82, Ancram, New York 12502; 518-329-1166. A 5-room restored Victorian village inn with an additional 5 rooms available in a nearby manor house. Located about midway between Salisbury, Conn., Hudson and Rhinebeck, N.Y., and Gt. Barrington, Mass. European plan includes Continental breakfast. Guests required to eat in dining room Saturday night. Breakfast, lunch, and afternoon tea served daily to travelers except Monday and Tuesday. Reservations required for all meals. Closed January 15 to April 1. Not especially for children. Small well-trained pets welcome. Ice skating and fishing on grounds; swimming, horseback riding, skiing, golfing, antiquing, and back roading nearby. J.P. Hayden, Jr., and Donald Chapin, Innkeepers.

Directions: From New York City: exit Taconic Parkway North at Jackson Corners, turn east and follow the signs 7 mi. to Ancram. From Massachusetts: turn west from Rte. 22 into Copake and turn right at the village clock following signs to Ancram.

Catamount ski area

SWISS HUTTE
Hillsdale, New York

Fran and Roger Wunderlich and I were having dinner at the Swiss Hutte. I've mentioned Roger before; he is the sales representative for Berkshire Traveller Press books in the Northeast. He and Fran and I try to get together several times a year at one of our country inns to enjoy a small holiday.

This was Fran's first visit to the Swiss Hutte. "You've been saying that it is a Swiss chalet, but I never expected anything quite so enchanting," she said. "Everything looks like a picture postcard of Switzerland! Look at those beautiful pine trees behind us, and the little brook and all the flowers. I think Tom Breen is as interested in growing flowers as he is in being a chef."

A few years ago, Tom and Linda Breen, after spending some time in Europe, particularly in the Alps, decided that they would like to find the ideal place to open up a small European-style inn that specialized in French and German food. "We knew that Tom could supervise the cooking," explained Linda, "but our biggest problem was to find the right setting. One day we were driving through

Hillsdale on Route 23 and came to a place where the road widened and we could pull off and look at the Catamount Ski Area. We both knew that we would never find a more suitable location for our little Swiss inn.

"Fortunately, there was an old farmhouse for sale. We bought it, and over the years we have added many other buildings. We tried to build lodging rooms like the kind found in the Alps. Each one has a Swiss motif, and we've made them as bright and cheerful as possible. Each has a balcony overlooking the valley and the ski area. We find that they are quite ideal for families, not only during skiing season, but during the summer as well."

In the summer, the Swiss Hutte offers icy-cold swimming in the mountain brook, but it also provides a swimming pool with more temperate water. The tennis courts get a great deal of attention, and for those who prefer to relax and enjoy the Swiss-like scenery, there are many comfortable chairs scattered about.

The dirndl-clad waitress, her hair done up in peasant-style braids, brought in our dinners. Roger had delicious-looking crêpes stuffed with chicken. His side dish was asparagus in what he described as a very delicate sauce. Fran had the veal piccata with freshly made fetuccini. I had a very tasty sauerbraten served with red cabbage and beautifully browned potatoes.

We were dining on the garden terrace outside, enjoying the cool evening air. As darkness fell, the moon came up, casting its glow over the valley and over the mountain.

Tom Breen came out of the kitchen long enough to say hello to his guests. When he got to our table, Fran and Roger were ecstatic in their praise.

"I loved the way you arranged everything on the plate with the watercress. It just looked too good to eat!" exclaimed Fran.

In all it was a beautiful night, deserving of her most heartfelt praise.

SWISS HUTTE, Hillsdale, N.Y. 12529; 518-325-3333. A 21-room Alpine country inn overlooking Catamount ski area, 6 mi. from Gt. Barrington, Mass. Modified American plan omits lunch. Breakfast, lunch and dinner served to travelers daily. Closed month of April and from Nov. 15 to Dec. 15. Pool, tennis, putting green, Alpine and xc skiing on grounds. Tom and Linda Breen, Innkeepers.

Directions: From Boston, travel on Mass. Tpke. and take Exit 2. Follow Rte. 102 to Rte. 7. Proceed on Rte. 7 to Rte. 23. From New York City, follow Taconic Pkwy. and Rte. 23. From Albany, follow N.Y. Thruway and Taconic Pkwy. Inn is 10 mi. east of Pkwy. on Rte. 23.

ALMSHOUSE INN
Ghent, New York

Author's Note: In a loss keenly felt by CIBR fellow innkeepers as well as by the communities of Ghent and Chatham, New York, the Almshouse Inn was destroyed by fire in mid-February, 1979. However, as this book went to press, owners Dr. and Mrs. Cullen Burris, Joseph Leon, and Robin Litton were already making plans to rebuild. Undoubtedly, there will be a full report in the 1980 edition.

Because the original Almshouse Inn can never be duplicated, I would like to share the experience of my last visit there.

The handwritten individual menu announced that the dinner for Friday, December eighth, consisted of a cream of mushroom soup followed by a fresh green salad, roast Long Island duckling, English style, served with miniature potatoes, braised Brussels sprouts, and parsnip purée.

The Christmas decorations were all in place in the many drawing rooms of the inn including figures of the three wise men on the top of the baby grand piano. They were beautifully dressed in colored velvet cloaks, one in gold lamé. There was a ceiling-high Christmas tree with a gold angel at the top, decorated with all types of old-fashioned ornaments including a little brass bugle and some straw figures from Mexico.

In one parlor, there was a lovely pine tree with lighted icicles. There were many della Robbia wreaths in all of the parlors and sitting rooms and quite a few Christmas balls hanging from the doorways, enhanced, no doubt, by mistletoe.

The Almshouse was once the county poorhouse. It has two dining rooms which are quite different in character: the paneled Oak Room is sedately furnished with antiques and paintings, while the Garden Room is done in black and white, with a contemporary design and wallpaper of exotic birds with long tails.

There are but three very cozy lodging rooms and these are frequently spoken for well in advance. One has the famous bathroom with a fireplace. As with dinner, reservations are not only advisable, but usually mandatory.

Here's a portion of a recent letter from Robin Litton, one of the four owner-innkeepers. "Our one-entrée dinners continue to be very popular and the Sunday brunch is, in the language of show biz, a sellout!

"We've had guests from almost every state of the union with the exception of Wyoming, Montana, and Alaska. Furthermore, we've had guests from many countries and continents. I can't forget a delightful couple and their nine-month-old daughter from Sydney, Australia, making a world tour staying at inns listed in your two books.

"Thanksgiving is more popular than ever, thanks to your account of it in the 1977 edition. We've been sold out for two months.

"The New Year's Eve party is as much fun for us as for our guests. We serve a late dinner at eight-thirty and then everyone congregates in the music room for a cabaret entertainment at eleven o'clock. Just before midnight, we light all the candles, turn out the lights, and toast in the New Year. We follow that with a sing-along and at one o'clock, we have a second show, followed by a buffet.

"Joe Leon (one of the owners) has a running part in ABC's television soap opera, "Ryan's Hope", and has good prospects of opening as a co-star of a Broadway show soon.

"Shirley Burris continues to step out of the kitchen looking as though she were a guest rather than the chef who prepared dinner. She and her husband, Dr. Cullen Burris, greet our guests and chat with them over coffee. I continue as the welcoming committee, and I love to tell stories of the early days of the inn, and of my days as a T.V. producer."

Thank you Robin, for that update. The Almshouse is certainly not the poorhouse any longer!

CLOSED

MILLHOF INN
Stephentown, New York

It was a wonderfully clear December night. The almost-full moon cast a silvery light on the snow-laden landscape. At the junction of Route 43, I turned east off Route 22 at the signs for Williamstown and Jiminy Peak, and in almost a trice I was at the entrance to the Millhof Inn. I recalled an earlier visit in August, when young Gregory Tallet had shown me around the grounds and proudly taken me up to see the new swimming pool which is located in a sylvan dell at the rear of the inn property. On that day we were joined by his sister Lisa, who is twelve, and Debbie, who is a grown-up seventeen. They pointed out the large stacks of firewood laid by for the living room fireplace on winter nights. The gardens had many flowers, including geraniums, petunias, and hollyhocks, and there were elm, maple, linden, spruce, apple, and birch trees aplenty.

Now, cold snow crunched underneath my boots as I walked from my car through the gaily decorated front door of the inn. Inside, innkeeper Frank Tallet gave me a robust handshake and said, "Welcome to the Millhof Inn, we had it snow just for you!" Almost as soon as I had settled down in front of the crackling fire, Ronnie Tallet dashed in and greeted me ebulliently, "What a wonderful night for you to come! We have some skiers here and maybe we'll pop some corn."

The Millhof is similar to many European country inns that I have visited. Like Black Forest farmhouses, it has broad over-hanging eaves under which are balconies off the bedrooms, over-looking the brook on one side and the forest on the other. The railings and window shutters have been hand-carved and colorfully decorated. The word "Millhof" really means "millhouse," and this building was actually used as a sawmill for many years. As Frank pointed out, "We have had to make many alterations and additions,

166

but the basic structure is the same as it was when it was the McVeigh's sawmill. We saw some great possibilities in it and since I'm from a French background, and Ronnie was born in Yugoslavia, we have lots of furnishings and decorations from the old country." He added, "Ronnie is an artist and has done quite a few of the paintings here in the living room herself."

The Millhof is a family operation. "Everybody really has to share," said Ronnie, "Debbie and Lisa help me in the kitchen, and little Gregory is a walking fund of information about where to go and what to see in the Berkshires."

Ronnie also does the cooking, and some of her admired dishes include chicken al Alba, blanquette de veau and Rock Cornish hen. The hearty breakfasts very often have wheat cakes made from stoneground meal, and omelets. Desserts include strudel, carrot cake, and apple pie.

The European alpine theme extends throughout the inn, and particularly into the lodging rooms, each of which are individually decorated and all have plants, books, and magazines. Frank has done almost all of the redesigning and redecorating of these rooms himself, and they are a tribute to his skill and ingenuity.

Late in the summer of 1978 I received a letter about the Millhof, and I would like to share a portion of it with you: "We were at the Millhof last week to attend the Tanglewood concerts. From the very beginning, Mr. and Mrs. Tallet were perfect hosts. The inn is small and warm-hearted in atmosphere, and because of the personalities of the host and hostess, it is just like being in somebody's home. They recommended restaurants, made the reservations for us, and helped us with some backroading adventures. The food was divine, and Mrs. Tallett's strudel is a knockout."

I had a short reunion with Debbie, Lisa, and Gregory before their homework intervened, and then Frank, Ronnie, and I settled down for a long evening of good conversation by the fire.

Winter or summer, its fun to visit the Millhof.

MILLHOF INN, Route 43, Stephentown, N.Y. 12168; 518-733-5606. A 10-room central-European-style country inn. 14 mi. from Pittsfield and 12 mi. from Williamstown. A pleasant drive from both Tanglewood in the summer, and Jiminy Peak and Brodie Mountain in the winter. European plan. Lodgings include a Continental breakfast. In wintertime, breakfast is served every morning, and dinner is served on the weekends and during holiday weeks by reservation; breakfast and lunch are served daily during the summer. (There is always a meal for the hungry guest.) Open every day from May 26 through March 31. Swimming pool on grounds,. Hiking,

*skiing, backroading, and all of the famous Berkshire recreational
and cultural attractions nearby. Quite suitable for children. No pets.
Frank and Ronnie Tallet, Innkeepers.*

*Directions: From New York: exit the Taconic Parkway at Rte. 295.
Travel east to Rte. 22 north. Turn east at Stephentown on Rte. 43.
The inn is one mile on the left. From Boston: exit Mass. Turnpike at
New Lebanon. North on Rte. 22 to Rte. 43, etc.*

THE FINGER LAKES

In his book, Slim Fingers Beckon *(now in its twelfth printing),
Arch Merrill points out that there is an old Indian legend of how the
Finger Lakes came into being as a result of the Great Spirit
imprinting his hand in a blessing on upper New York state. The
geographers and scientists maintain that the slim streaks of blue in
the center of the state go back to the glacial age, and when the great
ice sheet melted, its deposits dammed the parallel north and south
valleys which filled with water from springs and streams.*

*There are six major Finger Lakes, all with Indian names most
interesting to pronounce. The beauty of the region resembles
Switzerland, and it is generously sprinkled with many waterfalls and
high hills. There are gorges, glens, and caverns. Furthermore, it is a
land occupied by the Indians for untold numbers of years and as a
result, has many legends and stories about the Iroquois, the
Onondagas, Cayugas, and the Senecas. These names are repeated in
the towns, rivers, lakes, and streams in the area.*

*The region also has towns with fascinating classical names such
as Scipio, Romulus, Marcellus, Ithaca, Utica, Ovid, and Lodi.*

*Today, this area remains relatively unspoiled for the traveler. Its
archeology, history, and recreational advantages make it an ideal
area for meandering the backroads and discovering great scenic
views, beautiful farms, impressive parks, and, fortunately, a few
excellent country inns.*

LINCKLAEN HOUSE
Cazenovia, New York

Helen Tobin was sitting on the fireplace fender of the main
dining room of the Lincklaen House as we all enjoyed some
afternoon tea, a regular feature of this inn located on Route 20 in
Central New York State. Cakes were being passed to Bill and
Barbara Dove of the Springside Inn, Ruth Stevens of the Greenville
Arms, and Bob Lenz from the Asa Ransom House, all attractive
country inns in *CIBR.*

"We've been serving afternoon tea for some time," said Helen, "it's always so well-received, and many times I use my lace cloth and the silver tea set, and we serve pretty food. It's my opportunity to introduce many of the guests to each other. Now we do it every day between two and six. Many of our guests enjoy it before going up to stretch out after their journey. I offer tea, coffee, and hot chocolate, and even when we have our conferences, the men love to stop at the table. It's definitely a hit."

About five inches of new snow blanketed the trees and houses of the village. "I've never seen Cazenovia looking so beautiful," said Barbara Dove. "The ride over here from Auburn took us to the highest point in three counties, and there was a delicate coating of ice on the trees."

During the past ten years, I guess I've visited the Lincklaen House during every month of the year, and I would be hard-pressed to choose between a beautiful snow-laden day like today or one in early June or mid-September as my favorite time of year. The village with its beautiful mid-nineteenth-century homes, many of them centered around Cazenovia College and bordering the lake, is engaging in all seasons.

When innkeepers get together, the talk invariably turns to menus. Helen, when her turn came, had this to say about the Lincklaen House: "I think our Sunday brunch is very popular because we serve a very unique eggs Benedict and we serve popovers at lunch and dinner every day. Today, at lunch, we had something unusual—a cheese soufflé served with Canadian bacon. We also do a Quiche Lorraine and feature crêpes periodically. In the evening, we have sweetbreads on our menu frequently. We also serve fresh poached salmon, scallops Delmonico, chicken Kiev, and curried lamb.

"We bring our salads in on a large tray, and people can select from at least three different kinds. Our desserts are always something very special, too. For instance, we have a very untraditional lemon pie for which people are always asking the recipe."

Earlier, accompanied by the gentle golden retriever, Penny Tobin, Bob Lenz and I had made an informal tour of the second and third floor lodging rooms, and he commented that he liked to be able to look down at the main streets from village inns because it was such fun watching all the activity. As we descended the graceful, slightly curving stairway, I couldn't help but admire the paneled ceiling and walls. "They just don't do work like that anymore," he said.

The Lincklaen House has generous helpings of the ingredients that I look for in country inns: A genuine and hospitable warmth, attention and care in the kitchen, historical ambience, and a sense of personal involvement.

This last has been supplied by Helen Tobin herself for many years. I became conscious of it on my first visit back in the 1960s when Helen waited up well after midnight for me after I had been delayed on the road. She is everywhere, talking to the guests, introducing them, explaining about all the mid-New York state natural attractions and making everyone feel as if their visit were truly the most important thing in her life.

LINCKLAEN HOUSE, Cazenovia, N.Y. 13035; 315-655-3461. A 27-room village inn, 20 mi. east of Syracuse. Near several state parks, the Erie Canal Museum and the Canal Trail. European plan. Modified American plan upon request. Breakfast, lunch, and dinner served to travelers daily. Open year-round. Tennis, golf, bicycles, Alpine and xc skiing nearby. Helen Tobin, Innkeeper.

Directions: From west on N.Y. Thruway, take Exit 34A, follow Rte. 481 south, take Exit 3E and follow Rte. 92 east to Cazenovia. From east on N.Y. Thruway, take Exit 34 and follow Rte. 13 south to Cazenovia. From Rte. 81, take Exit 15 (LaFayette) and follow Rte. 20 East, 18 mi. to inn.

THE SHERWOOD INN
Skaneateles, New York

Joy Eberhardt was reminiscing about the first few years after she and her husband Bill had acquired the Sherwood Inn. This venerable building which has a beautiful view of Lake Skaneateles has an interesting history which dates back to the early nineteenth century.

"At first the two of us had to be prepared to do everything, including make the beds, cook the dinners, show people to their tables, and run the dishwasher. Fortunately, even as young as we were, both of us had some experience, particularly in the kitchen. When I think back on those days, it really makes me smile, and then I look around and see what wonderful progress was made. Almost from the first day we met which, by the way, was when we both worked in another restaurant, we knew that we wanted to own a country inn. We looked at a number of them, and then found the Sherwood and knew it was right for us."

We were having lunch in the same lively dining room where I had taken dinner the night before. The day was beautifully snowy in the Finger Lakes area in early February. I had traversed Route 20 from Cazenovia, thoroughly enjoying the roller coaster feature of the road as it dips into the valleys formed by ancient lakes, now departed. The central New York state farms, their staunch buildings and barns and silos filled with produce and silage, all looked prosperous. The orchards which are laden with blossoms in the spring, and rich fruit in the fall, now stood mute in the blowing snow.

I stepped into the cheery warmth of the inn lobby to find a small group of people gathered in front of the fireplace. Next to the piano there was an exhibition of art which I subsequently learned had just replaced the gingerbread Christmas village which was already a tradition at the Sherwood Inn.

A winding open staircase ascended to the second floor and I remembered that it had encircled a bountifully-laden Christmas tree during an earlier holiday visit.

Joy Eberhardt was there to greet me, apologizing for Bill's absence. She suggested that there was still time enough before lunch to see some of the newly decorated lodging rooms on the second and third floors. "We're really very happy about them," she said. "When we took the inn over we had a master plan for redecorating, and after taking care of many other essential changes, it finally became the turn of the bedrooms." (This is something I hear frequently from other innkeepers who have acquired inn property that has to be rehabilitated step by step.)

The beautifully finished floor boards of different widths caught my eye immediately as we reached the second floor. The original pristine character of the pine shines through. "There must have been eight coats of paint on them." she asserted.

Because I had seen the second-floor rooms a few years earlier, I was highly impressed by the transformation. The selection of wallpapers, furniture, and decorations appealed to me very much. There are eleven lodging rooms and three large apartments at the Sherwood Inn now. Joy showed me the honeymoon suite which is done in shades of blue, and the pattern of the quilt on the four-poster, canopied bed, matches both the drapes and the wallpaper. There is a beautiful view of the lake. Joy explained that all but three of the rooms have a lake view.

Now we were in the dining room enjoying a really delicious quiche which she told me was prepared by Pinky Lipe who had also created the gingerbread village during the holiday season, and who does all the desserts.

"As you can see, our menu is pretty much oriented to central New York state. We have roast duckling, London broil, roast beef, turkey, and lamb dishes. We serve a traditional Sunday dinner here and also a full Sunday brunch. On Fridays and Saturdays we have sing-alongs and everybody joins in."

Today, the Sherwood Inn which started its life as a stagecoach tavern is probably in the best possible hands. These young innkeepers have already established themselves as part of the community, and like so many other inns, it is the center of much village activity. The good people of Skaneateles take a more than proprietary interest in it.

THE SHERWOOD INN, 26 West Genesee St., Skaneateles, N.Y. 13152; 315-685-3405. A 12-room village inn on the shores of Lake Skaneateles in the Finger Lakes district of New York State. Continental breakfast included in room tariff. Lunch and dinner served daily to travelers. Open every day except Christmas. Tennis, swimming, and golf available nearby. Near Everson Museum, Barrow Art Gallery, and William Seward House. William and Joy Eberhardt, Innkeepers.

Directions: From New York State Thruway use Weedsport exit and follow Rte. 34 south to Auburn (6 mi.). Turn east on Rte. 20, 7 mi. to Skaneateles. Inn is located in center of village.

SPRINGSIDE INN
Auburn, New York

Barbara Dove was counting on her fingers, "Oh, we have lots of plans for 1979. If all goes well, we're going to build a lodge on Galpin Hill which, as you know, is behind the main building. It will provide twenty more lodging rooms and have a living room with a stone fireplace. Won't that be wonderful!"

Barbara and I were taking a few moments of quiet at the Maryland Inn at Annapolis. We were gathered for a few days with other innkeepers in *CIBR* to exchange ideas and meet old friends.

The Springside is at the northern end of Owasco Lake, one of the New York Finger Lakes. Each of the lodging rooms is decorated to give a different feeling. One is in shades of pink with a pink bedspread and matching curtains. Another has twin Victorian beds and lamps with red bows. A room on the top floor is done in shades of tan and yellow with formal valances at the window, a Tiffany-type lamp, hooked rugs, and twin beds.

"Flowers continue to play a big part in our atmosphere," Barbara said. "Our guests really enjoyed the beautiful hanging geraniums in the summer, and in the fall we had a mass of dried wild flowers, thistles, and corn stalks which were picked and put together with our loving scratched hands. On the Christmas holidays we set out eight Douglas Firs all with Christmas tree lights. They were beautiful."

In the Auburn and Finger Lakes area, Springside has a reputation as an excellent restaurant. The roast duckling, lobster Newburg, filet of sole Florentine, cheese soufflé, popovers, and the Black Forest torte which is made with shaved German chocolate, rank high among local diners.

"We had quite a few people from Toronto and Montreal this past year," said Barbara. "Like the other houseguests, they enjoy our breakfast in a basket. The first one down in the morning plugs in the coffee pot and we have warm blueberry muffins with sweet butter, served with fresh fruit. Most of them sit out on our summer veranda which overlooks our own little pond.

"In 1978, we had a group of autumn arts and crafts shows beginning in September and continuing through November, including a jewelry show, a stained glass show, an art show, a picture-taking emporium which supplies souvenir tintypes, and Christmas flower show. These were received with a great deal of enthusiasm and we're going to do them during the fall of 1979 as well."

Something started at the Springside Inn a few years ago that has now become a central New York tradition is the dinner-theatre presented for several weeks during the summer. As Barb explained, "We usually have a different special dinner with each presentation. Sometimes it fits and sometimes it doesn't. For example, during the run of *Mame*, we featured prime rib and a second choice of Long Island duckling. For *Carnival*, there was Alaskan king crab legs. For *Cabaret*, it was *coq au vin*, For *Six Rms Riv Vu* it was lobster Newburg; and for *Applause* it was *sole bon femme* ."

There is history here, too, at this inn which began as a boy's school in 1851. Old-timers say that at one time it was part of the underground railroad for runaway slaves. There is also much Indian lore throughout the Finger Lakes.

Fall is an ideal time to visit the Finger Lakes area. The lake scenery with the rolling hills and the beautiful fall colors is a gorgeous sight. The area has many roadside stands which offer tempting apples, peaches, pears, pumpkins, and other fruits and vegetables.

As we joined some of the other innkeepers in the main dining room, Barbara said, "Be sure to come and see us during the winter. You know, we have cross-country skiing on our own hill."

SPRINGSIDE INN, 41 West Lake Rd., Auburn, N.Y. 13021; 315-252-7247. A 7-room country inn, 1 mi. south of Auburn with a view of Owasco Lake. In the heart of the historical Finger Lakes. Lodgings include Continental breakfast. Some rooms with shared baths. Open Tuesday through Sunday, May 1 to Sep. 30. Open Wed. through Sunday, Oct. 1 to April 30. Closed Memorial Day, July 4th, Labor Day, Christmas, and New Year's Day. Boating, swimining, bicycles on grounds. Golf, riding, Alpine and xc skiing nearby. Bill and Barbara Dove, Innkeepers.

Directions: From N.Y. Thruway, take Exit 40 and follow Rte. 34 south through downtown Auburn to Rte. 38. Follow Rte. 38 south to traffic circle at Lake and take 2nd exit right at West Shore of Owasco Lake, Drive ¼ mi. to inn.

THE HOLLOWAY HOUSE
East Bloomfield, New York

I was headed west on Route 20 toward Buffalo and Niagara Falls. I had just visited the Sonnenberg Gardens in Canandaigua where there are over 5000 rosebushes set against a background of evergreens and a gleaming white Grecian temple — quite unusual for central New York State. Passing through the little town of East Bloomfield, I was attracted to a beautiful white clapboard house set back among large old maple trees. The sign told me that it was "The Holloway *Houfe*," a country restaurant.

I pulled into the parking space, walked up the stone steps into the front hallway, and found myself in what resembled a most gracious home. There were several fireplaces and lots of comfortable furniture. Lunch was still being served, so I decided to remain and asked for a table by the window.

An attractive woman came over and introduced herself. That's how I met Doreen Wayne. She and Fred are the keepers of the Holloway House, and both of them were kind enough to give me a tour after lunch and explain how all of this came about.

"Peter Holloway, the village blacksmith, built this house in 1808 and operated it as a tavern," explained Doreen. "You can still see the many hand-hewn beams and square nails.

"In those days cooking was done in the cellar and as a kind of reminder, this large open fireplace with a Dutch oven was built. In reconstructing our country dining room, old homemade bricks were used, and we have tried to preserve the early 19th-century feeling."

I found that the Waynes have been at the Holloway for 19 years

175

and have a marvelous reputation for serving delicious and interesting food. Among the items on the menu is Killarney Kress, a sweet pickle sauerkraut which is green in color. They also serve homemade Sally Lunn bread every day. "The original recipe came from Bath, England," Doreen explained. "It's cooked with a great many eggs and has a cakelike texture. It's made daily by our baker who has been with us for fourteen years."

The menu has unusual depth. It includes fried chicken and biscuits, baked ham, and turkey. Fred said that turkey is the most popular item on the menu. There is also a choice of beef and seafood dishes as well. "Lots of people come on Sundays because that's when we serve black-bottom pie and creamed mushrooms."

The kitchen at Holloway House is absolutely immaculate, roomy, and cool, and anyone is welcome to look in on it at any time. The kitchen floor and varnished tables are shining clean. I would feel at home dining there myself.

Innkeeping runs in the family at this inn in East Bloomfield. Son Steve, who is a Cornell Hotel School graduate, runs the grill and also serves as host. David, eighteen years old, is now at Cornell in the Hotel School. He and I had a brief reunion when I visited Cornell in the fall of 1978. The third member of the family, Linda, is also a Cornell graduate. "In another field", as Doreen says.

THE HOLLOWAY HOUSE, Rtes. 5 & 20, East Bloomfield, N.Y. 14443; 716-657-7120. A country restaurant 8 miles west of Canandaigua, N.Y. No lodgings. Lunch and dinner served daily except Mondays. Open April 1- Dec. 1. Sonnenberg Gardens, golf courses, and Finger Lake Racetrack nearby. Fred, Doreen and Mildred Wayne, Innkeepers.

Directions: From N.Y. State Thruway take Exit 45, follow Rte. 96E 3 mi. to Victor N.Y. Go south on Victor-Holcomb Rd. 5 mi. Turn right at light in Holcomb then second left to Rte. 5 & 20.

GLEN IRIS INN
Castile, New York

I was standing on the pillared porch of this beautiful inn with the morning sun streaming across the circular bed of radiant iris.. The sun, through the evergreens, maples, and oaks of the forest created a dappled pattern at the edge of the broad lawn. It was a clear morning in mid-June and I had just finished one of Peter Pizzutelli's hearty breakfasts and would be off in a few moments for a tour of Letchworth State Park.

Wherever I walked on the grounds, I could hear the sounds of the falls. In fact, the previous evening some people coming out of the dining room had thought that it was raining. The roar of the falls does, indeed, sound like a heavy downpour which, actually, they are. These are the Middle Falls of the Genesee River which cuts through this section of New York State, creating a series of S-turns and cutbacks between the banks that very much resemble the conformation of the Grand Canyon in Arizona, except, of course, they are not as deep.

There are two new additions to report at the Glen Iris: a new expanded terrace off the main dining room provides more comfortable seating arrangements for more people. The many large windows seem to bring the outdoors right inside. The original Letchworth dining room, which was a gift shop for many years, has now been returned to its former status of a small, pleasant dining room. It has very appropriate furniture to go with the beige and brown wallpaper.

The Glen Iris, originally a two-story frame house, was the former home of William Prior Letchworth, nineteenth-century philanthropist. The bedrooms are reached by a twisting, turning staircase of dark chestnut wood and instead of having numbers, they have names of trees found in the park. All are comfortably furnished in nineteenth-century style. A motel unit is located in a nearby grove for additional overnight guests.

The unusual combination of a beautiful country inn next to a spectacular waterfall in a totally protected state park located in a historical section of western New York State attracts large numbers of visitors to the area; I cannot emphasize too strongly the advisability of having reservations for any of the meals or lodgings.

Guests visiting the Glen Iris for an overnight stay or a meal, are reminded to give the waitress the $1.50 park toll ticket, which is deducted from whatever is spent at the inn.

The bill of fare at the Glen Iris offers many tempting choices. One of the selections is called chicken Virginia - boneless whole breast of chicken, sautéed to a golden brown, topped with a creamy wine sauce with mushrooms and then served over sliced ham. The roast beef choices include a hefty cut for a full appetite and a lighter cut for the not-so-hungry diner. They're served with fresh-baked popovers. It was at the Glen Iris that I made my first acquaintance with a non-alcoholic pina-colada made from fresh coconut and pineapple juice — it has changed my life.

Cora Pizzutelli joined me on the front terrace. "Oh, I wish you could be here in October. Last year the foliage was especially gorgeous. There were record numbers of people coming to view it and also to have lunch. We have an amazing number of repeat dinner and overnight guests who have become like family members. Our guests are very special to us. Each fall at closing time, when the trees are stripped bare and the park begins to show signs of winter approaching, many guests make a special visit to say 'good-bye' for another season and to wish us well. It's very touching."

GLEN IRIS INN, Castile, N.Y. 14427; 716-493-2622. A 20-room country inn located at the Middle Falls of the Genesee River in Letchworth State Park. European plan. Breakfast, lunch, and dinner served to travelers daily. Open from Easter Sunday to Nov. 6. Footpaths, swimming, and bicycles nearby. Historical sites in Park and spectacular views within walking distance. Peter and Cora Pizzutelli, Innkeepers.

Directions: Inn is located off Rtes. 436, 19A and 39 in Letchworth State Park, 55 mi. from Buffalo and Rochester.

ASA RANSOM HOUSE
Clarence, New York

Sparkly-eyed Judy Lenz and I were standing in the Clarence Hollow dining room of the Asa Ransom House. "We're changing the inn all of the time," she said. "We subtract and add different ideas. For example, when we set aside the Ransom Room for non-smokers a few years ago, it was quite innovative. Furthermore, we've kept the atmosphere in the two rooms quite different."

Yes, indeed, they are. The Clarence Hollow Room has blue table mats and ladder-back chairs. There are framed maps of Western New York State, a plate rail with plates and tea pots interspersed with a lantern or two that Bob and Judy have collected over the years. The curtains are blue and there's a big fireplace at one end. The Ransom Room has green tablecloths, ball-fringed curtains, many growing flowers, and two matching antique lamps hanging from the ceiling.

"When it came to decorating the guest rooms, Bob and I had a wonderful time. First, we decided that instead of numbers, they should have names to fit their personalities. For example, the Red Room is proud of the 1825 Cannonball double bed. The Blue Room is a soft, lovely bedroom with a canopied bed and is very popular

with honeymooning couples. The larger Gold Room is outfitted with twin iron-and-brass beds with a table between them. We have finally completed the new room, and I must say I'm so pleased with the hours of stenciling that I did on the walls. It has an American Eagle theme with each individual color and individual shading of pineapple below the ceiling. One wall is of natural brick which is a marvelous contrast. We always have lots of books and flowers in the rooms and whenever possible, bowls of fruit. Of course, each room has its own bath, and I'm happy to say that they're so popular that most of the time they're booked in advance."

The Asa Ransom House reflects Bob and Judy's innovative flair. For example, their religious convictions prohibit serving pork and shellfish. As a pork substitute, "one of our favorite dishes" asserted Bob, "is smoked cornbeef with apple raisin sauce." There are also "country pies" including salmon pond which is a house specialty, and chicken pot pie, and steak and kidney pie. In the kitchen of the inn, they whip their own cream, use honey and natural raw milk cheese from a local cheese factory, and never any MSG.

Lodgings include a breakfast of fresh fruit, muffins, and a beverage, as well as Judy's special breakfast egg pie. (I get lots of letters about the breakfasts).

Ever innovative, Judy said, "Last May we started serving lunch on Wednesdays, and it proved so popular, we're doing it regularly. We serve at the two tables on our front porch for both lunch and dinner when the weather permits. Jennifer, our seven-year-old daughter, likes to stop in after school on Wednesdays, and help clear the dishes in the kitchen. I hope this continues until her late teens!"

There are many more delightful original ideas at the Asa Ransom House, including Sunshine Square, a most interesting gift shop which is made in the form of a village of gifts. The herb garden has now reached such a proportion that Bob and Judy had to provide a diagram showing the many varieties. These, of course, are used in the kitchen.

The Asa Ransom House is closed on Fridays and Saturdays because Bob and Judy are members of the Worldwide Church of God. However, Sunday evening, the inn is filled again with happy diners.

ASA RANSOM HOUSE, Rte. 5, Clarence, N.Y. 14031; 716-759-2315. A 4-room village inn approximately 15 mi. from Buffalo near the Albright Knox Art Gallery, The Studio Arena Theatre, the Art Park, and Niagara Falls. European plan. Dinner served Monday through Thursdays 4:30 to 9 p.m.; Sundays, 12:30 to 8 p.m. Lunch is available on Wednesday only. Closed Friday and Saturday. No pets. Tennis, golf, fishing, swimming nearby. Bob and Judy Lenz, Innkeepers.

Directions: From the New York Thruway traveling west, use exit 48A-Pembrook. Turn right to Rte. 5 and proceed 11 mi. to Clarence. Traveling east on the N.Y. Thruway, use Exit 49; turn left on Rte. 78, go 1 mi. to Rte. 5 and continue 5¼ mi. Coming from the east via Rte. 20, just east of Lancaster, N.Y., turn right on Ransom Rd., go to end and turn left.

CLARKSON HOUSE
Lewiston, New York

A light snow was falling on an early December evening when I first visited the Clarkson House in Lewiston, New York, a number of years ago. The Christmas tree lights were already blinking out their happy message, and there was a small group of sculptured figures depicting the Holy Family across from the inn. I ventured down the street to see the appealing miniature Christmas tree lights draped around each of the trees in the business district. It all made a very happy holiday effect.

This was my first visit to this corner of New York State dominated by the presence of Niagara Falls. I learned about the Clarkson House from my good friend, Robert Lenz, now the innkeeper of the Asa Ransom House in Clarence, New York. Bob said that it was very special, and he proved to be right.

I found the Clarkson House to be an excellent restaurant — something I knew the moment I smelled a most delicious aroma which I discovered came from the charcoal grill right in the middle of the dining area, where the filets and lamb chops were sizzling away merrily. Around it, there is an unusual arrangement of booths and tables, and on the walls a collection of tools and gadgets used more than 100 years ago. "They haven't discovered the use for some of them!" said Marilyn Clarkson. There are old-fashioned kerosene lamps on the tables, and the walls have several good paintings interspersed with wall lamps.

On that first trip I discovered that Bob Clarkson is a great believer in having things under control. For example, there are 22 tables, all carefully spaced out on the wooden floor which is scrubbed every day. This means that reservations are most advisable as only a limited number of diners can be accommodated.

Secondly, the menu has been judiciously pared down to a few

entrees which are very carefully prepared and most tastefully arranged on the plates. There is an emphasis on beef, including sirloin, filet and prime rib. There are also delicious French-cut lamb chops. A combination of beef filet and lobster tail, or half of a Maine lobster (flown in fresh) are also offered. That, plus four desserts, including cherries jubilee and baked Alaska, is the menu. I mustn't forget to mention that there was a little sign on one of those delicious-looking baked potatoes that said, "Eat all you like, I've been scrubbed and tubbed."

The newest thing at the Clarkson House is a lobster tank which holds up to two hundred lobsters in artificial sea water. "We've always served lobsters," explained Bob, "and now we can serve lobsters fresh from the sea!"

I have revisited the Clarkson House several times since that December evening a number of years ago, and have noted with great satisfaction the continued growth of the Niagara Falls area, including the Art Park. They have a wide variety of programs ranging from Broadway plays to popular dance, ballet, opera, and jazz, featuring some of the leading artists from the United States and Canada. Nigara-on-the-Lake with the Shaw Festival is just a short, pleasant drive into Canada.

THE CLARKSON HOUSE, 810 Center St., Lewiston, N.Y. 14092; 716-754-4544. A country restaurant, 7 mi. from Niagara Falls and Olde Fort Niagara. No lodgings. Dinner served daily except Mondays. Closed Christmas. Bob and Marilyn Clarkson, Innkeepers.

Directions: From I-190 exit at Lewiston and follow Rte. 104E for 1½ mi. Turn right on Rte. 18F and travel 2 blocks west to restaurant.

Pennsylvania

THE CENTURY INN
Scenery Hill, Pennsylvania

"My husband and I cannot say enough about the Century Inn," said the letter. "In fact, I'm sure our friends are getting tired of hearing about it. One of the most important things was that we felt so welcome. The innkeepers were so pleasant and willing to talk about the inn. We are antique buffs, so we truly enjoy that marvelous collection."

Another letter said, "Our first stay was at the Century Inn, and what a beautiful old place this is. We had a lovely bedroom furnished with delightful antiques and enjoyed a huge, delicious home-cooked

dinner. The coleslaw has got to be the best ever. Our breakfast was equally good and we ate it in the fascinating 'Keeping Room.' We left the Century Inn with regret, saying that we would return again."

The Century Inn was built before 1794 and is the oldest continuously operating tavern on the National Pike, most of which is today's U.S. 40. Consequently, the inn has played an important role in the history of southwest Pennsylvania. General Lafayette stopped here on May 26, 1825, and Andrew Jackson was a guest twice, once on his way to his inauguration as President of the United States.

As the letters imply, the interior of this handsome old inn is filled with rare antiques, and there is a story behind almost every piece. Typical of the collection is a Chippendale highboy which was brought from Carlisle, Pennsylvania, probably by Conestoga wagon, in the late 18th century. It is in marvelous condition, and, oddly, the carved shell at the top is upside down. All the antique treasures are in a perfect setting created by the original exposed stone walls, wood paneling, low ceilings, and numerous fireplaces (in some cases, two to a room!).

Among delicious temptations on the menu are turkey which comes from a farm just down the road, and baked stuffed pork chops. There's also Virginia ham, chicken croquets, ham and asparagus roll, and a mouth-watering hot turkey sandwich.

Desserts include fresh strawberry shortcake, pecan balls with butter sauce, and a wide variety of homemade pies.

Today, the innkeepers are Bob and Nancy Scheirer who are continuing in the tradition of Nancy's mother and father, Gordon and Mary Harrington, who restored this inn and generously supplied it with not only their own antiques, but the gifts of many friends.

183

One of the most impressive antiques at this inn is the original flag flown during the Whiskey Rebellion which took place in western Pennsylvania in 1794. The flag is framed and hangs on the wall of the front parlor.

The Century Inn will be looking forward to its own bicentennial soon.

THE CENTURY INN, Scenery Hill, Pa. 15360; 412-945-6600 or 5180. A 10-room village inn on Rte. 40, 12 mi. east of Washington, Pa., 35 mi. south of Pittsburgh. European plan. Breakfast served to house guests only. Lunch and dinner served to travelers daily. Closed approximately Dec. 21 until April 1. Contact inn for exact opening and closing dates. No pets. Nancy and Bob Scheirer, Innkeepers.

Directions: From the east, exit the Pa. Tpke. at New Stanton. Take I-70W to Rte. 917S (Bentleyville exit) to Rte. 40E and go 1 mi. east to inn. From the north, take Rte. 19S to Rte. 519S to Rte. 40E and go 5 mi. east to inn or take I-79S to Rte. 40E and go 9 mi. east to inn. From the west, take I-70E to I-79S to Rte. 40E and go 9 mi. east to inn.

ON TO EAGLES MERE

The heat at the Harrisburg airport was sweltering, and I was happy to pick up an air conditioned rental car. Following Routes 15 and 11 north along the Susquehanna River provided me with an even furthur insight into this most interesting American waterway. At one time it was used to float log rafts down from the lumber operations on north and west branches. At Northumberland, the two branches come together and continue down into the Chesapeake Bay.

I turned and drove over the river from Selinsgrove to Sunbury, and followed the new highway (147) north to Muncy, turning off on Route 220 which rises gradually and most pleasantly into the mountains. I turned off the air conditioning, opened the car windows, and could feel the temperature drop.

My objective was to visit the village of Eagles Mere, which for many years has been a favorite resort area for Pennsylvania people. The road winds through ridge after ridge of mountains. The occasional farms have many old interesting barns weathered by variations of mountain climate.

At Muncy Valley, I turned left on Route 42 for the last six miles before Eagles Mere. Route 42 is a no-nonsense road. It simply points up into the clouds, then with a series of S-curves, weaves through the woods. I could well imagine that it has breathtaking color in the fall. It is real Pennsylvania deer country, and people traveling at night would do well to watch both sides of the road for the light reflected in the deer's eyes. Where there is one deer there may be a half-dozen more. Now, I arrived in the Land of Endless Mountains—Eagles Mere, Pennsylvania.

EAGLES MERE INN
Eagles Mere, Pennsylvania

Kathleen Oliver and I were on a combination walking/driving tour of Eagles Mere Lake, which is one of the many attractive features of this two-thousand-foot-high resort area. "The lake was formed by the receding glacier," she explained. "It is actually located on the top of a mountain. The Indians first hunted and camped here. The great eagles nested in the trees and later the French influence gave the place its name."

We walked down to the edge of the sandy beach, and I noted the unusual number of canoes and sailboats available for hire. A motor launch left from one of the docks transporting passengers to the other end of the lake.

"Everyone uses the lake," she said. "We swim, canoe, sail, skate, and fish on it. It means so much to many people."

As we continued our journey, she explained that the community is made up of people who have been coming to Eagles Mere for many years. "The entire community supports things such as our Athletic Association which maintains a summer program for young people in which our inn guests can also participate. There are riding stables

185

nearby and the riding paths convert into at least 65 miles of cross-country skiing in the winter. Guests of the inn also have the privilege of playing on the lovely 18-hole golf course of the Eagles Mere Country Club.

"Speaking of winter, this is when Eagles Mere is really at its most unusual, because we have a toboggan slide operated by the volunteer fire department on the weekends which provides at least a 1200-foot ride on specially constructed toboggans down the hill to the lake surface. The speeds get up to 65 miles an hour. Our inn guests love this too."

Kathleen and I continued our stroll on the footpath which completely encircles the lake. I learned that this lovely Irish colleen met her husband Bob, who is a rather hearty outdoor type, when they were both students at St. Lawrence University. "Our inn is really very much a part of the community."

Even if Eagles Mere were not a small community, I have a feeling that people would naturally gravitate towards the inn anyway, because it has a homey feeling which was very obvious to me as soon as I stepped in the front door. The sitting rooms and parlors on the main floor were all most comfortably furnished and, much to my surprise, I found a Baldwin piano tuned to concert pitch. "Once I had aspirations to become a concert pianist," explained Kathleen, "however when we came to Eagles Mere, I decided to set that aside for a while."

Meals at the inn are prepared by a lady from the village who has quite a way with things like roast pork, beef Bourguignon, and stuffed flounder. Bob told me that they were anticipating canning lots of chili sauce, blueberry jam, peach rum jam, and other goodies in the fall. "I'm working on the putting green and enlarging the gift shop; they'll both be ready by the summer of 1979. Incidentally, during the summer of 1979 there will be a policy of a two-night stay on weekends during the peak season and a 3-night stay on holiday weekends."

All of the Olivers at the Eagles Mere Inn—Bob; Kathleen; Maureen, who is 17; Eileen, 14; Karen, 12; and Kevin, 5—create a wonderful, natural, and relaxed atmosphere at this warm-hearted inn.

Eagles Mere, itself, may be one of the last unspoiled vacation places in the East.

EAGLES MERE INN, Mary and Sullivan Aves., Eagles Mere, Pa. 17731; 717-525-3273. A 9-room, all with private baths, small village inn high in the Allegheny Mountain range about an hour's drive north of Williamsport. 16 mi. from Dushore and Hughesville. Near Eagles Mere Lake, World's End State Park, Sullivan County

Historical Museum, and the LaPorte Little Theater. Modified American plan in season; European plan (room and breakfast) out of season. Breakfast and dinner served to travelers. Open every day from May 15 to Oct. 15; 2-day minimum stay at peak summer season. Reservations requested. Open from Friday dinners through Sunday breakfasts, Dec. 26 to March 15. All summer and winter sports available nearby. No pets. Robert and Kathleen Oliver, Innkeepers.

Directions: Exit 34 (Buckhorn) from I-80. Follow Rte. 42 north 32 mi. to Eagles Mere. Turn right on Mary Avenue to inn.

FAIRFIELD INN
Fairfield, Pennsylvania

If I quote from quite a few letters in this book, it's because I feel that often times they are the best way to obtain a deeper insight to the true nature of an inn. A case in point is this letter from David Thomas, the young, enthusiastic innkeeper at the Fairfield Inn.

"This has been a most busy and fruitful year here in Fairfield. In January we began to restore the oldest room in the Inn—the 1757 Room. Actually, the room was originally a separate building from the mansion house. The room probably was the first tavern on the property, and was a one-and-one-half-story structure. It was quite fascinating and surprising to find the remains of what was a baking oven in the fireplace. A large number of oyster shells, some old coins, and china fragments were found when the floor boards were lifted

187

and the old hand-hewn support logs were exposed. The town "locals" performed much of the work done in the room. They spent many hours consulting with neighbors and friends as to the best procedure to follow in the restoration work. By July the room was completed, and is now used as an additional dining area.

"Somewhere along the line, we found time to co-sponsor, with the local garden club, an Arbor Day Tea. Children from the local elementary school planted a tri-color beech tree at the rear of the property. The young people were escorted down Main Street to the Inn by the Fairfield High School Marching Band. It turned out to be a special event, and one which we hope will be repeated.

"Last Christmas we started what I hope will become a tradition at the Inn. On the first Sunday of December, we celebrate the Feast of Christmas. There are strolling carollers throughout the building, the yule log is brought in, and all the guests are seated for a candlelight dinner. The foods served are items that one doesn't normally find on our menu. Last year's feast was a gratifying success. Many of the guests are what we term 'regular', even though many are from Washington, Richmond, Philadelphia, and surrounding areas. What could be more fun, or a nicer way to begin the yuletide season?

"The coming year—who knows what it will bring! There are several projects floating around in the back of my mind. With several more rooms left to restore, who knows what will develop?"

There are just two lodging rooms at the Fairfield, so the main reason people stop is the food. Three meals are served each day except Sunday when, as David says, "We suggest that our guests go to Nancy Jeane Hammett's Hickory Bridge Farm."

Everything served is made from scratch, including chicken and biscuits, country ham steak (the salty kind), a "fizzled city ham," and family-style meals which include everything from appetizers to desserts. Desserts always include deep dish apple pie served with a pitcher of cream or a wedge of cheese, and other seasonal treats.

The inn building has a long and fascinating history. It was built by the Miller family who settled in Fairfield in 1755. It was once a stagecoach stop on the Great Road from York to Hagerstown. During the Civil War, Jebb Stuart lingered long enough to steal seven hundred horses from the valley.

A year later, the Confederates occupied the town for ten days during the Battle of Gettysburg. General Lee and his men retreated to Fairfield after the battle was over. The women of the town made huge kettles of bean soup and fed the starving troops as they retreated south. By the way, ham and bean soup is one of the specialties of the inn today.

I'm sure with a young, ambitious innkeeper like David, many

things will develop at the Fairfield Inn in the future.

FAIRFIELD INN, Main St., Fairfield, Pa. 17320; 717-642-5410. A country restaurant near Gettysburg with 2 lodging rooms available. Breakfast, lunch, and dinner served daily. Closed on major holidays, Sundays, and last week in August. Dinner reservations advised. No pets. Nearby region is rich in history, including Gettysburg Battlefield. David W. Thomas, Innkeeper.

Directions: Fairfield is 8 mi. west of Gettysburg on Rte. 116.

Riding between the cornfields from Fairfield to Orrtanna, a few miles west of Gettysburg, I was again impressed with the picturebook neatness of the beautiful Pennsylvania stone farmhouses and buildings. To the west, some of the mountains had orchards and I could see a ski area up in one corner. This is an area rich in history, not only from colonial days, but during the War Between the States where soldiers stopped by and got the famous black bean soup from the inhabitants of Fairfield during the famous hot summer of the Battle of Gettysburg.

The architecture of this region is an interesting mixture of Pennsylvania farmhouses and northern Virginia country homes, with some of the characteristics of each being evident, including second floor outdoor galleries which are quite common farther south in the Middleburg-Charlottesville area. This is great apple country with acres of orchards and many apple storage houses.

THE HICKORY BRIDGE FARM
Orrtanna, Pennsylvania

Rounding the bend I came to the sign for the Hickory Bridge Farm which is located on Jack Road. I went past a sturdy stone wall and then up and over the railroad tracks to a little woods and a stream with an old farmhouse. On the other side of the road, there's a great, wonderful red barn with a garden next to it and mammoth sunflowers in bloom.

189

Nancy Jean Hammet, wearing a calico milkmaid's dress with a white sunbonnet, gave me her usual ebullient greeting, and I was off on another wonderful tour of this most unusual country inn.

"Our big news," she said, "is that in addition to the lodgings which are in the two cottages across the creek, we have two adjoining bedrooms available for guests in the farmhouse. We're also going to have bicycles available. This is just some of the best biking country in the world."

We moved inside the big barn with the wide floorboards, heavy beams, and rustic pillars. There are long harvest tables with six or eight settings on each side, and a most impressive collection of old farm tools, seed posters, and other agricultural artifacts hanging from pegs on the walls.

We passed through another low-ceilinged dining room which has been created out of what once were stables. There are highly varnished knotty pine walls decorated with a plate rail displaying the familiar country agate ware. I saw quite a few old-fashioned high chairs which I'm sure are used frequently.

In the neat kitchen I met Wayne, who was preparing the evening meal which would feature country steaks served with mushrooms. There is always a choice of two entreés, homebaked bread and rolls, many different vegetables and fruit which come from the garden. Meals usually begin with an apple shrub or an apple juice, and then the guests are invited to help themselves at the salad sled. A typical Sunday dinner would have both roast turkey and baked ham with sweet potatoes, apple fritters, and apple sauce. There's also chicken, corn soup, Dutch lettuce, stewed apples, corn fritters, apple butter, schmier kase, apple pan-dowdy, and shoo-fly pie. Everything is made from scratch and they collect their own honey and blueberries.

As Nancy Jean and I continued wandering around the grounds, she said, "We have two very successful festivals here every year. One is on the first weekend in May in apple blossom time. The other one is the second week in October for the apple harvest. Many local craftsmen, musicians, and farmers participate, and last year we had over two thousand people. We have country music, square dancing, and hay rides. A country store museum is in one of our out-buildings.

We walked along the old country dirt road and stopped to chat with Luther Lightner, a gentleman who lives nearby and, as a hobby, has put a great deal of the old-time farm machinery into working order once again.

The little footbridge led to the cottages, and Nancy Jean reminded me that a complimentary breakfast of hot rolls, juice, and fruit in season is brought to guests in these cottages.

We circled back through the woods, and went into the farmhouse to look at the new upstairs bedrooms. I noticed a sampler with a quotation from Robert Browning, and thought, "How appropriate for The Hickory Bridge Farm."

> *The year's at the spring*
> *And day's at the morn;*
> *Morning's at seven;*
> *The hill-side's dew pearl'd;*
> *The lark's on the wing;*
> *The snail's on the thorn;*
> *God's in his heaven—*
> *All's right with the world!*

HICKORY BRIDGE FARM INN, Orrtanna, Pa. 17353; 717-642-5261. A country inn on a former farm 3 mi. from Fairfield and 8 mi. from Gettysburg. Near Gettysburg Battlefield National Park, Totem Pole Playhouse. Farm dinners served Wed. thru Sat., 5 to 8 p.m.; Sun. from 12 to 6. Open from Mar. 1 to Dec. 20. 6 lodging rooms available in 2 cottages and the farmhouse nightly from Mar. 1 to Dec. 20. Breakfast available to guests. Hiking, biking, hayrides, square dancing, fishing, hunting on grounds. Golf, swimming available nearby. The Hammett Family, Innkeepers.

Directions: From Gettysburg take Rte. 116 west to Fairfield and follow signs 3 mi. north to Orrtanna.

INN AT STARLIGHT LAKE
Starlight, Pennsylvania

"One thing we definitely feel after almost five years as inn-keepers: time goes by more quickly with each passing year, and more and more, it is a satisfying life - hard, yes; frustrating, yes—but the rewards are many and the goals we set are worth it."

Jack and Judy McMahon, innkeepers at this rustically informal inn, sharing a few of their impressions.

"We think that being in show business has provided us with an excellent background for becoming innkeepers," said Jack McMahon. "We're certainly sensitive to the moods and needs of our guests, and after all, running a country inn is something like putting on a show — a different show every day, bringing all of the parts together into one continuous production."

The Inn at Starlight Lake is situated on a back road in the rolling hills of Northeastern Pennsylvania. It has been in operation since 1909 and originally was intended to be a summer refuge for people living in New York and New Jersey. In May 1974, Jack and Judy McMahon bought it and resolved to preserve the character of the early period when it flourished.

The inn is a rambling, old-fashioned, comfortable place with the accumulated furniture of years. The lobby is a big room with a fireplace in one corner and a piano and guitar in another corner. It looks like a good place for children. There's an indoor game room and four McMahons for company.

Along with the usual sports offered at resort-inns—swimming, boating, canoeing, sailing, tennis, and hiking, there is another family-type activity that I was glad to see. The inn has extensive cross-country ski trails that run two, five, and six miles into the natural forests of the area.

"We also have one of the largest wild deer herds in the area," said Judy. "We often see deer from our front porch and from the dock in front of the lake. Many of our guests love the idea that the wild creatures are so close."

In the McMahon family, true to the background of show business, everybody "gets into the act." Cecilia, fifteen, finds time between being the president of her sophomore class to waitress and help out in the kitchen and laundry. She's head of the babysitting department. Will, thirteen, is sanitation engineer (taking out the garbage) and his favorite season is winter. He lends a hand with the guided ski tours and lessons. Patty, nine, is a fourth-grader and good at entertaining younger children. She's taking piano lessons and can't wait to start waitressing. Johnny, six, is just getting into the innkeeping business.

The food is most interesting. There are a number of German specialties including a Jagerschnitzel and weinerschnitzel. Some other dishes I sampled were cream of cauliflower soup, Hungarian goulash, sauerbraten, buckwheat cakes, and blueberry pie. "We like holidays here," said Judy, "when families gather for Thanksgiving and Christmas. We're open and everyone's welcome."

There is also great emphasis on serving only fresh meats and vegetables, and homemade breads. Even the coffee is freshly-ground before each pot is brewed.

I remember on my first visit we all sat around the fire vying with each other for points in a game of nostalgia. We began with old popular songs. Jack picked up the guitar and sang a few bars. Soon everyone was joining in.

The McMahons may no longer be in show business, but they are a smash in Wayne County, Pennsylvania.

THE INN AT STARLIGHT LAKE, Starlight, Pa. 18461; 717-798-2519. A 30-room resort-inn located 5 mi. from Hancock, N.Y. Modified American plan. Breakfast, lunch, dinner served daily between May 15 and April 1. Closed Easter if it falls within above dates. Swimming, boating, canoeing, sailing, fishing, hunting, tennis, hiking, bicycling, xc skiing, and lawn sports on grounds. Canoeing, hunting, fishing, golfing nearby. Judy and Jack McMahon, Innkeepers.

Directions: From N.Y. Rte. 17, exit at Hancock, N.Y. Take Rte. 191S over Delaware River to Rte. 370. Turn right, proceed 3½ mi., turn right, 1 mi. to inn. From I-81, take exit 62 and go east on Rte. 107. Turn left on Rte. 247 to Forest City. Turn left on Rte. 171, go 10 mi. to Rte. 370. Turn right, proceed 12 mi. Turn left, 1 mi. to inn.

MOSELEM SPRINGS INN
Moselem Springs, Pennsylvania

As I look back on the years that I have been writing this book, one of my happiest memories is of the day I met Walter and Madeline Stoudt, the innkeepers at Moselem Springs Inn. The three of us instantly became friends, and I am happy to say that the friendship has continued to grow over the years.

The Stoudts both have Pennsylvania Dutch backgrounds, and they and the Moselem Springs Inn are the antitheses of the commercialism and exploitation that I sometimes see in southeastern Pennsylvania. There is enough of an accent in their speech to make it distinctive, and their good humor and boundless optimism are most infectious.

These were a few of the reasons why I was anticipating my visit with them with such pleasure. I drove east from Harrisburg on Route 22 shortly before lunchtime on an early fall day. I turned off the Interstate at Shoemakersville (Route 61) and continued south to Route 662 where I made a left turn. Route 662 is one of Pennsylvania's most pleasant back roads. It winds among sprawling farmhouses, orchards, grazing cattle, and marvelous barns. It drops down out of the hills and comes to the four corners where the inn is located.

There were corn stalks tied around the inn's pillars and pumpkins on the porch. The many cars in the parking lot indicated that quite a few people had stopped there for lunch.

The Moselem Springs building has stood at the four corners since the mid-1800s. It has served a number of purposes over the years, but certainly none more noble than its present one of providing excellent food for travelers and local people. There are no lodging rooms available, but the Stoudts can recommend nearby accommodations, if necessary.

At luncheon, Walter was full of new ideas. "You know, we have a great many friends, and people come here for lunch or dinner frequently, so naturally we can't rest on our laurels. We've got to keep adding new dishes to the menu and new ideas for serving the food. We try to do as many extra things as possible."

"We are very much involved in serving natural things," explained Madeline. "We don't use any preservatives at all. We have three kinds of tea and don't serve instant ice tea. Our coffees include a natural dandelion coffee, which is delicious. Everything is served with real cream if the guest prefers. Our Smoke House is the oldest original building on the lot dating back to 1852. We still smoke all of our bacon, sausage, and corn beef. These are things that have become traditional here at Moselem Springs."

Walter said, "Another one of our unusual offerings is Dutch pickled tripe which you don't find very often. We also have smoked beef sausage served with apple fritters and horseradish, and corn pie served with hot buttered milk."

"Some of the foods we serve are sold in our Gourmet Meat Shop including the smoked meat, cheese, molasses, and sausages," added Madeline.

"Many of our guests who come here for the first time are surprised that we are not open on Fridays and Saturdays, but after we explain that it is because of our religious persuasion, they always understand, and our business on other days is fantastic," said Walter. This custom is also true of the Asa Ransom House in Clarence, New York.

MOSELEM SPRINGS INN, R.R. 4033. Box 10, Fleetwood, Pa. 19522; 215-944-8213. An historic country inn restored to 19th century opulence on U.S. 222, 13 mi. from Reading and 18 mi. from Allentown. No lodgings. Lunch and dinner served daily except Fridays and Saturdays. Full dinners served all day Sundays. Closed Christmas and special holy days. Near Mt. Doe and Mt. Hahn ski areas. Open year-round. Walter and Madeline Stoudt, Innkeepers.

Directions: From I-76 and U.S. Rte. 22, exit at Pa. Rte. 100 and travel south to U.S. Rte. 222. Follow Rte. 222 south to Pa. Rte. 662. Inn is located at this junction.

OVERLOOK INN
Canadensis, Pennsylvania

For those readers who have been following the steady progress of Bob and Lolly Tupper and the Overlook Inn, which is located in the pine-scented forests of the Pocono Mountains of Eastern Pennsylvania, here are excerpts from the most recent letter from Lolly, which I believe mirrors the inn and its qualities very well.

"It's been a good year! We completed all of our 1978 projects and now have private baths for almost all of our rooms and have enlarged a number of them as well. (They all have books and plants, adding to the 'home away from home' feeling.)

"We converted the right side of the front porch into a new dining area and next summer when the cool breezes waft through large screen windows, we will be serving breakfast and lunch there.

"Our chef, Joe Vibercik, has added quiches, clams casino, veal, and Overlook chicken to our menu and we now serve only fresh homemade soup and always all fresh vegetables, many of these from our garden that is maintained by Fred, the second chef, and Bob, our manager.

"It's really been fun to be open for all the holidays. At Thanksgiving, we had a buffet with turkeys and hams carved by Joe in the dining room, and everybody feels like 'family' about five minutes after they arrive.

"Christmas is a mixture of young and old and in-betweens. The inn is festooned with handmade and old-fashioned ornaments and treasures from the past. Three trees are adorned with lights, pop corn, and cranberry strings. The tables are set with Joe's handmade Christmas tree candles and the door of each room has its own pine cone spray or wreath. Each guest also receives a 'gift of love' from the Overlook—peach preserves made during the past summer at the inn.

"New Year's is wonderful, too. Although it's low key, we all have the *best time*. There's a midnight spread of goodies, a fire, and lots of singing around the piano.

"When the snow comes we have our own cross-country skiing and good ice skating on local ponds. There's even indoor tennis, nearby. In the summer our own pool and woods provide lots of diversions for our guests and we have tennis, golf, fishing, and riding just over the hill and through the woods.

"One of the high spots was the visit from your German innkeeping friends, and we did enjoy meeting your son Keith. We really had a beautiful time together and they all seemed to like our old-fashioned early American lodging rooms as well."

Lolly's reference to Chef Vibercik brought back a conversation I had with him about what he liked to cook the most. He reeled off everything from duckling with French orange sauce to marinated chicken. He also has a considerable assortment of desserts, including homemade cheesecakes and fresh fruit pies. He has, wonder of wonders, a delicious rice pudding which is very hard to find these days.

I did mention in the 1978 edition that the inn always receives several telephone calls and letters in the late fall from people who are looking for a place to spend the Christmas holidays. Apparently, the Christmas guests at the Overlook were delighted with the wonderful Christmas snowstorm on Christmas Eve of 1978.

An inn with much love, the Overlook Inn.

OVERLOOK INN, Dutch Hill Rd., Canadensis, Pa. 18325; 717-595-7519. A 23-room resort-inn in the heart of the Poconos, 15 mi. from Stroudsburg, Pa. Mod. American plan. Dinners served to travelers. Open every day of the year. Not ideal for children. No pets. Pool, archery, shuffleboard, bocci, hiking on grounds; golf, tennis, Alpine slide, ice skating, downhill and xc skiing, indoor tennis, antiquing, backroading, summer theatre nearby. Bob and Lolly Tupper, Innkeepers.

Directions: From the north (New England, New York state and Canada) use I-84 and take Rte. 390 south through "Promised Land" about 12 mi. to traffic light in Canadensis. Make right hand turn on Rte. 447 north- go 1/3 mi. to first right hand turn (Dutch Hill Road). Inn is 1½ mi. up hill. Look for new sign on right. From New York City, take George Washington Bridge to I-80 west. Turn off at Pennsylvania Exit 52. Follow Rte. 447 north to Canadensis traffic light. Turn left and right on Dutch Hill Road as above.

THE PINE BARN INN
Danville, Pennsylvania

The Pine Barn is another family-oriented country inn, and both Shube Walzer and his son Marty realized a dream when they completed the restoration of a large 19th-century Pennsylvania barn in 1967. A considerable amount of the original heavy stone walls was preserved, as well as the exposed beams and pillars. Today the dining room has handsome reproductions of Pennsylvania Windsor chairs, candles on each table, and a scattering of old country furniture to add to the atmosphere. One dining room has wooden shutters on the inside, polished stone floors, and heavy wooden pillars and posts to continue the Pennsylvania barn theme.

The accommodations at the Pine Barn are quite unusual. Although somewhat motel in style, the rooms are furnished with attractive cherry reproductions and there are many thoughtful touches which I always enjoy finding in a country inn, including magazines and books for guests to read. There are also plants in the rooms.

The menu at the inn includes homemade pies, breads and rolls, and other dishes such as roast beef, roast leg of lamb, and salads that are large enough to actually be a whole meal.

One of the memorable features about the Pine Barn is the unusual number of flowers. When I mentioned this to Marty, he laughed and said, "I tell people that this is one of the few inns with an outside horticulturist (my father), and an inside one (my wife, Barb). Dad's planning is a study in timing. From tulips and daffodils in the spring, to our fall marigolds, we are a virtual blanket of color with Dad out early each morning urging roses and peonies to fill the gaps. Our guests were amused to find tomatoes and Brussels sprouts outside their door intermingled with snapdragons, dahlias, zinnias and four o'clocks.

"Barbara keeps the sun porch and all the tables filled with plants and flowers from the garden, and the plants in the rooms seem to do very well."

Another real country inn touch at the Pine Barn is the Barn Swallow Gift Shop. It is now two years old and guests "ooh and ah" over the unique gifts, especially those that represent the nearby central Pennsylvania crafts. It began with only a few handmade dolls, wreaths, and candles, and has been growing steadily. I bought two very attractive dolls on my last visit and also a jar of local honey.

"I hope you will be able to come next time on a Tuesday, Thursday, or Saturday," asserted Marty Walzer. "It is the day the farmers' curbside market is held as it has been since 1871. The farmers arrive before 7 a.m., and display their produce throughout the morning. Those are the days that either Barbara or myself will take our truck and a few of the women from the kitchen and cover the main street from one end to the other buying the freshest of fruits and vegetables from the hills and valleys around us. If you have never been to a farmers' market, I can assure you that here in Danville, we have one of the finest."

Located just off I-80, Danville is a convenient distance from The Tavern in New Wilmington, Pennsylvania, near the Ohio border, and several other country inns in this book in the Pocono Mountains. It's also a very short, pleasant drive to the Inn at Starlight Lake to the north. Danville is close to three colleges, Bucknell, Susquehanna, and Bloomsburg.

PINE BARN INN, Danville, Pa. 17821; 717-275-2071. A picturesque country restaurant with 45 attractive motel rooms in central Pennsylvania. European plan. Breakfast, lunch, and dinner served daily except Christmas, July 4th, and Memorial Day. Pets allowed in some rooms. Near several colleges and historic sites. Golf, tennis, water skiing, sailing, and canoeing nearby. Martin and Barbara Walzer, Innkeepers.

Directions: From Exit 33 of I-80, go south 3 mi. to Danville. Take a left at the first traffic light. Proceed 10 blocks and follow signs to Geisinger Medical Center. Pine Barn adjoins the Center.

THE PUMP HOUSE
Canadensis, Pennsylvania

Fourteen years ago the Drucquer family, who had lived and worked in New Jersey for a number of years, were touring the Poconos looking for some property for a second home. As they came up the road near Skytop they saw a farmhouse for sale. It sat on

199

about seven acres of rolling land. There were huge trees, a sizable lawn, and, as an extra bonus, a view of the mountains from the front porch.

"As I think back now," explained Todd Drucquer, "the idea came to almost all of us at the same time. What a wonderful place for a country inn."

To make a long story short, they purchased the property, refurbished it, decorated it with loving care, and the Pump House Inn is now a way of life for all Drucquers including Todd and his wife, Penny, his brother Mark, his father Henri, and Todd's two growing sons, Chris and Cole.

Almost from the start the Pump House has had a reputation for innovation. For example, the first menu reflected the Drucquer family's French heritage, and even today the day's specials listed on the blackboard are written in French. Another novel idea was to create a dining room that actually had a waterfall in it. "This came about because there was one large rock that we just couldn't move," said Todd. "So we decided to make it into a waterfall. It is called the 'Thirsty Deer Room.'"

Other changes came with the passing years, and I've been sharing them with readers since my first visit in the late sixties.

In 1976, the Pump House established the Saturday night fixed-price dinner. They offer a choice of entrées including roast rack of lamb Persille, roast tenderloin Chasseur, duckling Normande and red snapper poached in leeks and wine. There is a wide choice of appetizers including shrimps in beer batter served in a pungent fruit sauce, fresh artichokes, and smoked trout. All of the soups are homemade and there is a large assortment of fresh vegetables.

This year's innovation involves Thursday evenings during winter until the middle of March. Todd explained that that's when they have Epicurean evenings." We take only twelve people, and all bookings have to be made by the previous Monday night so that Mark Kaplan, our chef, can plan the meal in the best possible way. We serve two hors d'oeuvres, one cold and one hot. It might be cold salmon aspic and stuffed mushrooms with lobster and crabmeat. Then there is a soup course which is sometimes lobster bisque or pumpkin soup. This is followed by a fish course, something simple like filet of sole. Then there is a meat course which is usually a steak, tournedos of beef, or rib eye steak with green peppers and onions that is prepared in a chafing dish at the table. We round the meal out with fresh vegetables, homemade bread, a salad, dessert, and coffee. There are eight courses in all and everything is done in a leisurely, elegant manner. It's more expensive than the average country inn dinner."

Although the emphasis at the Pump House is on the menu, there are four very pleasant country inn bedrooms on the second floor, some some of which are suites with baths. When all the rooms in the inn are booked, Todd directs people to the Overlook Inn which is just around the corner or to the Sterling Inn which is just a few miles away. Both of these are also in *CIBR*.

The Pump House is a sophisticated country inn in the Poconos. Its food and ambience have received accolades from many well-known publications including *Gourmet Magazine* and the *New York Times*. One reporter said that the cuisine outranked any other resort-dining room in the Poconos.

THE PUMP HOUSE INN, Canadensis, Pa. 18325; 717-595-7501. A 4-room country inn high in the Poconos, 1½ mi. north of Canadensis village and 16 mi. northeast of Stroudsburg. European plan. Sophisticated country dining. Dinner served to travelers daily. Closed Mondays in summer and Mondays and Tuesdays in winter. Closed Christmas and New Year's Day. Bicycles and golf nearby. The Drucquer Family, Owners. H. Todd Drucquer, Innkeeper.

Directions: From the north, follow I-84 to Rte. 390 south. Inn is located 13 mi. south on Rte. 390. From the south, follow I-80 to Rte. 191. Travel north on Rte. 191 to Rte. 390 north. Follow signs to Canadensis. Inn is 1½ mi. north from light in Canadensis.

1740 HOUSE
Lumberville, Pennsylvania

"Many people have a preconceived idea of what a country inn should be," says Harry Nessler, the innkeeper of the 1740 House, "and we do our best to live up to it. We do as many of the important little things as we possibly can."

The inn has an interesting history. Harry Nessler decided many years ago that he would like to get away from New York, and dreamed of owning a country inn. He searched and eventually found an 18th-century farm on the banks of the Delaware River, a few

miles north of New Hope, Pennsylvania. This was the beginning. It took time and patience to create the unique charm that is now the 1740 House. There is a remarkable blend of old and new, in a setting of great serenity and comfort. Everything is furnished with exceptional care and taste, with attention to interesting fabrics and textures, and even to such details as appropriate Allen Saalburg prints on the walls. Every room has a balcony or terrace overlooking the river and canal.

Harry explains his painstaking attention to detail quite simply. "This is my home," he says. "It is an extension of everything I hold dear . . . good taste, good food, and good manners. We welcome everyone who shares these enthusiasms."

Speaking of good food, the inn has it in abundance. An ample and varied buffet breakfast is included in the room rate (the British idea of "bed and breakfast"). It is served in the cheery, airy dining room overlooking the river. Dinner is served by candlelight on pink tablecloths. I've enjoyed the chateaubriand with sauce Bearnaise and the duck a l'orange many times, and Harry's chef does interesting things with fresh vegetables. The homemade desserts are scrumptious.

Bucks County and the surrounding area are rich in Revolutionary lore. Lumberville is just a few miles from the site of Washington's famous crossing of the Delaware on Christmas night, 1776. Soldiers of both armies crisscrossed this land many times. What is perhaps most remarkable is that some of the clapboard and stone buildings dating back to Colonial times are so well preserved. Harry provides his guests with good local maps and suggestions for back roading. He is well traveled and is also an informative guide to the many antique shops in the area.

Evening is one of the most enjoyable times at the 1740 House. After dinner, some guests gather in the paneled living room with its large fireplace to get acquainted and share the day's adventures. Others settle in the card room for bridge or Scrabble, or choose a book from the shelves to take to their room later.

For me, it is a joy to awaken early and take a quiet walk along the old canal towpath or paddle a canoe on the canal. Thickets along the river are a never-ending source of bird life and small game. While walking, I have flushed out many a pheasant. It's a beautiful opportunity to regain a sense of privacy.

1740 HOUSE, River Rd., Lumberville, Pa. 18933; 215-297-5661. A 24-room riverside inn, 6½ mi. north of New Hope, in the heart of historic Bucks County. Lodgings include breakfast which is served to house guests daily; dinner served daily except Sundays and Mondays, by reservation only. Open year-round. Pool and boating on grounds. Golf and tennis nearby. Harry Nessler, Innkeeper.

Directions: From N.Y.C., travel south on N.J. Tpke., and take Exit 10. Follow Rte. 287 north to Easton exit. Proceed west on Rte. 22 to Flemington, then Rte. 202 south over Delaware Toll Bridge. After an immediate turn onto Rte. 32N, drive 5 mi. to inn. From Pa. Tpke., exit at Willow Grove and proceed north on Rte. 611 to Rte. 202. Follow Rte. 202 north to Rte. 32 and turn north to inn.

STERLING INN
South Sterling, Pennsylvania

I could not resist it any longer—I had been listening to the gurgling waters of the Wallenpaupack Creek for about twenty minutes on a warm, lazy afternoon. I was sitting on a lawn chair about fifty paces from the back of the Sterling Inn, just two feet from the bank of the creek. The smell of the freshly-cut lawn mingled with the scent of the forest on the other side of the water. What a place, I thought, to propose to some pretty girl.

I kicked off my shoes, rolled up my pants, and waded out to stand on the flat, smooth shelf of rock in the middle of the creek. The water was clean and cool. There was a little pool about twenty-five feet away, deep enough for me to sit in and have the water come up to my chest. A flash of red and another of blue signaled a cardinal and a bluejay darting into the woods, deep in the Pocono Mountains of Pennsylvania.

I climbed back on the bank and was drying my feet when one of the other guests came and plunked down on a nearby chair. "I think this is one of the best-kept, neatest places that I have ever visited," she said. "It's as American as apple pie and fresh vegetables. The rooms are so comfortable, and I'm very glad I came. Don't you just love it here?"

203

Even if her enthusiasm hadn't been catching, I would have had to agree.

This was the friendly and unpretentious atmosphere that Alice Julian had in mind over forty years ago when she acquired the Sterling Inn. This is the way that her daughter and son-in-law, Carmen and Henry Arneberg, are keeping it today.

The Sterling Inn is on a back road in the Poconos. There are enticing hiking and walking trails on the inn property and nearby. One of them, Henry told me, leads to a waterfall on the ridge behind the inn. There is a very pleasant nine-hole putting green, a swimming area with a sandy beach, and a little pond with willow trees and a few ducks.

Lodgings are to be found in several very attractive buildings in this parklike atmosphere. The Wayside, Lodge, Meadowlark, Hilltop, and Spring Run are all beautifully situated with extremely attractive rooms that have been colorfully decorated. There are sixty-seven accommodations which are well-dispersed and give no feeling of being crowded together.

The menu includes such entrées as roast lamb, pot roast and standing rib roast, because, as Carmen Arneberg says, "This is the kind of food that some people serve only when they are having guests for dinner."

Although the Sterling has been here for more than forty-five years and has many old friends that return almost yearly, there are a great many honeymooners who find the quiet atmosphere much to their liking. It's a very good place for children because, even on rainy days, there's lots for them to do.

To tell the truth, I discovered the Sterling Inn one day when I took a wrong turn and got lost in the Poconos. I returned the next year to see if it was all true.

Believe me, it was.

STERLING INN. Rte. 191, South Sterling, Pa. 18460; 717-676-3311. A 67-room secluded resort-inn in the Pocono Mountains, 8 mi. from I-84 and 12 mi. from I-380. American plan. Reservation and check-in office closes at 10 p.m. Breakfast, lunch, and dinner served to travelers daily. Breakfast served 8-9 a.m.; lunch served 12:30-1:30 p.m.; dinner served 6-7:15 p.m. Jackets required for dinner. No liquor served. Open weekends only, beginning May 4 (Friday to Monday a.m.) until May 24; open every day thereafter until October 22 closing date. No pets. Swimming, putting greens, shuffleboard, all-weather tennis court, and woodland walks on grounds. Golf courses and horseback riding nearby. No credit cards. Henry and Carmen Areneberg, Innkeepers.

Directions: From I-80, follow I-380 to Rte. 940 to Mount Pocono. At light, cross Rte. 611 and proceed on Rte. 196 north to Rte. 423. Drive north on Rte. 423 to Rte. 191 and travel ½ mile north to inn. From I-84, follow Rte. 507 south through Greentown and New-foundland. In Newfoundland, pick up Rte. 191 and travel 4 mi. south to inn.

THE TAVERN
New Wilmington, Pennsylvania

The year was 1973. For years I had been fascinated with the "plain people" who live in eastern Pennsylvania. These include the Amish, Dunkards, Moravians, and Schwenkfelders. I had always enjoyed the back roads of Lancaster and Berks counties and admired the picturebook farms and industrious people.

Now at the western end of Pennsylvania, I was once again in "Dutch Country." I had heard there was a sizable community of Amish here, but I was surprised at the scope.

The purpose of my visit was to meet Mrs. Ernst Durrast and visit The Tavern in New Wilmington. When I drove through the town, I saw the familiar black buggies and plain dress of these pious folk who originally fled from Europe in the 18th century to obtain religious freedom.

"Oh, yes," Mrs. Durrast explained over a cup of tea, "this is Amish country, and they are a people who are quite proud of their ancestry. I hope that while you're here you'll drive out to the countryside to see those neat farms and spotless buildings." We

205

talked about New Wilmington and Westminster College and some of the joys of living in western Pennsylvania. "Well, I've had this inn for forty-five years," she said, "and I just can't imagine living anywhere else. This is a lovely little town. I like it especially because there's a constant flow of young people from the college."

The talk then shifted to the startling number of entrées on the luncheon menu. Just for fun, I counted twenty-seven, plus an appetizer, vegetables, fritters, salad, rolls, dessert, and a beverage. It was real country fare including gourmet beef balls, creamed chicken on a biscuit, cabbage rolls, grilled smoked pork chops, ham steaks, cheese and cheese souffle' with creamed chicken. Two warm honey buns with whipped butter are always served.

As I could see, lunch was a substantial meal. Mrs. D. explained to me that a great many of her noontime patrons are older people and prefer to eat their meal at midday.

Dinners include a great many of the luncheon offerings plus about twelve other main dishes. There's usually a most unusual combination of white meat of chicken and lobster tail served in a special sherry sauce. How does that sound?

There's a small lodge across the village street with a few sleeping rooms available. One of these is frequently occupied by my dear friends Claire and Lucy Dee Dee of Grand Rapids, Michigan. They first recommended Mrs. Durrast's splendid establishment to me back in 1972.

New Wilmington is just a few minutes from I-80, the east-west highway that traverses northern Pennsylvania. It's about two hundred and forty miles from the Poconos where there are at least three country inns that I have found most comfortable.

"It wonders me," said Mrs. Durrast, borrowing a quaint Amish saying, "why it has taken you so long to find us."

THE TAVERN, Box 153, New Wilmington, Pa. 16142; 412-946-2020. A bustling country restaurant on the town square with 5 sleeping rooms in a lodge directly across the street. European plan. Lunch and dinner served daily except Tuesdays. Reservations required. Closed Thanksgiving and Christmas. Sports and cultural events at Westminister College nearby. Mrs. Ernst Durrast, Innkeeper.

Directions: From I-80, take Exit 1-S, and follow Rte. 18 south to Rte. 208. Proceed east on 208 to town square. From I-79, follow Rte. 208 west for 14 mi. to New Wilmington.

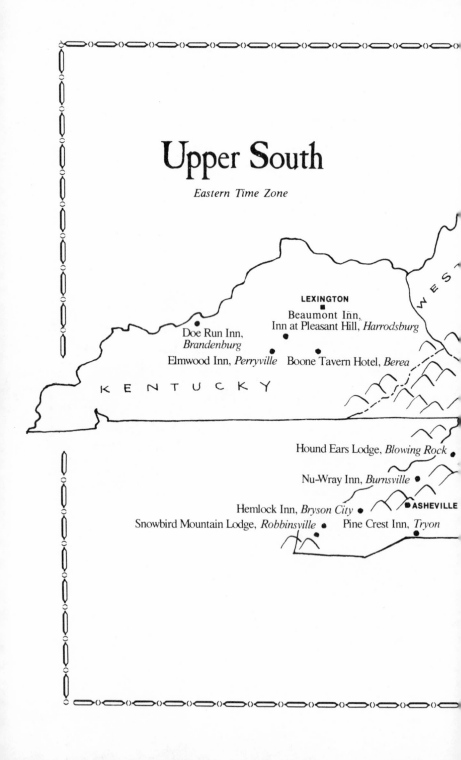

Upper South

Eastern Time Zone

LEXINGTON

Doe Run Inn,
Brandenburg

Beaumont Inn,
Inn at Pleasant Hill, *Harrodsburg*

Elmwood Inn, *Perryville*   Boone Tavern Hotel, *Berea*

K E N T U C K Y

W E S T

Hound Ears Lodge, *Blowing Rock*

Nu-Wray Inn, *Burnsville*

Hemlock Inn, *Bryson City*   **ASHEVILLE**

Snowbird Mountain Lodge, *Robbinsville*   Pine Crest Inn, *Tryon*

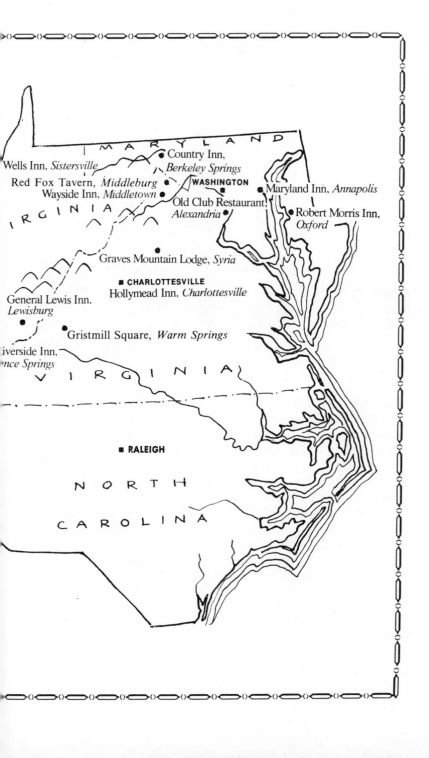

Maryland

MARYLAND INN
Annapolis, Maryland

In November of 1978, at least one hundred and seventy people, innkeepers and their wives from North America and Europe, gathered together for a two-day annual meeting of *CIBR* inns at the Maryland Inn. I'm sure that in the almost two-hundred-year history of the inn, it had never before played host at one time to such a large group of country inn aficionados.

Everyone agreed the food, accommodations, entertainment, and cooperation of the inn staff were superb. Personally, I can't think of a better recommendation.

We arrived to find that the ambitious program of restoration undertaken years ago by proprietor Paul Pearson is now nearly completed. Paul took us outside to show us the work that's being done on the roof with the intricate copper cornice gutters completely replaced and the slate mansards completely restored, partially with slate, he said, from the great dome from the nearby State House.

"The inn is in many ways a museum piece," he remarked. "The earliest part was built during the Revolution and then expanded about a hundred years ago. However, there are no 'do not touch' signs. Guests may feel and touch to their hearts' content."

There is much to feel and touch—original stone walls in the basement dining room, wood beams, and brick chimney arches in the 1784 King of France Tavern, where we all enjoyed the music of Charlie Byrd, the great jazz guitarist, who spends several weeks a year entertaining for his Maryland friends.

Innkeeper Peg Bednarsky was a tower of strength during our meeting, and other innkeepers spoke glowingly of the views from their rooms, including the State House, the Bay, Church Circle, and the Governor's mansion. Imagine trying to please a group of innkeepers!

Ever mindful of the role that good food plays in their success, our innkeepers were glowing in their praise of the Maryland Inn Crab Imperial as well as the broiled rock fish, oysters Rockefeller, and the Duke of Gloucester, which is baked filet of flounder stuffed with a delicately seasoned crabmeat.

There were lots of opportunities for us to take walking tours of the city of Annapolis, which started as a Colonial seaport and has seventeen miles of waterfront within its boundaries. The inn is conveniently located in the midst of the great historic city of Annapolis, where there are tours of some of the finest Colonial townhouses in America, including the newly-restored home and gardens of Governor Paca, one of the signers of the Declaration of Independence. Tours can also be arranged to the nearby Naval Academy.

During one of the quieter moments of our meeting, a group of us were standing on the porch of the inn with Paul Pearson, talking about the traditions of the city, and he pointed out some of the Maryland Inn's own traditions: "We commemorate such occasions as Bastille Day, with dancing in the street; Halloween, when we have sort of a zany, costumed 'freakers ball'; and Heritage Weekend with its big celebration à la Charles Dickens at Christmastime."

After breakfast on the third day, when most of us were packing our cars and getting ready to return to inns in all parts of North America and beyond, many of the innkeepers made a special point of saying how much they had enjoyed our time together, and wondering out loud how soon we would be returning to the Maryland Inn.

MARYLAND INN, Church Circle, Annapolis, Md. 21401; 301-263-2641. A 44-room 18th-century village inn in a history-laden town, 20 mi. from Baltimore and Washington, D.C. Near U.S. Naval Academy and Chesapeake Bay. European plan. Breakfast, lunch, and dinner served to travelers daily. Sunday brunch served year-round. Jazz Club, music nightly except Mondays in the King of France Tavern. Tours arranged to historic and scenic points of interest. Tennis and sailing school available. Paul Pearson, Proprietor; Peg Bednarsky, Innkeeper.

Directions: From Baltimore, take Rte. 2 south to first directional turnoff "Washington/Annapolis." From Washington, take Rte. 50 east to exit "Annapolis, Naval Academy, Rowe Blvd."

ROBERT MORRIS INN
Oxford, Maryland

In early January, 1979, I was reading a beautiful long letter from Wendy Gibson. She and her husband Ken are the proprietors and innkeepers of the Robert Morris Inn on the banks of the Tred Avon River in Oxford, on Maryland's eastern shore.

I went back to earlier editions of *CIBR* and discovered that I first shared some of Wendy's thoughts in our 1971 book when she and Ken first became associated with the Robert Morris.

In those days, the Gibsons had only been married a very short time, but before taking over the Robert Morris, they spent some time in one of Montreal's famous hostelries learning something about the problems of running an inn.

Both the Gibson family, and the size and the reputation of the Robert Morris have grown every year since. Here are some excerpts from Wendy's recent letter which will serve to update all of us.

"Ever since Robert Michener's book, *Chesapeake*, came out, our business has been tremendous. For the second year in a row we

212

received the Holiday-Travel Fine Dining award and we were also in Ripley's "Believe-it-or-Not," in connection with our staircase and the inn having been built in 1710.

"We've made many improvements since last year. The Lodge on the Point has been almost completely renovated. We put in three more rooms, and private baths in the existing room. In addition, we replaced all the windows and changed the heating and air conditioning systems. I can vouch for the windows as I personally washed all forty of them! I feel that when people are paying for a view of the water they should be able to see it. I will start on the inn windows next.

"We also renovated the old Carriage House which was nothing more than a broken-down shed when we started. We turned it into two lovely waterfront accommodations, one up and one down, complete with bay windows, paneling and waterfowl wallpaper. I must say, they are exquisite.

"I certainly owe a lot of thanks to my mother who makes the curtains for all of the rooms. Oh, I musn't forget that we completely painted the outside of the inn and most of the inside. It took a whole summer.

"Ken's brother, Jay, is doing a marvelous job and works very hard in all areas. Mr. Miller, our maitre d',has been with us since we took over eight years ago—he's as solid as a rock.

"Our boys, Ben who is five, and Kent who is seven, are slowly getting involved with the inn. They helped with the raising of the zinnias for the table vases, and they also pick up trash. They earn one cent for every cigarette butt they find. Ben often works with me in the rooms. He strips the beds and piles the sheets in the middle of the room and then dives in them. Kent is really my go-between. He takes messages back and forth from our house usually to the inn or to Ken.

"Morris, our bassett hound is fine. He had six weeks of basic training at obedience school and now can be seen walking behind me instead of vice-versa. The guests enjoy him."

Ken and Wendy's inn was named for the town of Oxford's most distinguished early citizen. Ships' timbers were used in the construction, and ballast stones can be seen in the fireplace. In addition to the lodging rooms in the main building, rooms are also available in the Lodge which is located on the Point just a few paces away.

Oysters prepared in many ways, as well as a wide variety of Chesapeake Bay seafood dishes, are the specialties of the menu. Breakfast includes scrapple and homefries as well as omelets and blueberry pancakes.

One way of reaching it is to take the Tred Avon ferry between

Oxford and Bellevue. It holds all of three cars on each trip.

ROBERT MORRIS INN, Oxford, Md. 21654; 301-226-5111. A 35-room village inn in a secluded colonial community on the Tred Avon, 10 mi. from Easton, Md. European plan. 15 rooms with private baths; 20 rooms with shared baths. 4 rooms with private porches overlooking the Tred Avon. Breakfast, lunch, and dinner served to travelers daily. Open year-round except Christmas Day. No pets. Tennis, golf, sailing, swimming, and bicycles nearby. Kenneth and Wendy Gibson, Innkeepers.

Directions: From Delaware Memorial Bridge, follow Rte. 13 south to Rte. 301 and proceed south to Rte. 50, then east on Rte. 50 to Easton. From Chesapeake Bay Bridge, follow Rte. 50-301 to Rte. 50 and proceed east to Easton. From Chesapeake Bay Bridge Tunnel, follow Rte. 13 north to Rte. 50 and proceed west to Easton. From Easton, follow Rte. 322 to Rte. 333 to Oxford and inn.

Virginia

TALLY-HO
The area around Middleburg, Virginia in Fauquier and adjoining Loudoun counties, has some of the best backroading I have ever experienced. Most of the roads are unpaved and there are honey-suckle-covered walls, and beautiful pastures and farmlands. It is this lush countryside that makes Middleburg a center for point-to-point and hunt race meets. The National Beagle trials are held here, and the nearby Upperville Horse Show is the oldest in the United States. There are also several steeplechase courses, one of them just a few moments from Middleburg. Incidentally, an excellent map for backroading is available at the front desk of the Red Fox Tavern.

RED FOX TAVERN
Middleburg, Virginia

There are not many country inns in North America that have remained in the same building more than 200 years. However, the Red Fox Tavern in Middleburg, Virginia, which started as a simple way station when the road to the west was known as "Ashby's Gap Turnpike," has passed the midway point of its third century, and is an integral part of American history.

Joseph Chinn was the first proprietor and it became known as

Chinn's Ordinary. His first cousin was George Washington, who was engaged by Lord Fairfax to survey the area around the tavern, which in turn became known as Chinn's Crossroads.

It's probably true that soldiers from both the American and British lines stopped at this local tavern during the war for American Independence.

The Assembly of Virginia chose Chinn's Crossroads as a specific town and established Middleburg on 50 acres of land November 2, 1787. Mr. Leven Powell, then owner of the property, subdivided the land and named the streets after his Federalist friends, some of whose names still survive.

In 1812, Chinn's Ordinary became the Beveridge House and was enlarged to thirty-five rooms. It was the political, social, and economic focal point of Middleburg, which was already an important grain and farming area.

During the War Between the States, Confederate General J.E.B. Stuart needed lodgings for the night and chose the large rooms above the tavern. It was in these rooms that Colonel John Mosby and his Raiders had a celebrated meeting with Stuart, and it was downstairs in the tavern where many of the wounded received care.

The inn became known as the Middleburg Inn around 1877, and was changed to the Red Fox Tavern in 1937, no doubt to recognize one of the most famous four-footed residents in this part of the country, for Middleburg had already gained a reputation as one of the nation's foremost areas for thoroughbred horse breeding and fox hunting.

There are ten tastefully decorated lodging rooms; six are in the main building, some with sitting areas and 18th-century, documented wallpapers and paint colors. Each room is furnished with period antiques and have canopied beds and working fireplaces. There are additional rooms in an ancient stone building a few doors away.

215

On the second floor of the tavern there is a very comfortable pine paneled lounge with two fireplaces, deep leather couches and chairs, and a warm feeling that draws everyone close together.

The main entrance leads directly into one of the two low-ceilinged dining rooms where the thirty-inch-thick walls are appropriately decorated with fox hunting regalia. Cheery fires are always lit during the chilly months. A secluded terrace to the rear of the inn underneath the trees has an intimate outdoor feeling and is very popular during the spring, summer, and fall months.

The menu includes such traditional Virginia dishes as country ham with red-eye gravy, peanut soup, as well as crab cakes, bourbon apple and pecan pie.

It was at the Night Fox, a small bistro located behind the main building that I discovered the skill of playing darts has reached a new dimension. Not only are there friendly games each evening, but frequent tournaments are held. The true devotee owns his own darts and carries them about in a mahogany or walnut box. There are as many dart rules as there are croquet rules, both English and American. The Night Fox has a little second floor porch with white iron furniture and a very intimate and romantic air.

Of course, there have been some renovations and additions and modernization of Chinn's Tavern, but I'm sure that Joseph Chinn would thoroughly approve of everything: particularly the fact that travelers to Middleburg are still received with gracious Virginia hospitality at the Red Fox Tavern.

RED FOX TAVERN, Middleburg, Va. 22117; 703-687-6301. A 10-room historic village inn near the Blue Ridge Mountains approximately 40 miles from Washington, D.C. Near Manassas Battlefield, Oatlands, and Oak Hill (President Monroe's White House). European plan. Breakfast, lunch, and dinner served to travelers. Open every day of the year. Spectator sports such as polo, steeplechasing, available nearby. No activities available for small children. Consult innkeeper for policy on pets. The Reuter Family, Innkeepers.

Directions: Leave the Washington D.C. Beltway (495) at Rte. 66 West, to Rte. 50. Follow Rte. 50 West for 22 miles to Middleburg.

OLD CLUB RESTAURANT
Alexandria, Virginia

For me the Old Club is a gateway to the South. I try to stop as often as possible to renew my taste for southern cooking. Take ham for example: on my last visit, Innkeeper Lee Palmer and I were discussing the subject. He explained his hams are "real

country" hams from Culpeper, Virginia. "We soak it overnight, boil for about three hours, cool it and then put in the oven with vinegar, and let glaze for two hours.

"Country ham is best served thinly sliced and salty. Our guests like it warm over bread with black-eyed peas and candied sweet potatoes."

The oldest part of this colonial mansion in Alexandria was built by George Washington and his friends as a private club, hence the name. The little brick building on the north was said to have been young Washington's office while he was surveying this area. There are dozens of stories connected with this sedate restaurant, including the fact that during the War of 1812, when the British were at the gates of Alexandria, all the handsome wooden furniture was buried in what is now the vegetable garden.

The Old Club has been included in CIBR since the late 1960s and, as on that first visit, I have always led off my meal with a cup of peanut soup, which is a feature of this historic restaurant. I find that a cup is sufficient, because there is still enough appetite left for the choices on the menu, which has changed very little during my tenure. Besides the Virginia country ham served over cornbread, covered with maple syrup, there is Allegheny mountain trout, which is boned and stuffed with mushrooms and rice, and topped with tartar sauce. I have also enjoyed chicken Laura Lee, which is a chicken breast on hickory ham served with a mushroom sauce.

The Old Club is located in the historic section of Alexandria where there are many buildings dating back to colonial days. In recent years, Alexandria has had an excellent program of restoration and preservation, which includes at least twenty-seven historic sites and buildings that are really architectural jewels. There is an excellent walking tour available with an explanation of such landmarks as Christ Church, Captain's Row, Gadsby's Tavern, and Carlyle House. Mount Vernon is just a few miles away by car.

I had finished my helping of country ham on cornbread, and Lee suggested I top it off with some deep dish apple pie. "It is made with a little apple wine and a little ice cream. Our guests sing its praises all the time."

We finished dinner and walked out on the flagstone patio and Lee explained that the Old Club is becoming a popular place for rehearsal dinners and wedding receptions. "As a matter of fact," he said, "we have had six marriages at the Old Club this year."

We said good-bye and Lee said, "Come back real soon."

I certainly would, and the next time it would be with touring German innkeepers.

OLD CLUB RESTAURANT, 555 So. Washington St., Alexandria, Va. 22314; 703-549-4555. Just across the river from Washington, D.C. in one of the country's best preserved colonial cities. No lodgings. Lunch and dinner served daily except Mondays and Christmas. Convenient to Christ Church, Robert E. Lee House, Gadsby's Tavern, Old Apothecary Shop, and Potomac River. Mt. Vernon and Gunston Hall nearby. Lee Palmer, Innkeeper.

Directions: North and southbound traffic on 495 take Exit #1 North to Rte. 1. Turn right on Franklin St. and left on Washington St., 1 block to inn. (Mount Vernon Memorial Hwy. is Washington St. in the city.)

WAYSIDE INN
Middletown, Virginia

The flickering candlelight in the Slave Kitchen cast our shadows on the smoke-blackened beams overhead and was reflected in the pewter plates, pitchers, and old windows. The fireplace radiated a warm glow and two cast iron pots on the crane gurgled and boiled.

"This room was hidden," explained Leo Bernstein, owner of the Wayside Inn. "It was discovered by accident, and restoring it was a great deal of fun. Those are the original brick walls, and I see you've already noticed the adz marks on the beams. All of the tools are from the colonial period."

The Wayside Inn dates from at least 1797. It is correctly referred to as an historic restoration. It was carefully restored to its present form after 1960 when Leo, a lawyer and banker from nearby Washington, happened to drive through the main street in Middletown and recognized the inn's tremendous possibilities. The inn is an antique lover's paradise. Its rooms are packed with a mind-boggling collection of tables, chests, paintings, and *objets d'art*.

The menu includes some very old country recipes, such as spoon bread and peanut soup, whole, baked tomatoes, Virginia country ham with red-eye gravy, and both smothered and pan-fried chicken. Homemade bread and real whipped butter accompany every dinner. Young people wearing the costume of the era serve these tempting dishes.

Three meals plus afternoon tea are served seven days a week in dining rooms decorated in accordance with their names: the Front Room, Lord Fairfax Room, President's Room, and Senseney Room. In earlier days the Wayside Inn served as a way station where fresh teams of horses waited to harness up to arriving stagecoaches traveling the Shenandoah Valley Turnpike. Soldiers from both the north and the south frequented the inn, then known as Wilkinson's Tavern, seeking refuge, comfort, and friendship during the War Between the States.

Later on, it became known as America's first motor inn—and who could have foreseen the trend which was to follow?

Rooms at the inn are decorated in many different styles, because Leo, an avid collector, has an eye for antiques of any kind. Hence, each lodging room is quite apt to be a potpourri of anything from Byzantine to Victorian.

In the summertime, Middletown also enjoys the Wayside Summer Theatre with a professional company of actors. Dinners are served earlier in order to provide guests ample time to walk the two or three blocks to the theatre.

Middletown actually provides the traveler with an introduction to the northern Shenandoah Valley. It is a short drive to the northern

terminus of the Skyline Drive, and there is ample skiing, hiking, fishing, swimming, horseback riding, and golf, besides the wealth of history to be found on the back roads.

WAYSIDE INN, Middletown, Va. 22645; 703-869-1797. A 21-room country resort-inn since 1797 in the Shenandoah Valley. About 1½ hrs. from Washington, D.C. European plan. Breakfast, lunch, and dinner served daily to travelers. Open every day of the year. Professional summer stock theatre and arts center, Belle Grove, Cedar Creek Battlefield, Blue Ridge Parkway, Crystal Caverns, Hotel Strasburg, and Shenandoah Valley historical sites nearby. Marjorie Alcarese, Innkeeper.

Directions: Take Exit 77 off I-81 to Rte. 11. Follow signs to inn.

HOLLYMEAD INN
Charlottesville, Virginia

"After the defeat of Gentleman Johnny Burgoyne at Saratoga in 1777, many Hessian mercenaries were marched down from upper New York State to an improvised internment camp in Charlottesville, Virginia. As their numbers increased, so did their need for housing, and that's how this house came to be built."

Peggy Bute and I were seated in the Hessian Room of the Hollymead Inn, and she was telling me a little about the fascinating history of the building and the area.

"The timber in this room is original and dates back to about 1780. The center part of the house was constructed between 1810 and 1820 and was used for a period of time as a private boys' school. About ten boys lived in the two rooms on the third floor. Their lessons were held in what is now one of our private dining rooms."

There is a great deal of American history in this part of Virginia. Monticello, the home of Thomas Jefferson, is just a few minutes from the inn, as are Ash Lawn (the home and garden of James Monroe), the University of Virginia with its famous serpentine walls and beautiful architecture, and Castle Hill, a Virginia landmark built in 1765.

Where the Hollymead really shines is in offering exceptional hospitality and good food. Peg does most of the cooking herself and supervises everything in the kitchen. "We are very particular about many things here," she said. "For example, we believe in serving the food while it is still piping hot. There is nothing more distressing than cold rolls or lukewarm beef Wellington. We take a great deal of time and care with dishes like our trout stuffed with crabmeat, flounder stuffed with shrimp, boneless breast of chicken in sauce, and other house specialties. We want nothing less than perfection."

The Hollymead is aptly named because it sits in a grove of holly trees which you can see from the windows in the dining rooms. The rolling Virginia hills with maple, magnolia, and oak trees stretch out in all directions. The building is a white clapboard colonial with a red brick walk leading up to the front door.

In the basement of the inn there is a country butcher shop where Virginia hams and beef are sold. It is called the Hook and Cleaver. There is also a sportswear and gift shop.

Since my last visit, there has been an interesting development at the Hollymead. Now, in addition to dinner, lunch is available Tuesdays through Saturdays. "We had so much demand for it," said Peg, "that we've decided to offer it. Now we have quite a number of the University of Virginia faculty at noon."

HOLLYMEAD INN, Rte. 8, Box 367A, Charlottesville, Va. 22901; 804-973-8488. A country restaurant a few minutes north of Charlottesville on Rte. 29. Near Monticello, Ash Lawn, University of Virginia, and Skyline Drive in Blue Ridge Mts. No lodgings. Dinner served Tuesdays through Saturdays. Lunch served Tuesday through Friday. Open year-round. Closed Christmas Eve, Christmas Day, and New Year's Day. Mr. and Mrs. Joseph Bute, Innkeepers.

Directions: Proceed 6 mi. north of Charlottesville, Va., on Rte. 29 North.

GRAVES MOUNTAIN LODGE
Syria, Virginia

"Many people who come back again request the rooms with fireplaces," Rachel Graves explained, as she passed a plate of pancakes fresh from the kitchen. I helped myself to several of the

pancakes and some scrambled eggs and crisp strips of bacon from another platter.

Jim Graves added, "This is the time of the year when the fireplace feels mighty good at the end of the day. I think the foliage is just about at its peak." He pointed down to the valley where the creek was flowing serenely. "The stream looks gentle now," he said, "but we had two serious floods a few years ago. In fact for awhile we were marooned on this side of the water."

"I wish you could have been here during our Apple Festival," remarked Rachel, pouring another cup of coffee. "We had a big pot of Brunswick stew on the fire and people came from all over and picked their own apples. You know, some of the kids had never seen apple trees before. Later they went over to the farm to look at the pigs and the cattle. For many of them it was their first farm experience."

Graves Mountain Lodge nestles at the end of a road in Syria, Virginia, in the Blue Ridge Mountains. At one time the road ran to the other side of the mountains, but when the Shenandoah National Park was built during the 30s the road was closed. Now this valley is a secluded spot with a three-thousand-acre working farm and a country inn.

There is a wide variety of accommodations. The several different rustic lodgings located in what were at one time farm outbuildings are popular with the younger generation. These include farmhouses, cabins, and cottages, many with their own fireplaces. There are also lodgings available in two modern motel units located on the side of the mountain above the Main Lodge.

The Main Lodge, as is the case with all the buildings, is built out of lumber taken right out of the hills. It contains the big country dining rooms where food is served family-style on long tables, a large recreation room and gift shop, and the W.C. Bader Room, named for the man who does the beautiful wood inlays of all kinds of birds and outdoor scenes which adorn the walls. There is a welcome apple barrel in one corner of the room as well.

"We find that a great many people like to come here during what we call our 'off season,' because it is so quiet and peaceful then, and it is possible to get close to nature."

Graves Mountain Lodge is an easy two-hour drive from Washington, D.C., but is as far removed as possible from an urban environment. On this gorgeous November day the colors were at their best, while the grass and willow trees were still green.

I decided to spend the day wandering around the farm and hiking back up into the foothills of the Blue Ridge, planning to return in time for a magnificent family-style dinner that evening.

GRAVES MOUNTAIN LODGE, Syria, Va. 22743; 703-923-4231. A 38-room secluded resort-inn on Rte. 670, off Rte. 231, 10 mi. north of Madison, Va., 38 mi. N.W. of Charlottesville, Va. American plan. Rustic lodgings including 11 cottages and cabins and two modern motel units. Breakfast, lunch, dinner served to travelers by reservation only. Closed Dec. 1 to late March. Swimming, tennis, riding, fishing, basketball on grounds. Golf nearby. Jim and Rachel Graves, Innkeepers.

Directions: Coming south from Wash., D.C., take I-66 to Gainsville. Follow Rte. 29 south to Madison, turn right onto Rte. 231 West, go 7 mi. to Banco, turn left onto Rte. 670 and follow 670 for 4½ mi. to lodge.

GRISTMILL SQUARE
Warm Springs, Virginia

In 1973, Cathy and Philip Hirsh began the restoration of Gristmill Square, which is twenty-five-hundred feet up in the Allegheny Mountains. A complete refurbishing of several buildings has replaced the former decay and dilapidation that existed in the center of this little town. Among those buildings is a mill which has been turned into a rustic, yet elegant, restaurant. All around the square are small shops and guest accommodations, including two-bedroom apartments, each with a bath, kitchen, living room, balcony or sundeck, and a wood-burning fireplace. Other accommodations include double rooms or small suites, also

223

available with fireplaces. The furnishings are extremely tasteful with a number of the rooms done in authentic antiques.

Since the Waterwheel Restaurant first opened, its food has attracted people from some distance. Philip Hirsh is in complete charge of the kitchen and many of the dishes are his recipes (quite a change from being a corporate executive just a few years ago). Some of his specialties include curried chicken, fresh rainbow trout from nearby hatcheries, vine-ripened tomatoes, and crisp zucchini from Philip and Kathy's own garden, shepherd's pie, and absolutely super chili.

"We're really a resort inn," explained Kathy, "with three all-weather tennis courts and swimming pool, plus guest privileges at the Bath and Tennis club. There's good horseback riding in our mountains, as well as fishing, hunting, and hiking. In winter there's skiing just a few hours away. Golfers are a few minutes away from the famous Cascade and lower Cascade courses at Hot Springs."

Since our last edition, the Hirshes have added Craig's Cottage, which is on their farm four miles west of Gristmill Square. Among other things, it has a high-ceilinged bedroom with a big stone fireplace and a large picture window looking over meadows and mountains. Guests at the cottage often take walks to the river or to the barn to see the ducks, geese, chickens, goats, and friendly dogs. (No pets are allowed at Craig's Cottage.)

One of the spring attractions at Warm Springs during the second or third weekend in March is the Maple Festival in nearby Highland County. Every restaurant in the area features pancakes and Highland County maple syrup. There are crafts to see and farms to explore.

Springtime in Warm Springs brings out the dogwood and redbud. In June there is laurel and rhododendron, trailing arbutus, lady's-slippers, trillium, bloodroot, dogtooth violets, and wild azaleas.

Fall foliage festivals are held in Monterey and Clifton Forge in mid-October.

A lovely place in all seasons, Gristmill Square.

GRISTMILL SQUARE, Warm Springs, Va. 24484; 703-839-2231. An unusual restoration which includes a restaurant, accommodations, small shops, and many resort attractions, in a small country town approx. 19 mi. from Covington in the Allegheny Mts. European plan. Lunch and dinner served daily Tuesday — Saturday. Sunday brunch only. Closed Mondays. Many different types of accommodations available. Suggest telephone for details. Children welcome. Pets allowed but not permitted loose on grounds. Tennis,

swimming pool on grounds. Golf, skiing, skating, riding, hiking, fishing, hunting, antiquing, back roading nearby. Philip and Catherine Hirsh, Innkeepers.

Directions: From Staunton, Va., follow Rte. 254 to Buffalo Gap, Rte. 42 to Millboro Spring, Rte. 39 to Warm Springs. From Lexington, take Rte. 39 to Warm Springs. From Roanoke, take Rte. 220 to Warm Springs. From Lewisburg, W. Va. take I-64 to Covington, Rte. 220 north to Warm Springs. From northern W. Va. travel south to Rte. 39 east to Warm Springs.

North Carolina

PINE CREST INN
Tryon, North Carolina

I asked Innkeeper Bob Hull about the famous Tryon "thermal belt."

"This is caused by a temperature inversion," he explained, "resulting in a temperate zone which escapes the frost of the valley and the deep freeze of the mountains. The foliage here is fresh and green compared with that above and below. Scientists have studied this unusual condition for years. We love it."

The Pine Crest is in the foothills of the Blue Ridge Mountains near Asheville, in the town of Tryon, which in itself is a very

225

interesting place. Many artists and writers have moved there over the recent years, finding inspiration in these mountains where nature has been so generous. Because of its advantageous location and its healthful climate, Tryon is an ideal place to spend a vacation. Many guests return to the Pine Crest year after year and make arrangements to meet each other on the next trip.

The rooms in the individual cottages are furnished in Carolina furniture which is handmade locally, and many of them have splendid views of the mountains. One of them, by the way, is called "Swayback" and was at one time occupied by F. Scott Fitzgerald. All have distinctive names, and most have fireplaces.

The innkeepers at Pine Crest are Fran and Bob Hull who say of themselves, "We left Fairfield County, Connecticut, and corporate living about seven years ago, and have found a completely different way of life here keeping a country inn."

"Fran," said Bob, "is in charge of the kitchen. It is something that she really likes to do. She wouldn't feel right unless she knew what was going on. Our guests seem to expect it. She can make practically everything from scratch, including bread, rolls, desserts, pies, and cakes."

In the dining room there is a big stone fireplace at one end and beautiful oak tables which need no tablecloths to enhance them. There are flowers and candles on the tables, and as everybody agrees, the food is marvelous. Many of the waiters have been here for over twenty years. In fact one of them, Theron Barton

226

who is seventy-seven years old, has been at the Pine Crest for sixty-four years. He has an award for being the third oldest waiter in the United States.

Apparently this way of life agrees with Bob and Fran, and with their guests as well. "We like to do things in our own way," says Bob. "We like jackets and ties on gentlemen at dinner, although ties can be eliminated in warm weather. We now require a minimum visit of two nights, and reservations are required at all times. We think it's important to have the morning paper at the table at breakfast, and a delivery of ice to the room late in the afternoon."

PINE CREST INN, P.O. Box 1030, Tryon, N.C. 28782; 704-859-9135. A 34-room resort-inn midway between Asheville, N.C. and Greenville/Spartanburg, S.C. Breakfast, lunch, and dinner served daily by reservation to travelers. Coats required for gentlemen at dinner. Closed Jan. 2 to Feb. 15. Closed Christmas. Attended, leashed pets allowed. Golf, tennis, and swimming at nearby country clubs. Reservations required at all times. Minimum visit 2 nights. Robert and Fran Hull, Innkeepers.

Directions: From Asheville, take I-26 to Tryon exit, then 108 to Tryon. Go through town. Do not cross railroad tracks but bear left to Pine Crest Lane. The inn is at the end of the lane. From Spartanburg/Greenville take I-85 north to I-26. Exit at Columbus, N.C. Take Rte. 108 toward Tryon—go through town. Do not cross railroad tracks but bear left to Pine Crest Lane. The inn is at the end of the lane.

THE NU-WRAY INN
Burnsville, North Carolina

Innkeeper Rush Wray was telling me what he serves for dinner at the Nu-Wray Inn: "We always have fried chicken or country-baked ham and four or five vegetables, biscuits and honey, and salads. The desserts are homemade cobblers, including peach or cherry, or different custards, ice cream, or homemade cakes.

"One of our main features is our fried chicken, which we feel is a little different than most because we fry it in a large pan. It is cooked slowly and takes quite some time, which I think enhances the flavor. It is always done on the inside. Often your deep-fried chicken is done on the outside but not on the inside. "We have our own hams which are baked and served cold in the evening. We rotate ham and chicken because they seems to be most in demand by our guests. We have special dishes like our own baked beans. These are not the same as your New England baked beans. We put a little more seasoning in ours, like tomato sauce. It could be more like Spanish beans, in a

way, and of course we use a little larger bean, whereas the New England beans are usually the pea beans. We bake our beans for quite some time just as you do in New England. People often enjoy them because they're a little different and we put in a little bit of onion, green pepper, seasoning, and strips of bacon."

We were enjoying breakfast at the Nu-Wray Inn which, like dinner, is served at long tables where everybody "passes" the plates and gets acquainted quickly. At eight o'clock I had been roused from my sleep by the famous Nu-Wray bell; at eight thirty, it had rung again, and we all made for the dining room from whence was drifting tantalizing aromas of coffee, scrambled eggs, ham, pancakes, and delicious honey in the comb!

Now, Rush continued, "For people who are staying longer than just a few days we vary the menu and work out different things. A lot of our guests stay on the American plan . . some for two and three weeks. We've had some people for a month or two, and even three months. We had a couple who came back for fifteen years and stayed for three months at a time. There's a lady coming on Sunday who will be here for eight weeks. A lot of people like to come and 'stay put,' instead of moving around.

"On the other hand, there are a lot of young people traveling with *CIBR*. They're so excited and they feel they've just discovered something that no one else knows about. They say they'll never stay at another commercial highway inn. It's just a thrill to hear them talk about it. These people love to go from place to place, inn-hopping, and it's always good that I can recommend other inns. I had a wonderful letter yesterday from a young girl in California. She said that the Nu-Wray was the highlight of her whole trip."

Almost all the letters I get about the Nu-Wray say that it's different. I've been visiting there for some years. In past editions I've written about the great backroading in the beautiful mountains; I've described the flora and the fauna; and the beautiful antiques. This time I thought readers would enjoy hearing about the country food.

The inn is now closed January, February, and March. Otherwise it's open every day of the year.

THE NU-WRAY INN, Burnsville, N.C. 28714; 704-682-2329. A 35-room village inn on town square on Rte. 19E, 38 mi. north of Asheville. A few miles from Mt. Mitchell. Modified American plan omits lunch and Sunday night supper. Breakfast and dinner served every weekday to travelers. Noon dinner served on Sundays only. Open daily mid-April through Dec. Golf, swimming, hiking, and skiing nearby. Rush T. Wray, Innkeeper. Mrs. Annie Wray Bennett, Hostess.

Directions: From Asheville, go north on Rte. 19-23 for 18 miles, then continue on 19. Five miles from Burnsville, 19 becomes 19E. From the north via Bristol or Johnson City, Tenn., take Rte. 19-23 to Unicoi. Turn left on 107 to N.C. State Line. Take 226 and turn right on Rte. 197 at Red Hill to Burnsville.

HOUND EARS LODGE
Blowing Rock, North Carolina

The balcony of my room at Hound Ears seemed to rest almost in the top branches of an oak tree. By now the sun was directly overhead casting a dappled pattern on the floor of the porch. In the distance, Grandfather Mountain was shimmering and to my left, perched on various levels of the lower mountains, were the attractively designed homes of the Hound Ears community.

Below, in the foreground, were some young people walking to the swimming pool, which I intended to visit shortly. However, dominating the valley floor, with many of the trees and greens visible from my vantage point, was the Hound Ears golf course.

Perhaps it was this picture of verdant greens and fairways punctuated by clear, white, menacing sand traps that momentarily made it difficult to realize that there had been eight or nine inches of snow here last Christmas and that the other face of Hound Ears, the winter visage, is one that includes spectacular skiing, roaring fireplaces, and the exhilaration of pure winter air.

After a cool night's sleep, I strolled across the flower-lined walk to the main lodge for breakfast, and was on the first leg of the Hound Ears tour.

As I moved from the accommodations in the main lodge to the chalets, and from the swimming pool to several of the private homes of native stone and wood, I found excellent taste everywhere.

229

The furnishings, appointments, and interiors and exteriors were carefully harmonized. For example, my room was done in complementary shades of brown with yellow sheets on my bed. All of the buildings were set among rhododendrons and evergreens, and in many places huge handsome boulders were allowed to remain where they rested. The road was built around them, curving and twisting and climbing.

Hound Ears is a luxurious American plan resort-inn, and the rates reflect the additional services and elegance.

The whole concept of Hound Ears which, by the way, is named for a rock formation on the mountain behind the lodge, is the inspiration of the Robbins brothers, all of whom were born and raised in this part of North Carolina. They saw the marvelous possibilities of making a resort-inn to which were added skiing and golf facilities.

Other resort-inns with extensive golf facilities include the Spalding Inn Club, Ojai Valley Inn, and the Inn at Rancho Santa Fe.

HOUND EARS LODGE and CLUB, P.O. Box 188, Blowing Rock, N.C. 28605; 704-963-4321. A luxurious 25-room resort-inn on Rte. 105, 6 mi. from Boone. Near natural attractions. American plan. Meals served to houseguests only. Open year-round. 18-hole golf course, swimming, skiing, and tennis on grounds. Bill Jeffcoat, Innkeeper.

Directions: From Winston-Salem, follow Rte. 421 west to Boone, then travel south on Rte. 105 to inn. From Ashville, follow Rtes. 19 and 19 E to Pineola, then Rte. 181 to Linville and Rte. 105 north to inn. From Bristol, Va., and I-81, follow Rte. 421 east to Vilas (mountainous), then Rte. 321 east to Boone. In Boone, pick up Rte. 105 and turn on Shulls Mills Rd.

HEMLOCK INN
Bryson City, North Carolina

Morning in the southern highlands. My watch said 7:30. I still had time for a brief walk in the woods before the breakfast bell would sound. A bluebird flitted past my window beckoning me to sample the forest of dew-laden flowers, bushes, and trees.

Hurriedly dressing, I walked over to see if I could get something warm to drink. What aromas! Country ham frying in the pan, fresh biscuits, and apple fritters! But at that moment Ella Jo Shell came in and picked up the thread or our conversation from the night before. My thought of a morning walk died aborning.

"Since you mentioned that you needed a list of birds and flowers," she said, "I sat down and wrote out as many as I could think of. But we have so many that I don't believe we can count them all. Why, just take flowers. We have violets, May apples, Dutchman's pipe, columbine, trillium, dogwood, lady's-slippers, little brown jug, wild geraniums, yellow fringed orchids, lillies of the valley, butterfly weeds, jack-in-the-pulpit, black-eye Susans . . ." I put up my hand and cried, "Uncle!"

Ella Jo's enthusiasm was not to be daunted. "As far as birds are concerned," she went on, "we have all kinds of thrushes, thrashers, mockingbirds, warblers, wrens, cardinals, goldfinches, titmice, several different kinds of owls—the list just goes on."

The Hemlock Inn is a very cozy, comfortable resort-inn in the Great Smokies. It's a rustic place, without what John refers to as "fancy frills." In fact, I find that it's almost like visiting relatives. Breakfasts and dinners are served around lazy Susan tables, and the bell rings at 8:30 in the morning and at 6:00 at night. People wander in and stand behind chairs and John asks the blessing. It's that kind of place.

Speaking of food, the Hemlock serves marvelous southern cooking. There's country fried steak, beef and chicken pies, coarse-ground grits, chess pie, Quaker pie, homemade cobblers, and all kinds of fritters, including okra. Have you ever had okra fritters?

At the Hemlock, everyone gets introduced to everyone else. It's a place where you can fill your days with hikes in the woods, or driving and sightseeing in the mountains. On the other hand, if you just care to sit and look at the scenery or read and be quiet or maybe play a little shuffleboard or ping-pong, that's okay too. There's no organized plan of recreation. John says, "It's just folks being folks."

Ella Jo, now thoroughly warmed up to her task, was telling me again about the various plants in the woods nearby. "Well, we have flame azaleas, rhododendron, boxwood, laurel, holly, all kinds of ferns . . ." She was full of lists this morning.

231

HEMLOCK INN, Bryson City, N.C. 28713; 704-488-9820. A 25-room Smoky Mountain inn 4 mi. from Bryson City and 60 mi. from Asheville. Near Fontana Village, Cherokee, and Pisgah National Forest. Modified American plan omits lunch. Breakfast and dinner served to travelers by reservation only. Sunday dinner served at noontime. Open from early May to early November. No pets. Shuffleboard, skittles, ping-pong, hiking trails on grounds. Tubing, rafting, and golf nearby. Ella Jo and John Shell, Innkeepers.

Directions: Located 1 mi. off Rte. 19 between Cherokee and Bryson City, N.C. Take paved road to top of mountain.

SNOWBIRD MOUNTAIN LODGE
Robbinsville, North Carolina

I really couldn't speak. The entire aspect was so awesome and so majestic that the spoken word seemed crushing to the mood. I was standing on the broad balcony of the Snowbird Mountain Lodge at twilight. Against a backdrop of delicate, iridescent blue, the silhouettes of the mute mountain peaks seemed to thunder at me. I could almost reach out and touch at least fifteen of them. Their heights were awesome — 4000 ft., 4500 ft., 4700 ft., 5400 ft.! The drop-off in front of me was 1000 feet straight down into a lake whose waters were so clear that in full daylight I could see the bottom. A mountain whippoorwill greeted a quarter moon that even now was becoming more bright.

I stepped back inside the beautiful, high-vaulted living room and went over to join the people standing and sitting around the mammoth fireplace. It was easy to slip into the conversation, because most of them were talking about the day's hiking and comparing notes about the various flowers and birds. This is seventh heaven for birders. Among the flowers are flame azaleas and mountain laurel.

Reaching the SML, I found, required persistence, patience, and trust. I drove from Saluda on Rte. 19, through the Cherokee Reservation and the Nantahala Gorge. There, I saw people riding the rapids in rubber rafts right next to the highway. I found that Rte. 129 cut back into the mountains to Robbinsville, and from then on I trusted the signs.

I came to the foot of a hill where there was a little sign pointing to the left that said: "Snowbird Mountain Lodge." This was a paved, single-lane road with many signs that said: "Blow Your Horn." At the top of the mountain is perched this remote resort inn.

Because this is a mountain inn, there is naturally a great deal of emphasis on hiking and back roading. To that end, Mary and Ed can supply all of their guests with maps for both hiking and driving in the area. Incidentally, there is a small Indian reservation nearby. The atmosphere is quite informal and sport clothes are the order of the day. However, I was glad I had some warm clothes, because even in summer the temperatures averaged in the 70s.

It didn't take Ed and Mary long to discover that every one of their guests would return at the end of the day with a ravenous appetite. The menu for both luncheon and dinner is set. Mary explained that entrée changes are arranged to accommodate the guests that stay for a longer period of time. Among the dishes are fresh mountain trout amandine, roast beef, fresh ham, and steaks. All the baking is done in the kitchen.

Ed had a comment to make about the changing nature of the guests at the inn, "There are a lot of young people here now. When we first came there were a lot of older folks, but now it's about 50-50. We

don't take children under 12, so that kind of limits the young marrieds, but the older children find it very enjoyable."

SNOWBIRD MOUNTAIN LODGE, Joyce Kilmer Forest Rd., Robbinsville, N.C. 28771; 704-479-3433. A 16-room inn on top of the Great Smokies, 12 mi. from Robbinsville. American plan. Lunch and dinner served to travelers by reservation only. No children under age 12. No pets. Open May 19 through October 29. Swimming, fishing, hiking, nearby. For nature lovers. Mary and Ed Williams, Innkeepers.

Directions: Approaching from the northeast or south, take U.S. 19 and 129; from the northwest take U.S. 129.

West Virginia

THE COUNTRY INN
Berkeley Springs, West Virginia

I watched the grey squirrel with his feathery tail busily hiding acorns. The midmorning sun had dispersed the light mist, and the day promised to be bright and cheerful. It was hard to realize that I was such a short distance from Washington, D.C.

I was in Berkeley Springs, West Virginia, seated on a bench in the park immediately adjacent to The Country Inn. This historic little town is located in the gorgeous Potomac highlands country to the west of our nation's capitol. The area offers back roads, history, antiquing, and scenery.

Adele Barker threaded her way among the sycamores and oak trees and joined me on the bench. "There seems to be an unusual number of inn guests going to the baths this morning," she remarked, "have you noticed?" The springs, for which the town is named, are located just a few steps from the inn. Roman baths, hot tubs, and massages can be obtained at a most reasonable cost.

"There were springs here long before the white man came," Adele went on. "George Washington on his first surveying trip 'took the waters.' His enthusiasm was partly responsible for its fame as a resort. In 1776, the town was named Bath by the Virginia Assembly, but the name was later changed to Berkeley Springs."

I am a firm believer that country inns take on the personalities of their innkeepers, and perhaps that accounts for so many people telling me how much they enjoy their stay at The Country Inn. Jack and Adele Barker are two of the most sincere, goodhearted people

that I have ever met. I was completely taken with Adele when I first saw her during the fall of 1972, when my son Keith and I were on an "inn trip" through Maryland, West Virginia, and Pennsylvania.

Incidentally Keith visited The Country Inn in the fall of 1978 when he was escorting a group of German innkeepers to various inns in *CIBR*. They remained overnight, and he and the Barkers had a wonderful reunion.

Two most interesting things have been happening at The Country Inn recently. One is that Bill North, who is a Cornell Hotel School graduate, has joined the Barkers as manager. "His presence allows Adele and me greater freedom."

The Barkers have just finished fencing in the south garden which will have its grand opening in 1979. Adele says, "It will provide for our guests a secluded nature spot for meals, coffee with the morning paper, and a romantic place under the stars. It will be called the Country Garden and Cafe. It's all very exciting."

"We're trying to recreate the gracious colonial style of living," explained Jack.

My letters indicate that guests enjoy the homey atmosphere and especially the country hams, smothered chicken, salmon soup, duckling with orange sauce, and the homemade hot breads. The golfers enjoy the new 18-hole Robert Trent Jones Golf Course nearby, as well.

THE COUNTRY INN, Berkeley Springs, West Va. 25411; 304-258-2210. A 37-room resort inn on Rte. 522, 34 mi. from Winchester, Va. and 100 mi. from Washington, D.C., or Baltimore, Md. Berkeley Springs Spa adjoins inn. European plan. Most rooms with private baths. Breakfast, lunch, dinner served to travelers. Open every day of the year. Hunting, fishing, hiking, canoeing, antiquing, champion-ship golf nearby. Jack and Adele Barker, Innkeepers.

Directions: Take I-70 to Hancock, Md. Inn is 6 mi. south on Rte. 522.

GENERAL LEWIS INN
Lewisburg, West Virginia

I had just returned from a walking tour of Lewisburg with its 19th-century residences and generous sprinkling of historic markers. I paused for just a moment at the bottom of the crescent-shaped drive that leads to the inn to read a marker which said, "Confederate troops under General Henry Heth on May 23, 1862 were repulsed by Colonel George Crook's Brigade."

As I settled into one of the rocking chairs on the long, shaded veranda, innkeeper Larry Little came out and joined me. "Well, what do you think of our little town?" he asked. I readily admitted that I was completely captivated.

"It was established in 1782 and is the third oldest town in the state," he said. "It was named for General Andrew Lewis, who defeated the Indians at the first battle in the American Revolution in 1774.

"The old part of the inn where the dining room is located was built in 1798 as a private dwelling. Later on, additions were made, and in 1929 it was opened by Mr. and Mrs. Randolph Hock as an inn. It took them many years to collect all of these antiques, including that four-poster canopy bed you are going to sleep in tonight."

The General Lewis Inn is like a permanent flashback to old West Virginia. It is furnished almost entirely in antiques. There is a sizable collection of old kitchen utensils, spinning wheels, churns, and other tools used many years ago, as well as an unusual collection of chinaware and old prints. The parlor has a friendly fireplace flanked by some of the many different types of rocking chairs that are scattered throughout the inn. The atmosphere is made even more cozy by the low-beamed ceilings.

The inn is surrounded by broad lawns, and in the rear there are fragrant flower gardens, tall swaying trees, and even a small rock garden.

The menu has many things that I associate with country cooking—pork chops, apple butter, pan-fried chicken, and West Virginia ham, to name a few.

Dusk had fallen while Larry, Mary Hock, the General Lewis' owner, and I were talking, and the gaslights which illuminate the tree-lined streets began to dot the late twilight. Our talk turned to some of the famous golf courses here in the Greenbrier area, and we discussed some circle tours of the mountains that would include the fabulous scenery and a generous glimpse of rural West Virginia.

"More and more people are discovering what we've got down here," Larry said, "or up here, as the case may be."

GENERAL LEWIS INN, Lewisburg, W. Va. 24901; 304-645-2600. An antique-laden 30-room village inn on Rte. 60, 90 mi. from Roanoke, Va. European plan. (Modified American plan only during W. Va. State Fair.) Breakfast and evening meal served daily with an additional meal on Sundays at noon. Dining room closed Christmas Day. Famous golf courses nearby. Laurence Little, Innkeeper.

Directions: Take Lewisburg exit from I-64. Follow Rte. 219 south to first traffic light. Turn left on Rte. 60, two blocks to inn.

THE RIVERSIDE INN
Pence Springs, West Virginia

Ashby Berkley, wearing a leather vest and knee britches, and sporting a well-trimmed black beard, showed me to a heavy oaken table set with pewter plates and pistol-handled knives, saying, "Welcome to our house."

The light from the big fireplace at one end of the low-ceilinged log room was reflected in the candelabra of handcrafted tin. I felt as if I had stepped into Jamestown, Virginia, in the early 1600s, which is exactly the period which Ashby and Kelley Berkley have succeeded in creating. Here is the same intimacy of a colonial roadside tavern

where travel-weary guests refreshed themselves with the table fare of their host.

It was the table fare that next commanded my attention. It was a six-course dinner served at a pleasant pace not often found in these times. There were English country dishes such as colonial game pie, roast goose and wild rice with glazed grapes, pheasant and rabbit, hunter's style, and fresh, stuffed duckling for two. Ashby's mother still bakes the breads, and all of the pastries and soups are home-made as well.

The building of The Riverside Inn is a log cabin with screened-in front porches, a large fireplace, and a very fetching view of the Greenbrier River through the trees. There are some limited accommodations available from Memorial Day to Labor Day, but please make reservations or risk being disappointed.

A visit to The Riverside also includes visiting the Pence Springs Water Company which is an old mineral spa where naturally carbonated spring water bubbles up out of the ground. One of the main buildings has been turned into an old-fashioned ice cream parlor where more casual meals are served every day.

Sunday flea market, the largest in the state, often attracts as many as 2,000 people offering everything from junk to antiques.

The success of the John Henry Folk Festival on Labor Day weekend in 1978 has assured its continuance for many years to come.

A few years ago when Ashby and Kelley first took on the project of rehabilitating this old log building and making it into a rather elegant West Virginia country tavern, I can well imagine that there were those who thought that the venture was risky, if not foolhardy. When I mentioned this to Ashby, he laughed uproariously and said, "Yes, you're right—the idea of people traveling this far away to dine in a Jamestown atmosphere seemed almost like a wild dream. However, I'm happy to say that it's been most successful. It just goes to prove what your friend John Conway from the Farmhouse in Port Townsend, Washington, says, 'people will travel any distance at all for a good meal as long as there's a place to park!'"

Time is standing still, at least for a moment on the banks of the Greenbrier River in Pence Springs, West Virginia.

RIVERSIDE INN, Rte. 3, Pence Springs, W. Va. 24962; 304-445-7469. A country restaurant 12 mi. from Hinton, W. Va., located in the beautiful West Va. mountains on the Greenbrier River on Rte. 3 between Hinton and Alderson. 12 mi. from Lake Bluestone. Limited lodgings. Dinner served daily except Mondays. Lunch served by special reservation only. Open daily from May 15 thru Labor Day for lunch and dinner. Open for dinner on weekends only from Mar. thru May 15 and from Sept. thru Dec. Closed Thanksgiving, Christmas, and Easter. Skiing, boating, hiking, swimming, spelunking, white water canoeing nearby. O. Ashby and Kelley Berkley, Innkeepers.

Directions: From the east, take Alta exit off I-64, follow Rte. 12-S to Alderson then Rte. 3-W 8 mi. to Pence Springs. From the west, from W. Va. Tpke. follow Rte. 3 from Beckley through Hinton to Pence Springs. The inn is located in Pence Springs on Rte. 3 between Hinton and Alderson.

THE WELLS INN
Sistersville, West Virginia

The Wells Inn is a flashback to days of late 19th-century opulence, with its Victorian parlor, where there is a Tiffany lamp, striped wallpaper, mahogany wainscoting, marble-top tables, and handsome settees. On the wall is an oil portrait of Ephraim Wells, the builder of the hotel and the grandson of the founder of Sistersville.

The main dining room has original gas chandeliers, now converted, hanging from an old-fashioned ceiling of molded metal. The walls are covered with rich, flocked paper in a red and gold pattern that presents a most interesting contrast to the green velvet upholstered dining room chairs.

My bedroom on my last visit had a brass bed, thick carpeting, and a kerosene-type lamp suspended gracefully on a draped chain from the ceiling.

"Here is your old friend, Victoria" said Max Taylor. "She hasn't spoken a word during your absence."

I must say Victoria, an alabaster statue in the lobby of the inn was very much in style. Her pristine whiteness showed up strikingly well against the gold velours of the walls, the rich, "gay nineties"

carpeting, and the velvet cushions on the circular bench where we were seated.

The original Wells Hotel was built in 1894 but faded into obscurity about 1912. It was remodeled in 1929 and had a second grand opening. In 1965, Wells Kinkaid, a grandson of the original builder, bought the hotel at auction; by this time it had fallen into a state of some disrepair. He and his son, Jack, made the happy decision to make it a turn-of-the-century hostelry. Period furniture was obtained, some of the 1894 furnishings were donated by townspeople, and major reconstruction took place with one thing in mind: providing modern conveniences in an authentic gay nineties style of decor. So, there was a third grand opening.

I have been visiting the Wells Inn since 1970, and on each visit I have found something more to share with our readers. In 1977, it was the arrival of Max Taylor, who has had a considerable background in the innkeeping business, and his very attractive wife, Diana. Since Max's new association with my good friend, Jack Kinkaid, some interesting things have been happening to the Wells Inn menu. Because Max has had a great deal of experience as a maitre d' hotel and is training the dining room staff in the European art of preparing food at the table, the menu of this inn has taken on new dimensions. In 1970, I never would have expected to see frogs legs Provencale, oriental pepper steak, sukiyaki, turkey tetrazzini, veal Cordon Bleu, bananas Foster, peaches Melba, cherries jubilee, and flaming coffees. Those are some of the inspired new offerings.

During late 1978 still more interesting things happened, including thermosol units for the lodging rooms. These include whirlpool baths and steam. The former "Black Gold Room" will now be called "The Back Porch." It is an informal coffee shop and is already quite popular with the Sistersville townspeople.

However, I am sorry to say that none of this has had any effect on the obdurate immovability of Victoria. Again, she refused my invitation to dinner, and not even mentioning the rainbow trout amandine had any visible effect on her. However, there was one ray of hope: when I offered to drape my jacket around her Praxitelesian shoulders, I fancied I saw a faint twitch of her lips and a flicker of an alabaster eyelid!

THE WELLS INN, 316 Charles St., Sistersville, W. Va. 26175; 304-652-3111. A restored Victorian 36-room village inn, 50 mi. south of Wheeling, 38 mi. north of Parkersburg. Sistersville is a former oil boom town of the 90s. European plan. Breakfast, lunch, dinner served daily. Open year-round. Skiing nearby. Max Taylor, Innkeeper.

Directions: From the south, leave I-77 at Parkersburg and proceed north on Rte. 2. From the north, leave I-70 at Wheeling and travel south on Rte. 2.

Kentucky

THE BEAUMONT INN
Harrodsburg, Kentucky

"And now Robert E. Lee's favorite dessert!" I looked into the faces of the Dedman family: Bud and Mary, and their son Chuck and his wife, Helen. I had reason to suspect they might be joshing me, because during the afternoon and evening when we had been touring the Beaumont Inn, there had been many jokes and lots of laughter. The Dedman family all have the great capacity to laugh.

A most delicious-looking confection appeared on the table. A four-layered, lemon-orange cake which was served with a small scoop of ice cream. "Yes, General Lee is reputed to have expressed great preference for this recipe," said Mary Dedman. "I believe it has been used at this inn for as long as anybody can remember."

"As long as anybody can remember" covers a lot of territory here at the Beaumont Inn. The truly handsome brick building with the six supporting Ionic columns was built in 1845 as a school for young ladies. Later, it became known as Daughters' College, and still later as Beaumont College. In 1916, it was purchased by Mr. and

241

Mrs. Glave Goddard and converted into the Beaumont Inn. The ownership and management passed from Mrs. Goddard to her daughter, Mrs. Dedman, and then to Mrs. Dedman's two sons. Today, Bud Dedman is the owner-manager and his son, Chuck, is following tradition and becomes the fourth generation trained in the inkeeper's art.

The inn, as befits its previous academic history, is set in the campus-like atmosphere surrounded by maples, dogwood, walnut, and catalpa trees. One of the catalpa trees in the front has been used literally for generations by families and guests for appropriate photographs.

The decorations and furniture in all the parlors and lodging rooms reflect American history. The hallways on the main floor have several cabinets with beautiful old china and silverware. The sitting rooms have elegant fireplaces and wallpaper decorated with roses. The entrance hall is dedicated to Robert E. Lee and has many pictures of this noble gentleman, some of them dating back to his youth. There is also a framed copy of General Lee's farewell address to the army of northern Virginia.

One might expect that with so many venerable pieces in such an impressive old building there would be an attempt to preserve the inn as a kind of museum. "Not a bit of it," explained Chuck Dedman. "There were five children in our family and this was our home. Mother and dad taught us respect for old things, but we were expected to enjoy them. We want our guests to feel the same way."

"There's so much for everybody to enjoy nearby," chimed in his pretty wife Helen. "Old Fort Harrod, the Lincoln Marriage Temple, the Perryville Battlefield, and, of course, Shakertown is just a few miles away."

"And don't forget the Keeneland Racetrack and the Kentucky Horse Park," added Mary Dedman.

Children are quite happy at the Beaumont Inn. "We have a children's playground, swimming pool, and tennis courts," explained Mary. "There's lots of room and youngsters enjoy it."

Besides General Lee's favorite dessert, the Beaumont is famous for its food, including mock scalloped oysters, corn pudding, Kentucky fried chicken—which Bud Dedman assures me is "the real thing," and especially two-year-old Kentucky hams.

There's a whole building set aside for the hams which are delivered in June and stored until the following April. About 800 hams are hung here each year and not used for about fifteen months.

The Beaumont Inn is almost in the center of Kentucky, a pleasant drive from Lexington. "In the 1920s," said Bud, "we used to figure it was about two blow-outs from Louisville!"

BEAUMONT INN, Harrodsburg, Ky. 40330; 606-734-3381. A 27-room country inn in the heart of Kentucky's historic bluegrass country. All lodging plans available. Lunch and dinner served to travelers. All three meals to houseguests. Open every day from March 1 through November 30. Tennis, swimming pool, shuffleboard on grounds. Golf courses and a wide range of recreational and historic attractions nearby. No pets. Lodging rate includes Continental breakfast. The Dedman family, Innkeepers.

Directions: From Louisville: Exit 48 from east I-64. Go south on Ky. 151, to U.S. 127 south to Harrodsburg. From Lexington: U.S. 60 west, then west on Bluegrass Parkway to U.S. 127. From Nashville: Exit I-65 to Bluegrass Parkway near Elizabethtown, Ky., then east to U.S. 127. From Knoxville: Exit north I-75 at Mt. Vernon, Ky., then north on U.S. 150 to U.S. 127. Use bypass at Danville, Ky. Go north on U.S. 127 to Beaumont Inn entrance which is on east side of highway as you enter Harrodsburg.

INN AT PLEASANT HILL
Shakertown, Kentucky

Ann Voris, the innkeeper at Pleasant Hill, had joined me for the evening meal in the Trustees' House, where guests had stayed during the Shaker period.

I asked her about the life of the Shakers in this beautiful community. She explained:

243

"The founders of Pleasant Hill belonged to a religious sect, the United Society of Believers in Christ's Second Appearing. They were actually an offshoot of the Quakers. Pleasant Hill was established in 1805, and by 1820 they had a prosperous colony of 500 persons. The Shakers lived in communal dedication to their religious beliefs of celibacy, public confession of sins (which culminated in the frenetic trembling dances which gave them the name of Shakers), renunciation of worldliness, and common ownership of property.

"There were five families at Pleasant Hill, each with its own house, shops, barns, farming lands, and orchards," Ann continued. "'Family' had a particular meaning since the Shakers did not believe in marriage. Men and women, they maintained, could live more happily as brothers and sisters, helping one another, but living personally apart.

"The Shakers also held some advanced social ideas. They were pacifists and believed in equality of sexes and races. They were hospitable to visitors and took in orphans and unwanted children.

"One of their most fundamental beliefs was in hard work and austere discipline that sought perfection. There were so many innovations made by Shakers, it always amazes me.

"The Civil War, plus nineteenth-century industrialism and worldliness seeped into the Pleasant Hill Shakers, and the celibacy rule prevented natural increase in their numbers. In 1910 they were dissolved."

The Trustees' House is one of 25 buildings clustered along the single country road, all furnished with Shaker pieces or reproductions. To construct buildings of enduring strength, some with walls three of four feet thick, the Shakers quarried limestone from the river bluffs and hauled granite slabs a mile uphill from the river. Most of the buildings are of deep red brick or limestone with a Federalist design.

I saw demonstrations of Shaker crafts and brought several things back to the Berkshires with me, including two handsome, marvelously simple glass chimneys which now shelter the candles on my dining room table.

The experience of sleeping in a room of such simplicity was refreshing. There were two single Shaker beds, each with its own trundle bed underneath. The Shaker rockers were classic, and the extra chairs were hung by pegs on the walls. I reached the second floor by one of the twin spiral staircases that are unmatched for craftsmanship.

Many of the foods served at Pleasant Hill are prepared from Shaker recipes. One is Pleasant Hill chicken and another is a combination of chicken and country ham. Many of the Shaker recipes on the menu have been included in two very good cookbooks authored by Elizabeth Kremer, who is the director of foods at Shaker Hill. Among the recipes are dove breasts in cream gravy, rabbit, sausage and egg casserole, turkey turnovers, oatmeal pie and many special salad dressings. For the most part, vegetables on the menu come from the garden.

I decided to take an early evening stroll around the village, and the sweet scent of honeysuckle, sage, and bluegrass caught us all up in the spirit. "There was worship in their work here," said Ann.

The entire Shaker experience at Pleasant Hill brought real meaning to their creed: "Lift your hands to work and your hearts to God."

INN AT PLEASANT HILL, Shakertown, Ky., P.O. address: Rte. 4, Harrodsburg, Ky. 40330; 606-734-5411. A 63-room country inn in a restored Shaker village on Rte. 68, 7 mi. northeast of Harrodsburg, 25 mi. southwest of Lexington. European plan. Breakfast, lunch, dinner served daily to travelers. Open year-round. Suggest contacting Inn about winter schedule. Closed Christmas Eve and Christmas Day. Ann Voris, Innkeeper.

Directions: From Lexington take Rte. 68 south toward Harrodsburg. From Louisville, take I-64 to Lawrenceburg and Graeffenburg exit (not numbered). Follow Rte. 127 south to Harrodsburg and Rte. 68 northeast to Shakertown.

DOE RUN INN,
Brandenburg, Kentucky

Let me share a letter with you that I received recently.

"Dear Berkshire Traveller, we would like to compliment you on your good taste in choosing the Doe Run Inn for your book. We have just spent a lovely week-long honeymoon there. We spent two nights in the honeymoon suite and the remainder in the Cardinal Room where I understand you stayed.

"Curtis and Lucille Brown are certainly most gracious hosts. The food was outstanding and the service was courteous and attentive. We wholeheartedly agree with your choice of the Doe Run Inn as a truly representative country inn.

"We hope to make a hobby of visiting your inns through the years. We are very thankful for your thoughtful book and look forward to more pleasant times such as we had at the Doe Run Inn."

There's nothing unusual in the experience of these two young people at the Doe Run Inn. I've received lots of mail indicating that Curt and Lucille Brown extend their country-style hospitality to everyone.

The Doe Run is an ideal place to spend a honeymoon or, for that matter, any kind of a holiday or vacation. On the banks of Doe Run Creek, it is surrounded by great numbers of trees including oak, dogwood, redbud, maple, persimmon, tulip, sycamore, black walnut, and cedars. There are dozens and dozens of different varieties of birds including the southern mockingbirds who make their homes in these trees. It's fun to go walking in the woods or fishing in the Creek.

Mention of the Cardinal Room brings back memories of many good times. I'll always remember the first time I stayed in that room. It was furnished completely in antiques, with a small wood stove at one end. The three-foot-thick outer stone wall made me feel as if I were in a fort. The building was originally a water-powered woolen mill, and later a grist mill.

There are dozens of antiques generously scattered throughout the inn. Many of them have real pedigrees. One is the walnut bed in the honeymoon room. It is over 150 years old.

As for food, imagine country ham and hot biscuits with red-eye gravy, or golden fried chicken, green beans, fried apples, chicken livers, and desserts like old-fashioned lemon pie. All the baking and cooking are done right in the Doe Run kitchen.

By the way, on Fridays and Sundays, a tremendous smorgasbord is served. I counted over 60 different dishes.

Abraham Lincoln's father was one of the men who worked on the construction of the mill building in 1816, and I believe it's quite appropriate that we include Mr. Lincoln's National Thanksgiving Proclamation of 1863:

> *The year that is drawing towards its close has been filled with the blessings of fruitful fields and healthful skies. These bounties. . . . are so constantly enjoyed that we are prone to forget the source from which they come. . . . It has seemed to me fit and proper that they should be solemnly, reverently, and gratefully acknowledged as with one heart and one voice by the whole American people.*

DOE RUN INN, Rte. 2, Brandenburg, Ky. 40108; 502-422-9982. A 17-room country inn reminiscent of the backwoods on Rte. 448, 4 mi. south of Brandenburg, 38 mi. south of Louisville. Near Fort Knox. European plan. 5 rooms with private bath; 12 rooms with shared baths. Breakfast, lunch, and dinner served to travelers daily. Closed Christmas Eve and Christmas Day. Hiking, fishing, and swimming nearby. Curtis and Lucille Brown, Innkeepers.

Directions: From Louisville take 64W through Indiana to 135S. Cross the toll bridge to Kentucky and follow 1051 to the dead end. Turn right on 448 and follow signs to Doe Run Inn.

ELMWOOD INN
Perryville, Kentucky

The luncheon salad looked delicious. It had many varieties of fresh fruits arranged around a generous scoop of sherbet. There were also freshly made hot biscuits filled with Kentucky fried ham. Ham and hot biscuits—what a treat for a visitor from New England!

I could have ordered the southern fried chicken with cream gravy. "That's what Colonel Sanders always orders when he eats here," innkeeper Gladys Coyle explained. "He loves the chicken, hot biscuits, new small potatoes, a big salad, and a huge helping of peas. He's been here five times and says it's the best chicken he's ever eaten."

The Elmwood Inn could only happen in Kentucky. Surrounded by a grove of maple and sweetgum trees beside the Chaplin River in Perryville, the inn features traditional southern dishes in an atmo-

sphere of Greek Revival elegance. The building was constructed in 1842 and became a field hospital following the Battle of Perryville during the Civil War.

The main entrance with its twin two-story columns faces the river. The lawns sloping down to the river are filled with sugar maples, black locust, hemlock, pine, ash, gingko, and willows. Next to the building there is a very large and colorful bed of tulips which must be breathtaking when in full bloom.

The inn has been carefully furnished in antiques and Kentucky and Civil War memorabilia. Each of the six serving rooms has been named for some worthy individual, well-known to the region or community. For example, there is the T.C. Poynter Room, named for the founder of a school which occupied the building for many years.

After lunch I took advantage of a few extra moments to visit some of the important sites in Perryville. One is the restoration of the old Perryville historic district. It was here that I learned that Perryville was originally known as Harberson's Station and was founded by some settlers from Pennsylvania. Many of the buildings are being restored, including the Karrick-Parks House which is directly across the river from the Elmwood Inn. A footbridge is planned to connect this historic section of Perryville with the inn.

I also visited the Perryville Battlefield which is just a few miles from the town and was the scene of one of the most desperate battles of the Civil War. It is very popular with tourists and history buffs.

At the end of a pleasant afternoon filled with Kentucky history, I was happy to return for the evening meal at the Elmwood. Confronted by myriad choices, including sweetbreads, fried shrimp,

Florida pompano, and other tempting dishes, I decided to try the fried chicken with cream gravy.

I think I know why Colonel Sanders keeps coming back.

ELMWOOD INN, Perryville, Ky. 40468; 606-332-2271. A country restaurant in an historically important Kentucky town on Rtes. 150 and 68, 9 mi. from Harrodsburg and Danville. Near the Perryville Battlefield State Shrine. No lodgings. Lunch and dinner served daily except Mondays. Closed Christmas Eve and Christmas Day. Open year-round. Gladys Coyle, Innkeeper.

Directions: Exit Bluegrass Pkwy. at Bardstown and take Hwy. 150 into Perryville. From Harrodsburg take Rte. 68 to Perryville.

BOONE TAVERN HOTEL
Berea, Kentucky

It may have been former Innkeeper Dick Hougen who first remarked, "I'd classify our food as southern gourmet rather than southern fried." Well, whoever said it, it's a perfect description of the menu at the Boone Tavern. Fortunately, a great many of the recipes still in use, are in three of Mr. Hougen's own cookbooks: Southern Peanut Soup, Plantation Ham, Boone Tavern Chicken Pie, Georgian Sweet Potato, Hollyberry Salad, Black Walnut Pie and Kentucky Blackberry Dumpling with Milk Dip, among others. And, of course, spoonbread. Spoonbread makes a southerner out of a "damn Yankee" in about thirty seconds.

I was astonished to learn that over 200,000 visitors stop at the inn each year for lodgings and meals. It is on Route I-75, south of Lexington and only 120 miles from Cincinnati.

At Berea, the college, the inn, and the town are all interlocked. It is impossible to speak of one without speaking of the other two. The college is a unique educational experience because the tuition is comparatively low. However, all students are expected to engage in a work program and I'm happy to report that it actually works!

To the promising young men and women from Appalachia (many of whom find here their only opportunity for college), Berea offers a liberal arts education of the highest academic standard.

On a student-conducted tour, I saw students working in woodcraft, making brooms, weaving, pottery, lapidary, and several other crafts.

Ninety percent of the inn staff are students, many of whom are majoring in hotel management. In fact, with the exception of the cooks and key personnel in the front office, the students run the whole show.

Berea College Campus

The inn is comfortable and inviting, and has among other things, a skittles game and chinese checkers set up in the lobby. These are both manufactured in one of the college craft shops and are sold commercially. The craft shop is also the source for the furniture in the inn, including tables, corner cupboards, beds, benches, and the like. Many of the designs were given to the college by the famous New England furniture designer, Wallace Nutting.

While I was in the library doing a little research on the background of the college, I found that one of the founders, Cassius M. Clay, had been converted to emancipation by a speech of the famous William Lloyd Garrison. This stand for racial freedom was a part of the original foundation of the college. Incidentally, the location—Berea—comes from the Bible town mentioned in *Acts XVIII:10 "where men were open-minded."*

BOONE TAVERN HOTEL, Berea, Ky. 4043; 606-986-9341. A 60-room village inn in a unique college community on I-75, 40 mi. south of Lexington, Ky. European plan. Breakfast, lunch, dinner served daily to travelers by sittings only. Dinner and Sunday noon coats required for men, dresses or pant suits for ladies. Open every day of the year. All campus activities open to guests; campus tours twice daily except Saturdays and Sundays. Tennis on grounds. Golf, pool, and bicycles nearby. Berea is on Eastern Time. Curtis Reppert and Cecil M. Connor, Innkeepers.

Directions: Take Berea exit from I-75. One mi. north to hotel.

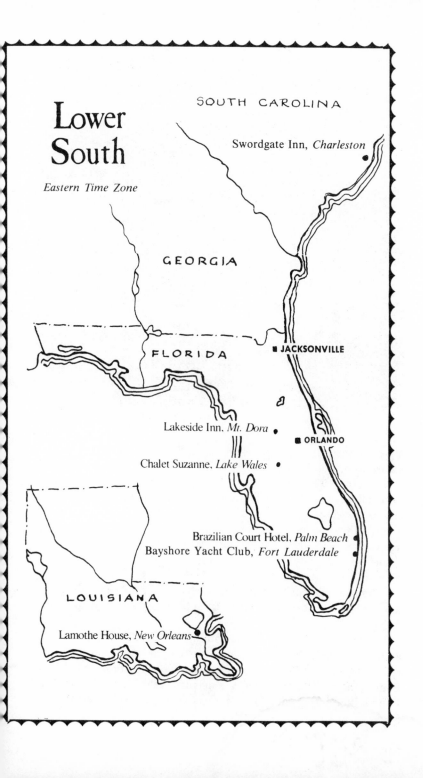

Lower
South

Eastern Time Zone

SOUTH CAROLINA

Swordgate Inn, *Charleston*

GEORGIA

FLORIDA

■ JACKSONVILLE

Lakeside Inn, *Mt. Dora*

■ ORLANDO

Chalet Suzanne, *Lake Wales*

Brazilian Court Hotel, *Palm Beach*
Bayshore Yacht Club, *Fort Lauderdale*

LOUISIANA

Lamothe House, *New Orleans*

South Carolina

Old Charleston Mansion

THE SWORDGATE INN
Charleston, South Carolina

Suzanne and David Redd, the innkeepers at the Swordgate, were telling me about the pleasures of keeping an inn in the historic city of Charleston.

"We try to run the inn as a family. Our daughter Martha Sue, age twelve, is really a young lady and makes reservations, checks guests in, and enjoys telling the history of this old house, especially the part about the ghost.

"Our son David Jr. is nine and is chief of the coke machine. The only problem so far is that little David likes to pass cokes out to his friends.

"We're very excited about adding our collection of French antiques to the French ballroom. This is a splendid room and very refreshing here in Charleston where many of the houses have only English furniture. The ballroom is included in the historic Charleston Foundation spring and fall tours sponsored by the Preservation Society."

"My family are antique dealers," explained Suzanne, "so we are making plans to add some fine antique pieces to the rooms. My mother was here for Christmas and is now looking for just the right furniture for each room."

David is a native Charlestonian and a professional organist. He is minister of music at the First Baptist Church of Charleston, which is a beautiful building just a few squares away from the inn. It is one of the oldest Baptist churches in the South. He's also organist for the Citadel Military College located in Charleston.

In speaking of the breakfasts, Suzanne said, "I think this is one of the most enjoyable times for our guests. In most of the months of the year they can sit out in our garden and before you know it, they are getting acquainted and planning to do things with each other."

"Our muffins are hot from the oven and we have Charleston grits that have been cooking overnight. There's jam and homemade bread as well."

The five guest rooms of the Swordgate Inn are individually decorated. Each has its own distinctive sheets, pillowcases, bedspreads, and ruffles. Fresh fruits and flowers are placed in the guest rooms daily, and there is a newspaper at the door each morning. Four of the rooms are on the first floor of the old mansion. The fifth room on the third floor has a canopy bed and a view of the fascinating rooftops of the city.

All of the guests are invited to view the grand ballroom on the second floor and this is an opportunity to see what a stately old Charleston mansion really is. It has a handsome marble carved fireplace on one end and at the opposite end, a gold-leaf classic mirror that runs from the floor to the ceiling. I can imagine what great parties were held there during the nineteenth century. The gentle Charleston climate encourages azaleas, camellias, and gardenias which are in profusion in the courtyard as well as magnolias and holly trees.

Charleston seems to have something going on almost continually and one of the highlights is the Spoleto Festival which is held in May and June. It is a real outpouring of music and art. Early reservations at the Swordgate would be highly advisable. Old Charleston is a place of balustrades, cupolas, dormers, fences, walls, scrollwork, cobblestones, old street lamps, trees that bend over the roads, gorgeous mellowed red brick walls, overhanging galleries, and even a gazebo in the park. There are, I understand, seventy-three pre-Revolutionary homes in the area. But actually, the architecture reflects different stages of American architectural taste.

The Swordgate Inn is a fitting complement to such well-preserved, quiet elegance.

SWORDGATE INN, 111 Tradd St., Charleston, S.C. 29401; 803-723-8518. A quiet 5-room elegant inn located in the center of an historic area of the city, amidst distinguished 18th and 19th century homes. Within walking and biking distance of most of Charleston's cultural and historic landmarks. Bicycles furnished without charge to guests. Lodgings include informal breakfast. No other meal served. Open every day of the year. No children or pets. Beaches, sailing, and fresh water and deep sea fishing nearby. David and Suzanne Redd, Innkeepers.

Directions: Take I-26 to Meeting St. South Exit. Turn right on Meeting St., 12 blocks to Broad St.; turn right on Broad, two blocks to Legare St. Turn left on Legare for one block; turn left on Tradd St. Look for small sign on right that says Swordgate Inn.

Florida

BAY SHORE YACHT CLUB
Fort Lauderdale, Florida

A country inn in Fort Lauderdale, Florida? Don't even smile. I've discovered warm, hospitable inns with a feeling of personal involvement in such metropolitan areas as New York, Palm Beach, and St. Louis. The emphasis is on the "inn" rather than the "country." But what really makes such a big difference to me are the innkeepers, Janet and Bert Carvalho. They are sort of aunt and uncle to everybody who stays there, and they are such good fun to be with.

It was in late winter of 1976 when I finally made it to Fort Lauderdale, and the BSYC proved to be everything that I had been told and even more.

Being located on the Intracoastal Bay Shore provides three docks for convenient mooring of visiting yachts and cruisers. Although not a yacht club per se, as a fun, tongue-in-cheek gesture, the guests are presented with membership cards signed by the "Commodore" which entitle them to the rights and privileges of the the "Club."

The BSYC is a white, four-story building facing the blue waters of the Intracoastal Waterway which traverses Fort Lauderdale. A great many of the accommodations have a very impressive view of the continuous water traffic. There are over 200 feet of landscaped waterfront gardens. The tropical gardens include gardenias, ixora, crotons, dieffenbachia, schefflera, coconut and Christmas palms, fern palms, and many others. In this beautiful, warm climate near the ocean there are cardinals, bluejays, woodpeckers, mourning and ground doves, and spot-breasted orioles who make their homes in the trees.

Most of the accommodations are efficiencies or apartments with kitchens, so it is possible for guests to prepare their own meals or take advantage of the many restaurants in the Fort Lauderdale area. The guests' comforts are well provided for in tastefully decorated apartments furnished with fine furniture and carpeting. The cabinets are stocked with china and silverware, and the facilities include central air conditioning, heating, sheltered parking (most important with that Florida sun), and maid service.

Janet and Bert make all of this beautiful atmosphere and sunshiny ambience really come to life—they're the big difference that makes the BSYC an inn. I think it is a fair statement that they consider each guest to be their friend and do everything they can to make everybody as comfortable as possible. They introduce all the guests, and join them at the pool.

During my stay, one of the guests who had been at the BSYC for quite awhile had a reunion with her son, who had driven down from Washington to spend a couple of days. The boy arrived while his mother happened to be out, and Janet made him feel at home immediately and took care of things until his mother returned.

Fort Lauderdale is a city that frankly awes me. Naturally, being on the sunny tip of Florida where the famous beach stretches out for miles, there are thousands of people who visit during the cold weather in the north. I asked Bert about the best time to visit Fort Lauderdale and he said, "February and March are the popular months, but Janet and I think that April, May, September and October are ideal because it is very comfortable, not nearly as many people, and prices on everything are really much lower."

The BSYC is not Henniker, New Hampshire, but it is a place where people from Henniker, Bellows Falls, Great Barrington, and Litchfield meet to thaw out.

BAY SHORE YACHT CLUB, 341 N. Birch Rd., Ft. Lauderdale, Fla. 33304; 305-463-2821. A comfortable homelike environment with many types of accommodations, including 4 efficiencies, 2 hotel rooms, 31 apartments with kitchens and baths located on the Intracoastal Waterway. Tennis, golf, sailing, ocean swimming nearby. Shuffleboard, fishing from dock, heated pool on grounds. Open year-round. Children welcome from April thru Dec. No meals served. Kitchen facilities with efficiencies and apts. No pets. Janet and Bert Carvalho, Jr. Innkeepers.

Directions: From Florida Tpke. exit at MacArthur Interchange, turn left (east) to Sunrise Blvd., go approx. 7½ mi. to ocean. Turn right on Atlantic Blvd., turn right at second light to Bay Shore Drive. Proceed one block to Birch Rd. and turn left to Bay Shore Yacht Club. From I-95S exit at Cypress Creek Rd., follow to Sunrise Blvd., then east for 7 mi. Turn left at ocean to Atlantic Blvd. and follow directions above.

BRAZILIAN COURT HOTEL
Palm Beach, Florida

I had found the other side of Palm Beach—not the glittering social facade, but the side with more genuine people. Furthermore, I was amazed to find a Palm Beach hotel with the simplicity and good taste that appealed to such people. It is called the Brazilian Court although most everyone refers to it as the "BC."

It was built back in the 1920s, and the Palm Beach residential area with sedate homes and beautifully landscaped gardens grew up around it. The building is a two-story Palm Beach Mission design with two completely enclosed patios. One patio, with several varieties of palm trees, begonias, and poinsettias, is a marvelous place to catch the morning sun.

The other patio really sets the tone for this discreet hotel. Dispersed among the royal palms, orange, banana, and African tulip trees are dining tables, many with umbrellas. Weather permitting, all three meals are served here, and each time of day has its own captivating mood.

In the evening, small lights twinkle on the inside of each umbrella and indirect colored lighting dramatically underscores the trees and exotic tropical plants. As night falls the lights become more brilliant against the dark blue sky. Now add a three-piece orchestra playing softly in the background and you have the complete picture.

The BC is reminiscent of the Black Point and the Asticou in Maine. And the climate brings to mind the Inn at Rancho Santa Fe, California.

Because there are many long-staying guests, the selections on the menu are numerous and varied. The broiled pompano amandine is delicious. The red snapper and Florida lobster Newburg are very appetizing also. There are several dishes prepared with Florida fresh fruit offered at each meal.

Although the BC is two blocks from the ocean, there's a special sundeck atop one of the buildings. As innkeeper Bright Johnson explained, "This is for people who don't want to go down to the ocean every day to get a good tan."

The lodging rooms and suites are furnished with quiet elegance. They overlook the residential area of town or the attractive inner patios.

The BC is basically a conservative resort-inn with quite a few of the amenities that guests find enjoyable. Great emphasis is placed on both the food and the service. The famous Worth Avenue shops of Palm Beach are just a few minutes away.

The Brazilian Court is part of my select group of inns and hotels in larger cities including the Algonquin in New York, the Botsford on the Detroit city line, the Cheshire in St. Louis and Lamothe House in

New Orleans. I think they meet a need for personal hospitality.

BRAZILIAN COURT HOTEL, 300 Brazilian Ave., Palm Beach, Fla. 33480; 305-655-7740. A 125-room hotel in the heart of Palm Beach. A secluded patioed garden spot just a short walk from the ocean and Worth Avenue shops. All plans available. Breakfast, lunch, and dinner served to travelers daily. Open from December to April. No pets. Swimming, boating, fishing, tennis, golf, and bicycles nearby. Bright Johnson, Innkeeper.

Directions: From Sunshine State Pkwy., take Exit 40 to Okeechobee Blvd. Turn left and proceed 6 mi. to Royal Palmway Bridge. Cross bridge and take first right, then turn left after 1 block on to Brazilian Ave. Hotel is two blocks east on Brazilian Ave.

CHALET SUZANNE
Lake Wales, Florida

I sat next to the swimming pool at Chalet Suzanne among the fabulous flowers and trees, wondering where to begin describing this place.

I decided to start with the Great Depression of the 30s. At that time Bertha Hinshaw was a new widow with two children, $1700 from a cancelled insurance policy, two old cars, and a six-room house about a mile and a half from the main highway. She decided to open a restaurant. For ten days no one came, and then finally a family of five arrived and stayed for Christmas. Chalet Suzanne was in business.

A fire in 1943 turned out to be a blessing because Bertha started all over again—this time with some pretty unique ideas. She created an atmosphere that looked like a set from a movie. There is a conglomeration of little houses, lodges, and chalets that could belong in nearby Disney World. It's Oriental, Persian, Bavarian, Swiss, and chocolate layer cake. There are little bridges, penthouses, cupolas, balconies, minarettes, peaked roofs, flat roofs, and here and there little tiny windows that lack only a Snow White peeking through them. Just to make it more fun, these strange places contain lodging rooms!

These are all connected by brick walls and cobblestone paths. Guests can choose accommodations for their moods — Byzantine or medieval, carpenter gothic or *Erewhon*.

Truly exceptional food is served at Chalet Suzanne in five different dining rooms, all in a sort of Hans Christian Andersen setting. The late Clementine Paddleford tasted the soups and wrote in her column in the *New York Herald Tribune*, "It's good! good! good!" In fact, the soups led to still another business and now Chalet Suzanne Soups, including at least nineteen different kinds, are available in food specialty shops and supermarkets all over the country.

Besides the soup, the cannery in 1977 added six new citrus sauces which are delicious as an accompaniment to all meats, poultry, and hot or cold entrees. Chalet Suzanne products are available in the gourmet pantries of local supermarkets, and in gourmet-type shops.

Bertha's son, Carl, is the major-domo of the kitchen, and the opening course for dinner at Chalet Suzanne is always an invention by Carl's wife, Vita. One such concoction is a chicken liver canape' centered in the original Chalet baked grapefruit. Among other specialties is their famous Chicken Suzanne, glazed with its own natural juices to a beautiful amber color. Other main courses are lobster Newburg, lump crab and shrimp curry. Crêpes Suzanne are served just before the dessert. These are rolled-up tiny pancakes topped with one of the new sauces.

Incidentally, Carl is also operator of the Chalet Suzanne air field (Unicom 122.8), with its 2450-foot lighted runway, which is immediately adjacent to the inn.

One important further thought — children love Chalet Suzanne. After all, why not? All those funny buildings, a lake, a swimming pool, airplanes arriving and taking off, and even a little golf cart to ride around on. It "out-Disneys" Disney World.

CHALET SUZANNE, P.O. Box AC, Lake Wales, Fla. 33853; 813-676-1477. A 30-room phantasmagoric country inn and gourmet restaurant, 4 mi. north of Lake Wales, between Cypress Gardens and the Bok Singing Tower near Disney World. European plan. Dining room open from 8 a.m. to 9:30 p.m. daily. Closed Mondays June through October. Pool on grounds. Golf, tennis, riding nearby. Not inexpensive. The Hinshaw Family, Innkeepers.

Directions: From Interstate 4 turn south on U.S. 27 toward Lake Wales. From Sunshine State Pkwy. exit at Yeehaw Junction and head west on Rte. 60 to U.S. 27 (60 mi.). Proceed north on U.S. 27 at Lake Wales. Inn is 4 mi. north of Lake Wales on County Road 17A.

LAKESIDE INN
Mount Dora, Florida

It was just after dinner at the Lakeside Inn. One of the guests sitting on the porch invited me to play some shuffleboard, and another new acquaintance asked me to be a fourth at bridge. Those were fun prospects, but I was in the mood for an early evening stroll.

As I walked through the gardens leading to a pool on the edge of the lake, I inhaled the heavy aroma of tropical blooms. There were camphor trees, azaleas, sabal palms, and orange blossoms. A light breeze swept through the trees which were literally filled with singing birds. There are well over two hundred and fifty varieties in Mount Dora.

If I felt a little homesick for New England, Mount Dora could certainly relieve it. This is the most New England of Florida towns. I needed only a sign saying "Lower Waterford, 14 miles" to convince me. A great many of the houses would be at home in Norfolk, Connecticut or Lyme, New Hampshire. Even the tropical foliage is interspersed with oaks and fir trees on a hilly terrain.

I left the lakeshore and walked a few paces over to the lawn-bowling area. There are superb courts here, well-lighted for night play, and several guests in the traditional lawn-bowling whites were enjoying an evening of sport. I remembered seeing quite a few of them on the Mount Dora golf course that morning.

If the community of Mount Dora is a bit of New England, the Lakeside Inn puts frosting on the cake. Many people on the staff are from Vermont and Massachusetts, and quite a few are employed in Maine during the summer. The guest list is generously sprinkled with people from the New England area.

Dick Edgerton, the owner of the Lakeside Inn was telling me earlier at dinner, "We don't have tourists—we have winter visitors. People come and stay as guests, and many stay for quite awhile. Our houseguests are on the American plan, but we serve all three meals to travelers.

"We've been very popular with retired people, but in the last few years there has been a steady increase in the number of younger guests who frequently come with their children. I think part of this is because we have so many activities available here or around the inn. Along with the pool and a wide variety of outdoor games, we have great fishing and boating. The Mount Dora Golf Club has four excellent tennis courts nearby where our guests can play.

"It is possible to reach the inn on the Florida Inland Waterway system. Our lake can handle boats with a draft up to 3 feet and about 28 feet long."

Lakeside Inn last year was "discovered" as a romantic setting by the television commercial crew of "N.B.E. Productions, Ltd." of New York. The British colonial Tudor architecture of the wings so typical of Bermuda and New Zealand, has attracted a British moviemaking group this year.

I left the lawn bowlers to their game, and took the long way back through the village streets with their many attractive shops. I still have two brass candlesticks that I purchased at one of the antique shops several years ago.

I arrived back at the Lakeside Inn just in time to make a fourth for bridge.

LAKESIDE INN, P.O. Box 175, Mount Dora, Fla. 32757; 904-383-2151. A 110-room resort-inn on Lake Dora in central Florida, 30 mi. northwest of Orlando. American plan. Breakfast, lunch, and dinner served to travelers daily. Open from Dec. 20 to April 6. Swimming pool, fishing, waterskiing, putting green, and shuffleboard on grounds. Golf, tennis, bicycles, lawn bowling, and sailing nearby. Marie and Dick Edgerton, Innkeepers.

Directions: Follow I-95 south to Daytona Beach, then I-4 to Rte. 46 west to Mount Dora. Or, follow I-75 south to Wildwood, then Rte. 44 east to Rte. 441. Proceed on Rte. 441 to Mount Dora. After passing Lakeside Inn billboard on Rte. 441, turn south at first paved road (Donnelly St.) and proceed to Lakeside Inn.

Louisiana

LAMOTHE HOUSE
New Orleans, Louisiana

There are special sections in many cities and towns in North America that still reflect some of the grace and style of earlier times. Fortunately, some of these have been declared Historic Districts to preserve them for generations to come. Some which come to mind are the old sections of Charleston (South Carolina), Newport (Rhode Island), Alexandria (Virginia), Sistersville (West Virginia), Marshall (Michigan), Boston (Massachusetts), and Cape May (New Jersey). And certainly high on everyone's list is the French Quarter in New Orleans.

That's why it has been a source of constant joy to me to have found, a number of years ago, the Lamothe House which sits on the very edge of the French Quarter and is typical of old-fashioned New Orleans hospitality.

The Lamothe House was built by two brothers from San Domingo who came to the United States to escape an uprising. They established a sugar plantation and built the house in 1800. It has the same floor plans on both sides of the center hall which divides the three floors of the house completely in half. There are two lovely winding staircases to the upper floors. The old formal parlors on the first floor have been converted into handsome suites with elegant antique furnishings. Rooms with balconies are found surrounding the flagstone courtyard on the back of the house.

A couple of my readers wrote me a short note about their recent visit to the Lamothe House: "As we entered, we walked along the center hall and emerged into the courtyard with its flowers, fish pond, and banana plants. Mimi Langguth, the innkeeper, greeted us as old friends because we have been stopping at the Lamothe House for 15 years. She showed us the Scarlett O'Hara and Rhett Butler suites. They have five beds and are great for families or can be divided for separate sleeping accommodations.

"During our three-day stay," the letter continued, "I had a chance to see many of the rooms and was delighted to see the redecoration, new bedspreads and other touches which combine so well with the collection of antiques.

"The warm, personal charm of this inn comes through at *petit dejeuner* around the dining room table each morning where everyone has a chance to meet. This tradition was started by Mrs. Gertrude Munson and is being carried on by her daughter, Mimi.

The canopy beds found in most rooms appeal to honeymooners and also to people returning on their anniversaries.

An old-fashioned family Christmas Eve party for the guests of the house features Mrs. Munson's old plantation punch recipe. The Lamothe House is a favorite for families at Thanksgiving and Christmas holidays because of its history, tradition, and family warmth.

For the benefit of many of our readers who have visited the Lamothe House, I am happy to report that Mrs. Munson, who established this inn and for so many years delighted guests with her stories about New Orleans and advice on what to see, is as indomitable as ever. She is no longer active everyday in the affairs of the inn, but is just as keen and interested as always.

For me she will always be the toast of New Orleans!

LAMOTHE HOUSE, 621 Esplanade Ave., New Orleans, La. 70116; 504-947-1161. A small, elegant, 14-room inn in the French Quarter within walking distance of many fascinating New Orleans restaurants and attractions. European plan with complimentary petit dejeuner. No other meals served. Closed mid-July to Sept. 1. No pets. Near Lake Pontchartrain, Mississippi River, bayou and river cruises, plantations and mansions on the Great River Road. Golf, tennis, fishing, and bicycles nearby. Mrs. Kenneth ("Mimi") Langguth, Innkeeper.

Directions: From the west or east on I-10, take the Orleans Ave. exit to Claiborne Ave. which runs under I-10 at that point. Proceed east for 7 blocks or until the intersection of Esplanade Ave. Turn right on Esplanade and proceed 10 blocks. Or take Esplanade Ave. exit from I-10.

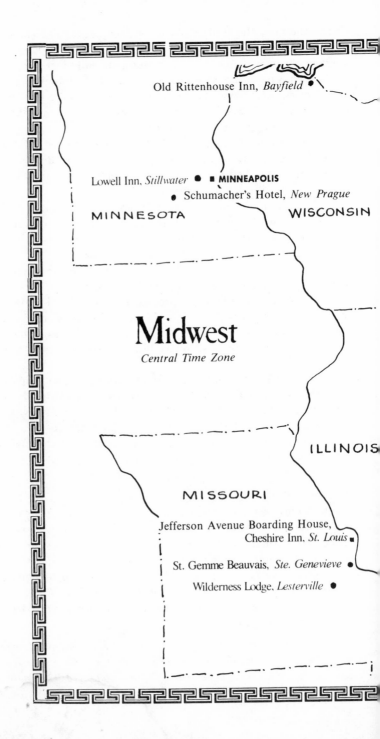

Old Rittenhouse Inn, *Bayfield* ●

Lowell Inn, *Stillwater* ● ■ **MINNEAPOLIS**

● Schumacher's Hotel, *New Prague*

MINNESOTA   WISCONSIN

Midwest

Central Time Zone

ILLINOIS

MISSOURI

Jefferson Avenue Boarding House,
Cheshire Inn, *St. Louis* ■

St. Gemme Beauvais, *Ste. Genevieve* ●

Wilderness Lodge, *Lesterville* ●

Stafford's Bay View Inn, *Petoskey*

White Gull Inn, *Fish Creek*

MICHIGAN

DETROIT

Botsford Inn, *Farmington*

National House, *Marshall*

CLEVELAND

The Patchwork Quilt, *Middlebury*

Welshfield Inn, *Burton*

OHIO

COLUMBUS

Buxton Inn, *Granville*

INDIANAPOLIS

Durbin Hotel, *Rushville*

INDIANA

Golden Lamb, *Lebanon*

CINCINNATI

EVANSVILLE

Ohio

THE BUXTON INN
Granville, Ohio

Five of us were in the downstairs tavern at the Buxton Inn playing *Gone With the Wind*. It seemed like a natural game, because we already had a Melanie, who is now sixteen. Amy, going on thirteen, was an obvious choice to play Scarlett. Orville, tall and handsome, had to be Ashley Dukes, and we decided Audrey, the mother of Amy and Melanie, should continue that role in our game. Amy, for some reason or other, said that I would be the perfect Rhett Butler. I never quite understood that.

All the Orrs, as well as the waiters and waitresses were dressed in costumes worn in 1812, which is the date that an inn was first opened here.

It was a great treat to be back at the Buxton Inn once again for a really wonderful reunion with all of the Orrs by whatever names. I made my first visit there in 1975 and was completely captivated. Apparently, a great many of our readers felt the same way, because in the past four years Orville has reported a steady stream of "Berkshire Travellers" visiting his inn, which is in one of the most attractive towns in central Ohio.

If first impressions are the strongest and most important, then Granville should be remembered by everyone who has visited it. The main street is broad and lined with trees, the sidewalks are clean, and here and there are little fences in front of homes. There are very attractive-looking shops; the library, bank building, and other public buildings are most handsome — and best of all, the Buxton Inn is just a short walk away.

The five of us had lunch together in the front dining room which has low ceilings, candelabra-type fixtures, and deep windows overlooking the street. There is an old-fashioned fender in front of the fireplace, prints of Martha and George Washington, and a cabinet with a collection of very fine chinaware.

The menu is in the form of a newspaper and not only lists the famous Buxton bean soup, eggs Benedict, quiche du jour, and "croques" (sandwiches dipped in eggs and sauteed), but also notes some of the history of early Granville and the Buxton Inn, and the beginnings of Denison University which is located in Granville.

I wanted to see the new features of the inn, so Melanie offered to guide me. This very attractive young lady, like her sister, seems born to the innkeeping business. We walked into the back dining room with its marvelous old chandelier which is let down with a pulley, and once must have held candles. She pointed out the oil painting of young Abraham Lincoln. "His eyes just seem to be looking right through you, don't they?" I agreed.

We went upstairs to look at the guest bedrooms with their antique beds, old quilts, old chests of drawers, Victorian prints, and chandeliers. All of the floors were beautifully finished. There is a sitting bathtub in a corner of one of the rooms.

Back downstairs once again, she was very proud to show me through the really excellent gift shop which has some attractive glassware, tinware, pewter, candles, small china pieces, figurines, and many rings and jewelry. "I'm mostly in charge here," she reported.

So, the Orr's and the Buxton Inn continue to progress in Granville, Ohio.

THE BUXTON INN, 313 E. Broadway, Granville, Ohio 43023; 614-587-0001. An 8-room inn in a college town in central Ohio near Denison University, the Indian Mounds Museum and the Heisey Glass Museum. European plan. Lunch and dinner served daily. Closed Christmas Day. No pets. Golf, tennis, horseback riding, cultural activities nearby. Orville and Audrey Orr, Innkeepers.

Directions: Take Granville exit from I-70. Travel north 8 mi. on Rte. 37 into Granville.

THE GOLDEN LAMB
Lebanon, Ohio

While her husband was signing the register, I heard a lady who was visiting the Golden Lamb remark, "It's like a 19th-century sampler."

The point was well made. An antique music box was tinkling merrily in the lobby, and on the table there was a handsome bowl filled with punch. Decorative blue wooden interior shutters, a glowing fire in the fireplace, an old Shaker stove, flooring of intricate tile, and antique chairs and benches completed the picture.

The inn has played host to distinguished visitors from many lands, as well as many American presidents and notables. In fact, its history dates back more than 170 years.

Speaking of presidents, on this paraticular evening there was a little poster in the lobby describing the favorite meal of Martin Van Buren when he stayed at the Golden Lamb. It included crêpes, chicken in red wine, buttered noodles, French green beans, lettuce salad with hearts of artichokes, and peach Melba. Jack Reynolds, the innkeeper, said that it was still possible to get the very same dinner.

Since this lovely old inn is a part of the heartland of America, it stands to reason that the main dishes would be representative of American cooking. For example, there is filet mignon, rainbow trout, and fried Kentucky ham steak. Other dishes offered that we usually associate with America are roast duckling with wild rice dressing, flounder, Warren County turkey, and pork tenderloin. When possible, vegetables from the Ohio countryside are used. These include corn, rutabaga, Brussels sprouts, turnips, beans, peas, and other seasonal selections.

Rooms at the Golden Lamb would enhance a museum of early Americana. There are huge four-posters, intricately carved chests and tables, and an almost priceless collection of 19th-century prints. The rooms are named for the distinguished visitors of the past including Dickens, DeWitt Clinton, and Ulysses S. Grant.

This section of Ohio has really become quite a holiday and vacation focal point. There's the Little Miami, Ohio's first scenic river with fishing, canoeing, hiking, and riding. The Glendower State Museum is a restored Greek Revival mansion; and one of the most popular places is King's Island, centered around a 33-story replica of the Eiffel Tower, where there is a variety of rides and entertainment, as well as a Jack Nicklaus golf center.

I had a wonderful time that evening, and fortunately Jack Reynolds was able to take a few moments to join me. Quite naturally the talk got around to the many Shaker artifacts in the inn and the fact that there was quite a relationship between the Ohio Shakers and the New Lebanon, New York Shakers who lived just over the mountain from the Berkshires.

Jack suggested that I visit the Shaker Room at the Warren County Museum just a few doors away, He also mentioned the reproduction of a 19th-century village green surrounded by tiny shops of that era. "It's all in the Museum," he explained.

THE GOLDEN LAMB INN, 27 S. Broadway, Lebanon, Ohio 45036: 513-932-5065. A historic 20-room village inn in the heart of Ohio farming country on U.S. Hwys. 63, 42, and 48. European plan. 19 rooms with private bath. No pets. Breakfast served only on Sundays. Lunch and dinner served daily except Christmas. Golf and tennis nearby. Jackson Reynolds, Innkeeper.

Directions: From I-71, exit Rte. 48 N, 3 mi. west to Lebanon. From I-75, exit Rte. 63 E, 7 mi. east to Lebanon.

WELSHFIELD INN
Burton, Ohio

"It's a funny thing," I said, "I tried your recipe for skillet-fried chicken back home in the Berkshires, doing everything just as you told me. I even got the right kind of iron skillet, but somehow mine doesn't taste as good as yours. What's the problem?"

Brian Holmes pushed his chef's hat farther back on his head and said, "Well, I understand that you have some great chickens in Massachusetts, but I have a feeling they can't compare with the kind we raise here in Ohio."

I was standing in the extremely neat kitchen of the Welshfield Inn watching Brian put together different ingredients needed for

269

dinner that evening. In addition to the skillet-fried chicken, there was a raisin sauce for the baked ham bubbling on the stove, and the wonderful aroma of the apple pies already in the oven was filling the room. Brian paused long enough to call my attention to the pans of sole and salmon. "Even though we are 500 miles from the nearest ocean, we never serve any frozen fish here. Everything is absolutely fresh. The seafoods are some of our most popular menu choices."

There were pans filled with baked acorn squash, stuffed zucchini, and the makings of fresh strawberry shortcake. "Our recipe for Indian pudding came from Cape Cod," he said. "We took it as a compliment when one of our customers said it tasted exactly like the pudding at the Red Inn in Provincetown."

One of the waitresses, dressed in an attractive early American costume, rushed into the kitchen and apologized for being a little late. Brian said he understood and popped some freshly made rolls into the oven. "That's another thing," he said, "we never use mixes. Our rolls and bread are made from scratch."

At this point Brian said that he had time for a short break, so we went out to the dining room which has a collection of 19th-century antiques and bric-a-brac. The center of interest is the old nickelodeon. I dropped a coin in, and the machine started playing "Three O'clock in the Morning." The music had a nostalgic flavor and sounded like a combination of mandolin, flute, violin, and piano. The machine never played a song that I didn't know, and as I hummed along, Brian remarked that my record was unbroken.

Brian pointed to a seat in the corner and said, "That's where Van Johnson sits every time he's here, and over there is Vivian Vance's table. We had Lucille Ball here for a week. You know, we have a very good theatre nearby where all of the big names appear."

Guests started coming in, so Polly went out to greet them, and Brian went back to the kitchen. I was left alone with the nickelodeon.

I dropped in another coin, and this time the machine played "She Was Only a Bird in a Gilded Cage."

My record is still unbroken.

WELSHFIELD INN, Rte. 422, Burton, Ohio 44021; 216-834-4164. A country restaurant on Rte. 422, 28 mi. east of Cleveland. No lodgings. Lunch and dinner served weekdays. Dinner only served on Sundays and holidays. Closed the week of July 4th and three weeks after Jan. 1. Closed Mondays except Labor Day. Near Sea World and Holden Arboretum. Brian and Polly Holmes, Innkeepers.

Directions: On U.S. 422 at intersection of Ohio 700, midway between Cleveland and Youngstown, Ohio.

Indiana

DURBIN HOTEL
Rushville, Indiana

The Durbin Hotel is the essence of Midwest America. It is like corn on the cob, fried chicken, and James Whitcomb Riley's poetry. The Durbin family tradition of innkeeping has been going on for 52 years. It began when Leo Durbin, a traveling salesman from Ohio, and Mary Cain of Indianapolis, were married and went into the hotel business. They had seven children, a great many of whom, inspired by their upbringing in the hotel, went into the business in other places. The present innkeeper, their son David, has continued in Rushville and many of *his* seven children have been employed at various times in the family hotel.

When I arrived on my most recent visit, David immediately took me in tow to see some of the interesting changes that had been made recently. "We used to call this room the Gay Nineties Room, but after we uncovered the brick walls, exposing the beams, and made it into a reproduction of an old taproom, the rest of my family began to call it 'David's Folly'—the name has apparently stuck. By the way we have live music here every night except Sunday and Monday."

I followed him into a newly decorated corner dining room with very bright colors and an air of gaiety. "We call this room the Strawberry Patch," he said. "You know we are pretty homey folks out here, and everyone feels comfortable with familiar names."

Our tour continued through many of the newly decorated and refurnished bedrooms. Each of them has its own theme, and all are very attractive. I asked him whether or not some of the beds still had

the "Magic Fingers" mattresses. He smiled and said, "Well, you don't find them in very many hotels or inns, but our guests tell us that they love them."

We returned to the lobby again, and while David went to get a menu, I sat down and just enjoyed being here in this friendly atmosphere. There is a main counter with all kinds of postcards, old-fashioned stick candy in jars, books, maps, and even some crafts from that section of Indiana. The grandfather clock tolls every fifteen minutes, and the penny scale still works. There is an arrangement of comfortable furniture in one corner, which is appropriately decorated with many photographs of Mr. Wendell Willkie, the Republican presidential candidate during the early 1940s, who made the Durbin Hotel his campaign headquarters.

David returned and we immediately launched into a discussion of the hotel's home-cooking which is noted far and wide.

"To begin with," he said, "everything is made from scratch. We make our own pies, cakes, and breads right here in the kitchen. The menu is just good farm food, things like scalloped chicken, noodle casseroles, fried chicken, candied yams, baked beans, Danish lobster tails, filet mignon.

"Our menu changes with the season and, of course, we have fresh vegetables whenever they are available. One of our most popular dishes is a homemade ham loaf. We also serve lots of liver, either broiled or pan fried. Do you know that we serve 700 for dinner on many Sundays? By the way, in this part of Indiana when someone says 'dinner' it usually refers to the midday meal. Supper is served at night."

When I said good-bye to David, once again I was filled with good food, loaded down with the warm wishes of new friends, and delighted with all that has been happening at the Durbin Hotel. The way things are going I am sure it will be there for many more years!

DURBIN HOTEL, 137 W. Second Street, Rushville, Ind. 46173; 317-932-4161. A 28-room country hotel in a bustling town, about one hour from Indianapolis. European plan. Breakfast, lunch, dinner served daily except Christmas and New Year's. Leashed pets allowed. Rushville is the home of Wendell Willkie, the 1940 Presidential candidate. Several round barns and covered bridges in the area. David Durbin, Innkeeper.

Directions: From the Indianapolis Beltway take I-74 south to Rushville-Shelbyville exit. Or follow Rte. 52 from the Beltway directly to Rushville. Located on Rtes. 52 and 43, one block from Rte. 3.

PATCHWORK QUILT
Middlebury, Indiana

Here I was, back again at the Patchwork Quilt, and glad to be here. It was the same as before—the broad fields, the white house and the trim outbuildings of a real working farm.

Arletta Lovejoy handed me a glass of mulled cider and introduced me to the other guests awaiting the dinner bell. We were indeed a "mixed bag." There were quite a few people from such nearby Indiana towns as Elkhart and South Bend. There were also Chicagoans, people from Cleveland, and New England.

The signal was given and we all took our places in the Keeping Room. My seat was placed so that I could see into the remarkable kitchen with its Danish oak cabinets. The ladies of the neighborhood, many with cooking specialties, were each busy with some phase of preparing our meal.

Now, one of them came out to the salad-and-relish buffet table and made an announcement. "This evening we have applesauce, kidney bean salad, potato salad, pecan cheese roll, a five-bean salad, corn relish, pickle relish, ham salad, Waldorf salad, Hawaiian franks, pumpkin bread, Swedish fruit soup, and five different dressings." I could just feel the "ooh" go through the room. After all, this was really a prelude to the main event. I tried to use discretion in sampling all of these, although the Swedish fruit soup was too tempting. The United States Senate bean soup was served from a steaming caldron hanging on a crane in the blazing fireplace.

Next, another pretty lady from the kitchen announced the main dishes, which were all served family style and are changed about every day. There were ham, steak Robert, and, of course, the prize-winning buttermilk pecan chicken. The plate with the meats was garnished with parsley and small red tomatoes. There were also green beans served with mushrooms and almonds, and corn served with bits of red pimentoes.

The only meal served at the Patchwork Quilt, which is a real working farm, is dinner, and it is always necessary to reserve in advance. It is closed on Sundays and there is a fixed-price dinner on Fridays and Saturdays. There are no guest rooms available, but the upstairs bedroom displays extremely attractive furnishings, including beautiful quilts that are for sale.

The other innkeepers from *CIBR* and I missed Milton and Arletta Lovejoy, and Herb and Treva Swarm at our annual meeting in the fall of 1978, because they were touring Morocco. "It was too good an opportunity to pass up," said Arletta's letter.

Finally, a large serving cart brought blueberry pie, pecan pie, candied violet cake, grasshopper pie, apricot chiffon pie, cherry cake, cherry walnut torte, and my eye caught the coffee toffee pie made with butter, eggs, chocolate crust (nuts), and chocolate filling.

Would you believe that the whole table actually stood up and applauded!

PATCHWORK QUILT COUNTRY INN, 11748 C.R. #2, Middle-bury, Ind. 46450; 219-825-2417. A working farm restaurant in the tradition of midwestern hospitality, about 20 mi. east of Elkhart. No lodgings. Dinner served daily by reservation only. Closed Sundays, Mondays, Thanksgiving, Christmas, and New Year's. Arletta Lovejoy, Innkeeper.

Directions: From east or west, exit Indiana Toll Road at Middlebury (Exit 10) and go north ¼ mi. to County Rd. #2 and proceed west 1 mi. to inn. From Middlebury follow Indiana Rte. 13 for 8 mi. north to County Rd.#2 and west 1 mi.

Michigan

MARSHALL, MICHIGAN

Marshall should certainly take its place, along with Cape May, New Jersey and Port Townsend, Washington, as one of the most significant centers of Victorian restoration in the world. There are dozens and dozens of gorgeous Victorian homes being lived in by the good people of Marshall today. Fifteen have been designated as state historic sites and six are in the National Register. The residential sections of the town all have beautiful, tall shade trees and sidewalks bordering carefully trimmed lawns and hedges. Everywhere are evidences of civic pride.

The most significant individual in Marshall's restoration and revival is Mr. Harold C. Brooks, a former mayor and true benefactor of the community. He became involved in the preservation more than fifty years ago. He bought several of the important vacant Victorian homes in Marshall and held them until an owner arrived on the scene who was interested in preserving and restoring the building. It appears that very stringent zoning laws and building restrictions have been enacted by the wise citizens of the town in order to preserve this truly magnificent reminder of America's opulent building period. Aided by a very explicit brochure, visitors to Marshall can enjoy a walking tour of the entire community.

The highlight of Marshall's year comes on the first weekend after Labor Day. It is the Annual Historic Home Tour in which Marshall homes are open for visitors. Over 35 organizations and 1400 volunteers work on this project and this is astonishing when we consider that the city has a population of only 7400. Thousands of people are in Marshall during these two days.

Some buildings, including the famous Honolulu House Museum, which has a fantastic collection of Victorian furniture and artifacts, are open May through October. The name "Honolulu House" stems from the fact that it was built by a former U.S. Consul to the then Sandwich Islands who decided to live "Hawaiian style" in Marshall.

For lovers of all Victoriana including the Italianate, Greek Revival, Gothic Revival, Queen Anne, and Italian-villa-style houses, Marshall is indeed a feast. Perhaps more than that, it is an inspiration for all communities to recognize, preserve, and use the irreplaceable reminders of the past.

THE NATIONAL HOUSE
Marshall, Michigan

Norman Kinney, the innkeeper at the National House Inn was helping me to assimilate the experience of this unusual town. "Mr. Brooks was the most important factor," he said. "He was the man who had the vision of Marshall. But everybody in town has joined in. We are proud of the homes and the museums and we all work together. I am sure that we could not have restored the National House if it hadn't been a community effort. People helped out in so many ways.

"This is probably the oldest remaining hotel building in Michigan," he pointed out. "We learned that it was open in 1835 and undoubtedly was the first brick building of any kind in our country.

"At one time it was a windmill and wagon factory, and more recently an apartment building," Norman continued. "My good friend, Hal Minick and I, along with his wife Jacqueline and my wife, Kathryn, decided to restore the building and return it to its original purpose.

"It has really been hard work, but underneath the dirt and grime of dozens of years, we found the solid, beautiful structure of the original brick as well as the irreplaceable woodwork. We converted the apartments into sixteen bedrooms and baths.

"As you can see, Marshall is very much a Victorian restoration. We searched everywhere — culled all the antique shops and removed furniture from our own homes. Many of our friends contributed some of their beloved pieces in order to help us recreate the atmosphere of Marshall before the turn of the century."

One of the most striking features of the National House is the passionate attention to detail. For example, each bedroom has its own ambience and there are colorful comforters, old trunks, marble top tables, bureaus, dried flower arrangements, electric lamps that are reproductions of gas lamps, candle sconces with reflectors, little corner sofas, special care with door knobs, and special attention is given to the linens. The bedroom windows overlook either the residential part of town, or a beautiful fountain in the town center park.

Breakfast is the only meal served, and is offered every morning

in the dining room which has a most fetching collection of chairs and tables from great-grandfather's day. The color tones are warm brown and beige. The breakfast offerings include homebaked coffee cakes and muffins, nut breads, and the like. I spent an hour and a half at breakfast talking with many different people.

The Kinneys and Minicks have devoted a great deal of loving care, pride, and considerable investment in restoring this beautiful building to its original state. The people of Marshall can well be proud of the National House Inn.

THE NATIONAL HOUSE INN, 102 South Parkview, Marshall, Mi. 49068; 616-781-7374. An elegantly restored 16-room Victorian-period village inn. Marshall is the finest example of 19th-century architecture in the Midwest. It has 15 State Historic Sites and 6 National Register Sites. European plan includes Continental breakfast. No other meals served. Open year-round. Closed Christmas Eve and Christmas Day. Tennis, golf, swimming, boating, xc skiing nearby. Norman D. Kinney, Steve Poole, Innkeepers.

Directions: From I-69 exit at Michigan Ave. in Marshall and go straight 1½ mi. to inn. From I-94 use exit 110, follow old 27 south 1½ mi. to inn.

STAFFORD'S BAY VIEW INN
Petoskey, Michigan

Janice Smith and I were rocking in the red rockers with the yellow cushions on the porch at Stafford's Bay View Inn. While we were gazing over Little Traverse Bay she said, "Oh look, there's a sailboat race—and they're setting their spinnakers." Sure enough, while we watched the boats came about, and for this leg of the race they broke out their colorful balloon-like sails.

It had been a very interesting day—Jan and I had gone to Petoskey, particularly so that I could see the famous Gaslight district with its branches of many smart stores which I have also seen in Chicago, Naples, Fort Lauderdale, and Palm Beach. It's part of the reason why Petoskey is known as Michigan's Cote d' Azur.

"The Michigan Historical Society is having it's yearly convention at the inn this fall," she said, "and the inn will be awarded its one-hundred year sign. We're the oldest inn in continuous operation in the state and we're registered as a historical place."

I asked her how the inn happened to be built. "It was a part of the Bay View section of Petoskey," she replied." Bay View is a summer resort community with a program of music and drama along with religious lectures and services. The community began in the late 1880s, when people rode on the Grand Rapids and Indiana Railroad or on the lake steamers to reach Petoskey."

She laughed for a moment, saying, "It must have required a bit of faith to see the future glory of the area because there were nearly two hundred miles of unbroken forest to the south.

"However," she went on, "the early residents built the fine Victorian homes which are scattered throughout Bay View today. The cultural and religious programs which started then are still going on, providing our guests with the additional opportunity for summertime enlightenment and enjoyment.

"Duffer (Stafford) and I met here at the inn in 1960 when I was the hostess and he was the assistant manager. We fell in love with each other and the inn, and a year later had scraped up enough money to make a down payment on it and also to get married. The inn has been a major part of our life. Our children, Reg, 15; Mary Catherine, 13; and Dean, 8; have grown up with it.

"This is the year that we completely redesigned and reconstructed the entire kitchen area. Stafford is so proud of it, that he takes almost everyone of our guests on a tour of the kitchen."

I suggested a walk on the shore of the lake, and as we crossed the country railroad tracks which go around the bay, she said, "It's great fun to cross-country ski up these tracks—there's lots of trails up around the bend."

We strolled along the lake, and I realized it provided a striking view of the inn—a white building, three stories high with a green mansard on the third story. Many of the rooms look out over Little Traverse Bay.

Meanwhile, a car with Indiana plates pulled up to the inn and a

family with three children began unpacking tennis rackets, scuba diving gear, and bicycles.

"Oh, excuse me for a moment," said Jan, "these people have been coming here for at least five years. I want to say hello!"

STAFFORD'S BAY VIEW INN, Box 3, Petoskey, Mich. 49770; 616-347-2771. A 23-room resort-inn on Little Traverse Bay in the Bay View section of Petoskey. Modified American plan omits lunch. Breakfast, lunch, and dinner served daily to travelers. Open daily Memorial Day to mid-October, Christmas week and long weekends during the winter sports season. Lake swimming and xc skiing on grounds. Golfing, boating, fish;ing, hiking, and Alpine ski trails nearby. Stafford and Janice Smith, Innkeepers.

Directions: From Detroit, take Gaylord Exit from I-75 and follow Mich. Rte. 32 to Rte. 131, north to Petoskey. From Chicago, use U.S. 131 north to Petoskey.

THE BOTSFORD INN
Farmington Hills, Michigan

John Anhut, the innkeeper, and I were standing in the attractive fully paneled private dining room of the Botsford, and I commented on the unusual patina of the walls.

"That's an interesting story," replied John. "Under Henry Ford's direction, these panels were installed carefully by expert cabinetmakers and the entire room was then sealed off. The fireplace was filled with corncobs and then lighted. Can you imagine this room filled with corncob smoke? Well, the fire burned for a long time and the wood was allowed to cure. The result is an antique finish which can only be obtained by this type of treatment. By the way, the colonial sideboard is supposed to have come from General Lee's home in Virginia."

The Botsford Inn has a fascinating history which began 141 years ago when it was a stagecoach stop on the road between Detroit and Lansing. Like other country and village inns of the 19th century (and even today), the public room was the scene for lots of stories and jokes and probably a great deal of business. Incidentally, the doors have remained open continuously since the first day. It is Michigan's oldest inn.

The late Henry Ford became interested in its preservation in 1924 and, upon purchasing it, placed a great many of his own 19th-century antiques and treasures in it. Among them are furnishings from his country home, including a beautiful little inlaid spinet, a handsome horsehair sofa, his music boxes, a Simon Willard clock, an exquisitely inlaid mahogany table, and an attractive oil painting of the Botsford Inn showing people in costumes of the late 19th century.

I walked through the other rooms including one with very low ceilings and huge beams. The fireplace had mammoth andirons and there was a cross section of the wall left bare by Mr. Ford in order to show the split lathes of 150 years ago.

John had a few words to say about the menu: "We believe in serving predominantly American food; we aren't a French restaurant and we have never tried to be one. Consequently, we have a lot of things on the menu that people come to associate with country living here in the Midwest. We have a salad bowl with lettuce, pea beans, celery, carrots, and tomato sections." There are lots of casserole

dishes, and on that particular night I enjoyed short ribs. "As far as I know," John added, "now we're going to have dinner theater each week with an emphasis on light comedy."

He continued, "I think that we have many elements of a New England country inn here, but we're really a big city inn. We attempt to compensate for bucolic charm in other ways."

Later, while dressing in my room after a welcome swim, I was grateful for some modern conveniences in the Botsford Inn such as air conditioning on an afternoon of record heat. The throb of the Motor City had almost entirely receded. So near, and yet so far.

BOTSFORD INN, 28000 Grand River Avenue, Farmington Hills, Mich. 48024; 313-474-4800. A 62-room village inn on the city line of Detroit. European plan. Dinner served daily except Monday. Breakfast and lunch Tuesday thru Saturday. Sunday brunch. Closed Christmas and New Year's Day. Pool on grounds. Greenfield Village, skiing, and state parks nearby. John Anhut, Innkeeper.

Directions: Located in Farmington Hills on I-96 which is easily accessible from major highways in Michigan.

Wisconsin

I learned a great deal more about Wisconsin during two trips in the summer of 1978. My first visit was north of Milwaukee and Green Bay in Door County, which is on a peninsula jutting out into Lake Michigan. I'm sure that this part of Wisconsin is a most familiar and enjoyable vacation experience for many of our readers.

One of the highlights of that trip was meeting Andy and Jan Coulson and their young daughter Meredith, all of whom are happily ensconced at the White Gull Inn in Fish Creek.

My other experience was an equally pleasant one farther north and west in the town of Bayfield, which is on the shores of Lake Superior. It was not only my first glimpse of the Apostle Islands, but also my first meeting with Jerry and Mary Phillips and their lovely restored Victorian inn known as the Old Rittenhouse.

My search for inns led me to other sections of the state, and I was immediately attracted to its broad farmlands and its natural towns and villages. I'm sure that the many readers from Wisconsin will be glad to see we've included two inns from their state in this edition, and perhaps with furthur recommendations, we may have more in the future.

Nineteen seventy-eight was my year to meet several wonderfully enthusiastic young innkeepers. Besides Jan and Andy Coulson at the White Gull Inn, there were the Schumachers in New Prague, Minnesota; the Phillipses in Bayfield, Wisconsin; the Stanfords in Carmel, California; the Pavlovs in Deer Isle, Maine; the Tallets in Stephentown, New York, and several others which are new in this edition. In the hands of earnest, enthusiastic, and innovative innkeepers like these, American innkeeping should prosper for many years to come.

THE WHITE GULL INN
Fish Creek, Wisconsin

Jan and Andy Coulson and their one-year-old daughter, Meredith, and I were enjoying a breakfast of cherry pancakes deliciously saturated in Door County maple syrup. There was a wonderful air of expectancy about The White Gull which was enhanced by the summer staff of very delightful college people.

Andy was talking about plans for the future, "We're going to add another dining room and expand the kitchen, which will make quite a difference in our seating capacity. With the new dining room we will be able to seat up to 240 each night, regardless of the weather, and this will also appease some of our dinner guests who are disappointed if they forget to make a reservation for the Fish Boil two weeks in advance."

At this point I'd better explain about the Fish Boil, which is, as far as I know, a tradition limited to Wisconsin. The Fish Boil at The White Gull features freshly caught lake fish, boiled potatoes, homemade cole slaw, fresh-baked bread, and cherry pie.

Center stage is outdoors at the rear of the inn, where Russ, the master boiler, has built a roaring fire under two huge cauldrons in which the fish is boiled. This wood-smoke fire, combined with the aroma of the Lake Michigan fish, creates gargantuan appetites. In addition, Russ plays the accordion and leads everybody in lots of singing and clapping of hands. The White Gull has a Fish Boil every Wednesday, Friday, Saturday, and Sunday evening.

On Monday and Thursday nights, from mid-June through September, an early American buffet is served, including a selection of old-fashioned prepared dishes and fresh-baked goods. The menu includes turkey dumpling soup, glazed baked ham, corn and clam pie, maple-baked carrots, Boston baked beans, scalloped potatoes, and lots of homemade breads.

The inn is a white clapboard three-story building dating back to 1896. It doesn't "put on airs," and there's a definite open informality among the owners, the staff, and the guests. The rooms are tidy and neat, and some of them in the main house share a bath. There are also spacious cottages in the rear.

"All of this started more than 75 years ago," said Jan, "when The White Gull was part of a large resort area consisting of several of the present-day hotels in Fish Creek."

"I think we're still very much of a resort area," joined in Andy. "Fish Creek is still basically an unspoiled village, but there are dozens of ways for our guests to enjoy themselves. For example, we have Peninsula Park which has thousands of acres of forests, majestic cliffs, caves, and a rugged coast line. There are bridle paths and bathing beaches. We have more miles (250) of shore line in Door County than in any other country in the United States."

By this time, Jan picked up the pace by pointing out that not only were there all of these wonderful outdoor activities, but there were also professional companies of singers and actors, including the Peninsula Players who have been delighting audiences in this area for the past 44 years. "There's also the Birch Creek Farm Performing Arts Academy, as well as the Peninsula Music Festival," she said.

It was great fun to visit The White Gull and to meet the Coulsons, and to see beautiful Door County through their eyes. It was also reassuring to know that I would be visiting them for many years to come.

THE WHITE GULL INN, Fish Creek, Wis. 54212; 414-868-3517. A 9-room inn in a most scenic area in Door County, 23 mi. north of Sturgeon Bay. Considerable outdoor and cultural attractions nearby. Rooms with and without private baths. Open mid-May through late October. Winter season: December 26-January 1; weekends in January and February. European plan. Breakfast daily

throughout the season. Lunches mid-June to Labor Day. Fish Boils: Wednesday, Friday, Saturday, Sunday nights throughout the season. Early American buffet: Monday and Thursday. Dining room closed Tuesday nights. All meals open to travelers.
Reservations requested for evening meals. Golf, tennis, swimming, fishing, biking, sailing, and other summer and winter sports nearby. Excellent for children of all ages. Pets allowed in cottages but not in main lodge. Andy and Jan Coulson, Innkeepers.

Directions: From Chicago: take I-94 to Milwaukee. Follow Rte. I-43 (141) from Milwaukee to Manitowoc; Rte. 42 from Manitowoc to Fish Creek. Turn left at stop sign at the bottom of the hill, go 2½ blocks to inn. From Green Bay: take Rte. 57 to Sturgeon Bay; Rte. 42 to Fish Creek.

BAYFIELD COUNTY, WISCONSIN

My Rand McNally Road Atlas (incidentally an invaluable travel tool, especially in the large size) shows the northwest corner of the state of Wisconsin to be pinched in between Minnesota on the west and that inexplicable portion of western Michigan on the east. On a peninsula stretching out into Lake Superior is the town and county of Bayfield, the Red Cliff Indian reservation, and the Apostle Islands National Lakeshore. As a vacation and resort area, it may be one of the best-kept secrets in North America.

Naturally, being a New Englander, I date history from the arrival of the Pilgrims in 1620. However, it may well be that a French explorer named Etienne Brule probably nudged his canoe into the shores of Madeline Island off what is now Bayfield, in 1618. In any case, there was much activity by missionaries and fur traders during the 1600s, and Radisson and Groseilliers, the two famous brother-in-law adventurers, were on the scene as early as 1659. They were seeking furs from the Indians, for this had been the ancestral home of the Chippewa since about 1490. Other tribes, including the Huron, Ottawa, and Sioux, have shared the territory before and since that time.

Oddly enough, Bayfield was named for Lt. Henry R.T. Bayfield of the British Navy who made the first survey of Lake Superior in 1827, and whose charts are still used.

The area is dominated by the presence of the Apostle Islands, a 22-island archipelago. For the most part, the entire area is still unspoiled, but accessible. It's a vacation haven offering boating, swimming, golf, and camping, plus colorful natural and historical attractions seasoned with romantic mysterious legends.

The legend that appeals to me very much is how the islands were created: "A Manitou (Big Spirit) pursued a great stag. Unsuccessfully, he launched his arrow at the animal, but the deer escaped by plunging into Lake Superior. Angry, the Manitou picked up a handful of rocks and threw them at the deer. The rocks fell into the water and became the Apostle Islands."

The National Park Service maintains in Bayfield both headquarters and a very informative and energetic interpretative program that provides an even greater enjoyment of the area's great and natural beauty. For further information, contact the Madeline Island Ferry Line, Box 66, LaPointe, Wis. 54850; or write Bayfield County Historical Society for its excellent map and explanation of points of historical interest.

OLD RITTENHOUSE INN
Bayfield, Wisconsin

I arrived in Bayfield to the accompaniment of a thunder and lightning storm of positively Wagnerian proportions. The electrical display lit up the shoreline of Lake Superior, providing spectacular but "eye-blink" views of the Apostle Islands lying offshore.

I came in on Route 13 and easily identified an impressive Victorian mansion as the Old Rittenhouse Inn. It is located on a tree-shaded street on a high bank considerably above the road. It has four stories with a white porch around the front and side. In midsummer there were many wicker furniture pieces.

I waited a few moments for the deluge to abate, and then, dodging raindrops, hurried through the front door into a world of delicate Victoriana. The first person I saw was Jerry Phillips, a handsome bearded gentleman wearing a white, turn-of-the-century suit with a double-breasted vest, a red shirt with ruffles at the cuff, and a black, oversized butterfly tie.

"Welcome to the Old Rittenhouse Inn," he said. "We've tried to turn out for you in real style."

"Style" was exactly what I found in great abundance during my visit with Jerry and Mary Phillips, the keepers of the Old Rittenhouse Inn. I'm sure that the innkeepers of our other handsome Victorian inns, Norman Kinney of the National House Inn at Marshall, Michigan; Tom Carroll of the Mainstay in Cape May, New Jersey; and Lowell Bogart of the James House in Port Townsend, Washington, would agree that this elegant hostelry measures up in every respect.

Jerry showed me to my table and explained that he and Mary, who does all the cooking (with the exception of the desserts which are Jerry's province), would join me for a long after-dinner talk. Meanwhile, Bruce, my waiter who moved with the grace of a trained dancer, never made a sound placing plates on the table or tray. He, like the other bearded waiters, wore a white shirt with a black bow tie, black trousers and a black vest. The waitresses wore long flowered dresses.

I was served at a round oak table with a single candle. The cream and sugar and salt and pepper were a silver set. There was a green napkin on my plate in the middle of which was placed a small red blossom. Jerry presented the spoken menu, explaining very carefully the details concerning every individual course and the delicate content of each recipe. That evening, my first course was a mushroom Burgundy soup made with clarified beef stock. I could have opted for a fruit soup, served warm. The second course had a choice of three salads, including a fruit salad made with fresh wild blackberries, raspberries, blueberries, peaches, and apples.

I had a difficult decision to make among the six main courses, which included Lake Superior whitefish baked in wine and garnished with almonds and served in a champagne butter sauce; ham baked in a spiced orange glaze and garnished with fresh fruits; ocean scallops sauteed in a very delicate curried drawn butter; leg of lamb roasted with fresh rosemary, garlic, and lemon served in its own sauce. There were four freshly baked breads available that evening as well.

After dinner, when Jerry and Mary joined me, they explained that the house had been built in 1890 as a summer home. When they bought it, much restoring and redecorating were needed. "Furnishing it with Victorian furniture was fun," said Mary. "We've met every antique dealer between Duluth and Milwaukee, getting the right furniture for five bedrooms and three dining rooms."

Yes, the word for the Old Rittenhouse Inn is *style*, to which I must inevitably add the word *grace*. I found them both in abundant quantities at this inn in Bayfield, Wisconsin on the shores of Lake Superior.

OLD RITTENHOUSE INN, 301 Rittenhouse Ave., Bayfield, Wis. 54814; 715-779-5765. A five-room Victorian inn in an area of historic and natural beauty, 70 mi. east of Duluth, Minn., on the shores of Lake Superior. European plan. Breakfast and dinner served to travelers. Open all year except the first three weeks in November; Christmas Eve and Christmas Day. No pets. Not comfortable for small children. Extensive recreational activity of all kinds available throughout the year, including tours, hiking and cycling on the nearby Apostle and Madeline Islands. Jerry and Mary Phillips, Innkeepers.

Directions: From the Duluth Airport, follow Rte. 53-S through the city of Duluth over the bridge to Superior, Wisconsin. Turn east on Rte. 2 near Ashland (1½ hrs.), turn north on 13-N to Bayfield.

Missouri

CHESHIRE INN
St. Louis, Missouri

The Cheshire Inn is as British as anything one might find this side of London's Piccadilly Circus. Imagine finding two red double-deck London buses and a Tudor-style building with half timbers just a few miles from the Mississippi River!

For the most part, furnishings and decorations of the inn are the result of a passion for collecting shared by proprietors Steve and

Barbara Apted, and this passion extends to the lodging rooms, some of which are named for prominent English literary figures such as Johnson, Galsworthy, Dickens, and Tennyson.

I stayed in the Richard the Lionhearted Room which had a canopied bed with curtains around it, taking me back to medieval times. When the sun came up, the matching rich red curtains at the windows created a marvelous red glow. The television set was hidden in an old oak chest.

Houseguests enjoy a breakfast buffet which offers an endless array of eggs (poached, scrambled, fried, soft boiled and hard boiled), bacon, and several different kinds of fresh breads, delicious hot chocolate, and a very pleasant and accommodating morning staff which makes even the dullest days seem bright.

The first page of the very extensive dinner menu explains why the Cheshire Inn has been created in an English atmosphere. It says in part: "Times were hard in 'Merrie Olde England'. People worked hard for long hours and to compensate, learned how to live and live well on the simple pleasures of everyday life. At sundown they would repair to their hearthsides for a warming bowl of soup followed by rich roast beef.

"At Cheshire we try to recreate this jolly period with costumes, recipes from old books, music, and a general air of 'hail stranger, hail friend, sit down and rest yourself, partake of what we offer!'"

The descriptions of the main courses are enough to give one the appetite of Henry VIII. One of the specialties of the house is roast prime rib of beef served with Yorkshire pudding and horseradish sauce. The meat is roasted on a slowly turning spit to keep in the natural juices and flavor.

Another specialty is roast duck which, according to the menu, is prepared "in the manner preferred by Charles Dickens." The glazed pork chops Buckingham are brushed with a sweet-sour sauce and topped with a grilled pineapple ring. There are many, many more selections on the menu, including trout stuffed with crabmeat, short ribs of beef, fish, lobster tails, and many types of steaks. The most popular dessert is the English trifle; or perhaps it is the Missouri apple pie served warm with cheese or ice cream; or maybe it's both.

I enjoy staying at the Cheshire Inn when visiting St. Louis because it's right across the street from the park where there's so much happening in both summer and winter. It's out of the hustle and bustle of downtown St. Louis, however Highway 40 runs right into the center of the city, and it's just a few moments to the Beltway around St. Louis (270) which provides ready access to all directions.

CHESHIRE INN and LODGE, 6300 Clayton Rd., St. Louis, Mo.

63117; 314-647-7300. A 110-room English style inn, 1 block off Hwy. 40 near Forest Park. European plan only. Breakfast, lunch, and dinner served to travelers daily. Accomodations available every day of the year. Restaurant closed on New Year's Day, Memorial Day, July 4th, Labor Day, and Christmas Day. Pool, bicycles on grounds. Boating, golf, tennis, and riding nearby. St. Louis Art Museum, zoo, Gateway Arch, and opera nearby. Jim Prentice, Innkeeper.

Directions: Just off Hwy. 40 at Clayton Rd. and Skinker Blvd. on southwest corner of Forest Park. From the east, take Clayton Rd. exit. From the west, take McCausland Ave. exit, north two blocks to Clayton Rd.

THE JEFFERSON AVENUE BOARDING HOUSE
St. Louis, Missouri

It was three-thirty p.m., and since The Jefferson Avenue Boarding House was not open for dinner as yet, I used the rear entrance through a spotlessly clean kitchen where there were a number of people involved in the preparation of the evening meal. I stepped into the dining room which was a combination of late Victorian and early Art Noveau. There were bentwood chairs, lots of delicately stained glass, and oil paintings and prints that would have pleased Aubrey Beardsley. From the far end of the room, I heard my name being called and then a man came forward saying "Hi, I'm Rich Perry, welcome to The Jefferson Avenue Boarding House." Thus began another interesting adventure which culminated that evening in a most enjoyable dinner with Jim Mellow and his family.

Since there are no lodging rooms at the JABH, I asked Rich about the menu. I knew there had been some changes since my previous visit.

"Our guests can choose from at least three different entrees at each meal; moreover in the true boarding house fashion, they can have just one of the entrees or some of each if they wish. Among our main typical courses are St. Louis World's Fair Steak, chicken a la Tony Faust, and baked trout almondine. We're very proud of the things we do with seafood. Most of the time we have some type of beef on the menu.

"We start with an appetizer which might be oysters on the half-shell or oysters Rockefeller, boiled shrimp, and some special soup or quiche. Our breads are all homemade and served with whipped butter. We're very proud of our salads, and we always use fresh raw vegetables and our own country dressing."

I picked up one of the menus on the table and commented, "I see that you also serve breakfast on Sunday mornings."

Rich continued most enthusiastically. "Yes, that's something that we think is a great deal of fun. We start off with a nice fresh fruit and for the second course there might be hot cereal or a breakfast quiche. The main course always is some variation of eggs and a breakfast meat like sausage or bacon. Our maple syrup is from nearby Bloomington, Illinois, across the river. After the main breakfast course, we continue with a homemade pastry and finish up again with a fruit.

"Here on the first floor we call this the Café Faust which is open from six until midnight every night except Monday and Saturday. We serve without reservations here, and we're open late enough so that people can come in after the theater. Reservations for the second-floor dining room are for regular seatings at 6:30 and 8:30."

Rich glanced at his watch, and I took the hint that it was time for him to join the others in the kitchen. Since I would be returning that evening we said, "So long," for just a couple of hours.

Dinner was a great success. I'm happy to say that all the Mellows were present except for young Jim, the sculptor, with whom I had had dinner at the Red Lion Inn in Stockbridge earlier in the year. We toasted his success.

The meal was served by Rich and his partner, Jim Belshaw, who, along with the other waiters, wore blue jeans, and a denim work shirt colorfully set off by a large white apron. After the beef barley soup, which was served from the cast iron pots with dippers, I had braised pork, and Jim Belshaw explained as he served it, "We take half-pound pork chops, braise them and then bake them with a combination of sour cream and applesauce." They were, indeed, delicious.

THE JEFFERSON AVENUE BOARDING HOUSE, 3265 So. Jefferson Ave., St. Louis, Mo. 63118; 314-771-4100. A most unusual informal restaurant located about 15 minutes from downtown St. Louis. Dinner is served Tuesday through Sunday at 6:30 and 8:30 p.m. Additional seatings are available on Saturdays. Luncheon guests are seated from 11:30 a.m. until 1:30 p.m., Tuesdays through Fridays. Sunday breakfast is served from 10:00 a.m. Reservations are heartily encouraged. Café Faust is open from 6 p.m. until midnight on Tuesdays through Fridays and Sundays: Reservations are not accepted. There are no meals served on Monday, Christmas, or New Year's Day. No lodgings available. Richard D. Perry and James C. Belshaw, props.

Directions: Exit I-44 to So. Jefferson Ave. and follow the numbers on the west side to the corner of Jefferson And Utah Street. Easy to find.

ST. GEMME BEAUVAIS INN
Ste. Genevieve, Missouri

The magazine was called *Missouri Life* and it was the July-August, 1978, issue. Boats Donze handed it to me with a twinkle in his eye, "I think you'll find something interesting on the inside."

I leafed through the rather handsomely designed pages and came to a full-page color photograph of the St. Gemme Beauvais Inn framed by a tree and a beautiful wrought iron fence in the foreground. On the opposite page was a smaller photograph of a man in a very elegant-looking yellow brocaded coat and a ruffled shirt standing at the top of the four brick steps that lead to the entrance of

291

the inn. I peered at it closely and said, "Why Boats, that's you!" He smiled somewhat deprecatingly and admitted that it was.

It is perfectly natural for Boats Donze to be wearing an antebellum French costume while standing in front of his inn, because the inn is his boyhood home. "My father bought it in 1923," he said. "It was the property of the daughter of Felix Rozier who built it in 1848. Before that, the property was owned by first families of the village, including St. Gemmes' and Beauvais'—hence its name."

The inn is really a showcase for the Mississippi River village of Ste. Genevieve, which is fifty miles south of St. Louis. The people of the village have lived under three different flags. Settled by the French in the latter part of the seventeenth century, in 1763, the treaty of Fontainebleau gave the territory west of the Mississippi to Spain, which then returned it to France in 1800. As part of the Louisiana Purchase in 1803, Ste. Genevieve became a part of the United States.

It is to its French heritage, however, that the town addresses most of itself. It is the only place in Missouri where so much of the state's French culture has been preserved. Thirty buildings were built before 1800 and almost all of them remain the same as they were two hundred years ago. Quite a few are open to the public, and a complete walking tour is available.

The Donzes have furnished the inn mainly with 19th century regional pieces. There are six-foot-high carved headboards, marble top dressers, floral wallpapers and bright carpets. Most of the lodgings are two bedroom suites. One is a corner bedroom which was occupied by Paul Harvey, the well-known radio commentator. Frankye told me that Harvey talked about this inn and the village on his program. The adjoining room has a beautiful high golden oak headboard and a similar matching chest of drawers. All of the windows are hung with Country Curtains from Stockbridge, Massachusetts. Each of these little suites has its own bathroom.

A favorite room is on the top floor where the windows overlook the uppermost branches of a Douglas fir tree. "They are quite rare in this part of the country," explained Frankye.

Frankye and Boats are great travelers, and many of the things they have collected are now decorating the inn, including impressive chandeliers from Florence.

My lunch that day consisted of a tasty quiche Lorraine (most appropriate for a French inn), carrots with a distinctive herbal touch, string beans cooked with bacon bits, and a salad. The dessert was a homemade cobbler. One of the house specialties is chicken-filled crêpes.

Frankye and Boats have lovingly restored three other old buildings of Ste. Genevieve including the Amoureaux House, the Beauvais House, and the Green Tree Tavern which was built about 1790. It was the first inn in Ste. Genevieve. "All of this restoration was done with private funds and not supported by any foundation money," asserted Boats.

He sums up their feeling quite well. "We think that these houses should be living areas instead of cold and lifeless museums. It's much more fun to be able to touch things and communicate with the past."

All in all, I think that's what happens at Ste. Genevieve and at its handsome inn, St. Gemme Beauvais—it's a communication with the past.

ST. GEMME BEAUVAIS, 78 N. Main St., Ste. Genevieve, Mo. 63670; 314-883-5744. An 8-room village inn about 1½ hrs. from St. Louis. Modified American plan includes breakfast only. Breakfast served daily. Lunch served Mon.—Sat. Open year-round. Closed Thanksgiving and Christmas Day. No pets. Golf, hunting, and fishing nearby. Frankye and Boats Donze, Innkeepers.

Directions: From St. Louis, south on I-55 to Hwy. 32. Exit east on 32 to Hwy. 61 to the Ste. Genevieve exit.

WILDERNESS LODGE
Lesterville, Missouri

"We're having a wonderful time here, I wish we could stay forever." I was having breakfast at Wilderness Lodge and making the acquaintance of a young honeymoon couple who were kind enough to say that they had chosen this Ozark resort-inn because they read about it in *CIBR*.

"Aside from being on our honeymoon," said Sue, her eyes dancing, "we're having a beautiful time here because we love the floating." Tom joined in, never relinquishing a loving hold on his wife's hand. "Yes, I like to fish, but I hate to paddle, and Sue doesn't like to fish, but loves to paddle, so I think we're off to a great start!"

As the waitress served the pancakes, Tom said, "It seems to me that we've been eating every minute since we got here, and every meal is better than the last. On Friday night we had corn relish, cream slaw, fried chicken, green beans,and mashed potatoes and gravy. Saturday breakfast was cereal, orange juice, hot biscuits, fried eggs, bacon, coffee, and cake. For dinner on Saturday—what did we have, Sue?"

"There were stuffed pork chops, baked apples, and chocolate pie. On Sunday night they have spaghetti with Italian salad and garlic bread. An old dinner bell calls everybody for all the meals including an eight o'clock breakfast!"

For people who love horseback riding, floating, platform tennis, canoeing, hiking, fishing, and other outdoor activities the Wilderness Lodge in the Missouri Ozarks is ideal. There is a wide variety of accommodations. My hillside room in a rustic cabin made of native wood had a big fireplace with the wood already laid in the grate. A rear balcony was perched high in the trees overlooking the river. The

furniture was all country-made. This is not an ordinary hunting lodge, but something very special with conveniences built right in. Even the air conditioners are tucked out of sight.

The buildings of the Lodge are spread out on a hill that slopes down to the banks of the Black River. Their basic construction is of horizontal logs with the bark stripped off and white mortar in between.

The center of activities is the dining hall which is also a gathering place for the guests at the beginning and the end of the day.

Besides being a great place for honeymooners, Wilderness Lodge provides a super vacation for kids. It has just about everything in the world for them to do.

I mentioned "floating." This is a wonderful outdoor experience enjoyed on the Black River. Guests and canoes are taken upriver anywhere from five to fifteen miles. The canoe is put in the water and then begins to float with the current down the river to the Lodge. Paddles help out here and there. Box lunches are provided. It's great fun to drift slowly underneath the trees on the riverbank or perhaps lift the canoe up on the sandy shore and stretch out on the grass in the warm sunshine.

As we were leaving the dining room, Tom and Sue invited me to join them in a game of platform tennis. I looked at my watch, remembered my pressing appointment at the Cheshire Inn in St. Louis, which is just about two and a half hours away and reluctantly declined.

"But, here's an idea, I'll meet you here a year from today on your first anniversary." The three of us shook hands on it.

WILDERNESS LODGE, P.O. Box 87, Lesterville, Mo. 63654; 314-637-2295. A 24-room resort-inn located in the heart of the scenic Ozarks approximately 2½ hrs. from St. Louis. Modified American plan. Breakfast and dinner to travelers. Closed from Christmas to the day before New Year's. Box lunches available. No pets. Tennis, platform tennis, bocci, horseback riding, canoeing, float trips, walking and nature trails, fishing, archery, and many other sports on grounds. Stephen and Barbara Apted, Innkeepers.

Directions: From I-244 take Hwy. 55 south and just past Festus, take Hwy. 67 south. After the junction of Hwy. 32, Hwy. 67 becomes two lanes only. Follow 67 and very shortly look for a sign: "W," Farmington. Take this exit and turn right. You'll be on W west. Remain on W for approximately 8 mi. and there will be a sign, Jct. V. Turn left onto V for 9 mi. and it ends at Hwy. 21 in Ironton, where you turn left. Follow 21 and 1 mi. past town of Hogan be careful. This is Jct. of 21 and Hwy. 49. 49 will continue straight ahead and 21 will swerve to the right. No big thing if you look for it, just be sure to go right, toward Lesterville. As you approach Lesterville, you'll pass Lake Taum Sauk signs; ¼ mi. further, on the left, are a Dairy Queen and an old package store (both small white buildings), and a group of resort signs. Turn left, before the signs, follow the hard surface road. You'll cross over the Black River bridge and follow the road turning left at the next set of signs, and just a little farther, on the right, is Wilderness Lodge.

Minnesota

LOWELL INN
Stillwater, Minnesota

The plane made a wide circle around the Minneapolis-St. Paul Airport and obligingly dipped a wing so that I could get a full view of the golden grain country of Minnesota. I asked my seat-mate to point out the St. Croix River and the little town of Stillwater. "If you're going to visit the Lowell Inn," he said, "you're bound to like it."

A short time later, I drove to Stillwater from the airport and soon the Mount Vernon exterior of the inn with its tall white pillars and beautiful red brick walls came into view.

I stepped inside and it was like being in a rather large home. As Innkeeper Arthur Palmer explained to me, "We really consider the inn a home, and the lobby is our living room." Everything was decorated with an eye toward comfortable elegance. The large Colonial fireplace was surrounded with quilted couches, blue leather chairs, and a grandfather's clock. The side parlor's furniture had summer slipcovers with flower designs and a beautiful breakfront with Dresden china on display.

Maureen Palmer explained that many of the fine furnishings were collected by Arthur's parents, Nelle and Arthur, Sr., during the 1930s. Nelle was an actress and talented coronet player and Arthur, a pianist. They met and married when both worked with Nelle's sisters' traveling troupe, "The Obrecht Sisters." When the opportunity arose to manage the Lowell Inn, they decided it was time to settle down and become innkeepers, something they had always wanted to do. After leasing the inn for a number of years, their final dream came true when they purchased the inn in 1945.

I found the originality of this Midwestern inn most exceptional. For example, there are three dining rooms, each with its own theme.

Probably the most striking experience of all is to dine in the Matterhorn Room which would be unique even in Switzerland. It reflects the Palmers' Swiss family background. The room is filled from floor to ceiling with authentic Swiss woodcarvings. The staff is dressed in Swiss costume and the feature of the five-course, fixed-price dinner is fondue Bourguignonne, cubes of select prime beef which each person cooks to his own taste in individual fondue pots.

Weather permitting, the front terrace of the inn is now used as a sidewalk cafe. The menu includes French crepes and a light, modestly priced lunch. There are petunias under the front window and there's a very gay atmosphere with yellow umbrellas, trees, and plants.

Lodging rooms at the Lowell Inn are quite luxurious. Many have leaded glass doors to the hallway, and several of the rooms have French telephones. Each room is decorated separately with its own set of sheets and pillow cases. A clock radio eliminates the necessity for wake-up calls. There are fresh flowers everywhere.

Something new and exciting is always happening at the Lowell Inn, and I find several pleasant surprises on each visit. "I think that's because I've inherited my mother and father's love of show business," explained Arthur, "Besides serving the very best food in the most pleasant manner that we can, and providing exceptional lodgings, we think the Lowell Inn should be, above all, an enjoyable experience for the guests. We dress our waitresses in petticoats and flowered gowns and some of them even have Colonial caps. We try to do all of the extra things that make staying here at the inn a joyous experience." Arthur, Maureen, and all of the assorted Palmers . . . you've certainly succeeded.

THE LOWELL INN, 102 N. Second St., Stillwater, Minn. 55082; 612-439-1100. A 22-room village inn 18 mi. from St. Paul, near all the cultural attractions of the Twin Cities. European plan. Lunch and dinner served daily except Christmas Eve and Christmas Day. Open year-round. No pets. Canoeing, tennis, hiking, skiing, and swimming nearby, including 4 ski resorts within 15 mi. Arthur and Maureen Palmer, Innkeepers.

Directions: Stillwater is on the St. Croix River at the junction of Minn. 95 (north and south) and Minn. 36 (east and west). It is 7 mi. north of I-94 on Hwy. 95.

SCHUMACHER'S NEW PRAGUE HOTEL
New Prague, Minnesota

John and Nancy Schumacher are representative of a dedicated genre of new younger innkeepers who gain great satisfaction and personal fulfillment in running a country inn. "For John and myself," said Nancy, tossing her golden mane, "it's been a wonderful experience since 1974 when we first discovered New Prague and the hotel. It's been hard work, but so much fun and certainly a wonderful future."

Perhaps the best way to tell the story of this inn is to share some of John's comments about Nancy, and vice versa: "Nancy is an artist. She writes the menu, designs the brochures, decorates the rooms, buys the furniture, and when we need a hostess, she can fill in. She also does all of the bookeeping. This operation is fifty percent Nancy Schumacher!"

Nancy says of John: "The food is John's department; even though he seems young, he's been a cook and a baker since 1964. He has a great flair for creating new dishes. He went to the Culinary Institute of America and graduated at the top of his class. Each of the dinners is prepared as ordered. It may take a bit longer, but it tastes so much better. We bake our own breads and pastries. All side dishes, main courses, and desserts are made from fresh vegetables, fresh fruit, and fresh meats. Recipes are from John and the little Czechoslovakian ladies of the village."

Nancy has decorated the twelve lodging rooms, named after each month, and they greatly resemble inns and hotels I have visited in Bavaria and Austria. Each room is almost totally different. One of the most welcome features are the eiderdown-filled comforters on all of the beds, a custom I found throughout northern and central

Europe. Each room is minutely described in the colorful brochure of the inn.

The menu has approximately fifty-five main dishes, most of them having Central European origins. The fish, poultry, and game courses all have Czechoslovakian names. These include boneless breast of chicken topped with blue cheese; roast duck cooked in caraway seeds served with dumplings and red cabbage, and two of the house specialties—creamed rabbit and the bock beer batter shrimp. There are also several different types of schnitzels served with dumplings, red cabbage, and German potato salad.

The staff is dressed in central European costumes with colorful vests and dirndl dresses. "More of Nancy's designs," said John.

One final note: John and Nancy visited both Czechosolvakia and Germany in late fall 1978 in order to get a more intimate feeling of both the culture and cuisine of the regions. Through Jens Deikmann, they visited many of the Romantik Hotels in Germany about which I wrote in *CIBR-Europe*. For them it was also a reunion with several of the German innkeepers who were our guests at a meeting of other *CIBR* innkeepers at Annapolis, Maryland. (See Introduction)

Nancy reported that it was a beautiful trip: "John and I literally ate our way across Central Europe. We got many ideas and made quite a few purchases of things we will use at the inn. We plan to go back as frequently as possible, and invited all of them to come and visit us. It's really wonderful to visit other innkeepers of other countries."

Inspired perhaps by this trip, plans for the restoration of the original front porch, and a Bavarian bar, as well as a Central European butcher and bakery shop, are now under way in this eighty-year-old hotel.

SHUMACHER'S NEW PRAGUE HOTEL, 212 West Main St., New Prague, Mn. 56071; 612-758-2133. (Metro line: 612-445-7285.) A 12-room Czechoslovakian and German inn located in a small country town approximately 35 mi. south of Minneapolis and St. Paul in the verdant Minnesota countryside. European plan. Lunch and dinner served to travelers all year except two days at Christmas. No pets. No entertainment available to amuse children. Good bicycling and backroading nearby; also xc skiing, tennis, and golf. John and Nancy Schumacher, Innkeepers.

Directions: From Minneapolis, take 494 west to 169 south to Jordan exit. Turn south on Rte. 21 for 9 mi. to New Prague. Turn left to Main St. at the stop sign, and the hotel is in the second block on the right.

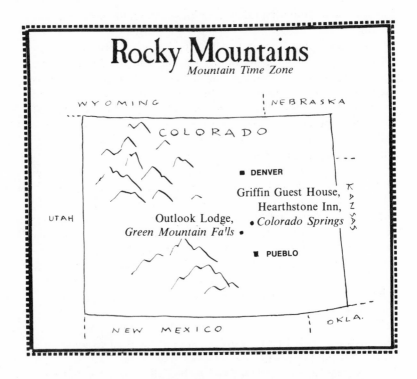

Rocky Mountains
Mountain Time Zone

WYOMING | NEBRASKA

COLORADO

■ DENVER

Griffin Guest House,
Hearthstone Inn,
• *Colorado Springs*

UTAH

Outlook Lodge,
Green Mountain Falls •

KANSAS

■ PUEBLO

NEW MEXICO | OKLA.

Colorado

COLORADO SPRINGS

I'll always be grateful to Dorothy Williams and Ruth Williams, innkeepers of the Hearthstone Inn in Colorado Springs, for convincing me to fly from Hartford one early December weekend to visit this most remarkable community.

I couldn't possibly have imagined the grandeur of the mountains, the bursting cultural borders of Colorado Springs and vicinity, and the wealth of tourist attractions within less than a day's drive in all directions.

Dorothy, Ruth, and I were driving through the Garden of the Gods, which is one of the world's most unusual city parks — a thousand acres of giant red rock formations of various shapes and sizes.

The tour of the Garden of the Gods was just a portion of a very busy and fruitful weekend which just lightly touched the points of interest. We visited the Broadmoor which is a resort complex providing a varied selection of dining, entertainment, and rec-

reational activities, including 18-hole golf courses, tennis courts, indoor ice skating, a ski area, and a concert hall.

We drove out to the Air Force Academy to look at the chapel and planetarium, and visited the Outlook Lodge in Green Mountain Falls, about which I will have more to say a few pages on. We also took in a few of the very attractive shops in downtown Colorado Springs, including the Chinook Bookstore and the Whickerbill Shop.

I asked Dorothy how Colorado Springs came to be. "It was founded by General William Jackson Palmer, the promoter of the Denver and Rio Grande Western Railroad, when he decided in 1871 to make Colorado Springs a railroad terminus.

"Palmer created a proper city of parks, wide tree-shaded streets, a college, schools, churches, and a health resort; but he failed to reckon with the stampede that followed. Miners, gamblers, industrialists, promoters, and camp followers arrived — ironically enough — by railroad.

"Then artists and writers came, because it's such a paintable and free place," said Ruth. "At one time there was more wealth here per capita than any place else in the country. The socialites got art and money, and some of the artists got rich and social. Some of the miners became more cultured and respectable with every nugget they panned."

I asked about Colorado Springs today. "I think it's primarily a young community of people on the move," said Ruth. "It has a relatively high turnover of population, and yet there's a very stable, solid group of people who call themselves natives and are the backbone of the community. Even though it has almost 300,000 people, Colorado Springs has the feel of a very small town. It has some of the arts and culture and things that you find in larger communities, but overall, it is a small town.

"The Fine Arts Center has a resident troupe that performs four or five plays all summer, and they change the art show every two or three weeks," said Ruth, "and, of course, we have our symphony orchestra which celebrated its fiftieth anniversary in 1978.

"We're actually a gateway to the mountains. This is a very casual community in terms of clothing and atmosphere. There are places where you would dress for dinner, but a majority of the activities and places to go in Colorado Springs are very much in the casual, easy-going style.

"The weather is phenomenal. Summer weather is really very nice. We have a few hot days, but most of the homes in Colorado Springs are not air conditioned because they don't need to be.

"As far as winter weather is concerned, I think the people back

East think that Colorado Springs must be under a blanket of snow all winter, which is not true. Of course, we do have snowfalls, but the snow blows off the streets. It's so dry, it's more like powdered sugar; there are probably two or three days in the winter when it's difficult to get around. Maybe there are a half a dozen to ten days in the winter when it's cloudy all day, otherwise, even though it snows, the sun will come out and it will be very clear. Even on cold days, the sun is warm. Good skiers ski in their cut-offs and short sleeves. We're at the base of the Rocky Mountains about two hours from good skiing, and now they have man-made snow at the Broadmoor. Of course there's lots of cross-counrty skiing here, too. Most of the mountain parks have cross-counrty ski trails."

THE HEARTHSTONE INN
Colorado Springs, Colorado

A group of us were having breakfast on Sunday morning at the Hearthstone Inn. Dorothy Williams and Ruth Williams, the Hearthstone innkeepers were there; also Stella Arkell from the Griffin Guest House, and Don and Anna Ahern from the Outlook Lodge in nearby Green Mountain Falls. We were all enjoying a tasty quiche Lorraine and some of the fresh, warm orange-nut bread being served that morning. Since all three of these inns were to be in *Country Inns and Back Roads, 1979,* we already felt a common bond of understanding.

Someone asked Dorothy about the history of the Hearthstone Inn. "Well, the house was built in 1885 by Judson Moss Bemis, a man from Boston," Dorothy recounted. "Mrs. Bemis needed to come to Colorado Springs for the healthful climate, and the family became an important part of the community, making many generous gifts to the city, including the Fine Arts Center and several buildings at Colorado College, three blocks away.

"The architecture of the Hearthstone Inn is Queen Anne, although most people just call it Victorian. After we bought the building in 1977 to renovate it as an inn, we decided to furnish and decorate it as it would have been in 1885. We didn't want a museum-- we wanted a homelike atmosphere for people to enjoy. We are often asked about the exterior colors--three shades of lavender, taupe, peach, and rose on a basically grey building. They are the colors of Victorian inks and dyes seen in turn-of-the-century wallpapers and fabrics. It also helps people find us!" she laughed.

As we were getting up from the table, other guests were sitting down to breakfast and enjoying meeting one another. As we all looked through the inn, we noticed the elegant handcarved beds, brass lighting fixtures, marble top dressers and sinks, and the cheery fireplaces. There are 19th-century paintings and photographs throughout the inn, and a great many of them connect with the early days of Colorado Springs. One is a portrait of Sylvannus Ferris, father of George Ferris, the inventor of the Ferris Wheel, and Dorothy's great-great-grandfather.

Ruth showed us a fascinating scrapbook which graphically traces the progress of the Hearthstone building through the years, including the "before and after" photographs showing Dorothy's and Ruth's alterations.

Our tour of the bedrooms brought a chorus of "oh's and ah's." In various sizes and shapes, they are all true to the Victorian atmosphere, with such names as The Library, The Drawing Room, The Peak View, and the Garden Room. They are reminders of gentler days. Thirteen of the fifteen have their own bathrooms, and all have colorful handmade quilts. "It's just like my grandmother's house," was a frequent comment.

We all remarked on the beautifully cared-for gardens and lawns where there are plantings of pansies, fuchsia, red and pink geraniums, marigolds, and iris. There's a beautiful red maple tree, as well as spruce and elms. The Hearthstone is on one of Colorado Springs' two most beautiful residential streets.

As we all walked out on the sunny front porch, I invited Dorothy to take a ride on the bicycle built for two. "It's great fun," she said, "our guests use it all the time."

The Hearthstone, with its delightful atmosphere, is being run with admirable *esprit* and true concern for guests' comfort and convenience. Although breakfast is the only meal served, both Dorothy and Ruth love good food, and are happy to talk about the restaurants in Colorado Springs.

Mr. Bemis, your house is in good hands once again.

THE HEARTHSTONE INN, 506 N. Cascade Ave., Colorado Springs, Co. 80903; 303-473-4413. A 15-room bed-and-breakfast inn within sight of Pike's Peak, located in the residential section of Colorado Springs. A full breakfast is included in the price of the room; only meal served. Open every day all year. Convenient to spectacular Colorado mountain scenery as well as the Air Force Academy, Garden of the Gods, Cave of the Winds, the McAllister House Museum, Fine Arts Center and Broadmoor Resort. Golf, tennis, swimming, hiking, backroading nearby. Check innkeepers for pet policy. Dorothy Williams and Ruth William, Innkeepers.

Directions: From I-25 (the major North/South Hwy.) use Exit 143 (Unitah St.) travel east (opposite direction from mountains) to third stop light. (Cascade Ave.) Turn right for 7 blocks. The inn will be on the right at the corner of St. Vrain and Cascade. A big Victorian house, grey with lilac trim.

THE GRIFFIN GUEST HOUSE
Colorado Springs, Colorado

Stella Arkell and I were having a proper English tea in the parlor of the Griffin Guest House when I admired the beautiful English tea set. She replied, "I brought a great many things from England which I think make the place very homey, don't you think so?" Since I had already recognized many English touches in this Colorado Springs bed-and-breakfast inn, including a very handsome dining room set with carved-back chairs, I readily agreed.

"Oh course, as you can see, I'm really British myself, and I kept an inn in Torbay, South Devon for many years. Over there we started as a bed-and-breakfast and it became a hotel and supper club."

Stella, a very vivacious, attractive woman, already quite active in the rather extensive British community in Colorado Springs, continued enthusiastically, "I think we are really quite British," she asserted, "we serve fresh-squeezed orange juice, homemade zucchini and pumpkin breads in the morning, and tea served in the traditional English way, not in tea bags. We British are very plant-minded and you've probably noticed we have many, many plants throughout our

little place, including the lodging rooms and even the bathrooms.

"My daughter Tricia who lives nearby, discovered this place, and after a lot of transatlantic telephoning and long letters, I came for a visit and we decided to open a 'bed-and-breakfast.'"

"The house, I think, is particularly adaptable beacause we love a fireplace in the living room and this warm oak woodwork reminds me of my home. We've set up chess and backgammon games and I see you've already been reading our English newspapers and magazines. It's interesting, we're so far away from England, and yet our guests love them.

"We decided to call it 'The Griffin Guest House' in honor of my late husband who was Welsh. We selected as a logo, the griffin, which is a mythical Welsh dragon. Usually griffins look fierce, but we have a smiling griffin."

Most of the bedroom accommodations are two-room suites done in oak and mahogany. Some have four-poster beds and fireplaces. There are trays of chocolate kisses, and many flowers and plants. "We try to pamper people as much as we can," she said.

The Griffin Guest House is on a boulevard street in a residential area. There's a little white fence around it and an antique sleigh in the front yard. A broad front porch with lots of comfortable furniture and a resident English cat finish off the picture of hospitality. There are a total of nine bedrooms, one of them with a private shower. The other eight share a bath down the hall.

"There's one thing I really miss very much," Stella said, as she poured me a second cup of tea, "and that is Devonshire clotted cream. Wouldn't that be just perfect for scones and jam in the afternoon?" Remembering my own experiences in Devon and Cornwall at those famous creamed teas, I agreed enthusiastically.

THE GRIFFIN GUEST HOUSE, 1414 No. Nevada Ave., Colorado Springs, Colo. 80907; 303-635-8819. A 9-room bed-and-breakfast inn on a very quiet residential street in Colorado Springs, readily adjacent to Colorado College, the Air Force Academy, the Broadmoor, Pike's Peak, Manitou and the Garden of the Gods. Breakfast is the only meal served. Open every day of the year. No pets. Stella Arkell and Tricia Ludt, Innkeepers.

Directions: Use Exit 143 from I-25. Proceed on Unitah Street to Nevada Ave. and turn left. Griffin House is on the left side of the street.

THE OUTLOOK LODGE
Green Mountain Falls, Colorado

"This is a rather historical bathroom because it was supposedly the first one in Green Mountain Falls and people would line up to pay fifty cents to take a bath!"

Don and Anna Ahern were showing me through the Outlook Lodge and we were now on the second floor. There were four lodging rooms, including one called the Tree House which has a little sitting room. Don explained that guests lying in bed can see the sun coming up over the mountains.

"We call ourselves country Victorian," said Anna, "We do a few things that are a little different. For example, if guests leave their shoes outside the door before 10 p.m., they'll find them shined when they wake up in the morning. I'll bet you don't find many inns in your book that do that, do you?"

"The fact is that nostalgia is a very heavy theme here," said Don, who is an instructor in English at the nearby Air Force Academy. "We try to entertain our guests in the old-fashioned ways with plenty of opportunity to sit around the table and talk, and even roast marshmallows over the fire."

We wended our way back downstairs to the sitting rooms where Anna pointed to a piano. "Impy, Don's mother, plays and Don holds forth on the guitar," she said. "We've got tons of sheet music and guests love to gather around and have informal sing-alongs. I'm sorry Impy isn't here right now because she is very much a part of what Outlook Lodge is all about."

"Yes," explained Don, "after my father retired, she got a degree in creative writing from Arizona and writes both fiction and non-

fiction. She was the one that wrote you about us in the first place."

The dining room has an adjoining kitchen with an old propane oven. "One of the other things that makes us popular is the fact that our guests have refrigerator and stove privileges. It's a sort of old mountain custom that for the most part has died out, but we think it's important. Lots of people prepare their own dinner in our kitchen and then remain here for the evening. You know Impy is a great mixer and many guests have made lots of new friends while they were staying with us."

Outlook Lodge is literally on the lower slopes of Pike's Peak. It's only eight miles from Colorado Springs, but worlds apart in a great many other ways. The village is located at an altitude of almost 8,000 feet and dates from the 1880s. The inn is located next to the historic "Church in the Wildwood," although I'm not certain there's any connection to the hymn of the same name. In other days, the Lodge was a parsonage for the church. It consists of two buildings with a total of twelve rooms. Lodgings include a complimentary Continental breakfast which features homemade breads, such as cranberry and banana-nut, and squash bread and gumdrop bread.

Besides all of the nostalgia and the really homelike feeling, the Outlook Lodge is also very convenient to a really awesome collection of sightseeing opportunities during all seasons of the year. Those that come readily to my mind are Pike's Peak, the Cog Railway which runs to the top, the old gold mining town of Cripple Creek, and the Air Force Academy. Energetic guests can go horseback riding or hiking; enjoy tennis, swimming or other vigorous pursuits. The backroads have magnificent pine-scented views of the impressive mountain scenery. Colorado Springs with its many restaurants, its theater, and symphony concerts, and the Broadmoor with all of its activities, is just a few miles away.

"Outlook is close to big city entertainment and yet very much a part of the Rockies . . . rustic and homelike," concluded Don. "In fact, eight of our twelve rooms have shared baths. However, one thing has changed: We don't charge fifty cents anymore for the use of the historic bathtub!"

OUTLOOK LODGE, 6975 Howard, Green Mountain Falls, Colo. 80819; 303-684-2303. A 12-room rustic lodge on the slopes of Pike's Peak, 8 mi. from Colorado Springs. Immediately adjacent to all the copious mountain recreational activities as well as the U.S. Air Force Academy; Colorado Springs Fine Arts Center; Cripple Creek Gold Camp. European plan. All lodgings include Continental breakfast. No other meals served. 8 rooms with shared baths. Open from June 1st through Labor Day weekend. Tennis, swimming, horseback riding, hiking, backroading, all nearby. Don, Anna, and Impy Ahern, Innkeepers.

Directions: Green Mountain Falls is 8 mi. west of Colorado Springs on U.S. 24. Outlook Lodge is located next to the historic Church in the Wildwood.

Oak Bay Beach Hotel, *Victoria, British Columbia*

James House,

The Farmhouse, Captain Whidbey, *Coupeville*

Port Townsend

■ SEATTLE

Lake Quinault Lodge, *Quinault*

WASHINGTON

Far
West

Pacific Time Zone

Partridge Inn, *Underwood*

■ PORTLAND

● Benbow Inn,
Garberville

ARIZONA

● Heritage House, *Little River*
● Harbor House, *Elk*

Rancho de los Caballeros,
● *Wickenburg*

Wine Country Inn,
St. Helena ■ SACRAMENTO

■ PHOENIX

Sutter Creek Inn, *Sutter Creek*

SAN FRANCISCO ■

Lodge on the Desert,
Tanque Verde,
● *Tucson*

Bed and Breakfast Inn, *San Francisco*

Normandy Inn,
Vagabond House,
Rosita Lodge, *Carmel*

ORNIA

Ojai Valley Inn, *Ojai*

LOS ANGELES ■

The Inn, *Rancho Santa Fe*

■ SAN DIEGO

Arizona

TANQUE VERDE
Tucson, Arizona

"This is now the third time I have been to this ranch and I have talked to Herr Cote and am making reservations to return for the fourth time next March."

Guests returning to Tanque Verde for the fourth time are not particularly unusual, but this guest happened to be from Nuremburg, Germany. He explained that he stayed two days the first time, five days on the second visit, a week on the third, and in the spring was coming back for three weeks. "My wife and I, we just love it, and each time we bring some more friends, also."

We were in the cottonwood grove enjoying the weekly steak roast, which is one of the many opportunities that guests have to get together during their vacations at this historic guest ranch. In the background, I could hear a man playing a guitar, his pleasant voice lamenting the loss of his sweetheart to a man on a black horse who "carried her away." The big fire around which many guests were seated, gave off its friendly warm light and there was the compelling aroma of grilled steaks, succulent ranch beans, and coffee.

I talked with Crystal Puschak, who was a tour leader for a group of Europeans who were stopping at Tanque Verde on a swing through the West. "This is about the sixth time that I have visited here," she said. "It is by far one of our most popular stops. For one thing, my German and Swiss groups are thrilled to see the unusual desert country and the spectacular sunsets and scenery. They get into desert horseback riding immediately, and they particularly enjoy the breakfast rides, and watching the sun come up. It's a such a thrill to ride up through the desert to the mountain knowing there is a delicious breakfast of flapjacks, bacon, and hot coffee waiting."

Actually, in the many years that I have been coming to Tanque Verde, this was the first time that I've visited during the summer, and I was surprised at the number of guests from Europe. When I mentioned this to innkeeper Bob Cote, he said, "During July and August we have so many guests speaking so many different languages we could almost advertise it as a good place for children to get some tutoring in French and German. The small tour groups from Europe seem to come mostly in the summertime. During the winter we have a continual stream of Americans and Canadians with their children. Children especially take to ranch life, and it's a fact of life that kids and horses get along like two peas in a pod."

Tanque Verde has a one-hundred-year-old history as one of Arizona's pioneer guest cattle ranches, and even has stories about Indian raids. It is set back in a sunny circle of mountains about a thirty-minute drive from downtown Tucson and the airport. The predominant activity has always been horsebacking riding in the desert. However in recent years, four tennis courts, a complete indoor health spa, a fully automated exercise room, and an indoor swimming pool, have been added for guests' enjoyment.

Accommodations are in almost luxurious individual *casitas,* all of which have their own Spanish-style corner fireplaces.

Everyone eats at long tables in the vaulted dining room, and there's nothing like the desert air to encourage big appetites.

My new German friend summed up his and my feelings about Tanque Verde very well. "It has what we Germans call *gemütlichkeit!"*

TANQUE VERDE RANCH, Box 66, Rte. 8, Tucson, Ariz. 85710; 602-296-6275. A 65-room ranch-inn, 10 mi. from Tucson. American plan. Breakfast, lunch, and dinner served to travelers by reservation. Open year-round. Riding, indoor and outdoor pool, tennis, sauna, exercise room, and whirlpool bath on grounds. Robert and Dee Dee Cote, Innkeepers.

Directions: From U.S. 10, exit at Speedway Blvd. and travel east to dead end.

THE LODGE ON THE DESERT
Tucson, Arizona

The slanting rays of the western sun, providing spectacular backlighting for the great banks of clouds which seemed to skim the jagged peaks of the Santa Catalina Mountains, streamed through the casement window and lit up the interior of my spacious studio bedroom at the Lodge on the Desert.

Even though the afternoon temperature in September reached 85, I knew that later that evening I would want a fire in my fireplace to ease the chill of the cool desert night.

My bedroom was really most impressive, with three windows on two sides and a patio facing north. The two double beds had rich bedspreads that complemented the orange curtains, and an armful of freshly picked flowers lent an air of gaiety to the dark tones of the

carved wooden tables and chests. The full-sized closet reminded me that many people came here to spend weeks at a time, enjoying the benefits of a friendly climate in both summer and winter, plus the many opportunities for outdoor recreation, as well as the pursuit of the arts.

Tucson is one of the most sophisticated cities in the Southwest with many fine homes and good shops in the downtown area. The University of Arizona is an active cultural center with a continuing program of music, drama, and art and craft exhibitions.

"My father built the Lodge on the Desert outside Tucson in 1936," explained Schuyler Lininger, the *patron grande* of this resort inn. (I found that in the Southwest innkeepers adopted this rather impressive Spanish title.) "Now the city has grown up around us; fortunately, we have no tall buildings to disrupt our guests' view of the mountains, and yet we are set apart by the hedges around the property. However, many of our guests find nearness to the center of things in the city most desirable, even though it seems we are way out in the country."

Here in the Southwest desert during the outdoor weather everybody gathers around the swimming pool, and here is where many conversations and lasting friendships start.

For cooler days, the Lodge has a very spacious and inviting living room with lots of books which guests are free to take to their rooms, a chess game, a jigsaw puzzle, and many opportunities just to sit and relax.

The lodging rooms of the inn have been designed after the manner of Pueblo Indian farmhouses, the beige adobe color frequently relieved by very colorful Mexican tiles.

Although the dining room features many dishes of the Southwest, I found there were also such favorites as Chateaubriande for two, roast rack of lamb, and several veal dishes. Schuyler explained that he and Helen have gone to great lengths to bring milk-fed Wisconsin veal to the table in different versions. Incidentally, one of the most popular features of the inn is breakfast served on the guest room patios in the beautiful early morning sunshine.

I believe another guest succinctly summed up my feelings about the Lodge on the Desert while we were both taking advantage of that bright September sun to get a few more degrees of tan.

"What I like about it here," she said, "is the really endless variety of things that are going on in Tucson—the Art Center, the many different theaters, the new museum, the exhibition of Indian arts, the opera company, the ballet, the Tucson Symphony, the golf courses, the racetrack and all kinds of sports events—it's so *civilized!*"

THE LODGE ON THE DESERT, 306 N. Alvernon Way, Tucson, Ariz. 85733; 602-325-3366. A 35-room luxury inn within the city limits. Near several historic, cultural, and recreational attractions. American and European plans available in winter; European plan in summer. Breakfast, lunch, and dinner served to travelers every day of the year. Attended, leashed pets allowed. Swimming pool and lawn games on grounds. Tennis and golf nearby. Schuyler and Helen Lininger, Innkeepers.

Directions: Take Speedway exit from I-10. Travel about 5 mi. east to Alvernon Way, turn right (south) onto Alvernon (¾ mi.). Lodge is on left side between 5th St. and Broadway.

RANCHO de los CABALLEROS
Wickenburg, Arizona

I found myself with an interesting group, among which was a gentleman and his wife from Illinois who had been coming to the Rancho for at least ten years. They had become so attached to the high desert country in Wickenburg that, during the previous year, they had purchased one of the beautiful houses adjacent to the ranch property and were now part-time residents. Sometime during the last two or three years, they had met a second couple also staying at the ranch and found that they all liked tennis. This was actually a reunion for them.

We were all sitting in the lounge overlooking the tennis courts, swimming pool, and the Bradshaw Mountains, which seemed no farther than 25 miles distant in the clear air. I was surprised to learn that they were at least 50 miles away! The sun was going down behind Vulture Peak, and the convolutions and gradations of the mountains across the valley were constantly changing until they melted into one black silhouette against the night sky.

More people joined our circle and we talked about the day's activities. The newcomers who had been out on one of the trail rides were being kidded about feeling a bit stiff. The "old hands" enjoying their third or fourth day were comparing the personalities of the different horses. All of this "horsey" talk caused me to change my mind, and instead of more tennis the next morning, I told the head wrangler that I would be on the slow ride, at ten o'clock.

Rancho de los Caballeros is a most impressive ranch-inn. A great deal of care is taken with plantings, gardens, and lawns around the main house and the beautiful cacti and trees are filled with birds (at least 45 varieties), particularly in early morning.

The decor and furnishings are those of a luxurious, large *hacienda* and the individual lodgings are all done in an Arizona-Indian motif.

Many families have been returning for years, and there is a children's counselor to keep young people entertained. I'm always amazed at how the children take immediately to ranch life. They are the first ones out and the last to come in.

Our little group broke up in order to be ready for dinner. We arranged for a large table to accommodate all of us, and it looked like it would be another fine evening at the Rancho de los Caballeros.

RANCHO de los CABALLEROS, Wickenburg, Ariz. 85358; 602-684-5484. A luxury 62-room ranch-resort, 60 mi. north of Phoenix in the sunny dry desert. American plan. Rooms with private baths. A few with shared baths. Breakfast, lunch, and dinner served to travelers daily. Open from mid-October to early May. No pets. Pool, corral of 75 horses, hiking, skeet shooting, airstrip, putting, tennis on grounds. Golf nearby. Dallas Gant, Jr., Innkeeper.

Directions: Rtes. 60, 89, and 93 bring you to Wickenburg. Ranch is 2 mi. west of town on Rte. 60 and 2 mi. south on Vulture Mine Road.

California

HOW I FINALLY CAME TO LEAVE MY HEART IN SAN FRANCISCO

To me, San Francisco is one of the most livable cities in the world. I place it right up there with London, Stockholm, and Boston. It runs counter to the old comment, "It's a great place to visit, but I wouldn't want to live there." Many people have gone to San Francisco on a visit and stayed to make it their permanent home. Another thing, it's difficult to synthesize all of its qualities into a simple statement. Maybe Tony Bennett says it all.

Before I share my adventures in finding the Bed and Breakfast Inn, let me explain that a number of years ago, in response to requests from readers, I began to include a few "country inns in the city" in this book. I began by seeking out the antithesis of the usual big city hotel—the commerical slickness which makes no allowance for personal service and hospitality. Of necessity, these would all have to be rather small in comparison to the conventional city hotel.

In many visits to San Francisco, I just couldn't seem to find the right combination of size and personal involvement. There are some splendid hotels there, but I couldn't match them up with the Hotel Algonquin in New York, the Brazilian Court in Palm Beach, or the Maryland Inn in Annapolis. However, finally, with the guidance of CIBR innkeepers in California, I found - not a hotel - but a European pension.

THE BED AND BREAKFAST INN
San Francisco, California

It was a wonderfully warm morning in mid-September. The sun shone down from a completely cloudless sky, and happy San Franciscans moved briskly up and down the many hills of the city pursuing the day's occupations—the kind of a day in which I knew everything would go right, and it did.

I had walked a few blocks on Union Street, then turned on Charlton Court, and I was standing in front of one of San Francisco's Victorian houses, painted light green; wooden stairs ascended the

316

front of the building to the very top floor. There were beautiful golden marigolds in boxes and pots placed around the porches, and a birdhouse with a very chipper occupant. The sign said, "The Bed and Breakfast Inn."

The reception room apparently was used as one of the breakfast areas. It had a very light and airy feeling, enhanced by white wicker furniture, many flower arrangements, and light touches everywhere. The enticing aroma of fresh coffee filled the room, and some guests were just finishing delicious-looking croissants.

There followed in delightful order my first meeting with Marily Kavanaugh and her husband, Bob; a tour of all of the eight rooms in the inn; a leisurely chat on the garden deck, and a wonderful realization that I had at last found my country inn in San Francisco!

First the lodging rooms: some of them are named after various parts of London. There's Covent Garden, Chelsea, Green Park, and Kensington Garden. Other rooms are called the Library, Autumn Sun, the Willows, Mandalay, and the Celebration. When I was there, Bob and Marily were moving out of their apartment on the top floor, which was soon to be available for guests.

Each room provides an entirely different experience. For example, many have completely different sets of sheets, pillowcases, and towels. There are all varieties of beds from those with carved Victorian headboards to traditional shiny brass bedsteads. There are flowers everywhere, thermos jugs of ice-water, many books, baskets of fruit, an electric clock with an alarm, down pillows and gorgeous coverlets and spreads. Three of the bedrooms have their own bathrooms, and the others share. Three rooms have the garden view. I saw old-fashioned British ceiling fans in some of the rooms. "They're hard to find outside of Bombay," said Marily.

I liked the Kavanaughs immediately. Originally, they were from southern California where Bob was in building and real estate. "All of our lives," he said, "we wanted to live in San Francisco." Marily continued, "So, when the children grew up, we decided to combine our interests and talents and come to San Francisco and open up a small inn. We looked around a long time for just the right place, and I'm happy to say we found it."

The location of the Bed and Breakfast is another virtue. Charlton Court is a little dead end street off Union, between Buchanan and Laguna. It's within easy walking distance of Fisherman's Wharf. In fact, San Francisco is such a "walking place" that it's convenient to everything. The nicest part of it is that when people get tired of walking, they can always take the cable cars!

Marily and Bob are very proud and happy to be located in San Francisco, and they take great pleasure in providing guests with information about all of the things to do and restaurants to visit. However, one of their guests had this word of admonition for me: "You'd better warn your readers to reserve a room here as far ahead as possible."

THE BED AND BREAKFAST INN, Four Charlton Court, San Francisco, Ca. 94123; 415-921-9784. An 8-room European-style pension in downtown San Francisco. Convenient to all of the Bay area recreational, cultural, and gustatory attractions. Continental breakfast is the only meal offered. Open daily except late December and early January. Not comfortable for small children. No pets. Robert and Marily Kavanaugh, Innkeepers.

Directions: Take the Van Ness Exit from route 101 and proceed to Union Street. Turn left on Laguna. Charlton Court is a small courtyard street halfway between Laguna and Buchanan, off Union.

BENBOW INN
Garberville, California

This is the intriguing story of two California inns and their innkeepers: the Benbow in the magnificent redwood country of northern California, and the Vagabond House in Carmel.

The two inns are a study in contrasts. That's what makes this true story so fascinating. When I first visited Chuck and Patsy Watts at the Vagabond House in Carmel a few years ago, it seemed to be the perfect setting for their quiet diversions. They are both avid collectors of antiques: Chuck repairs old clocks along with his many other mechanical interests; and Patsy is a needlework fanatic.

However, I reckoned without one of their other great passions: their love of traveling and visiting country inns. It was on such a journey that they first visited the Benbow Inn in Garberville, and the hidden embers of more involved innkeeping became a blazing fire. In May 1978, I learned that Chuck and Patsy Watts had literally exchanged inns with Dennis Levett, who was one of the owners of the Benbow Inn! (For Dennis' story see the section on the Vagabond House.)

"But there's such a marked difference," I said to Chuck and Patsy as we were having dinner at the Benbow, "the Vagabond House is a small, cozy, bed-and-breakfast inn and here's the Benbow with 70 rooms serving three meals a day, and the two of you up to your necks in plans to redecorate rooms, plant new gardens, lay new carpets, paint and wallpaper, plan tennis courts, and even re-route the driveway . . . not to mention an elevator and a new library."

"That's exactly the fascinating part of innkeeping," said Chuck.

"We loved the Vagabond House, but as soon as we saw the Benbow, we knew that we were traditional-style innkeepers. We revel in the new responsibility, the fun of making out new menus, of dealing with much larger problems—and we are crazy about this great wonderful redwood country with its wild beauty and magnificent scenery."

"Yes," chimed in Patsy, "I wake up in the morning and can hardly wait to get the day started. We've enjoyed every minute of it, even though it's been a tremendous demand on our time and energy."

The Benbow was designed and built in the early 1920s by Albert Farr, a well-known San Francisco architect. The Tudor style was enjoying a very popular revival during those years, and the inn has furnishings that are reminiscent of those times, along with stonework and carved wood that is virtually impossible to duplicate today.

In one corner of the unusually large living room lobby there is a chess set which is often in use. A bright fire burns in the fireplace and there is a display of beautiful candles on either side of the mantel, while above it hangs an oil painting of the inn in the earlier days. Big comfortable chairs and sofas are arranged in various corners. Many of the clocks on the walls are part of Chuck's collection. The library tables have, in addition to picture books, lots of magazines.

"Ambitious" is the word that came to mind as I walked about the grounds with Chuck and Patsy, and we discussed all the changes which are a part of an ongoing program. "We think the inn stands on its own," said Patsy, "but we have some exciting ideas for the future. One of the big changes is that we are going to stay open from March 15 to December 1. We've also put in a new heating system."

Chuck and Patsy's many friends and guests will be happy to know that there is one irreplaceable member of the Vagabond House team who is having a simply wonderful time in making new friends every day at the Benbow. That's Muffin, the gorgeous blonde afghan hound, who has exchanged the long runs on Carmel Beach for equally rewarding romps in the invigorating air of the pine forests of northern California.

BENBOW INN, 2675 Benbow Drive, Garberville, Ca. 95440; 707-923-2124. A 70-room English Tudor inn in the redwood country of northern California. On Rte. 101 near the Benbow State Park. European plan. Breakfast, lunch, and dinner served to travelers daily. Open March 15 to Dec. 1. Swimming on grounds; golf adjacent. Hiking, magnificent backroading, and tennis nearby. Chuck, Patsy, and Muffin Watts, Innkeepers.

Directions: From San Francisco follow Rte. 101 north 200 mi. and exit at Benbow.

HARBOR HOUSE
Elk, California

Jane Way, Nora McNab, Dennis Levett, and I were breakfasting in the dining room at the Harbor House which has a spectacular view of the Pacific Ocean.

As Patricia Corcoran, the attractive innkeeper of the inn, joined us for a cup of coffee, Dennis, the enthusiastic innkeeper of the

Vagabond House in Carmel, stood up and led us in a round of applause for her hospitality and, as he said, "This delightful breakfast."

The Harbor House was built in 1916 by a lumber company as an executive residence. The construction was entirely of redwood taken from nearby forests. It is an enlarged replica of the redwood Model House at the 1915 Pan American Exposition. Four of the five rooms of the inn have fireplaces and there are four additional cottages on the south side, all with private baths.

My room in one of the cottages had a four-poster bed, an old-fashioned cast-iron stove, and a collection of attractive water colors. I could walk right out on the deck and have an unobstructed view of the massive rock formations with their tunnels which extend out into the blue ocean.

The inn is located on a bluff overlooking Greenwood Landing, once a busy port for lumber schooners plying the Mendocino coast. The inn is operated on the modified American plan; the rates include dinner and breakfast.

The hand-carved and hand-fitted redwood ceiling and wall in the living room were coated with hot beeswax in 1916. The process preserved the quality and color of the wood for over sixty years.

Guests enjoy ocean swimming, abalone and shell hunting, fishing, hiking, biking, and some beautiful backroading along the coast and in the forest.

"We've had a simply wonderful year," said Pat. "We repapered the dining room and collected all of the antique oak chairs. Don't you think they go well with our turn-of-the-century feeling?"

Nora McNab, who is both the owner and the cook at the Partridge Inn in Washington asked Patricia about some of the dinner specialties. "We have fresh broiled salmon most of the time, as well as fresh vegetables from our garden a great many weeks of the year," Pat said. "We also have unusual things like Iberian pork chops and an unusual recipe for Moroccan chicken. Our guests seem to enjoy our homemade soups like broccoli and mushroom. I guess one of the things we're best known for is mocha coffee pie and a Bavarian layered dessert. We make all of our breads and rolls right here."

Jane Way from the Sutter Creek Inn remarked that she had gone for an early walk down to the beach which is sort of tucked away under the cliff in front of Harbor House. "I loved the feeling of seclusion," she said.

"We added redwood steps to the last thirty or forty feet down to the beach," explained Pat. "I am putting some natural wood benches on the path which will provide different viewpoints."

By this time we had all finished our eggs Benedict and were

settling in to talk about our favorite subject: country innkeeping. Dennis drew me to one side and said, "Isn't that view absolutely unbelievable? I'm finding this such a restful experience that I've decided to stay one more night and just settle down in the sun on the terrace and watch the sea and listen to the sea birds."

For all I know, he may still be there, and who could blame him?

HARBOR HOUSE BY THE SEA, Hwy. #1, Elk, Ca. 95432; 707-877-3203. An 8-room seaside inn, 16 mi. south of Mendocino, overlooking the Pacific. Modified American plan omits lunch. Breakfast and dinner to houseguests served daily. Open year-round. Ocean swimming, abalone and shell hunting, fishing, and hiking on grounds. Biking, boating, deep sea fishing, golf, canoeing nearby. Patricia Corcoran, Innkeeper.

Directions: Take Rte. 128 from I-101 to Coast. Turn south on Hwy. #1, 6 mi. to Harbor House.

HERITAGE HOUSE
Little River, California

"To Don and Hazel Dennen, the deans of northern California innkeeping!"

We all rose as one, glasses raised high, and Don Dennen, the innkeeper of Heritage House, modestly raised his hand acknowledging the well-deserved compliments from other innkeepers who had gathered here for a day of good conversation and exchange of ideas and a lovely dinner at this truly original inn on the spectacular northern California coast.

"It doesn't seem possible that it was 1949 when Hazel and I came through here, saw the location and remembered that the farmhouse was built in 1877 by my grandfather, John Dennen. We decided to open a quiet country inn. Actually the arrangements were made within an hour. In just a few months, we built the first guest cottages."

"Well, I'm certainly glad you did," said Jane Way of the Sutter Creek Inn. "I'm sure you remember the day I came up here and you encouraged me to open my inn over in the gold country."

Patricia Corcoran from nearby Harbor House in Elk, chimed in, "I don't think we could have made it if it hadn't been for Don and Hazel. They were tremendously encouraging."

Jim Smith from the Wine Country Inn in St. Helena said, "I know that my mother and father came here many times to talk to the Dennens about innkeeping. This is my first visit, but I've never seen anything quite like it."

That particular comment, "I've never seen anything quite like it," is typical of the compliments that I receive in great numbers from readers who visit Heritage House. Here's an excerpt from a lady who had been using *CIBR* to tour California: "We drove to Heritage House which is just a lovely dream. The chicken tarragon and corned beef with ginger glaze was incredible. We stayed in one of the little cottages you mentioned back in the 1971 edition, because it was on a point overlooking both the inlet and the ocean. We set our alarm so we would be sure to see the sunrise."

"Oh, I believe I remember them," said Hazel Dennen, her eyes lighting up with a nice smile. "They sent us a long letter and said they were going to write you."

The Heritage House is about a three-hour drive up the coast from San Francisco. Although there are a few guests' rooms in the main building, most of the accommodations are in the cottages tucked unobtrusively into the landscape with an unobstructed view of the ocean. They have names inspired by early-day buildings of the area. For example, "Scott's Opera House" was the center of entertainment on the coast with traveling minstrel shows and, later, a hand-cranked moving picture operation. It was moved to its present location over looking the ocean. Other cottages are named "Country Store," "Bonnet Shop," "Ice Cream Parlor," "Barber Pole," "Stable," and the like. Most of the furnishings have come from the area.

"We never advertise," said Don. "All of our guests come to us because some former guest has recommended us. Frankly, we like it that way, because the place attracts the kind of people we like and many of them have become warm friends. We keep our atmosphere informal and relaxed. We don't arrange any games or activities, because we feel our guests would prefer not to be regimented. There are numerous walks along the beaches and through the forest, and we can provide our guests with ample information about circle tours along the coast and into the great redwoods."

He smiled, pulled on his earlobe, then with a twinkle in his eye said, "I can honestly say, I have never known a guest to be bored."

HERITAGE HOUSE, Little River, Ca. 95456; 707-937-5885. An elegant oceanside inn with 52 accommodations on Coast Highway #1, 144 mi. north of San Francisco, 6 mi. south of Mendocino. Modified American plan omits lunch. Breakfast and dinner served to travelers daily by reservation. Open from February through November. Don Dennen, Innkeeper.

Directions: From San Francisco (a 3-hr. drive); follow Rte. 101 to Cloverdale then Rte. 128 to Coast Highway #1. Inn is 5 mi. north of this junction on Hwy. #1.

NORMANDY INN
Carmel, California

A few weeks before this edition went to press I was looking through some photographs that Jim Mellow had taken of the Normandy Inn when he stayed there a few years ago.

The first one showed the front entrance to the inn and that marvelous old tree that twists around like a boa constrictor.

The next one had the inner court, with the patio of fitted flat stone, and the second-floor gallery. The third photograph took me right back to a sunny afternoon I had spent around the swimming pool, which is in the rear of the inn in a little sylvan hideaway.

It was an interesting coincidence that I ran across a letter from a man in Atlanta. "Having twice benefited from your recommendations, I wanted to write and inform you how much my wife and I enjoyed the Whitehall Inn in Camden, Maine, and the Normandy Inn in Carmel.

"To our delight, your description of the Normandy Inn was most accurate. Rarely before have we been so absolutely charmed by an inn, especially our quarters—a twin-bedded square room with a fireplace, a vaulted ceiling, and an ocean view over the courtyard. The Continental breakfast was not only tasty but plentiful. The

Sunday papers on the table were a nice treat. At the front desk the people were cheerful and helpful in suggesting a good restaurant in Monterey."

The Normandy Inn is the symbol of gracious living conceived by its owners, architect Robert Stanton and decorator Virginia Stanton, who was party editor for *House Beautiful* a few years ago. Everything has been done with taste and comfort in mind—such as oversized twin, and extra-long, beds with down-filled pillows. Some of the bathrooms are particularly spacious and some suites have dressing rooms and fireplaces. The scenery, nearby ocean beaches, Carmel shops, and the famous golf courses, attract visitors to the Monterey penisula throughout every month of the year. I personally prefer to visit from October through April when the pace is a little slower. However, whenever I visit Carmel, it's always a delight to return to the quiet elegance of the Normandy Inn.

NORMANDY INN, Carmel, Ca. 93921; 408-624-3825. A 48-room French Provincial inn in the heart of Carmel, on Ocean Ave. between Monteverde and Casanova. Within walking distance of beach, shops, and restaurants and near Point Lobos State Park. European plan includes Continental breakfast served to inn guests only. No other meals served. Open year-round. No pets. Tennis, golf, fishing, bicycles nearby. Mike Stanton, Innkeeper.

Directions: Follow Rte. 101 to Salinas, then Rte. 68 into Monterey peninsula. Or, follow Coast Hwy. # 1 which travels through Carmel.

OJAI VALLEY INN
Ojai, California

It was early March in Ojai, which is springtime in southern California. The robins were nesting in the oak trees. The plantings on the patio of the Ojai Valley Inn were in early bloom, and the golf course and tennis courts were in readiness. The putting green had already been swept free of the dew, and the air was so clear and dry I felt as though I could drive every green or ace every serve.

The native Indians named this sunny valley, which is pronounced "o-hi." It means "the nest." It is most aptly named, for it sits in the center of a vast amphitheater of towering mountains. These mountains create an ideal climate year-round, and I understand that the average summer temperature is between 70 and 90 degrees. Winter daytime temperatures range from 60 to 85 degrees. There is no fog or smog or dampness because everything is 1000 feet up in the dry, invigorating air. The days are warm and brillliant with sunshine and the nights are cool. I've slept under a blanket even after the warmest days.

This inn is one of the very few American resorts where guests can enjoy the four major outdoor playtime activities—golf, tennis, riding, and swimming throughout the year.

The championship golf course, designed by Billy Bell, is 6,800 yards. "Tricky, but fair" is one description. There's a heated swimming pool with cabañas and terraces for sun bathing, and luncheon and refreshments are served at poolside. There are hundreds of miles of riding trails in the mountains, valleys, and canyons surrounding Ojai. Horses are available at the inn stable. The tennis pro is always glad to arrange games, and I've already made quite a few tennis friends among the regular residents of this attractive town.

One other important feature that delights me at this inn is the playground for children and other possibilities for their having fun; and babysitters can be arranged.

The architecture of Ojai Valley Inn is in Spanish mission style. It is surrounded by beautiful oaks, evergreens, eucalyptus and an occasional palm tree. There are more varieties of birds than I could possibly count.

Innkeeper Bill Briggs, a Massachusetts native who has been here at the inn for many, many years explained that because of its many sporting and recreational facilities, the inn is now quite popular for business meetings and small conventions.

The Ojai Valley Inn is somewhat larger than the average inn listed in *CIBR*. I first visited in the late 1960s, and on each visit since I have found it to be a very pleasurable resort experience, where there are certain obvious dress requirements such as gentlemen wearing jackets and ties for dinner. However, there is no attempt "to put on airs." It's the most natural thing in the world to dress for dinner here and ladies wearing long gowns like the party feeling.

Golfers were already getting ready for the morning round. As two of them passed on their way to the first tee, I heard one say, "Do you realize that we're only an hour and a half from L.A.?"

OJAI VALLEY INN & COUNTRY CLUB, Ojai, Ca. 93023; 805-646-5511. A 100-room resort-inn with its own championship golf course, 12 mi. northeast of Ventura on U.S. 33. American plan. Breakfast, lunch, and dinner served to travelers daily. Open year-round. No pets. Tennis, riding, heated pool, golf, and bicycles on the grounds. Bill Briggs, Innkeeper.

Directions: From the Ventura Freeway, exit at Hwy. 33.

THE ROSITA LODGE
Carmel-by-the-Sea, California

"What we've really been concerned about for the last three years is making the Rosita a really special place." Jeff Stanford leaned forward in his chair and it was evident that he was a very enthusiastic person. "I think that our close friendship with Chuck and Patsy Watts brought much assistance and advice in those early days," asserted his wife Joan. "When we came to Carmel, they were most encouraging. When they sold the Vagabond House and moved to the Benbow Inn, at first we felt devastated, but now we have new friends in Dennis Levett and Julie Brown, the new owners of the Vagabond. In fact, we're all having dinner together tonight."

Jeff, Joan, and I were seated on the wooden deck in a corner of the garden of Rosita Lodge; we were literally surrounded by fuchsia, begonias, bougainvillaea, jasmine, cyclamen, azaleas, camellias, and rhododendrons. Several strategically placed bird feeders provided treats for many different hummingbirds, and an occasional finch darted from branch to branch. This floral-paradise feeling was enhanced by a trellis-covered brick walkway between the lodging rooms.

Jeff obligingly handed me a plate of Danish rolls. These delicious confections are a part of a Continental breakfast served every morning. Guests may bring a tray to their own rooms or join other guests who sometimes gather on the deck. "Toronto," the Stanford's black dog, frequently overlooks the scene.

"We feel that Rosita Lodge is most typically Californian," said Jeff. "We have many plants in the rooms, and as you can see, the low ranch-style buildings with the shake roofs are traditional California architecture. We have furnished the lodging rooms with antique pine furniture, and paintings and serigraphs by local artists."

"Don't forget that we have some of your grandfather's work," said Joan "He painted with the Silvermine Artist Guild in Connecticut in the 1930s. We've also put lots of books and magazines in the rooms, and have extra pillows available for people who like to read in bed. I know that you feel this is very important."

All of us stopped for a moment to watch a squirrel who calmly contemplated us for about ten seconds before nervously scampering up one of the live oaks. "We have a raccoon here as well," said Jeff "I guess he lives under the deck."

Some of the lodging rooms have individual wood-burning fireplaces and private garden courtyards. Six of the nine rooms also have fully equipped individual kitchens, so that guests can prepare their own meals if they desire. Joan said she thought that this was one of the reasons so many of their guests stayed for several days on return visits. "We have innumerable restaurants here on the Monterey peninsula; however, many of our guests enjoy an occasional quiet dinner in their own garden or out here on the deck. Sometimes, after a day of golf or on the beach, they just don't feel like getting dressed up to go out."

There's a good feeling about the Rosita. Jeff and Joan are very attractive young people, quite ready to discuss everything from the quality of native abalone to Zoroaster. Both their backgrounds and personalities have equipped them to be excellent innkeepers.

Naturally, such conversation includes Carmel and the Monterey peninsula. Joan sums up her feelings in this way: "Carmel is whatever you most want. It's an ideal place to be. The escapist, the individual explorer, the artist, the photographer, the shopper, the golfer, the tennis player, and the gourmet will all find in Carmel their personal paradise."

They'll also find a very warm welcome and a wonderful sense of involvement at the Rosita Lodge.

THE ROSITA LODGE, P.O. Box 2077, 4th and Torres, Carmel-by-the-Sea, Ca. 93921; 408-624-6926. A nine-room bed-and-breakfast inn within a two-minute walk of the shops, galleries, and restaurants of Carmel. European plan includes Continental breakfast served to inn guests only. No other meals served. Open year around. Please check in advance for the regulations on pets. Tennis, golf, fishing, swimming, and all the Monterey peninsula recreational delights are nearby. Jeff and Joan Stanford, Innkeepers.

Directions: Turn off U.S. Rte. 1 at Ocean Ave. and proceed west to Junipero. Turn right and continue three blocks to 4th Ave. Turn right to Rosita Lodge.

SUTTER CREEK INN
Sutter Creek, California

It was breakfast time at the Sutter Creek Inn. We were all sitting around the three harvest tables in the old-fashioned kitchen where everyone passes the platters of fresh eggs, miners' hash, and wonderful, light baking powder biscuits which taste so good with the homemade jam. The talk was about the gold country and how history seems so recent out here. Innkeeper Jane Way was telling us about an old native of the town with whom she had had a recent conversation.

"He could remember sitting around the dinner table when he was a child, and his father saying that the gold was running out. 'We would all hold hands,' he said, 'and pray that the gold would go on. The next day more gold would be found. We depended upon God to feed us.'"

Ever since 1967 when I opened the gate in the white picket fence and strode up the narrow walk of this New Hampshire inn in northern California, I've been intrigued by gold rush country. On that first visit, Jane and I drove to many of the fascinating towns in

the area including Jackson, Volcano, Murphy's Angels' Camp and Sonora. . . . all names prominent in the living history of this area, which today still has tremendous deposits of gold underneath the verdant hills.

After breakfast, most of us decided to continue our conversation in the front parlor of the inn where book shelves cover one wall. The titles include everything from late novels to bound copies of American Heritage magazines. The room is a glowing testament to Jane Way's eclectic interests. There are many plants, much comfortable furniture, and a large center table loaded with different kinds of magazines. I noted reproductions of Brueghel, Cezanne, Manet, Rubens, and El Greco. There's also a most handsome collection of pewter spoons, a corner cupboard with an arrangement of beautiful old glassware, an unusual chess set in one corner, and a cribbage set in the other. Some guests ask Jane to read their palms or teacups.

Jane's lifelong devotion to beauty and the arts continues in the highly individualistic designs and furnishings in the inn bedrooms. For example, my room was the Garden Cottage, one of several outbuildings that have been converted into guest rooms. It had a fireplace, a canopied bed, cathedral ceiling, windows with tinted glass, and its own porch with a vine-covered trellis. There were two comfortable chairs and a shelf with dozens of books right next to the bed.

The bathroom had reproductions of Flemish prints and a print of a typical New Hampshire house. A special feature in all the rooms is the decorator sheets and towels.

The only meal served at this inn is breakfast, which is really an experience. When the bell rings at nine o'clock everyone troops in for a hearty mother lode repast and, incidentally, there is no smoking in the dining room.

Because the inn is rather intimate in nature, children are not encouraged as guests. Reservations in advance are almost always necessary. There's a two-day minimum stay on weekends, whether Friday and Saturday or Saturday and Sunday.

"Once in a while," explained Jane, "we do have last minute cancellations."

For many of her guests, Jane Way and the Sutter Creek Inn are the "first" country inn experience. "People frequently ask me," she said, "about the essential qualities for successful country innkeeping.

"I reply that there are three things that are most important: First is unlimited funds, the second is unlimited energy, and the third is unlimited love for people."

SUTTER CREEK INN, 75 Main St., Sutter Creek, Ca. 95685; 209-267-5606. A 16-room New England village inn on the main street of a historic mother lode town, 35 mi. from Sacramento. Lodgings include breakfast. No meals served to travelers. Closed all of January. No children under 10. No pets. Water skiing, riding, fishing, and boating nearby. Mrs. Jane Way, Innkeeper.

Directions: From Sacramento, travel on the Freeway (50) toward Placerville and exit at Power Inn Rd. Turn right and drive one block, note signs for Rte. 16 and Jackson. Turn left on Fulsom Rd., approximately ¼ mi., follow Rte. 16 signs to right for Jackson. Rte. 16 joins Rte. 49. Turn right to Sutter Creek. From San Francisco, follow Freeway (80) to Sacramento and take previous directions or drive via Stockton to Rte. 49.

THE INN
Rancho Santa Fe, California

The town of Rancho Santa Fe, California, is one of the most attractively designed that I have ever visited. It has been well-described as a "civilized planned community." The homes and estates have been created in perfect harmony with nature's generous endowment of climate and scenery. One of the dominating factors is the presence of the gigantic eucalyptus trees.

Innkeeper Dan Royce told me the story. "It's hard to imagine this place without these great trees, but back in 1906 it was nothing but an area of sand and occasional low trees and brush. At that time the Santa Fe Railroad purchased the land for the purpose of growing eucalyptus trees for railroad ties. About three million seedlings were planted, but the project failed when it was discovered that the wood was not suitable. Fortunately, the trees were left to flourish and today we have glorious shade and beauty. They provide homes for literally thousands of birds.

"The first building of The Inn was constructed in 1923 and is now a part of the main building of today's Inn. Beginning in 1941 it was expanded into a quiet resort where guests could enjoy the truly beautiful surroundings.

"In 1958, my father Steve acquired the property, and it's been a family operation ever since."

At this mention of Steve Royce, who was dean of southern California hotelmen for many years, I was reminded of my first visit to Rancho Santa Fe.

Steve had given me the pleasure of a tour of the entire community with its beautiful homes and orange groves. When I mentioned it to Danny, he smiled and said, "Yes, my father certainly made a great contribution to innkeeping. One thing I learned from him that will never leave me is to make a point of meeting personally every guest in The Inn during his or her stay. I think in the true definition of the word dad was a real innkeeper."

Although Dan may not be able to greet every newly-arrived guest, the chances are that Peggy Beatty, who has been associated with the Royce family for many years, will be on hand to extend best wishes for an enjoyable stay. Peggy has an incredible memory for names that is possbily unmatched by anyone I've ever met in the innkeeping business. "She certainly amazes me," said Dan.

This "family" feeling is extended even further when guests learn that the stunning framed needlepoints very much in evidence through the main lobby and living rooms of the inn, have been done by Danny's mother. For example, there is one very large, extremely handsome piece showing a large eucalyptus tree. It has become the symbol of the inn and is found on all of the stationery used. My favorite is a needlepoint clock located on one wall of the cathedral-ceilinged living room.

Cottages are scattered among the towering trees, and there's recreation for everyone here, including the younger set. The Inn has membership in nearby private 18-hole golf courses, and there are three tennis courts and a putting green on the grounds. The swimming pool has an outdoor terrace where luncheons and refreshments are available. Also, The Inn has a beach cottage at nearby Del Mar for use during the summer months.

Part of the pleasure of staying at The Inn is the opportunity to visit the shops in the village. They are all designed to be attractive, but unobtrusive. I stood in front of one building for three minutes without realizing that it was a supermarket!

All of this is happening today at Rancho Santa Fe because eucalyptus trees could not be used for railroad ties!

THE INN, Rancho Santa Fe, Ca. 92067; 714-756-1131. A 75-room resort-inn, 27 mi. north of San Diego Freeway #5, 5 mi. inland from Solana Beach, Del Mar. European plan. Breakfast, lunch, and dinner served to travelers daily. Open year-round. Pool, tennis, putting green, and bicycles on grounds. Golf and ocean nearby. Airport transportation provided. Daniel Royce, Innkeeper.

Directions: From I-5, take Exit S8 and drive inland about 6 mi.

VAGABOND HOUSE
Carmel, California

An entirely new *dramatis-personae* has taken over at this lovely sequestered inn in the residential section of Carmel. Former owners Chuck and Patsy Watts, and their blonde Afghan hound Muffin, are now at the Benbow Inn in Garberville, high in the redwood country. The new owners and innkeepers of the Vagabond House are Dennis Levett, one of the former owners of the Benbow, and Julie Brown, another Benbowite, who has joined the Vagabond as co-owner and hostess. There is even a new dog of some indefinite background named Festus.

Now this selfsame Festus and I were seated in the enclosed courtyard at the Vagabond House, amongst the gorgeous live oaks, magnolias, and mock orange trees from which were hung dozens of baskets of hanging flowers. There were flowers everywhere in the courtyard: camellias, primroses, impatiens, rhododendrons, azaleas, and many others. The hummingbirds, sparrows, and woodpeckers flitted about and Festus, with a red and white calico ribbon around his neck, kept a lazy eye on all of them, as well as the squirrels, who had thought for years the courtyard was their domain.

Julie Brown came out and joined us, carrying with her my

breakfast, a basket of delightfully warm pastries with sweet butter, and a glass of orange juice and a cup of coffee.

"This has really been a wonderful move for everybody concerned," she said. "I do miss the great redwoods, but the climate here in Carmel is so wonderfully inviting, and I just love the people here.

"We've found it necessary to make very few changes here at the inn. We continue to work on the gardens with the aid of Jeff Jenkins, and were fortunate enough to retain the services of Aiko and Herumi, who have kept things in such immaculate condition for a number of years.

"We're going to continue with some of the holiday traditions. For instance, the Halloween treat is already planned for each room, plus the jack-o-lanterns in the courtyard. Also, every room will have fruit-filled cornucopias at Thanksgiving, and its own Christmas tree at Christmas.

"The rooms will still be furnished with antiques, clocks, quilted bedspreads, plants, books, and needlework, plus some things that Dennis and I would like to add. I think that the quotation you used in the 1978 edition of *Country Inns and Back Roads:* 'the Tiffany diamond of country inns' is the thing that we continually bear in mind.

"We offer transportation to and from the bus station and airport, and we're always happy to mark special occasions such as birthdays, anniversaries, and honeymoons."

The Vagabond House has highly individualized rooms, most of which have woodburning fireplaces. There are attractive overstuffed swivel rockers, and among the other amenities, morning papers are delivered.

And so, the great switch was completed in the spring and summer of 1978. The wonderful part of it all is that everyone concerned — Chuck and Patsy, and Dennis and Julie — is deliciously pleased with the new arrangements. I think it worked out beautifully.

VAGABOND HOUSE, Fourth & Dolores Streets, P.O. Box 2747, Carmel, Ca. 93921; 408-624-7738 or 408-624-7403. A 12-room village inn serving Continental breakfasts to houseguests only. No other meals served. Open every day of the year. Not ideal for children. Attended, leashed pets allowed. Bike renting, golf, natural beauty nearby, enchanting shops. Dennis Levett, Jewell Brown, Innkeepers.

Directions: Turn off Hwy. 1 onto Ocean Avenue; turn right from Ocean Avenue onto Dolores, continue 2½ blocks. Parking provided for guests.

THE WINE COUNTRY INN
St. Helena, California

Jim Smith of the Wine Country Inn and I were taking a short walk after dinner with other northern California innkeepers at the Heritage House in Mendocino. It was one of those soft September evenings and both of us were filled with the wonderful feeling of contentment and good humor that follows a sumptuous meal with good friends.

Our talk naturally turned to the Wine Country Inn which is a few hours south of Mendocino in the beautiful Napa Valley. Jim and his wife Nita are the innkeepers. Jim's mother Marge and father Ned and I have been good friends ever since that day a number of years ago when they stopped to visit me in Stockbridge, and we had a long conversation about the ideals and objectives of innkeeping.

"Our big news is the construction of our new building which will change us from a fifteen to a twenty-room country inn," explained Jim. "Everything should be completed by April. It was designed, decorated, and furnished to go with our original building. I'm sure you know the story about that."

Indeed, I did. Ned and Marge Smith wanted a country inn in the beautiful Napa Valley, but there were no buildings available that could be adapted for such a purpose. They decided to build an inn from the ground up in St. Helena, which would be in harmony with the valley's surroundings, textures, and colors. They wanted every room to have a view; so now in both the original inn and new addition, some rooms have intimate balconies and others have patios leading to the lawn. Each room is individually decorated with country antique furnishings sought out and refinished by members of the family.

Many of the rooms have fireplaces, canopied beds, tufted bedspreads, and handmade quilts. There are no televisions or radios, but a generous supply of magazines, books, and big, fluffy, comfortable pillows encourage the pleasure of reading.

A Continental breakfast is served with fresh California fruit or delicious piping hot carmel-pecan rolls. It is the only meal served, but the Smiths make many helpful suggestions about nearby restaurants for the evening meal.

The inn gardens, which were just being planted during my first visit in 1975, have now been completely developed, and the Chinese pistachio trees and live oaks are now maturing. The wild mustard, lupines, oleanders, and petunias dress everything up beautifully.

Visitors in the Napa Valley enjoy visits to the many wineries, as well as mineral baths, geysers, a petrified forest, and several Robert Louis Stevenson memorial sites. There are a number of antique shops in the area, and the manicured agricultural beauty of the valley contrasts with the rugged, tree-covered hills surrounding it. It is dotted with century-old stone bridges, pumphouses, barns, and rock buildings, all of which are a delight to both painter and photographer alike.

"By the way," said Jim, as we paused for a moment to admire the sunset. "My brother Jeff is very enthusiastic about the inn. He's still in high school, but he'll be taking more responsibility in 1979 because I'm hoping to go to hotel school. I guess we're an innkeeping family all right."

Because of my early acquaintance with all of the Smiths, and my sharing of some of the joys and frustrations of their progress, I feel I have an almost vested interest in the Wine Country Inn. Since our very first meeting in Stockbridge, I knew it would be something exceptional, and it is.

THE WINE COUNTRY INN, 1152 Lodi Lane, St. Helena, Ca. 94574; 707-963-7077. A newly built 25-room country inn in the Napa Wine Valley of California, about 70 mi. from San Francisco. Continental breakfast served to houseguests, no other meals served. Open daily except December 22-27. No children; no pets. This inn is within driving distance of a great many wineries and also the Robert Louis Stevenson Museum. Golf and tennis nearby. Ned and Marge Smith, Innkeepers.

Directions: From San Francisco take the Oakland Bay Bridge to Hwy. 80. Travel north to the Napa cutoff. Stay on Hwy. 29 through the town of St. Helena, go 1¾ mi. north to Lodi Lane, then turn east ¼ mi. to inn.

Washington

THE CAPTAIN WHIDBEY INN
Coupeville, Washington

Let's go back in time a little to 1972, and my first visit to the Captain Whidbey; in fact, my first trip to the Northwest. I've been there several times since.

I remember walking through the big front door of this inn which is on the shores of Penn Cove, and there, greeting me in broad New England accents, stood innkeeper Steve Stone, complete with tweeds, white hair, and a corncob pipe. Steve, a Nantucket Island man, was the last thing I expected to see here in Coupeville, Washington, 3,000 miles away from the "grey lady of the sea."

I had seen a postcard of the Captain Whidbey which showed its rustic exterior, but I was completely surprised at the extensive collection of antiques, bric-a-brac, original oil paintings, pewter, silver, ship models, spinning wheels, books, and memorabilia which greeted me inside.

I had lunch in the Chart Room that day, and although it was a busy Saturday, Steve and Shirlie were both able to join me. It wasn't long before we found we had several friends in common, including David Wood, another Nantucketer, who is the curator of the Norman Rockwell museum in Stockbridge.

It was on that occasion that I had my first taste of the world-renowned Dungeness crab, the specialty of the inn, which was baked in its shell with butter and herbs. Since that time I've enjoyed almost all of the menu choices from filet mignon, to grilled halibut steak, and salmon.

Steve and Shirlie had explained that Coupeville is one of the oldest towns in Washington, and that the inn was built in 1907 of madrona logs, which are found in quantities on Whidbey Island. It's been a family inn for most of the past sixty years and has had surprisingly few innkeepers. I took a tour of the lodging rooms, and on the second floor, the first things that greeted me were a huge wall of books, an old spinning wheel, a marble-top music cabinet, and a long hall filled with all kinds of pieces to delight collectors. Most of these things came from the Stones' own collection.

Then, as now, some of the lodging rooms in the main house of the inn share a common gentlemen's and ladies' room which includes bath facilities. However, since my first visit, other rustic buildings have been built overlooking the lagoon—all of these have private baths.

The terrace facing the cove is highlighted with plantings of holly, Oregon grape, fir trees, Indian paintbrush, Scotch broom, English ivy, junipers, and fig trees.

The natural center of the inn is the living room with a very big fireplace made out of round stones. Here, everybody—houseguests and dinner guests alike—sit around talking and leafing through the dozens of various magazines. There's a fire almost every evening because, as Steve told me that first time, "It really draws people together."

That was many visits ago. Since then I have been a yearly visitor at this bit of New England on Puget Sound. Few things have changed, but there is one notable exception. Steve and Shirley's son John, who was a student at Western Washington State College when I first met him, has become the manager of the inn and furthermore, was married in the fall of 1978 to Mendy, a very pretty young lady whom I had the pleasure of meeting at our innkeepers' conference at Annapolis, Maryland, in November.

As we see, the Captain Whidbey family is growing.

THE CAPTAIN WHIDBEY INN, Rte. 1, Box 32, Coupeville, Wash. 98239; 206-678-4097. A 25-room country inn, 50 mi. north of Seattle, 3 mi. north of Coupeville. European plan. 4 cottages with private bath; 12 rooms with private bath. Breakfast, lunch, and dinner served daily to travelers. Open year-round. Pets allowed in cottages only. Boating and fishing on grounds. Golf nearby. Steve, Shirlie, and John Stone, Innkeepers.

Directions: Whidbey Island is reached year-round from the south by the Columbia Beach-Mukilteo Ferry, and during the summer and on weekends by the Port Townsend-Keystone Ferry. From the north (Vancouver, B.C. and Bellingham), take the Deception Pass Bridge to Whidbey Island.

THE PARTRIDGE INN
Underwood, Washington

"After three and a half years," I asked Nora McNab, "how do you feel about innkeeping?"

"I love it," she replied enthusiastically. "Occasionally on a very busy Sunday afternoon when I have a moment to stand unobtrusively and survey the dining room, I'm filled with so much joy with what I see and am able to provide. Here is a couple who dine out once a month. At the next table might be a minister and his wife relaxing after their busy morning. Over in the corner, a group of ladies, long-time friends plus a newcomer, chatting happily after their church service.

"At the big table there's a family group celebrating their mother's seventieth birthday. Nearby is a middle-aged group treating their mother to a dinner away from the nursing home. She has so much reminiscing to do, she forgets to eat.

"Now I see the 'full-of-life-and-love young couple' who came in from a hike. Some are from many miles away and some are from close by.

"For all of these people I am able to provide good food and a pleasant scenic atmosphere with all the warm homemade bread and pear butter they want, and to surprise them with unusual offerings for dessert such as hot lemon crunch pie, lemon and maple nut pie, or even baked fudge apple."

The Partridge Inn is a modest, unassuming restaurant with two lodging rooms available for guests' convenience. From Nora's front lawn the view to the south and east is up the glistening Columbia River to Hood River, Oregon and well beyond to the hills near The Dalles, Oregon. There are also spectacular views of Mount Hood and the Hood River Valley from vantage points nearby.

Nora continued, "We strive to keep the prices reasonable with consistently good food. We offer just plain country cooking. Besides

baked salmon, another specialty is barbequed Cornish hen. We also have swiss steak, homemade tamales, seafood thermidor, Underwood Mountain meat loaf, and usually roast beef and roast pork with bread dressing. By the way, I'm now preparing my own cookbook for publication.

"People from Vancouver and Portland drive out to have dinner with us quite frequently, but travelers from other parts of the country are usually very much surprised at what a wealth of attractions are located in our area. For example, at Underwood, we have the unique nine-mile-long lumber flume that speeds rough-cut lumber down the mountain to be finished. It crosses the highway at several points.

"Nearby, our little towns of Bingen and White Salmon resemble German towns along the Rhine River.

"I think one of our biggest attractions is the famous Dalles Dam with the fish ladders which allow migrating fish to continue their accustomed journey from the upper rivers to the sea and back again.

"I feel wonderful about innkeeping. I enjoy the cooking. I feel that the people who come to visit me are guests in my home, and I'm also happy to share our little shop, organized and maintained by my friend and neighbor, Sharon Harmsen. She displays jams, pickles, jellies, homemade gifts, and toys.

"When I look out the back window on a warm sunny afternoon, and see children and young people joyfully bouncing on our trampoline as their parents sit nearby looking at the view and visiting with other guests . . . for this kind of life I say 'thank you!'"

THE PARTRIDGE INN, Box 100, Underwood, Washington 98651; 509-493-2381. A country restaurant with two lodging rooms located 60 miles east of Portland, Oregon or Vancouver, Washington. Restaurant opened for dinner Wednesday through Saturdays at 5 p.m.; Sundays and holidays at noon. Breakfast served to houseguests only. Hiking trails and camping nearby. Free huckleberry-picking in season. Pears and apples for sale most of the year. Adult-sized trampoline for guests' enjoyment. Nora McNab, Innkeeper.

Directions: On Washington Highway 14, 60 miles east of Ft. Vancouver turn left on to Cook-Underwood Road at the confluence of the Columbia and White Salmon Rivers. (This road has 2 ends, do not turn off at Cook.) Follow yellow line up the hill for 2 miles. When the Columbia River is on the left begin to look for inn sign on the right. Coming from the Oregon side along Interstate 80N, 60 miles east of Portland cross the interstate bridge at the town of Hood River. Turn left and drive 2 miles to Cook-Underwood Road directly after crossing the White Salmon River. Follow directions up the hill as above. From coastal region take any highway leading to Portland, Oregon, then pick up 80N going east.

LAKE QUINAULT LODGE
Quinault, Washington

"A rain forest?" I asked. "I always associated the term with the Amazon River." Marge Lesley smiled and said, "Even though we're within a very short distance of snowcapped mountains, here in the Quinault rain forest, the temperature runs between forty and seventy degrees year around and we have an annual rainfall of between one-hundred-ten and one-hundred-sixty inches. These conditions produce the ideal growing environment of a greenhouse and there's a wide variety of plants from three-hundred-foot, centuries-old Douglas firs, to tiny mosses and delicate ferns."

"Marge and I were driving up Route 101 which leads from Aberdeen to Port Angeles on the extreme western coast of Washington. Great stretches of the road are cut between avenues of majestic trees, and it reminded me of northern California and the redwood country.

We were driving up to visit Marge and Larry Lesley's newest acquisition, Kalaloch Lodge, which overlooks the beautiful Pacific Ocean in the Olympic National Park.

"The two places are quite different," she said. "The Lake Quinault Lodge overlooks the placid waters of the lake and is surrounded by mountains with great fir forests. Our guests spend the days walking or driving in the woods.

"Kalaloch, on the other hand, is by the ocean and there, people enjoy beachcombing, clamming, and fishing. At Kalaloch, we have

hotel, motel, and cabin accommodations, whereas at the Lake Quinault Lodge, it's more like a traditional country inn."

I nodded in agreement remembering that late the previous afternoon I had walked through the big front door of the Lodge into a most welcome living room with a fire crackling in the fireplace. There was a fresh supply of wood stacked up on either side of the massive chimney. On one side great glass doors provided a view of the spacious lawns of the Lodge which lead down to the lake. I could see some children playing croquet.

There was a chess game going on in front of the fireplace, and other guests were reading magazines and taking a few moments of respite after what I presume was a busy, pleasant day in the forests.

Fran Still, at the reception desk, gave me a warm greeting and assured me that I had time for a quick swim in the indoor pool before dinner. "Marge and Larry will join you a little later on," she said. "They're all excited about going over to Europe this year as representatives of the State of Washington Committee on Tourism."

She pointed out that the Lesleys have been adding considerably to their collection of Indian objects, including wall hangings, rugs, and similar crafts. "We're all very proud of the Indian heritage of this section, and the Lesleys have really gone out of their way to preserve as many as possible of the old things and the old ways.

Most of the bedrooms at the Lodge are very colorful and comfortable, ranging from rustic to modern. Many have individual fireplaces and panoramic views of the lakes and the mountains.

One thing that always impresses me about this place is the number of ways devoted to keeping children happily occupied.

Besides some lakeside playground equipment such as swings and slides, there is a fully equipped game room in the basement with all kinds of electronic games and pinball machines, ping-pong, and billiards.

Naturally, one of the things that keeps all guests occupied for part of every day is eating. Marge spoke at length on this subject: "We're primarly known for seafood and steak. Our principal seafood dish is lobster. Everybody loves the salmon, too—either poached or grilled—which is caught fresh nearby."

By this time we were within sight of Kalaloch Lodge, and I could see the numerous oceanside cabins. There was a grocery store, gasoline station, and restaurant. Rollers from the Pacific were majestically parading in, and I couldn't help but remark to Marge that, indeed, it was quite different from the Lake Quinault Lodge.

LAKE QUINAULT LODGE, Southshore Rd., Quinault, Wash. 98575; 206-288-2571. A 55-room resort-inn in the Olympic National Forest of the State of Washington, about 40 mi. from Aberdeen. European plan. Breakfast, lunch, and dinner served daily to travelers. Open every day of the year. Fee for pets; must be attended. Indoor swimming pool, chipping green on grounds. Hiking, mountain climbing, fishing, nature walks nearby. Marge and Larry Lesley, Innkeepers.

Directions: Use Quinault exit from Rte. 101. Proceed 2 mi. on south shore of Lake Quinault to inn.

THE FARMHOUSE
Port Townsend, Washington

Ever since visiting The Farmhouse in 1973, I have been not only personally enriched by my friendship with John Ashby Conway and his wife Dorothy, but my mail has included letters of praise from many parts of the world commending the food, the view, and the unusual atmosphere. On my most recent visit, I shared the good times with several other innkeepers in *CIBR*, including the Lesleys from Lake Quinault Lodge, Nora McNab from the Partridge Inn, Steve and John Stone from the Captain Whidbey, and Lowell and Barbara Bogart from the James House.

We all gathered in the kitchen while John demonstrated sauce-making. Then we watched his young assistant put together the most delicious cake you can imagine. Just like kids in mom's kitchen, we had our chance to spoon up some of the icing, which was a delicious combination of chocolate, coffee, and sour cream.

In my most recent letter from John, just before this book went to

press, he said: "The Farmhouse is really the crossroads of the world! There was a birthday party in the dining room, and one of the guests was a French lady traveling with her husband and son. Imagine her surprise to see her nephew seated across the room. Neither of them knew the other had left Paris!

"On the same evening there were folks from Tokyo and Hong Kong, and four people from Dusseldorf. We never fail to be surprised that people from so far away find us. A man from Bangkok reminded me that he had visited us two years before. A Hungarian gentleman said it was the best Hungarian food he had ever eaten! (I should explain that John learned to cook in Budapest.)

The Farmhouse is truly a gourmet restaurant, and there are several ground rules which I would like to explain: There is one set menu each month. I hope that all of our readers will telephone in advance. Please do not "drop in" on The Farmhouse. While it is not an arduous trip from Seattle, it would be disappointing if there were no tables available. It might be convenient to reserve rooms overnight at the nearby James House.

Here are the monthly specialties for 1979: February — mandarin food from North China; March — a German menu; April — classic Greek food; May — curry and sambals from northern India.

In June, July, and August there is a summer schedule for Thursday, Friday, Saturday, and Sunday. Thursday's entrée is marinated leg of lamb; Friday's is seafood; Saturday's is usually roast beef; and Sunday, the entrée is fowl, served in a Persian style with pomegranate syrup from Damascus.

September, the inn is open weekends, including Friday, with an Italian menu. In October, it's Hungarian; November is classic Japanese, and the inn is closed in December and January.

During 1978, The Farmhouse received the prestigious and coveted Travel-Holiday Award for 1979.

Remember, don't go to The Farmhouse without a reservation.

THE FARMHOUSE, North Beach, Port Townsend, Wash. 98368; 206-385-1411. A unique gourmet country restaurant, 50 mi. from Seattle. Meals by reservation only. Dinner served Thursdays through Sundays in June, July, and August; dinner served Fridays, Saturdays, and Sundays from September through May. Closed months of December and January. Dorothy and John Ashby Conway, Innkeepers.

Directions: From Seattle take Edmonds-Kingston Ferry and follow Rte. 104 over Hood Canal Floating Bridge to Rte. 101 N. Exit at Port Townsend and make inquiries for The Farmhouse before driving into town.

JAMES HOUSE
Port Townsend, Washington

I have a letter from Lowell and Barbara Bogart of the James House which I would like to share with our readers. It contains a great many messages for people who love to visit country inns and for those who, like the Bogarts, came into country innkeeping from an entirely different way of life. First, however, let me explain a little about this bed-and-breakfast inn located in Port Townsend, Washington, a town well worth a visit for its own virtues.

The James House is a Victorian mansion overlooking Port Townsend Bay with the Cascade Mountains to the east and the Olympic Mountains to the west. There is no television and only the ticking of the old clock, the sound of the wind, and the whistles of the ferries disturb the peace and quiet.

There are ten bedrooms on four different levels, all with distinctively different Victorian furniture and decorations.

A Continental breakfast of orange juice, toasted homemade breads, and coffee or tea is served in the old-fashioned kitchen.

Port Townsend is known, not only for its collection of Victorian homes, brick and stone buildings, and natural beauties, but also as the developing art and cultural center of Washington state, with art galleries, antique shops, a chamber music festival, a summer dance laboratory, and little theatre productions.

Now to portions of Lowell's letter: "We were delighted to have you and other innkeepers here for the regional meeting. We got acquainted with some really fine folks.

"In the past year we've concentrated on making the atmosphere more homelike, creating a comfortable area in each room to read or

write, and making a greater variety of magazines and books easily accessible to the guests. We've added a private bath to the bridal suite, and redone one of the baths downstairs. We've also acquired a lovely music box circa 1895, and a walnut-burl sectional bookcase. I guess what I'm saying is that we have added more and more of those things that *we* like in a home, such as plants, books, good music, comfortable reading spots, etc.

"We appreciate Port Townsend so much, aside from the pleasure of meeting so many delightful guests. We find that we are enjoying the area and all the interesting and talented people who live here.

"Our daughter Jennifer, whom you met on your first visit, is happy, too, with her life in Port Townsend. Her social calendar is full! And she's into cheerleading and sports (not confusing fun with studies).

"We get almost daily requests for information on running an inn! It certainly indicates a widespread awareness of the virtues of alternative hospitality.

"Our plans for 1979? We have several ideas, not the least of which is to find the proper helpers to give us a vacation break. We hope to add a bathroom on the second floor which will give us four rooms with private baths on that floor. We'll be painting the trim on the windows, and we want to get everything painted except the shingles. We'll be fixing up the carriage house some time later."

Thank you Lowell, Barbara, and Jennifer. Things certainly seem to be in tiptop shape at the James House in Port Townsend!

JAMES HOUSE, 1238 Washington St., Port Townsend, Wash. 98368; 206-385-1238. A 10-room village inn, 50 mi. from Seattle on the Olympic Peninsula. Some rooms with shared baths. European plan with sit-down breakfast served to houseguests. No other meals served. Open year-round. No children under 12; no pets. State parks and beaches nearby. Lowell and Barbara Bogart, Innkeepers.

Directions: From Seattle take Winslow ferry. From Edmonds take Kingston Ferry. James House is adjacent to Post Office on bluff overlooking Port Townsend Bay.

British Columbia

OAK BAY BEACH HOTEL
Victoria, British Columbia

My host, during my first visit at the Oak Bay Beach Hotel in Victoria, was Kevin Walker who, at the age of 20, has already had seven years' experience in the inn business. "I think it's wonderful," he said. "I just can't imagine being involved in anything else. I have worked in almost every department, but I guess because my father is the owner, I've had to work that much harder."

Kevin and I were enjoying high tea in the beamed, low-ceilinged living room overlooking the Straits of Juan de Fuca. A fire crackled in the fireplace.

"We're the only seaside hotel in the area," he said. "Very often we can see killer whales, seals, and salmon. In fact, we have our own friendly neighborhood sea serpent who is a part of Indian legend and mythology.

"Right in from of us are the Straits of Haro with the United States-Canadian border running right at mid-channel." He pointed toward a small island, "That is Discovery Island named for Captain Vancouver's ship, and those are the San Juan Islands across the Strait. Mount Baker is to the east and it's more than 10,000 feet high. You ought to see it when the sun catches the snow-clad peaks and glaciers in the early morning or evening. We are a combination of water and mountains."

Even while we were watching, a cruise ship glided through the Straits, disdainfully ignoring a stubby tugboat towing one of British Columbia's most abundant resources: logs.

"We have a front seat for the annual Swiftsure race," he remarked. "Boats come from all parts of the world."

Kevin and I had just finished a tour of the hotel lodgings. Each room has a character of its own. For example, there's a newly decorated group on the third floor with names like "Georgian Suite" and "Samuel Pepys" room. "These accommodations are inspired by English history and literature," he explained. "In fact, most of the antique furnishings were acquired in England."

Still another very handsome room was called "Prince Albert." One suite overlooked the Oak Bay Marina.

"English" is indeed the word to describe the Oak Bay Beach Hotel. I've often remarked that Victoria was the most English of all Canadian cities, and this inn in many ways resembles several inns and country houses I have visited in England. One that comes to mind is the Mermaid in Rye, which also has the handsome Tudor-style half-timbers.

"May I offer you some more tea?" Kevin said, picking up the Spode teapot. I acquiesced immediately, and helped myself to more crumpets and jam, refraining momentarily from the selection of English Wensleydale, Cheshire, and Stilton cheeses.

There were other reminders of England here at this British Columbia inn. One was a public room with a water view known as "The Snug." Kevin explained that this was the Canadian equivalent of the Englishman's local." "Some people have been coming here for a long time as you can see from their names on the mugs hanging there. It's an English tradition."

Long before my visit to the Oak Bay Beach Hotel, I had heard from John Stone of Captain Whidbey's Inn, and Marge and Larry Lesley of the Lake Quinault Lodge, that it was indeed the kind of place I would like. Now, sitting here enjoying high tea with Kevin Walker, looking over the dinner menu which included Beef Wellington, Juan de Fuca filet of sole and Veal Oscar served with sauce Bernaise, I knew that they were entirely correct.

OAK BAY BEACH HOTEL, 1175 Beach Drive, Victoria, B.C. V8S2N2; 604-598-4556. A 48-room seaside inn located in one of the quiet suburbs of Victoria. A short distance from the spectacular scenery and recreational resources of British Columbia. European plan. Breakfast, lunch, and dinner served to travelers. Open every day in the year. Swimming on grounds. Golf, tennis, fishing, sailing available nearby. No pets. Bruce R. Walker, Innkeeper.

Directions: Take Johnson St. or Fort St. from downtown Victoria east to Oak Bay Ave., which leads into Newport Ave. Turn left into Windsor Ave. to Beach Dr. Turn right and continue to 1175 Beach Dr. If arriving by air at Victoria Airport, I suggest you take public transportation to the center of the city and then take a taxi to the hotel.

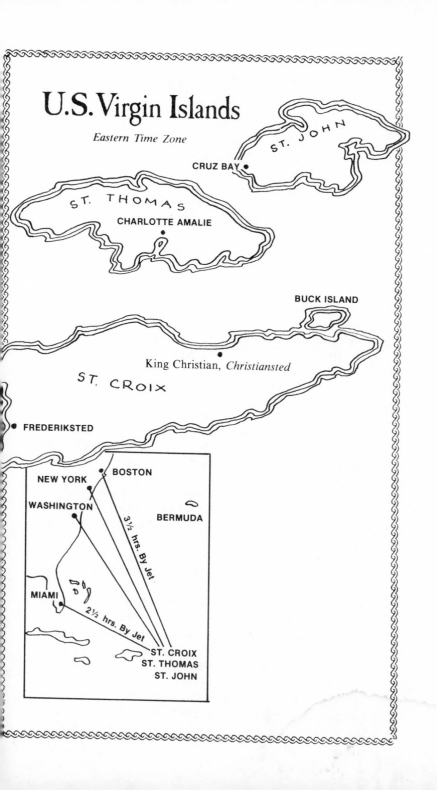

U.S. Virgin Islands

Eastern Time Zone

ST. JOHN

CRUZ BAY •

ST. THOMAS

CHARLOTTE AMALIE •

BUCK ISLAND

King Christian, *Christiansted* •

ST. CROIX

• FREDERIKSTED

BOSTON •
NEW YORK •
WASHINGTON •

BERMUDA

3½ hrs. By Jet

MIAMI •

2½ hrs. By Jet

ST. CROIX
ST. THOMAS
ST. JOHN

U.S. Virgin Islands

St. Croix has mountains and gorgeous beaches as well as excellent swimming, snorkeling, and scuba diving. It has two communities, Christiansted and Fredericksted. Each of these has picture book charm.

For further and more detailed information about both the American and British Virgin Islands, I recommend Margaret Zeller's book, The Inn Way . . . Caribbean, $4.95, at your bookstore, or from the Berkshire Traveller Press, Stockbridge, Massachusetts 01262. It contains her adventures in searching for country inns on all the islands in this sunny part of the world.

KING CHRISTIAN HOTEL
Christiansted, St. Croix, Virgin Islands

"I think we are very fortunate here on St. Croix," said Betty Sperber. "In addition to the King Christian, there are several excellent accommodations on many different parts of the island. More and more people are coming to St. Croix every year. I think it's because of the beaches, the tranquility, the golf course, and the fact that it is such an entirely different atmosphere."

Betty and I had been walking through the hotel and had stopped momentarily on a balcony overlooking the harbor. I remarked that the Kings Wharf seemed to be the center of a great deal of activity.

"Yes, it's fun right here on the waterfront," she said. "You know this is a working harbor, and in addition to the pleasure craft and boats that are available for rent, there are also fishermen who go out every day. Our guests seem to like the feeling of being near the water. We are within walking distance of museums, many art galleries, and shops. The beach is just 300 yards away. Did you know that Alexander Hamilton spent his boyhood in Christiansted and worked within two blocks of where we are now?"

Since my last visit, I received a letter from Betty bringing me up to date. She writes in part:

"We now have a New York Wats Line—800-221-4588. One of our new attractions is a year-round Learn to Sail package that includes sailing lessons and is becoming a popular part of a stay at the King Christian.

"The unending refurbishment that's part of keeping a hotel attractive and comfortable goes on. The National Park Service has undertaken a complete renovation of the old Scale House that's

adjacent to the King Christian, complete with 'yellow brick road,' and to make our hotel conform in character and mood, we've done some work on our own facade. We've also constructed a new boardwalk along the waterfront, wider, sturdier, and safer than the old one.

"We've made improvements to Limin' Inn, the restaurant/lounge on our own premises, so it's a more aesthetically pleasing environment for dining and for 'limin'—(West Indian for taking it easy)—and there's nightly entertainment.

"One of the highlights of the past year was an opportunity for the King Christian to host a group of *CIBR* innkeepers. Among other things, we had a party for them on our patio, which gave them a chance to get better acquainted with us and the other way 'round. The Kendalls from Kedron Inn in South Woodstock, Vermont, went fishing and brought in a record catch-of-the-day. Just about everybody snorkeled at Buck Island and thoroughly enjoyed its beauty. We have received many kind notes from members of the group since their visit, and I would like them to keep in touch."

KING CHRISTIAN HOTEL, King's Wharf, Christiansted, St. Croix, U.S.V.I. 00820; 809-773-2285 (N.Y. reservations 800-221-4588). A 38-room waterfront hotel in town. Open year-round. No pets. Restaurant, fresh-water pool, duty-free stores, dive shops on premises. Sailing, snorkeling, scuba diving, glass-bottom boat rides, Hertz car rental all arranged by the inn. Dine-around plan. Tennis and golf nearby. Betty Sperber, Innkeeper.

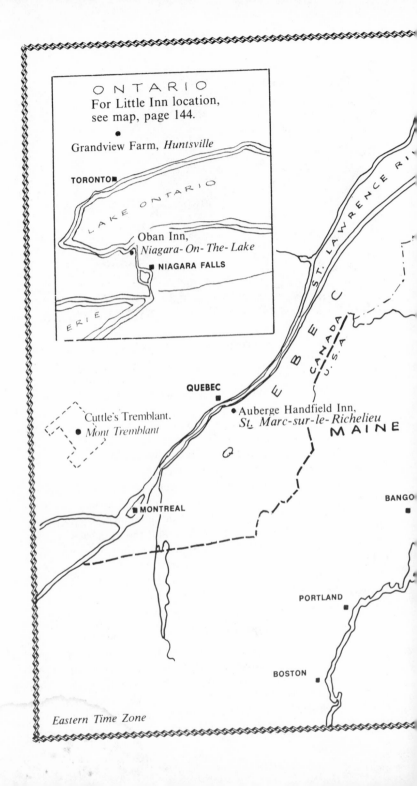

ONTARIO
For Little Inn location,
see map, page 144.

Grandview Farm, *Huntsville*

TORONTO

LAKE ONTARIO

Oban Inn,
Niagara-On-The-Lake

NIAGARA FALLS

ERIE

ST. LAWRENCE RIVER

QUEBEC

CANADA

U.S.A.

Cuttle's Tremblant.
Mont Tremblant

Auberge Handfield Inn,
St. Marc-sur-le-Richelieu

MAINE

Q

MONTREAL

BANGO

PORTLAND

BOSTON

Eastern Time Zone

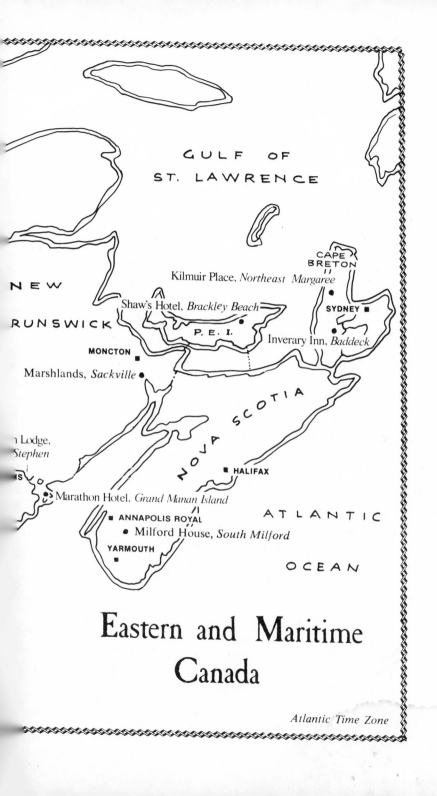

GULF OF
ST. LAWRENCE

NEW

RUNSWICK

CAPE
BRETON

Kilmuir Place, *Northeast Margaree*

Shaw's Hotel, *Brackley Beach*

SYDNEY ■

P. E. I.

Inverary Inn, *Baddeck*

MONCTON ■

Marshlands, *Sackville* ●

NOVA SCOTIA

n Lodge,
Stephen

■S

■ HALIFAX

● Marathon Hotel, *Grand Manan Island*

ATLANTIC

■ ANNAPOLIS ROYAL

● Milford House, *South Milford*

YARMOUTH ■

OCEAN

Eastern and Maritime
Canada

Atlantic Time Zone

Ontario

BAYFIELD, ONTARIO, BRIEFLY

Bayfield, Ontario is a small village on the edge of Lake Huron, built around a traditional central park with many trees, benches, and play areas. Around the outer circumference of the park are a few stores used by the local villagers, including clothing shops, gift shops, a woolen shop, a general store, and a few arts and crafts shops.

This is a quiet town with beautiful homes on tree-shaded streets and many gardens. Lake Huron has been of considerable importance in the town's history, and some early citizens wisely provided park areas bordering the lake which supply visitors and town folk alike with a very pleasant atmosphere for picnics and other diversions. Some of the streets of the town lead directly to the lake shore with walkways and wooden steps to reach the beach which stretches out in both directions for a considerable distance. I'm told that this portion of Lake Huron is extremely swimmable and, interestingly enough, it's located just a few steps from the residential part of town.

The railroad bypassed Bayfield, and the little village remained undisturbed, its chief industry for many years being commercial fishing from the small natural port where the river runs into the lake.

Since early in this century, Bayfield has been a quiet but popular summer resort for those who enjoy relaxing in a peaceful Canadian atmosphere.

Of further interest to the traveler are the two marinas which are located in the small river flowing into the lake. The day that I was there there were dozens and dozens of very picturesque sailboats and power boats all berthed overnight. The crews were talking together on the grassy walkways and several of them were preparing dinners at little barbecue pits thoughtfully provided by the marina owners. There's nothing quite like a group of boats, is there?

Bayfield is made even more attractive because of two nearby summer theatres; the famous Stratford Festival Theatre will be in its 27th season in 1979. The offerings are a combination of Shakespeare, Chekov, Shaw, and other significant dramatists. It opens in early June and closes in mid-October. One of the most popular shows in 1978 was Noel Coward's Private Lives with Brian Bedford and Maggie Smith. The other theatre is the Blyth Summer Festival which plays lighter fare during July and August.

THE LITTLE INN
Bayfield, Ontario

The kitchen at the Little Inn in Bayfield, Ontario was certainly a busy place on this Saturday morning. Mrs. Rose Scotchmer was baking the pies, cakes, and pastries necessary for the day. Innkeeper Ruth Wallace was preparing breakfast, including eggs of various kinds and also french toast and bacon. The morning waitress moved in and out of swinging doors with the orders. Two young men delivering cottage cheese, milk, and spices were also enjoying a quick cup of coffee and some banter with the waitress. The light and airy kitchen was indeed very busy and bustling. It also happened to be one of the cleanest kitchens I have ever seen and there was plenty of room for everybody to work. The young men from the dairy truck left, the waitress brought in more orders, and Ruth got busy. Even though I had just enjoyed a breakfast of two beautifully fried eggs and bacon, watching her cook the french toast was making me hungry once again!

"Our main dishes for dinner," she said as she deftly flipped over a piece of french toast, "are roast beef, barbecued pork chops, white fish, roast pork, leg of lamb, T-bone steaks, baked ham, baked chicken breasts, and turkey. Rose does most of the baking, and as you see this morning, there's an angel food cake that will end up as a fresh strawberry-banana torte. There's also a rum cake with butter rum icing, Dutch apple pie and fresh chocolate pie."

My stay at the Little Inn had begun on the previous afternoon when Ruth and I watched a parade pass in front of the inn with lots of little children and young people dressed up in Bayfield costumes of 100 years ago. Senior citizens came by in horse-drawn carriages. There were two bands, one of them a pipe band dressed in the uniform of the Seaforth Highlanders. Were they ever stirring! Scots pipes bring tears to my eyes. We stood in front of the Little Inn along with others under a beautiful willow tree and the parade was over too soon.

The Little Inn has a number of features that make it a very interesting experience for the traveler. First there is the inn itself, which dates back to 1862 and has since been in continuous operation. It's a two-story yellow brick building with the red overtones quite characteristic of other buildings in this portion of Ontario. There are tables and chairs on the front veranda, making a most comfortable and cozy place to relax.

The inn sign conveys an inviting message: it reads, "The Little Inn, Sunday Brunch, Afternoon Tea, Lunches, Dinners."

It has a classic country atmosphere with many things done in the old-fashioned way, including the fact that all the occupants of the lodging rooms have the fun of shared bathrooms. The decorations are Victorian and there are lots of books and oil paintings.

Ruth, herself, personifies the inn. She's a very pretty, well-informed, hard-working individual who still has the time to stop and chat with a few guests in the sitting room at the front corner of the inn.

"There's so much to do at the Little Inn," she said, "including nothing, if your fancy tends that way. Laze in the sun over a good book . . . swim and sun on the white sand beach a short stroll away . . . enjoy summer rambles along the shore and through the green countryside.

"When guests feel more active, there is golfing on excellent courses nearby . . . boating and fishing on the river and lake . . . treasure-hunting in the many attractive antique and gift shops in Bayfield and surrounding towns.

"1979 will be my eighth year," she said, and "I've loved every minute of it." I'd say that her guests share her enthusiasm as well.

THE LITTLE INN, Bayfield, Ontario, Canada NOM IGO; 519-565-2611. A most pleasant 10-room, 3-bathroom village inn in a natural Canadian village on the shores of Lake Huron about 12 miles from Goderich. All three lodging plans available. Lodging includes full breakfast. Breakfast, luncheon, dinner served to travelers. Open from May 24 to the Canadian Thanksgiving Day (2nd Mon. in Oct.).

No pets. Museums, Stratford and Blyth Summer Theatre, skiing, sailing, swimming, hiking and backroading nearby. Ruth Wallace, Innkeeper.

Directions: Traveling between Detroit and Port Huron follow Hwy. 7 to Hwy. 21 and then north 50 miles to Bayfield. It's about 150 miles from Detroit; 50 miles to London (Ont.); 73 miles to Sarnia; and 140 miles to Toronto. Well worth the trip.

GRANDVIEW FARM
Huntsville, Ontario

Bruce Craik throttled down the speed of the motor boat so that we were barely moving through the canal between Fairy Lake and Penn Lake. "There is a blue heron that lives here," he said, "and perhaps we can catch sight of him. These lakes, St. Mary's, Fairy, and Penn are all connected by this canal which was built many years ago as part of a transportation system from Toronto that included passage on a lake steamer and another short journey on a narrow-gauge railway. This has always been a popular resort area."

The water was very still at twilight, and he nudged me to point out a beaver who was busily engaged on a half-submerged log. It was about as close to a beaver in its natural habitat as I have ever been.

We were in the twilight of a near-perfect summer day. I had made the pleasant trip from Niagara Falls, New York, and arrived at

359

Grandview Farm just in time to see Bruce and part of a working crew load the last of the bales on the farm cart. There were horses in the meadow, and as I drove past the barn, once again the two goats, Homer and Jethro, poked their heads out of the window and eyed me with some justifiable suspicion. A few of the farm dogs barked their greetings.

I had time for a quick swim and then joined Bruce and Judy under the beautiful yellow canopy that covers the terrace in the summertime. In addition to being a resort-inn, with many activities during summer and winter, Grandview Farm Inn is also a restaurant serving three meals a day. Specialties include roast beef with Yorkshire pudding, which is served on Wednesday and Saturday nights. Other nights there are three different entrées such as chicken done in many different ways, fish, duck, stuffed roast pork, and veal.

For dinner the waitresses wear very attractive costumes with long skirts, which are replaced by entirely different costumes at breakfast and lunch.

Bruce and Judy and their six children have kept Grandview Farm Inn for the better part of the last ten years. The lake provides a great deal of the recreation including swimming, sailing, and motor boating. Bruce explained that most of the guests rent boats at the nearby marina for exploring the lake system. In winter, there are many kilometers of cross-country ski trails that start right at the front door.

Lodgings are in the main house and in six other attractive cottages set among some fine old trees either on or near the lakeshore.

All the rooms are very comfortable, from the corner room in the inn with the four-poster, to the fireplace rooms in the "Tree Tops", and those in the little waterside cottage called "Puffin Hill."

While I was browsing in the Rafters, the small gift shop at the inn, I picked up the Grandview Farm brochure. It was extremely handsome with full color photographs of all of the activities, the lake views, and the lodging rooms. I found it very helpful when writing this account.

Back on our odyssey through the lake, Bruce put his finger on his lips and pointed ahead. I saw a stately, graceful blue heron standing in the bulrushes along the side of the lake. "When he is frightened," Bruce whispered, "he stands up as straight as possible and that long neck blends into the background of the shore." Suddenly our friend flapped his large wings and took flight, skirting the shore. Bruce speeded up the boat to stay as close as possible, saying, "He likes to play like this and continues for quite a few minutes. I think he understands that we really mean no harm."

*GRANDVIEW FARM, Huntsville, Ontario, Canada POA 1KO;
705-789-7412. A 25-room resort-inn on Fairy Lake, 142 mi. north of
Toronto in a beautiful lake and mountain resort area. American and
Mod. American plans. Breakfast, lunch, and dinner served to
travelers daily. Open from mid-May to mid-October; Dec. 26 to
Mar. 31. Closed Christmas Eve and Christmas Day. No pets. Tennis,
swimming, sailing, waterskiing, canoeing, xc skiing trails; Alpine
skiing nearby. The Craik Family, Innkeepers.*

*Directions: From Niagara Falls, N.Y. (I-195): take Queenstown
Bridge through Canadian checkpoint, follow QEW north to Toronto,
then Rte. 427 north, Rte. 401 east, and Rte. 400 north, which runs
into Rte. 11 north, and then on to Huntsville. Turn right on Rte. 60 a
few more miles north of Huntsville. This is the main road from this
part of Canada to Ottawa. Grandview Farm is on the right a few
kilometers distant.*

THE OBAN INN
Niagara-on-the-Lake, Ontario

"To really understand Niagara-on-the-Lake," said innkeeper
Gary Burroughs, "I think that it's well to know its past, because in
many respects, the past, the present, and the future are existing here,
side by side. This village has been known as Loyal Village,
Buttlersville, West Niagara, Newark, Niagara, as well as its present
name."

Gary and I were seated for a moment in "Shaw's Corner" in the
Victorian pub at the Oban Inn in front of the lovely warm fireplace. It
was decorated with many photographs of actors and actresses who
have appeared at the nearby Shaw Festival. In the center of the buffet
bar was the star of the midday repast: a turkey pie with a big,
beautiful crust. There was also a large salad bowl, cold cauliflower,

361

mixed peas and lima beans, cold sliced meats, sliced eggs, and generous helpings of tomatoes, beets, and pickles. It was, indeed, quite British.

Gary was warming to his subject: "We have many 'firsts' here. This was where the first Canadian Parliament was held in 1792 when the town was known as Newark. I daresay that most Americans do not realize that this was the scene of battles during the War of 1812. Fort George was built in 1797 and then damaged by American fire and largely demolished during the War of 1812. It was restored by the Niagara Parks Commission, and a great many visitors enjoy walking around the replica. You see, the United States is just across the river.

"Our building has an interesting history. It was once the home of Captain Duncan Malloy, a laker captain whose home was in Oban, Scotland, a beautiful seaport town. It was built about 1824, and later turned into an inn. In 1914, there were additions made and the Oban Inn became a Canadian Officers' Mess."

The Oban is essentially a Canadian inn. However, because of its evident English heritage, it recalled English inns that I have visited such as the Crown in Chiddingfold which has the same cozy village air, and the Mermaid Tavern in Rye where the atmosphere is also drenched in history.

The menu indicates that the Oban really is a mix of the old world and the new. For example, among the appetizers was a homemade pate'which is a tradition in England and the Continent, and the main menu items have the ring of the English countryside: roast prime ribs of beef with Yorkshire pudding, and calves' sweetbreads with bacon served on toast.

There was a mixture of patrons during the noon hour, including businessmen from the town as well as a few Canadian and American visitors. I noted a piano in one corner, and Gary said that in the evening there were informal jolly sing-alongs, as well as quiet entertainment. With the fire crackling away on a rather chilly day, it was all very heartwarming and hospitable.

This hospitality at the Oban Inn extends to some very homelike lodging rooms. Some have a view of Lake Ontario and all are quite neat, typical of country inns, with individual color schemes and furniture.

In recent years, one of the principal reasons for visiting Niagara-on-the-Lake is to enjoy the Shaw Festival Theater, since 1962 one of the outstanding summer and fall theaters in North America. There is also the Canadian Mime Theater, Canada's first professional mime-in-residence group, which offers full-scale productions of the silent art from mid-May through August, every day except Monday.

While I am devoted to the theater, I personally prefer Niagara-on-the-Lake during the quiet off-season. Then it's possible to enjoy the town, the museums, and the beautiful homes in a more leisurely fashion.

THE OBAN INN, 160 Front St., Box 94, Niagara-on-the-Lake, Ontario LOS IJO 416-468-2165. A 23-room village inn on a quiet street in one of Canada's historic villages approx. 12 mi. from Niagara Falls, N. Y., on the shores of Lake Ontario. Near Ft. George and Ft. Niagara, the Shaw Festival, and Mime Theatre. All plans available. Breakfast, lunch, dinner served daily to travelers. Open every day of the year. Owner-controlled pets welcome. Golf, xc skiing, sailing, fishing, tennis nearby. Gary Burroughs, Innkeeper.

Directions: Exit Hwy. 55 at St. Catherines from the Queen Elizabeth Hwy. Follow signs to Niagara-on-the-Lake.

Quebec

Quebec is a land of 999,999 lakes, a vast spread of forests and fjords around an inland sea and an estuary that narrows into the mighty island-dotted St. Lawrence River, the historic lifeline of the Province. Quebec is also a land of rolling plains, fertile valleys, and a great peninsula with sandy beaches, hidden coves, and soaring mountains.

Quebec is European in the French manner — she is very old and very proud of her heritage. Long before Columbus sighted America, Basques fished in the Gulf of St. Lawrence. Twelve years before the Mayflower landed, 370 years ago, Champlain built the bustling fort that became Quebec City.

Such was the value of "precious furs" to the French kings that, by the turn of the 18th century, French trappers, explorers, and missionaries had reached the Rockies, the Mississippi Valley, and the Gulf of Mexico. The young city of Montreal had its own street plan nine years before William Penn laid out Philadelphia.

Today, Quebec is a happy historic mixture of blue jeans and haute couture, French bistros and hanging flower baskets, English tea rooms and American pool halls.

For the most part, Quebec is inhabited by the Quebecois, *a spirited, happy, French-speaking people with a tradition of exploring, trapping, farming, feasting, dancing, and merry-making.*

363

Besides visits to Hovey Manor which is located in the Eastern Townships, and Cuttles in the Mont Tremblant area, in this issue I am recounting the story of a visit to a Quebec inn where French is the principal language. I found it a broadening and enjoyable experience which I recommend to anyone.

HANDFIELD INN, (AUBERGE HANDFIELD)
St. Marc-sur-le-Richelieu, Quebec

In 1978 I visited the Handfield Inn twice. The first time was in late March when Tom Noonan of the Bird and Bottle Inn in Garrison, New York, flew me in his airplane to Montreal. The two of us went to a "sugaring off party" which was being held by innkeeper Conrad Handfield at his own maple sugar grove a few miles from the inn. The spell of winter was still on the land with much snow and many cross-country skiers.

Tom and I were bundled into a car and taken to the "sugar shack" a low-ceilinged rough building where there was a great fire roaring with great iron cauldrons of maple syrup boiling down. There were at least 80 French Canadian innkeepers and their wives all enjoying a great feast of pancakes and sliced maple-cured ham and eggs all served with the maple syrup. There was a fiddler in one corner and an accordion player in the other, and everyone was singing at the top of their lungs.

Innkeeper Handfield explained that these sugaring parties start at the beginning of March and run to the end of April and are very popular with the inn guests. "They are part of the fun of visiting Auberge Handfield at this time of year," he said.

He also persuaded me that I should return to see the inn at the height of the Quebec summer, and on the spot I fixed the date.

The second time, the Richelieu River (part of the waterway which carries boats down to the St. Lawrence and to the tip of Florida) was blue and sparkling in the summer sun. The Marina in front of the inn had several visiting boats, and there were people sitting around the swimming pool enjoying animated conversations in both French and English. The fields were bursting with ripening grain and I could see a number of farm animals, including sheep, goats, ducks, and geese.

I was greeted upon my arrival by Madame Huguette Handfield who enthusiastically explained all the things there were to do, both on the inn grounds and in the immediate area. She also explained that theatrical performances were given on the converted ferry boat, *l' Escale,* which is moored on the river a few hundred yards from the inn. (These performances are in French, but I had no difficulty in catching the drift.)

With her help in translating the menu, I found that among the main courses that evening were a homemade paté (quite traditional among the European restaurants), salmon from the Gaspé, duck, chicken in wine, filet mignon, and steak au Poivre.

Accommodations were in rustic rooms decorated and furnished in the old Quebec style, but with touches of modern comfort including tile bathrooms and controlled heating. My room had rough wooden walls and casement windows overlooking broad fields. Madame Handfield explained to me later that most of the inn is decorated either with antiques or furniture made by local craftsmen.

The village of St. Marc was wonderfully French and I had animated communication with the village baker, he in French, I in

Gathering sap for maple sugar

365

English, while the aroma of his bread and rolls sent my gastronomic senses reeling. The little supermarket reminded me of similar stores I had visited in France. St. Marc stretches along the Richelieu River, and has a twin village on the opposite side called St. Charles, which is reached by ferry.

The Handfield Inn is a great many things: it is a venerable mansion that has seen a century and a half of history; it is an enjoyable French restaurant; a four-season resort; and perhaps best of all, it is an opportunity to visit a French Canadian village which has remained relatively free from the invasion of developers with its ancient stone houses remaining untouched and its farms, where good stock and poultry are still being raised.

HANDFIELD INN (Auberge Handfield), St. Marc-sur-le-Richelieu (Saint Marc on the Richelieu River), Quebec, JOL-2EO, Canada; 514-584-2226. A 45-room French-Canadian country inn about 25 miles from Montreal. Different lodging plans available. Please consult with the inn in advance. Some rooms have shared baths. Breakfast, lunch and dinner served daily to travelers. Ladies are expected to wear a skirt or dress and gentlemen a coat at dinner. Open every day all year. No pets. All summer and winter active sports easily available. Many handcrafts, antique, and historical tours in the area. M. and Mme. Conrad Handfield, Innkeepers.

Directions: From Champlain, Victoria, or the Jacques Cartier bridges, take Hwy. 3 to Sorel, turn right at Hwy. 20. From the east end of Montreal go through the Hyppolite LaFontaine Tunnel. Rte. 20 passes through St. Julie, St. Bruno and Beloeil. Leave Hwy. 20 at Exit 112 turning left on Rte. 223 north. Handfield is 7 miles distant.

CUTTLE'S TREMBLANT CLUB
Mont Tremblant, Quebec

I cast off the trim Laser sailboat and immediately ran up the jib. Jim Cuttle kept us heading out into Lac Tremblant and trimmed the mainsheet. Things were all shipshape and we were set for a good sail. "These Lasers really respond very adroitly," I remarked. "Yes, they do," said Jim, "and we introduce many Americans to them for the first time. In fact, we have a sailing instructor who is particularly expert in handling them.

"Our newest sport here is windsurfing. It combines sailing, surfing, and skiing. We held the first Quebec regatta here last Labor Day. It's going to be an annual event."

From the center of the lake we enjoyed a most unusual perspective of the Laurentians. Straight ahead was Mont Tremblant,

one of the most famous ski areas in the world. Behind us was the grassy lakeside beach of Cuttle's Tremblant Club, where I counted several other sailboats and motorboats for waterskiing. Next to the beach house, the tennis courts were already busy on this early morning, and some young children were playing in the sandbox. The main house of the Club was farther up the side of the hill with a commanding view of the lake and mountain.

All of my visits with Jim and Betty Cuttle have been in the summer, so it was quite natural for me to be curious about what it was like in the winter. "Just imagine six to eight feet of snow," said Jim. "I'm sure you know that heavy snow is a way of life up here and everybody welcomes it. We've had our own ski school here at the Club for many years. In fact, Betty and I were instructors in the early days. Today our guests board our bus right after breakfast and head for the mountain where all of the teaching is done. The Club has eight instructors who are busy all day long. They use video cameras, and in the evening after dinner, everybody sits around in front of the fire and the tapes are shown which enables the guests to improve their technique. The evenings are really great fun; that's where everybody gets together and a lot of new friendships are made. We have lots of singing and dancing."

Winter is a magic time here at Cuttle's. In addition to the downhill skiing there is snowshoeing and excellent cross-country skiing. Many trails begin at the front door. Mont Tremblant Park offers fifty miles of marked and groomed trails for Nordic skiers of all abilities. Box lunches are available at the Club, and there is a waxing room and repair bench.

Jim painted an attractive word picture of Cuttle's in winter, but it has a great deal of appeal to me in summer and fall as well. Besides the active sports, I like to sit by the graceful pool in the sunshine and walk the green woods. Laurentian back roads are a joy, and the French-speaking natives in the little villages remind me of northern Provence.

With so many opportunities to spend days out of doors, the food at Cuttle's takes on an added importance. The emphasis is on French dishes, including onion soup, a cold seafood plate featuring fish from the Gaspé Peninsula, roast leg of veal, braised calves' sweetbreads, and boned chicken Bayonnaise. The menus are bilingual so everyone can practice his French.

Jim and I decided to head back to the pier where Charlie, the collie, and Meg, the Irish setter, were scampering up and down the shore awaiting our return. "They're lots of fun," he said. "Meg particularly likes to go for walks in the forest with our guests."

CUTTLE'S TREMBLANT CLUB, Mont Tremblant, Quebec, Canada JOT 1ZO, 819-425-2731. A 32-room resort inn on Lac Tremblant facing Mont Tremblant, the highest peak in the Laurentians. Modified American plan omits lunch. Breakfast, lunch and dinner served daily to travelers. Open year-round. No pets. Tennis, swimming, sailing, windsurfing, boating, fishing, and xc skiing on grounds. Golf, riding, trap shooting, Alpine skiing nearby. Jim and Betty Cuttle, Innkeepers.

Directions: From Montreal, 85 mi. northwest via Laurentian Auto Rte. 15 to St. Jovite. Turn right at church on Rte. 327N, 7 mi. to Lac Tremblant. Cuttle's is on the west shore facing the mountain.

New Brunswick

THE ST. STEPHEN-CALAIS BORDER FESTIVAL

There is an unusual spirit of friendship and cooperation up in northern Maine where the United States and Canadian borders join at Calais, Maine, and St. Stephen, New Brunswick.

Each year an international festival is held on both sides of the border during the first week in August. This has actually grown out of the tradition of Canadians and Americans helping each other for well over 100 years with barn raisings, quilting bees, church services, fighting fires, and lending tools and equipment.

This spirit was dramatized in events which took place many, many years ago. St. Stephen's garrison was well supplied with gun powder. However, the garrison commander was worried about having so much of this highly volatile material on hand. His problem was solved by the Americans who had no gunpowder to use for their Fourth of July celebration. An arrangement was made and the gun powder traded hands. It is said that the British gunpowder made a whale of a bang when it was set off. All of this took place during 1812 when Canada and America were supposed to be at war!

To me, the best part of this story is the fact that the Americans sent a huffy-puffy colonel named Benjamin Church to destroy an enemy that he discovered didn't exist. This ego-inflated military man is still an object of considerable satire in this area.

ELM LODGE INN
St. Stephen, New Brunswick

Following Patrick Garbutt's explicit directions I drove east on Route 9, which is known by the local people on both sides of the Maine-New Brunswick border as the "Airline Route." I watched for a little sign on the left that said Milltown-St. Stephen with an arrow pointing to the left. This leads to the border-crossing and the stop at customs. As Pat explained, "The local people use this border crossing because there is usually never more than a car or two in line. Down at the busy Calais-St. Stephen crossing, cars are lined up on both sides quite frequently."

Passing through Canadian customs, I went over the St. Croix River and into St. Stephen, a community that seemed to belong to an earlier century. There were broad streets, huge elm trees, graceful homes, and a pleasant park. Immediately in front of me was the elegant facade of a Victorian building which turned out to be the Elm Lodge Inn.

369

The inn is a beautifully restored building with three huge elm trees on the front lawn, handsome coach lamps flanking the entrance, and large green shutters which enhance the building considerably. There are flowerbeds on the lawn, including a number of rose bushes. On one of my visits, bluebells were in full array.

The interior of the inn tells a marvelous story. Pat and Zena Garbutt have worked very hard over the past few years restoring this truly elegant house. Floors, walls, and woodwork are all cleaned, polished, and refurbished until everything shines like a schoolboy's face. Victorian antiques and an improvisation of different types of furniture make each of the three little dining rooms a separate experience. Zena and Pat have been aided in their efforts by young enthusiastic people.

Upstairs are nine very handsome, comfortable rooms. Mine overlooked the lawn and the broad street, and had a canopied bed, which Pat explained was very popular with honeymooners.

That evening I found that the inn was a quiet place for the local people to gather and enjoy themselves. I learned about the friendship between the U.S. and Canada at this border-crossing that survived even the War of 1812. It is being observed to this day with mutual cooperation and annual celebrations.

One couple who had stopped at the Elm Lodge wrote me a letter which said in part: "It was late when we arrived, but there was still time to get some refreshment and we enjoyed talking to the local people in the pub room.

"We liked this inn very much. We were made to feel at home and invited to walk around anywhere we wished inside the inn. I took many pictures. One of my favorites is the one I took of my wife in the dining room that morning. We felt even more at home when one of the young men who works at the inn told us that he had been to our hometown in Minnesota just the summer before."

ELM LODGE INN, 477 Milltown Blvd., St. Stephen, New Brunswick, Canada; 506-466-3771. A 9-room village inn on a quiet street near the Canadian-American border-crossing at Calais, Maine. European plan and Modified American plan which omits lunch. Breakfast, lunch and dinner served daily. Open every day from Jan. 12 through Dec. 14. Dining room closed on Sundays from Jan. to May. Children welcome and pets who act like English gentlemen. Bicycles, sailing, swimming, nature trails, horseback riding, golf, canoeing, jogging nearby. Patrick and Zena Garbutt, Innkeepers.

Directions: From Bangor, Maine, follow Rte. 9. Cross at Milltown-St. Stephen border-crossing. Inn is kitty-cornered to and within sight of Canadian customs.

Grand Manan, Campobello, and Deer Islands are known as New Brunswick's Fundy Isles. Grand Manan was settled by United Empire Loyalists. It's even possible that the Vikings may have arrived hundreds of years earlier.

Grand Manan Island is reached by ferry from Black's Harbour, which is about 75 miles from Calais, Maine.

MARATHON INN
Grand Manan Island, New Brunswick

As the ferry from Black's Harbour approached the wharf at North Head on Grand Manan Island, I could readily see that this was a place where men made their living from the sea. There were fishing boats, seining weirs, and weathered docks on tall stilts, a necessity because of the very high tides in the Bay of Fundy.

Once again, I could see the Marathon Inn at the top of the hill — a gleaming three-story building with a mansard roof.

It is a quiet unspoiled island of great natural beauty, fifteen miles long and about four miles wide—a paradise for naturalists, bird watchers, photographers, artists, divers, bicyclists, and rock hounds. One of the best ways to experience its great natural unspoiled beauty is by walking.

The owner-innkeepers of the Marathon are Jim and Judy Leslie, and Jim's mother, Fern. There are also three children in the Leslie family — Rosalind, four; Owen, two; and Rachel, who was born in the fall of 1978, which makes her a real Grand Mananer.

The Leslies are all Canadians. Fern is from Saskatchewan, and both Judy and Jim were brought up in Toronto. They first met when they were youthful figure skaters together, and later went to the same high school.

There's no doubt that the Marathon Inn is a real family undertaking. "It's really the only way we can do it," said Jim, who is an enthusiastic individual. "Fern, my mother, is really in charge of the kitchen. I try to keep all of the new projects moving both inside and out, and Judy is very busy with the housekeeping details, checking people in and out and, of course, being a mother, as well.

"We have made a lot of progress. Now we have a heated swimming pool which our guests enjoy very much. Because many people prefer to park their car at Black's Harbour and come over as foot-passengers on the ferry, we have made it possible for them to rent automobiles to tour the island. We also have mopeds and bikes. I hope the tennis courts will be in use in the summer of 1979.

"Our guests often like to take advantage of the chance to go deep sea fishing for herring, pollock, and haddock with the island fishermen. There are also boating trips to Gannet Rock, Machias Seal Island, and Tent Island. Children seem to have such a wonderful time here, and that is very gratifying. I think one of the reasons that Judy, Fern, and I moved out to the island to begin with was that we thought it would be a wonderful place to raise children."

I had a long talk with Fern regarding the inn menus. "We always have a choice of fresh fish or another meat at every evening meal," she said. "We offer our seafood chowder and another soup, and there's a choice of desserts. We've received many compliments for our raisin and walnut pie, and also our rum pie. I make homemade buns every day and all of the desserts."

I think Jim sums it up very well. "We've tried to make the Marathon Inn everything you'd expect in a hotel originally built over a century ago by a retired sea captain. Fortunately, the inn has been well maintained over the years and we've refinished much of the furniture and redecorated many rooms. We've attempted to retain the charm and atmosphere of leisurely living of another age."

Ferry service from Black's Harbour has been doubled for the summer season. Ferries leave from both sides at eight a.m., ten a.m., two p.m., and at six p.m.

There's are lots of exciting things happening on Grand Manan Island now that the Leslie family is operating the Marathon Inn for twelve months of the year.

MARATHON INN, North Head at Grand Manan, New Brunswick, Canada E0G 2M0; 506-662-8144. A 38-room resort-inn on

Grand Manan Island in the Bay of Fundy, 40 mi. from St. John in New Brunswick. Modified American and European plans. Open all year. Breakfast and dinner served to travelers daily. Pets allowed on ground floor annex. Heated swimming pool on grounds. Beachcombing, bird watching, swimming, fishing, hiking, diving, bicycles, golf, and tennis nearby. Jim, Judy, and Fern Leslie, Innkeepers.

Directions: Grand Manan Island is reached by ferry from Black's Harbour which is just off Rte. 1, midway between Calais, Maine, and St. John, New Brunswick.

MARSHLANDS INN
Sackville, New Brunswick

Every year I hear from a great many people who drive across Maine into New Brunswick to reach Nova Scotia, Prince Edward Island, and Newfoundland the long way—by land.

Almost all of these letters make some reference to the Marshlands Inn, which is located just a few miles from the Nova Scotia border and the P.E.I. ferry. This is what one couple reported: "Our first stop was the Marshlands Inn. We had planned a three-week camping trip with an occasional overnight stop to get a bedroom and an adjoining bathroom, the pleasures you miss even in the best Provincial parks. Our itinerary brought us to the Marshlands Inn for a late lunch. We must admit the setting, decor, and food exceeded our expectations." (I have many letters from people who stop at the Marshlands and mention the fact that they never expected to find such a sophisticated inn so far north.)

"While paying our bill we found a copy of *Country Inns and Back Roads,* perused the table of contents, and noticed your entry regarding the Marshlands. We found that we were in complete agreement with your comments and enjoyed your personal observations. Believe it or not we never expected that such a purchase would determine the roads that we would eventually take." Incidentally, that couple also visited the Inverary Inn and the Milford House in Nova Scotia, both a single day's drive from Sackville.

My personal dilemma when visiting the Marshlands is to make a choice of entrées at dinner. The Atlantic and Miramichi salmon are very tempting, but the curried lamb with Marshlands chutney is very enjoyable, too. There are also lobsters, scallops, beefsteak and kidney pie, the famous fiddlehead greens, and many curry dishes. All the rolls, breads, ice cream and sherbets are homemade.

I am happy to say that Innkeepers Herb and Alice Read continue to pursue the Marshlands tradition of leaving a thermos pitcher of hot chocolate in the front parlor for guests who like a late snack.

Although the Marshlands seems like it is just a few miles from the North Pole to those of us who live below the Canadian border, it would be unusual in any setting. The dinnerware is sterling, the china is Spode, and all the waitresses wear dark blue uniforms with white collars and aprons.

The breakfast offerings include freshly-squeezed (honest) orange juice, baked apples, fresh homemade apple sauce, stewed foxberries, (*fox*berries?), slow-cooked oatmeal, cracked wheat porridge, creamed salt cod, buckwheat pancakes with maple syrup . . . should I continue? . . . should I continue?

Incidentally, Marshlands is named after the Tantramar Marshes that surround the town of Sackville. Tantramar comes from the Indian word, meaning "sound of bird wings." The marshes are home to millions of migrating waterfowl. This area, now largely controlled by Ducks Unlimited and the Marsh Reclamation Board, is one of the main flyways of North America. In the spring and fall huge flights of geese and ducks may be seen coming in to rest on the marshes.

The Marshlands is not only a place where East meets West, but also a place where North meets South—then all sit down to eat!

MARSHLANDS INN, Box 1440, Sackville, N.B., Canada EOA 3CO; 506-536-0170. A 16-room village inn near Tantramar Marshes and Fundy Tides. European plan. Eight rooms with private baths. Breakfast, lunch, and dinner served to travelers daily. Closed during the Christmas season. Golf, xc skiing, curling, hiking, and swimming nearby. Herb and Alice Read, Innkeepers.

Directions: Follwo Trans-Canada Highway to Sackville, then Rte. 6, 1 mi. to center of town.

Prince Edward Island

Prince Edward Island is one of the great surprises of North America. For one thing, ocean water temperatures along the wide P.E.I. beaches average 68 to 70 degrees in summer and the sun is excellent for tanning. It has one of Canada's finest national parks stretching 25 miles along the Gulf of St. Lawrence. There are wild seascapes, breathtaking views, and an atmosphere of hospitality, because this has been a resort area for more than a century.

During the summer months there is an excellent theatre at the Confederation Centre of the Arts in Charlottetown offering a choice of musicals which play to capacity houses almost every night. Cavendish Beach is the locale of Lucy Maude Montgomery's stories of Ann of Green Gables. *A small, gabled, green cottage has been built with some reminders of* Ann *stories.*

Prince Edward Island is very popular in July and August, so reserve well in advance and be sure to obtain ferry information.

SHAW'S HOTEL
Brackley Beach, Prince Edward Island

I never thought that I could be this far north and find swimming water so wonderfully warm and enjoyable. Here in the Gulf of St. Lawrence on the north side of Prince Edward Island it was so comfortable, pleasant, and warm that it reminded me of Fort Lauderdale in March.

I had arrived early in the afternoon, having taken the ferry from Caribou, Nova Scotia, filled with anticipation at seeing P.E.I. and Shaw's Hotel once again.

Shaw's was originally part of a pioneer farm, started in 1793. It became a hotel in 1860, and today it is still part of a working farm with large, beautiful barns.

Some of the accommodations are in the main building which is a Victorian house with a brilliant red mansard third story. There are also individual cottages which can accommodate from two to eight people each. These are spaced far enough apart on the property to ensure complete privacy. Half of them have fireplaces.

The place has many trees and rolling meadows, and the view from the dining room window often includes a sailboat bobbing about in the bay. At the time of my visit, there was a good mix of both Canadian and American guests, and we all agreed that the food, which featured fresh fish such as salmon, lobster, mackerel, and halibut, was excellent.

My arrival was timed with another one of a more auspicious nature. One of the two big sheep dogs had just given birth to a litter of six beautiful puppies. This was much to the delight of several children vacationing there.

Gordon Shaw said that he has had as many as thirty or forty children visiting at one time in the height of the season. "There's always plenty of elbow room," he added. "We don't have any trouble keeping the parents of all these children amused either. Besides the beach, there is riding available nearby which is fun, especially along the beach and on the bridle paths. We also have two sailboats on the bay, and golf and tennis nearby.

"We're located in the sticks, at the end of the road—the best location of any resort on P.E.I. The beach is the big attraction. The water is seventy degrees, and in the bay it gets even warmer. The temperature goes up to ninety here in midsummer."

Well, I could attest to that. It was mid-June, and there I was in swimming and loving every minute of it!

SHAW'S HOTEL and Cottages, Brackley Point Road, Brackley Beach, Prince Edward Island, Canada COA 2HO; 902-672-2022. A 24-room country hotel within walking distance of Brackley Beach, 15 mi. from Charlottetown. American plan. Some rooms with shared baths. 10 guest cottages. Breakfast, lunch, dinner served to travelers daily. Open from June 15 to Sept. 15. Pets allowed in cottages only. Tennis, golf, bicycles, riding, sailing, beach, and summer theatre nearby. Gordon Shaw, Innkeeper.

Directions: Prince Edward Island is reached either by ferry from Cape Tormentine, New Brunswick (near Moncton), or Caribou, Nova Scotia. In both cases, after arriving on P.E.I. follow Rte. 1 to Charlottetown, then Rte. 15 to Brackley Beach. P.E.I. is also reached by Eastern Provincial Airways, Canadian National Railways, and Air Canada.

Nova Scotia

The super back road in Nova Scotia is the Cabot Trail which winds around the top of the province next to the Gulf of St. Lawrence, through the great forests and back down to Lake Bras d'Or. It includes the Cape Breton Highlands National Park and should be traversed twice, once clockwise and the second time counterclockwise.

MILFORD HOUSE
South Milford, Nova Scotia

Once again, Wendy Miller and I were seated on the swings next to the Milford House. We first sat here during the summer of 1973, when Wendy was twelve years old and even then, was a very important part of all of the many activities at this Nova Scotian woodland country inn. Now, it was mid-June and the lady's-slippers, and other early summer flowers were blooming in profusion. A few of the many varieties of birds that frequent this part of Nova Scotia had already returned from winter quarters and were setting up housekeeping.

It was difficult for me to believe that this attractive young lady, who first showed me around all of the lakes and cabins, patiently explaining about the fireplaces, maid service, trout fishing, canoeing, and the walks along the woodland trails, had now graduated from high school and would be entering Dalhousie University in the fall.

Every year we've had good chats like this one. Sometimes walking through the woods, others while canoeing, and sometimes at dinner table. I think I've pictured the Milford House through

Wendy's eyes and her great love of this wonderfully sequestered natural country where it's still possible to see deer, otter, wild duck, and beaver.

"Tell me about a typical day here for the guests," I asked. "Well, they generally wander up to the main lodge for a breakfast of bacon, eggs, muffins, and coffee," she said. "Then there are just so many things to do like tennis, swimming, canoeing, volleyball, fishing, croquet, and maybe a picnic, or just lying in the sun. While they relax, the cabin is tidied, the beds are made, a load of logs is delivered to the fireplace, and another block of ice is delivered to the ice box."

The cottages are spread out along the shores of two lakes. Each of them has its own dock and a living room with a fireplace, electricity, and a bathroom with hot and cold running water and a shower or a tub.

"The only noises here are birds and frogs. We don't allow outboard motors on our lakes. But there is wonderful canoeing among the several lakes. The whole area is a fisherman's delight. There is speckled trout, native and stocked, and the salmon rivers aren't very far away.

"After a day's activities or a day of doing nothing, people return to the lodge for dinner. We serve home-baked bread, pastry, vegetables from our garden, roasts, fresh fish, blueberries, and raspberries. After dinner there is nothing to compare with a quiet evening on the porch of the cottage watching the sun go down, listening to the strange laughing call of a loon.

"I think one of the main reasons why people enjoy it here is that our *guests* are so special. For instance, there's Sara and Gordon Sikes — Gordon taught me, as well as hundreds of other kids, how to canoe. He's a hard taskmaster, but a word of praise from Mr. Sikes makes it all worthwhile. The biggest thing that could happen is that he would carve your initials in your canoe paddle. The Sikeses have been coming here since the 1920s. I think no matter where I go, I'll always want to come back."

On my very first trip in 1973, Wendy explained to me that when guests leave, all the remaining guests stand on the porch and wave their napkins or handkerchiefs, and the departing guest waves back until they pass the oak tree on the corner of the property.

Once again, Wendy, along with her father and mother, Innkeepers Margaret and Bud Miller, stood on the porch as I made another reluctant farewell. I always weep a little, but this year perhaps there was an extra tear or two of joy, because I realized that Wendy, now grown up and going out into the world, would always carry with her an abundance of the spirit of the Milford House.

MILFORD HOUSE, South Milford, R.R. #4. Annapolis Royal, N.S., Canada, B0S 1A0; 902-532-2617. A rustic resort-inn with 24 cabins on 600 acres of woodlands and lakes, 90 mi. from Yarmouth, N.S., near Kejimkujik National Park. Modified American plan. Breakfast and dinner served daily with picnic lunches available. Open from June 18 to Sept. 15. Tennis, fishing, croquet, canoeing, bird-watching, and swimming on grounds. Deep-sea fishing and golf nearby. Warren and Margaret Miller, Innkeepers.

Directions: From Yarmouth follow Rte. 1 to traffic lights in Annapolis Royal. Turn right and continue on to Rte. 8, 15 mi. to inn.

INVERARY INN
Baddeck, Nova Scotia

Bettie Gilbert, a dear friend, used to be the innkeeper at the Colby Hill Inn in Henniker, New Hampshire. However, a few years ago, she sold the inn to the Glover Family and decided to do a lot of inn-traveling. Among the other letters I received from her during the past couple of years, here is one that tells about her visit to the Inverary Inn.

"Isobel MacAulay's greeting was so warm that I felt at once as if she and I were old friends. She told me that you had been at the inn just a week earlier. I loved her tartan drapes and her welcoming fire in the evening. Our rooms were comfortable and spotless, and her dining room so cheerful and interesting. The food, of course, was delicious. I noticed Isobel greeted all of her guests at breakfast and dinner. We managed a nice visit in spite of her busy schedule, and I really felt homesick for the inn life and was tempted to take up her joking offer of a summer job! There is so much to do in Cape Breton and so little time."

I've been at the Inverary Inn several times and watched tired travelers arrive. Many of them had driven all day from Halifax or South Milford, Nova Scotia, or Sackville, New Brunswick. Newcomers didn't quite know what to expect but I could see that they were immediately pleased. The inn sits back from the road in a garden of lupine, honeysuckle, and wild roses. There are firs, white birches, and maples everywhere, and there is an apple orchard on the opposite side of the inn beside the unpolluted waters of Lake Bras d'Or.

Since the inn is located in one of the most picturesque sections of the Maritimes, every effort is made to inform guests about the Cabot Trail and its magnificent scenery.

The Scottish breakfasts, which Bettie also mentioned later on in her letter—spiced applesauce, oatmeal porridge, oat cakes, and bannochs, and other interesting Scottish delicacies that I always have trouble spelling—always seem to invite praise.

A typical Cape Breton dinner served at the inn is dried cod with pork scraps—sounds funny but it is really delicious. There are more familiar offerings such as the famous Cape Breton salmon.

In the years that I have been visiting the Inverary, I've seen Scott MacAulay grow from a small schoolboy into the full-fledged manager of the inn. He and I had a chance to stroll around the grounds and visit several of the lodgings rooms, including the cabins and the rooms in the carriage house. He is a fine young man and I am certain that Isobel and Dan MacAulay are very proud and pleased with the fact that he is taking such an interest in innkeeping.

"Have you ever noticed the back of one of our menus?" he asked. "We've reprinted a poem by Robert Burns entitled *On Incivility Shewn Him At Inverary*. Of course, he's talking about Inverary in Scotland; he evidently stayed at the castle there. It occurred to me that maybe your readers would find it amusing. Of course, nothing like that could happen at *this* Inverary!"

> *Whoe'er he be that sojourns here,*
> *I pity much his case,*
> *Unless he come to wait upon*
> *The lord their god, His Grace.*

> *There's naething here but Highland pride,*
> *And Highland cauld and hunger;*
> *If Providence has sent me here,*
> *'Twas surely in his anger.*

INVERARY INN, Box 190, Baddeck, Cape Breton, N.S., Canada 902-295-2674. A 40-room village inn on the Cabot Trail, 52 mi. from Sydney, N.S. On the shores of Lake Bras d'Or. European plan.

Some rooms with shared bath. Breakfast and dinner served to travelers daily. Open from May 15 to Nov. 1. Bicycles and children's playground on grounds. Boating and small golf course nearby. Isobel MacAulay, Innkeeper.

Directions: Follow Trans-Canada Hwy. to Canso Causeway to Baddeck.

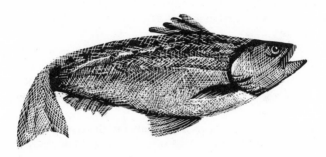

KILMUIR PLACE
Northeast Margaree, Cape Breton, Nova Scotia

"I've never used a mix in my life, and never will." Isabel Taylor stood with her hands on her hips, tossed her head back, and her eyes flashed. "After all, my mother and father started this place over 50 years ago and our guests love the old-fashioned ways. I can tell the difference when something is made from a mix, and I'm sure everybody else can, too."

"Indeed, they do. And I'm a guest who has been coming for 40 straight years."

This time the speaker was a lady from Philadelphia who walked into Isabel and Ross' cozy kitchen as if on cue.

"In those days it took some persistence and motivation to come out to the Margaree," she said, settling down into one of the comfortable upholstered chairs in one corner of the kitchen. "Now you can get here from Sydney in about an hour and a half and from Halifax in about three and a half hours. In the old days the roads weren't paved and sometimes Ross had to get a team to pull us out of the mud.

"One thing that pleases me is that we have so many young people. A lot in their early 20s. They're so *interested* in everything!"

Ross asked her if she would like to have another piece of his chocolate cake, reminding her that he had been up at the crack of dawn that morning making it. She demurred, saying that she couldn't possibly eat another bite.

While we were chatting, Isabel deftly carved a generous slice of roast beef and poured pan gravy over a big helping of mashed potatoes on my plate. She topped it off with some cauliflower.

"Here you are," she said, "if you don't mind eating in the kitchen." Well, I've never eaten anywhere but in the kitchen at the Kilmuir Place. It's the one way to find out what Ross and Isabel have been doing over the past winter.

"Well, one thing we do is feed birds all winter. They keep us company. All of the summer birds come back every year. Tell your friends to bring their binoculars and notebooks. This is really good bird country."

The Kilmuir Place became known for the fine salmon fishing on the Margaree. Ross knows all the good fishing holes in this most beautiful of rivers. Now, however, guests also come to the Kilmuir to tour the Cabot Trail and enjoy a few days of rest, reading, and conversation.

I must add that this is a very tiny inn. It has only three rooms with private baths and two of them without. Don't even think of coming without a reservation.

But when you do come, be prepared to wish fervently on the day you leave, that you could stay several days longer.

KILMUIR PLACE, Northeast Margaree, Cape Breton, N.S., Canada B0E 2H0; 902-248-2877. A 5-room country inn on Rte. 19, 28 mi. from Baddeck. Some rooms with shared baths. Modified American plan. Breakfast and dinner served to houseguests only. Open from June to mid-October. Salmon fishing in the Margaree River, touring the Cabot Trail, and both fresh water and salt water swimming nearby. Mr. and Mrs. Ross Taylor, Innkeepers.

Directions: After crossing Canso Causeway to Cape Breton, follow either Rte. 19 (coast road to Inverness) and turn right on Cabot Trail at Margaree Forks, or follow Rte. 105 and turn left on Cabot Trail at Nyanza.

INDEX

The Last Word . . .

Remember, to avoid disappointment, telephone ahead to all inns for reservations.

Country Inns and Back Roads, North America is completely rewritten each year. The new edition is available every March. Your bookstore will be happy to reserve your copy in advance, as well as to supply you with other books on inn travel including *Country Inns and Back Roads, Europe* and *The Inn Way . . . The Caribbean.* For a complete catalogue on Berkshire Traveller Books write to: The Berkshire Traveller Press, Pine Street, Stockbridge, Massachusetts 01262.

In addition to books on North American and European inns, the Berkshire Traveller Press also publishes books on other types of travel, on history, country living, Shaker lifestyles, and Shaker furniture design; works of fiction: juvenile, adult, historical; and also cookbooks.

Author's inquiries are invited; please send a two- to four-page outline of the work. Unsolicited manuscripts are not accepted.

Grafton, Vt.
89
Stonehenge - Vt